"This collection of essays is a fitting tribute to a giant of Pauline studies. Each essay honors Bob Jewett by both celebrating and moving beyond his own historical, exegetical, interdisciplinary, and cross-cultural contributions and commitments. It is especially appropriate today that voices from non-Western and indigenous cultures, like those included in this volume, be heard and engaged."

—**Michael J. Gorman**, St. Mary's Seminary & University

"From the question of the political dimension of Paul's Gospel, to the socio-historical situatedness of Robert Jewett's Romans: A Commentary, to the honor-shame competition of Rome's society and the Corinthian correspondence, this is a rich collection of stimulating essays that illustrate Robert Jewett's lasting contributions to Pauline scholarship."

—**Annette Weissenrieder**, Martin Luther University of Halle-Wittenberg

"Biblical scholars from around the world splendidly honor Robert Jewett as a complete biblical scholar by offering (1) essays prolonging his text-focused scholarship, (2) essays emphasizing that any exegesis of Paul's letters is necessarily framed by the interpreter's context, and (3) essays illustrating that any interpretation of Paul's letters necessarily prolongs Paul's discourse as a Word-to-live-by in a particular cultural setting."

—**Daniel Patte**, Vanderbilt University

"This volume offers a critical but serious engagement with the multifaceted scholarship of Robert 'Bob' Jewett. Representing a wide spectrum of disciplines, its contributions are a testimony to the inspiration that Jewett has been for many generations of scholars and a celebration of his influence on the study of Pauline writings. The result in this impressive volume is itself a major contribution to the field."

—**Christian A. Eberhart**, University of Houston

"Can curiosity be passed on to others? This book in honor of Robert Jewett, an impressive scholar and teacher who covered a large number of fields related to the Pauline epistles and contemporary issues in fruitful dialogue, has good opportunities to do so. It does not only bring the traces of Robert Jewett's legacy to the fore, but also invites readers who never met him to make their own discoveries."

—**Cristina Grenholm**, coeditor, Romans through History and Cultures series

"These outstanding essays demonstrate the sprawling impact of the pioneering work of Robert Jewett. Scholars from around the globe honor Jewett by deepening his contributions and extending the relevance of his insights to diverse social locations. Readers who knew him will revel in this tribute to the man and his scholarship. Younger scholars will discover one of the giants on whose shoulders they stand. Devour and savor."

—**David Rhoads**, Lutheran School of Theology at Chicago

Scripture, Cultures, and Criticism

Contrapuntal Readings of the Bible in World Christianity

Series Editors: K. K. Yeo, Melanie Baffes

Just as God knows no boundaries and incarnation happens in shared space, truth does not respect borders and its expression in various contexts is kaleidoscopic. As God's church is birthed forth from local cultures, it is called into a catholic community—namely world Christianity. This series values the twofold identity of biblical interpretations that seek to engage in contextual theology and, at the same time, become part of a global and "many-voiced" conversation for the sake of mutual understanding. By promoting contrapuntal readings that hold contextual and global biblical hermeneutics in tension, this series celebrates interpretations in three movements: (1) those based on the biblical text that honor multiple and interacting worldviews (reading the world biblically/theologically); (2) those that work at the translatability of the biblical text to uphold various dynamic vernaculars and faithful hermeneutics for the world (reading the Bible/theology contextually); and (3) those that respect the cross-cultural and shifting contexts in which faithful communities are embedded, and embody, real-life issues.

International Advisory Board

Walter Brueggemann, William Marcellus McPheeters Professor Emeritus of Old Testament, Columbia Theological Seminary (USA)

Adela Yarbro Collins, Buckingham Professor of New Testament Criticism and Interpretation, Yale Divinity School (USA)

Kathy Ehrensperger, Research Professor of New Testament in Jewish Perspective, University of Potsdam (Germany)

Justo L. González, Emeritus Professor of Historical Theology, Candler School of Theology, Emory University (USA)

Richard A. Horsley, Distinguished Professor of Liberal Arts and the Study of Religion Emeritus, University of Massachusetts—Boston (USA)

Robert Jewett (1933–2020), Emeritus Professor of New Testament, Heidelberg University (Germany)

Brigitte Kahl, Professor of New Testament, Union Theological Seminary (USA)

Peter Lampe, Professor of New Testament Theology, Heidelberg University (Germany)

Tremper Longman III, Robert H. Gundry Professor Emeritus of Biblical Studies, Westmont College (USA)

Daniel Patte, Professor Emeritus of Religious Studies, New Testament, and Christianity, Vanderbilt University (USA)

Volumes in the Series (2018–2022)

Volume 1: *Text and Context: Vernacular Approaches to the Bible in Global Christianity*, edited by Melanie Baffes

Volume 2: *What Has Jerusalem to Do with Beijing? Biblical Interpretation from a Chinese Perspective* (Twentieth Anniversary Edition), K. K. Yeo

Volume 3: *Chinese Biblical Anthropology: Persons and Ideas in the Old Testament and in Modern Chinese Literature*, Cao Jian

Volume 4: *Cross-textual Reading of Ecclesiastes with Analects: In Search of Political Wisdom in a Disordered World*, Elaine Wei-Fun Goh

Volume 5: *The Cambridge Dictionary of Christianity*, 2 vols., edited by Daniel Patte

Volume 6: *An Ethic of Hospitality: The Pilgrim Motif in Hebrews and the Refugee Problem in Kenya*, Emily Jeptepkeny Choge

Volume 7: *The Diffused Story of the Footwashing in John 13: A Textual Study of Bible Reception in Late Imperial China*, Yanrong Chen

Volume 8: *Who Is to Blame for Judges 19? Interplay Between the Text and a Chinese Context*, Grace Kwan Sik Tsoi

Volume 9: *Scripture, Cultures, and Criticism: Interpretive Steps and Critical Issues Raised by Robert Jewett*, edited by K. K. Yeo

Scripture, Cultures, and Criticism

Interpretive Steps and Critical Issues
Raised by Robert Jewett

EDITED BY
K. K. Yeo

FOREWORD BY
Kathy Ehrensperger

◆PICKWICK *Publications* · Eugene, Oregon

SCRIPTURE, CULTURES, AND CRITICISM
Interpretive Steps and Critical Issues Raised by Robert Jewett

Contrapuntal Readings of the Bible in World Christianity 9

Copyright © 2022 Wipf and Stock Publishers. All rights reserved. Except for brief quotations in critical publications or reviews, no part of this book may be reproduced in any manner without prior written permission from the publisher. Write: Permissions, Wipf and Stock Publishers, 199 W. 8th Ave., Suite 3, Eugene, OR 97401.

Pickwick Publications
An Imprint of Wipf and Stock Publishers
199 W. 8th Ave., Suite 3
Eugene, OR 97401

www.wipfandstock.com

PAPERBACK ISBN: 978-1-6667-9785-5
HARDCOVER ISBN: 978-1-6667-9784-8
EBOOK ISBN: 978-1-6667-9783-1

Cataloguing-in-Publication data:

Names: Yeo, K. K., editor. | Ehrensperger, Kathy, foreword.

Title: Scripture, cultures, and criticism : interpretive steps and critical issues raised by Robert Jewett / edited by K. K. Yeo ; foreword by Kathy Ehrensperger.

Description: Eugene, OR: Pickwick Publications, 2022. | Contrapuntal Readings of the Bible in World Christianity 9. | Includes bibliographical references and index.

Identifiers: ISBN 978-1-6667-9785-5 (paperback). | ISBN 978-1-6667-9784-8 (hardcover). | ISBN 978-1-6667-9783-1 (ebook).

Subjects: LSCH: Jewett, Robert. | Bible—Epistles of Paul. | Bible.—Romans—Criticism, interpretation, etc. | Motion pictures—Religious aspects—Christianity.

Classification: BS2655.52 S15 2022 (print) | BS2655.52 (ebook)

08/22/22

Scripture quotations marked (NRSV) are taken from the New Revised Standard Version of the Bible, copyright © 1989 National Council of the Churches of Christ in the United States of America. Used by permission. All rights reserved worldwide.

Scripture quotations marked (RSV) are taken from the Revised Standard Version of the Bible, copyright © 1946, 1952, and 1971 National Council of the Churches of Christ in the United States of America. Used by permission. All rights reserved worldwide.

Scripture quotations marked (ESV) are taken from the ESV® Bible (The Holy Bible, English Standard Version®), Copyright © 2001 by Crossway, a publishing ministry of Good News Publishers. Used by permission. All rights reserved.

This book is dedicated to
friends and students of Robert Jewett,
whose friendship and scholarship exhibit
faith, hope, and love

Contents

Foreword by Kathy Ehrensperger | xi
Acknowledgments | xv
Introduction by Ellen Jewett and K. K. Yeo | xvii
Abbreviations | xxviii
Contributors | xxix

Part I: Scripture, Paul, and Ancient Cultures

1. Beyond the Acts-Based Approach to Pauline Biography | 3
   —Douglas A. Campbell

2. Robert Jewett and the Corinthian Correspondence | 19
   —Frank W. Hughes

3. A Question of Perception: Food Debates in Corinth | 34
   —Kathy Ehrensperger

4. The Good Citizen: A Philological Analysis of *Politeuō* in Philippians 1:27 and 3:17—4:1 | 46
   —Najeeb T. Haddad

5. Human Trafficking in Romans 1:18–32 | 59
   —Sheila E. McGinn

6. Scripture and Echoes in Romans: Robert Jewett on Midrash and on Adam in Romans 7:7–12 | 72
   —A. Andrew Das

7. The Measure of Strength in Romans 14:1–15:6:
   Paul's Redefinition | 85

   —William S. Campbell

Part II: Pauline Theology and Interdisciplinary Study

8. To Imagine Otherwise: Interpreting Romans 7:14–25
   from the Perspective of Scriptural Criticism | 103

   —Meng Hun Goh

9. Shame and Honor Systems in the Book of Romans:
   A Psychological Analysis of the Struggle for Superiority Within
   and Between the Roman Tenement and House Churches | 117

   —Lallene J. Rector

10. A Metaphorical Interpretation of *Charis* and *Charisma* in Romans 12:
    A Cultural-Critical Understanding of "Gift" | 130

    —K. K. Yeo

11. The Hermeneutic of Love, Honor, and Hospitality:
    Redefining Relationships in Romans 12–13 | 145

    —Zakali Shohe

12. Robert Jewett Goes to the Movies:
    Teaching University Courses on Religion and Film | 159

    —Christopher Deacy

13. Superhero Myth(s), Movies, and Scripture:
    Robert Jewett as Cultural Exegete | 173

    —Robert K. Johnston

Part III: Pauline Study and Contemporary Cultures

14. Hospitality as a Means to Further God's Reign
    in the New Testament and Dominican Context | 191

    —Aída Besançon Spencer

15. Reimagining the Thessalonians at the End of the World with Ghost Dancers | 208

—T. Christopher Hoklotubbe

16. Reading Galatians with the Barbarians: West African and East European Perspectives | 223

—Brigitte Kahl and Aliou C. Niang

17. By Any Means Necessary, All Israel Will Be Saved: Paul, Malcolm, and Community Identity in the Letter to the Romans | 246

—Keith Augustus Burton

18. Christian Submission to Civil Authorities in the Ghanaian Context | 260

—Frederick Mawusi Amevenku

19. Reading Romans 13:1–7 as a Hidden Transcript in the Malaysian Context | 274

—Kong Hock Hii and Kar Yong Lim

Index of Authors | 289

Index of Subjects | 295

Index of Ancient Documents | 307

Foreword

It is a great honor for me to introduce this tribute volume in remembrance of Robert Jewett. I was introduced to him at the turn of the millennium by my husband, William S. Campbell, who was a longstanding friend of Bob's since 1971. They included me in their scholarly and personal friendship from the day we first met.

Robert Jewett was a towering scholar, one of those New Testament colleagues who was entirely immersed in his studies, thorough and knowledgeable in his field, but who knew with his heart and soul that scholarship cannot exist in an ivory tower; the world of studies is not the entire world. Out there were the world and the church, real people who celebrated, struggled, loved, and cried, and his scholarly work never lost sight of them. It actually was the reason for him being a scholar, and it was the horizon of the relevance of his work. The breadth of his knowledge, interest, and understanding did render him a Scholar with a capital S, or in German, he would be called *ein wahrer Gelehrter*. And the horizon of his life and work, although deeply molded by the width of the American plains and his love for the sea, did not stop there but led him to embark not only on journeys to other parts of the world (by boat and other means) but immerse himself into European ways of life for several years, firstly during his time as a doctoral student in Tübingen, and later in life, in Heidelberg. He was multi-cultural within himself, in a sense, before the arrival of the term or the awareness of the relevance of different life-worlds and perspectives that come with it. This is reflected in his publications, not least in his *Christian Tolerance: Paul's Message to the Modern Church* (1982), which is more relevant than ever. He made it clear that tolerance does not mean to merely "allow" the other to exist, but to value and cherish the other in their difference. This involves getting to know the other, learning from them and, where necessary, to change in light of the encounter with those who are and remain different from us.

This openness was not only evident in his scholarly work; he embodied it and lived it also in relation to his colleagues and friends. The fact that so many of them from all corners of the earth contributed to this tribute volume is telling evidence of his warm, open heart and tolerance, which included critical engagement and serious discussions. He listened and took his conversation partners seriously, whether he discussed, agreed, or disagreed with them. Of course, he had clear stances, and advocated his views with conviction and clear arguments. He was one of those scholars who, in the 1970s, initiated the reading of Paul's letters as real letters, addressed to specific people, raising particular issues, rather than reading them as a theological treatise. Thus, his goal in writing *Paul's Anthropological Terms* (1971) was that these terms should be read afresh in their immediate literary setting in each of Paul's letters, rather than as abstractions with generalized dictionary definitions. This is an indication that his exegetical work is rooted in contextualized theology, which pays attention to socio-historical situatedness and draws relevance for contemporary life. It is thus no surprise that he also was concerned with the practicalities of Paul's life and travels. He worked out travel routes and times, particularly those by sea, established a timeline for them and the letters in relation to these in his *Chronology of Paul's Life* (1979). By this focus, Bob drew attention to the fact that thoughts are not free-floating but are socially located, embodied by people in their everyday lives and dealings. He thereby emphasized the relevance of a strand of research that is now generally considered to be of high relevance, that is, social and economic history and everyday life studies.

The focus on real life is manifest also in his thorough and rigorous application of rhetorical analysis informed by in-depth knowledge of the classical sources of ancient rhetoric. In a magisterial way, he combined the method with the emphasis on the socio-historical situatedness in his masterpiece, the Hermeneia *Romans: A Commentary* (2007), a work that was in the making for twenty-five years. In this commentary, he integrated and discussed scholarship on Romans over this extensive period of time, thereby also providing an overview of Pauline scholarship on Romans over time. It is an example of a commentary that can hardly ever be repeated, and is a lasting contribution to Pauline scholarship. It correlates with another emphasis of Bob's work, which follows logically for him from his emphasis on the contextuality of Paul's letters: the political dimension of Paul's gospel. The Roman Empire and its elite ideology are the context reflected in the New Testament, and Paul engages with this context of his addressees throughout, in a critical way. Most important in Bob's view was Paul's inversion of the Roman honor-shame system, thereby engaging with a highly important aspect of Roman society. Since the majority of the addressees most likely were not part of the elite, but rather were located at the lower end of the social strata—possibly slaves or former slaves—their problem was lack of honor, that is shame, rather than guilt from which they would need to be redeemed. The competition for honor marked Roman society, with the negative effect of humiliating the weaker members. This, in Bob's view, was the major problem, the super-mindedness and boasting that denigrated and looked at the other with contempt. Sin consists of the refusal to relate to the other with the respect owed to them as being created in the image of God. The humiliation of the other affected directly the relationship with God. Although all people lack honor in relation to God, those shamed by the elite in their competitive behavior were the ones for whom Christ has restored their honor in relation to God. This was the powerful and liberating gospel for those held in contempt by a society dominated by elitist ideology. Thus, the power of the gospel is not merely inward oriented, but has a fundamental impact in society. Any humiliating or shaming of the other was sin, and thus rendered the "strong" guilty. In Romans, in particular, Bob sees Paul advocating the inversion of this dominating honor-shame competition as that which corresponds to being redeemed by Christ. Bob saw this expressed in the meals the Christ-followers shared, in his view on a daily basis, the agape meals, thereby providing real-life support as well as spiritual support for those at the bottom of Roman society—whom Bob saw as living mainly in tenement churches.

He also took aspects of feminist approaches seriously by highlighting the role of women in the early Christ-movement. He was one the first to argue that Phoebe played a decisive role as a leader and patron of the Christ-movement, and she was particularly instrumental in the logistics of the Spanish mission. To highlight the key role of a female leader for the work of the gospel was not common among male scholars in the 1980s. It was not merely an aspect he included in his own scholarly approach, but it also involved active support for young female scholars and their careers. His emphasis on the political and social relevance of the gospel had a significant impact in New Testament scholarship generally, and contributed to the rise of imperial critical approaches, although it raised critical questions from colleagues as well. Bob's work had a widespread impact, well beyond the realm of the so-called Western world. It nourished and will nourish scholars world-wide; this is something that cannot be said of many in our guild.

And his impact is of an actuality one could not have envisaged a few weeks ago. With a clarity that is almost prophetic, he was able to see the implications of competitive, humiliating behavior in contemporary Western societies and in American society in particular. Although I do not share all aspects of his analysis and his conclusions, the publication *Captain America* (1973) reads like a vision, or maybe a nightmare, of what was to emerge out of such behavior, and how destructive it is not only in personal relationships but on the political level as well in the form of religiously nourished nationalism. Bob attributed this attitude to the US being rooted in Puritan notions of purity, in particular. However, it is a kind of fundamentalist notion permeating populist political movements that is not confined to the US, but is destructive wherever it emerges. Bob's admonition to embrace the ambiguity of life also at a political level has not lost its relevance. As I am writing, we are confronted with the deadly consequences of behavior nurtured in a cycle of nationalistic fervor in Central Europe—yet again—that was unimaginable a few months ago.

Rational realism and the willingness to live life with the uncertainty of ambiguity speak from many of Bob's writings. They challenge us as New Testament scholars to be in-depth exegetes, applying the tools of our trade to the best of our knowledge and ability but to never forget that this is not a means in and of itself. We are part of our communities, entrusted with responsibility for our neighbors in mutual respect wherever we live our lives, in light of the message of the gospel.

Kathy Ehrensperger
Berlin
March 21, 2022

Acknowledgments

I AM GRATEFUL TO DR. Andrew Das and Dr. B. J. Oropeza for opening up precious space in their "Scripture and Paul Seminar" of the SBL for us to conduct the special tribute session for Robert Jewett at the San Antonio conference on November 21, 2021. Despite COVID-19 restrictions, the tribute session was well attended. I extend my appreciation to presenters at the conference and contributors to this volume for sharing their friendship and scholarship with students of the Bible in and through the life and works of Professor Bob Jewett.

I am especially grateful to Dr. Kathy Ehrensperger, who sits on the International Advisory Board of this series and has been a generous colleague in offering support and guidance and who has graciously contributed a chapter and the foreword despite her heavy research load.

I also am indebted to series co-editor, Dr. Melanie Baffes, for her impeccable attention to detail in copy-editing the entire manuscript and for overseeing the smooth production of this volume in collaboration with the editorial teams at Wipf & Stock Publishers. Last but not least, I'm grateful to Kungsiu and Phoebe Yeo for their meticulous compilation of the indices, allowing readers to easily and conveniently access this volume for their studies.

Introduction

Robert Jewett (December 31, 1933–December 4, 2020)

Ellen Jewett and K. K. Yeo

This Festschrift, a collection of essays written in honor of Professor Dr. Robert Jewett, is our simple gift to future generations, whom the life and works of our beloved "Bob" also bless. Nineteen representative essays—including those presented at the special session at Society of Biblical Literature conference in San Antonio on November 21, 2021, together with those from other colleagues—are collected in this tribute volume. They have been written in Jewett's blessed memory, testifying to how his works have impacted and will continue to leave an indelible mark on Pauline study, and testifying to the lives his life has touched.

Our tributes to Jewett's legacy express our gratitude to his "love without pretense . . . cleaving to the good . . . [and] taking the lead in honoring one another" (Rom 12:9–10, Jewett's translation). The apostle Paul and Professor Jewett are "twins" to many of us; yet, Jewett has also graciously invited us to know Paul, the follower of Jesus, in the wide and wildly expanding metaverse of intersecting spheres: civil religions, film, sailboats, songs, mountains, psychology, millenarian movements, and so forth. Jewett's expansive research interests have inspired each author in this tribute volume and have witnessed to the ways that helmsman Bob has navigated through the often-choppy ocean waters of biblical interpretation. Our hope is that future generations of Bible readers will find it easier to steer through the strong winds of exegetical, theological, and hermeneutical methods, and perhaps find faith, hope, and love (1 Thess 5:8).

Bob Jewett: Dad, Uncle, and Friend (by Ellen Jewett)

My father was born the first son of four children on December 31, 1933, in Lawrence, Massachusetts, and was given the name Robert Lee Jewett. His parents—Elizabeth, a high school teacher, and Walter, a wood-pattern maker turned Methodist minister—were from the Finger Lakes region of upstate New York and had probably never ventured very far south. But my grandfather was a great admirer of the Confederate of the same name, and I think my dad may have become aware early on in his life of the historical complexities embedded in a name. When dad was very young, grandpa got involved in an anti-gambling campaign that turned menacing, and they decided to move the family out west to Nebraska. Over the next years, they moved around the state, with my grandpa serving in a number of churches within the Methodist conference (even by horseback at times!). In WWII, he was called to serve as a chaplain at the US military base in Trinidad. The family decided to relocate for a few years to the state of Georgia in order for my grandfather to be able to visit periodically with the family. It seems that they were in quite a difficult financial situation, and my dad reported going months without proper shoes. Circumstances changed considerably, though, when the local army commander there learned that dad's name was Robert Lee—such a surprise from a Yankee northerner! And suddenly a nice, large, heated house became available to the family for the duration of the war. In adulthood, dad began to use "L" as an initial but dropped the Lee from his name altogether for his official publishing.

After the war, the family was offered either the family farmhouse in Hammondsport, New York (my grandma's side), or a car, and they chose the car and returned to Nebraska. As my grandpa also returned to the pulpit in larger churches now, he drew audiences with his wonderful storytelling. His specialties were the Old Testament tales; my dad would often relish in his retelling of grandpa's sermons—with him sitting in the front pew beside a line of middle-school-age children (especially the boys) who were spellbound with his "action packed" and theatrical descriptions (the bloodier the better). My grandma would sometimes admonish him for his graphic stories at Sunday dinner. Grandpa would also tell me stories about my dad, describing how when my dad was around the age of thirteen or fourteen, that he would run from his school to the public library to read all afternoon until dinner. He was a voracious reader from that time onward.

He met my mother, Janet Miller, at a church camp that was run by my grandparents in western Nebraska around that time. A few years later, they met again at college at Nebraska Wesleyan in Lincoln, where they both sang in the school's touring chamber choir. At the end of their studies there, they got engaged. In his junior year in 1954, he was selected for a prestigious semester program at the American University in Washington, DC. This intensive seminar brought together elite students from around the country to study government in action. (Michael Dukakis was one of his classmates.) He had a chance to observe sessions of Congress, as well as detailed legal discussions in the courts, and I am certain that this experience inspired his lifelong passion for American history and politics.

After my parents were married, they moved to Chicago to pursue graduate degrees--my father in theology and my mother in music. They attended a ton of classical concerts, and each worked a number of odd jobs in order to make ends meet. Dad was even a taxi driver for a while, which seemed to satisfy his adventurous personality. After receiving his degree from the University of Chicago, he won a scholarship from DAAD for his PhD studies in Tübingen, Germany. They stayed there for four years without returning to the US. In addition to learning German, they immersed themselves culturally and travelled as much as they could afford to. They returned by ship in the summer of 1964, bringing along a Volkswagen Beetle in the cargo hold. They drove west to Dakota City, Nebraska, where dad took a position as minister in a small Methodist church, and where I was born six months later.

After one year, he began to teach part-time at Morningside College in Sioux City, Iowa and quickly realized that he belonged in an academic environment. For the next thirty-three years, dad's rituals and lifestyle remained much the same. Being a prolific writer, scholar, and a well-loved teacher (his students called him "Uncle Bob"), his days started very early; he insisted on getting a few hours of writing done before breakfast and before teaching. There was always a lot of music in our lives--we sang together at home (with a bust of Beethoven behind the piano), in the car, around the campfire at our small cabin, and at large family get-togethers or gatherings with his students and colleagues. He nurtured my love of music and came to every one of my concerts he possibly could, from my childhood days in the Suzuki method up into my professional career. When we moved to Chicago, we had season tickets to the symphony and the opera; we especially loved summers at the Ravinia Festival, where we indulged in fancy picnicking and listening to wonderful music on our blankets under the stars.

He was happiest outdoors, and was almost as serious about new adventures as he was about his academic scholarship. Any summer teaching, outside lectures, or semester sabbaticals would offer a chance for extra travel and exploration. We shared many thrilling sailing experiences on our boat on Lake Okoboji and later on Lake Michigan. He would put me on the bottom side of the boat in strong winds, skimming the water and about ready to capsize, and we would laugh and laugh. We spent hundreds of hours on long walks, at home and abroad. Most often unhurried, these walks were a chance to rehash current and historical events, our own personal projects, hopes, fears, and dreams. Dad was careful, insistent, and Socratic with his questioning, and he certainly helped me to look at a topic from as many sides as possible. But we were always dreaming—about building straw bale houses situated off the grid, building secluded practice/writing cottages nestled in the woods, about a world without nuclear weapons, about building a Roman-era boat . . . the subjects were endless, but the art of shared conversation was most important. Both of my parents had large families, and we spent many happy holidays over the years, feasting, playing cards, and watching Huskers football. In 1999, my parents separated amicably, and my dad retired from his position at Garrett–Evangelical Theological Seminary, marking a new chapter in his life.

And They Came Down to Troas is the title of an autobiographical book my father had in his mind to write (one of many unfinished books in his mind). In the summer of 1999, he organized a tour to Turkey, mixing a group of scholars from Garrett-Evangelical and Germany. I was lucky enough to join them and, serendipitously, met my future husband Hüsam Süleymangil, who was their guide. This anchored us in Turkey for the rest of dad's life, and he loved being able to stay with us and travel leisurely throughout the country, re-imagining Paul's travels by road and by wind. He moved to Heidelberg, Germany, as a guest professor, and found a new love and new inspiration. Artist and writer Heike Goebels shared his passion for creative dialogue, and they collaborated on many projects together. They kept a beautiful home full of books and artwork and shared Heike's wonderful meals surrounded by abundant greenery and gardens. She was with him through the final stages of his Romans Commentary for the Hermeneia series, and he always said that he would never have finished without her precious guidance. She remained his steadfast confidante through his last days.

The advancement of Parkinson's disease had an isolating effect in his life, but I never heard him complain, even when it took forty-five minutes for him to dress. He had certainly inherited an optimistic and humble spirit, but I believe he also put a lot of effort into cultivating patience, acceptance, and kindness in his daily life. He passed away in his apartment adjoining the St. Mark's Methodist church in Lincoln, Nebraska on December 4, 2020, four days after testing positive for COVID-19. He was found kneeling on the ground with his face cradled in his arms on his favorite chair.

Dr. Jewett, Like Mentor, Like Friend (by K. K. Yeo)

A phone call from Ellen Jewett in Istanbul on the morning of December 4, 2020, delivered shocking news. I was in a state of disbelief and raw sadness. We had lost one of our Renaissance men, a people-promoter, a creative and prolific scholar, a faithful friend, my *Doktorvater*. A few flashbacks transported me to Dr. Robert Jewett's living room at St. Mark UMC: my wife and I last visited him in August 2019. I last received from him three DVDs of his research and writing material in October 2020, and in November I mailed him his requested research he needed on the book of Isaiah and the Lord's Prayer.

Within three days of his death, I received many of Jewett's friends and former students' tributes (personal emails used with permissions), tempering my sadness into a "communion of saints":

- *Anne Streaty Wimberly* (Christian Education professor emerita, Interdenominational Theological Center) and *Edward Powell Wimberly* (president emeritus, Interdenominational Theological Center) wrote, "Our loving friendship goes back so many, many years. Our admiration of him and gratitude for his presence in our lives, depth-filled conversations, co-teaching, and writing will be remembered and held dear always."

- *Hua Wei* (associate professor of philosophy and religious studies, Yuelu Academy, Hunan University, China) wrote, "I studied under Professor Jewett (and Professor Yeo) in 2007 in Beijing and met him again in 2009 at the Garrett library. His words of wisdom for my research in Romans and his care for my well-being continue to be my inspiration—as much as his Hermeneia Romans commentary, a life companion to me. A beloved grand-mentor!"

- *Philip Chia* (professor rank professional specialist, Chung Yuan Christian University, Taiwan) wrote, "Bob impressed me more than just a renowned biblical scholar, but truly a real patriot who loved his country with a deep sense of honor and shame, and of course, a mountain lover!"

- *Barbara Rossing* (professor of New Testament and environmental ministry coordinator, Lutheran School of Theology at Chicago) wrote, "I used Jewett's *Jesus Against the Rapture* in writing my own book *The Rapture Exposed*. And I continue to use essays by him regularly, every semester, in teaching . . . and everyone writing on Romans 8 engages with him—his breakthrough idea that Roman imperial abuse of the natural world and exploitation is being critiqued, in creation's co-groaning."

- *Wang Zi* (assistant professor, The Institute of Religions, Minzu University of China) wrote, "I have never met Dr. Jewett but feel like I know him for ages. I was a kid in the candy store when I read his Romans commentary . . . and he led me deep into the kaleidoscopic Roman world . . . that led me to my doctoral study of 1 Corinthians."

- *David Rhoads* (professor emeritus of New Testament, Luther School of Theology) wrote, "He was a giant in the field and at the same time humble and always ready to encourage and support. He struggled courageously through numerous health problems. I deeply valued my friendship with him as well and will miss him. My wife and I had many meals together with him. He was always so gracious."

- *Daniel Patte* (professor emeritus of religious studies, professor of New Testament and Early Christianity, Vanderbilt University) wrote, "Aline and I are also heartbroken to hear about Bob passing away. Since the 1970s, Bob has opened the path for a biblical scholarship (especially on Paul and Romans) that sets in constant dialogue the biblical text and its cultural context together with the readers of the Bible (including biblical scholars) and their cultural contexts—transforming biblical scholarship in the process, but also transforming the ways my students learned to read Paul. . . . Bob's passing leaves a big hole . . . but this big hole is already bridged by the scholarship of his many and many followers and students."

- *Lallene Rector* (president emerita, professor of religion and pastoral psychotherapy, Garrett-Evangelical Theological Seminary) wrote, "I knew him [Bob] as a supportive, creative, and thoughtful colleague; as one who always came with a written manuscript when he reported the Committee on Faculty's work to the entire faculty; and who engaged his students in his current research, often modifying his conclusions based on student interaction with it in the classroom. . . . His was a spirit that lives on in many of our hearts and minds."

- *Osvaldo Vena* (professor emeritus of New Testament, Garrett-Evangelical Theological Seminary) wrote, "Bob, you were a gracious man, and humble too, I would say. You took time to have coffee with me, a junior faculty member, and listened to my many concerns. But you also shared your own; you became vulnerable and so you taught me a great lesson, one which the apostle Paul had already taught us, that we are stronger when we are weak. . . . I know there are no desks in heaven, Bob. Desks are for acquiring knowledge, and that you don't need anymore. So, enjoy your desk-free time until the day when we meet again."

- *Brigitte Kahl* (professor of New Testament, Union Theological Seminary New York) wrote, "I am really heartbroken to hear about Bob passing away. And it is very moving that he apparently until his last day didn't give in and didn't give up on being one of the most game changing biblical scholars of our century. It'll still take us a while reading these 1,000 pages Romans commentary and understanding their impact . . ."

I had known Dr. Jewett since 1987 when I was a student at Garrett-Evangelical Theological Seminary, then as his colleague at the same school, starting in 1996. I could tell you about his long list of publications—including two hundred academic essays and reviews and twenty-three monographs—but his curriculum vitae and the many citations of his works in academic publishing can say it much better. I wish to tell you about Bob Jewett, "like mentor like friend," as the Chinese proverb says.

I enrolled at Garrett-Evangelical, and later at Northwestern University, between 1987 and 1992 and took seven New Testament courses from him as my early forays into making sense of the world of the apostle Paul. Every paper of mine that he graded came back with at least two single-spaced pages of feedback. He was a tremendous mentor to me, a valued colleague, and a dear friend. Bob's life is about the way a person's life touches another's; his gift to us has been his natural trust and investment in people.

His bow ties made an inspirational mark on my soul. For six years, as a student at Garrett-Evangelical Theological Seminary, I saw him wearing bow ties, signifying his signature of gold standard in theological education. I received a bow tie from him after I received my PhD in 1992 as I headed to Hong Kong for my first teaching assignment. What an encouragement! I hold onto it dearly and use it only on special occasions, because tying a bow tie is rather challenging for a Chinese person. I asked him, "How do I tie a bow tie, Dr. Jewett?" He replied, "Call me Bob; now we are colleagues." I replied, "Yes, Professor." Then he continued, "The trick is not to make the bow tie too asymmetrical, too perfect, and look too cheap. Relax when you tie, and give it your character." I learned from Bob then that the gold standard does not mean perfection; instead, it means to be unique, projecting your voice, letting one's works reflect one's character. This tip about professional life is invaluable.

I don't know how many recommendation letters he wrote for me for my scholarship and grant applications; they were undoubtedly very strong letters because I received most of the scholarships and grants for which I applied. I remember also that before he wrote the first letter, he asked for my resume. I thought he needed it to write a substantive letter. He actually scheduled a lunch meeting with me in the dining room of the seminary and went through my resume line-by-line, suggesting how I should write a curriculum vitae.

We organized international symposia around the world after he published his Romans Commentary. He and his commentary received a warm reception and critical assessment —in all he was thankful for the responses. And in 2013, all the proceedings of papers were published in a volume called *From Rome to Beijing*. For two months in 2007, we lived in a small apartment in Beijing where we co-taught Romans seminars at the Department of Philosophy and Religious Studies at Peking University. That summer, he donated and shipped forty-six boxes of his own Romans library to Peking University. He was actually the teacher of that course, and I was his translator, so in return I did not mind doing all the cooking and the laundry—and engaging in conversation with him about Paul and politics and cultures.

In Chinese culture, we say, "Once a teacher, always a teacher," and also *yishi yiyou* ("like mentor like friend"). A student's desire is to imitate his or her *Doktorvater*. Yet, Professor Jewett in class disapproved of his students being his clones. He would often present various approaches to a biblical text and then ask his students "to bite the bullet" about which view they would take, and why. Bob Jewett embodied a marvelous paradox of academic excellence and congenial spirit. His expansive heart is unmatched by any scholars I know. He enjoyed the sharing of minds and hearts with us all. He invited students to coffee or meals, showing a genuine interest in their families and a caring for their well-being. My children have fond memories of "Dr. Jewett" inviting us to spend time with him on his sailboat on Lake Michigan. We shall dearly miss this Christ-like human being, whose gift to us has simply been unconditional and graceful, or in one word—his favorite NT word—*agapic*.

The last piece (September 2020) we were working on is the "Lord's Prayer and Isaiah 25," where verse 6 says, "on this mountain the Lord of hosts will make for all peoples *a feast of rich food, and feast of well-aged wines* . . . ." (NRSV). I can still hear Bob Jewett's echoing of the apostle Paul in Romans 15:7, "Welcome one another as Christ welcomes you."

I'd like to use my good friend Troy W. Martin's words to end this section:

> My heart is heavy today with grief, but my mind is filled with wonderful memories of a bus tour throughout archaeological

sites in Turkey, quiet evenings around the dinner table at Bob's residences in Heidelberg and Rothenberg in Odenwald, stimulating discussions while walking the German countryside, and a most memorable trip to the Frankfort airport in Bob's old moving van. My grief is further tempered by our common hope in the salvation from this realm of sin and death that is guaranteed by Jesus Christ so that someday both Bob and all of us may taunt along with the Apostle Paul, "O Death, where is your victory? O Death, where is your sting?" (personal email)

Indeed, Bob Jewett still speaks through his life stories and through the pages of his numerous writings (see the list of selected publications below).

Selected Publications by Robert Jewett

Books

1. *Paul's Anthropological Terms: A Study of Their Use in Conflict* Settings. Arbeiten zur Geschichte des antiken Judentums und des Urchristentums 10. Leiden: Brill, 1971.

2. *The Captain America Complex: The Dilemma of Zealous Nationalism.* Louisville: Westminster, 1973; revised edition by Bear & Company, 1984. Korean translation by Young-Il Kim, Seoul: Voice, 1996.

3. *The American Monomyth*, with John Shelton Lawrence, foreword by Isaac Asimov. New York: Doubleday/Anchor, 1977. Second edition, by University Press of America, 1988. Italian translation by Bompiano; Japanese publication by Kaibun Sha Ltd.

4. *A Chronology of Paul's Life*. Minneapolis: Fortress, 1979. Published by London: SCM, as *Dating Paul's Life*. German translation by Gisela Koester by Kaiser Verlag, 1982.

5. *Jesus Against the Rapture: Seven Unexpected Prophecies*. Louisville: Westminster, 1979.

6. *Letter to Pilgrims: A Commentary on the Epistle to the Hebrews*. Cleveland: Pilgrim, 1981.

7. *Christian Tolerance: Paul's Message to the Modern Church*. Louisville: Westminster, 1982.

8. *Romans*, Teacher Book and Student Book for the "Genesis to Revelation Adult Bible Series." Vol 20. Nashville: The Graded Press of the United Methodist Publishing House, 1986.

9. *The Thessalonian Correspondence: Pauline Rhetoric and Millenarian Piety*. Foundations and Facets. Minneapolis: Fortress, 1986.

10. *Romans*, in the "Cokesbury Basic Bible Commentary" series. Nashville: United Methodist Publishing House, 1988; reprinted 1994 in the "Basic Bible Commentary" series.

11. *Saint Paul at the Movies: The Apostle's Dialogue with American Culture*. Louisville: Westminster John Knox, 1993.

12. *Paul the Apostle to America: Cultural Trends and Pauline Scholarship*. Louisville: Westminster John Knox, 1994.

13. *Saint Paul Returns to the Movies: Triumph over Shame*. Grand Rapids: Eerdmans, 1999.

14. *The Myth of the American Superhero*, with John Shelton Lawrence. Grand Rapids: Eerdmans, 2002.

15. *Captain America and the Crusade against Evil: The Dilemma of Zealous Nationalism*, with John Shelton Lawrence. Grand Rapids: Eerdmans, 2003.

16. *Romans: A Commentary*. Hermeneia. Minneapolis: Fortress, 2007.

17. *Mission and Menace: Four Centuries of Religious Zeal in America*, with Ole Wangerin. Minneapolis: Fortress, 2008. German translation, *Mission und Verführung. Amerikas religiöser Weg in vier Jahrhunderten*. Göttingen: Vandenhoeck & Ruprecht, 2008.

18. *Robert Jewett on Romans* [in Chinese]. Hong Kong: Logos, 2009.

19. *The Shame Factor: How Shame Shapes Society*, co-edited with Wayne L. Alloway and John G. Lacey. Eugene, OR: Cascade Books, 2010.

20. *The Bible and the American Future*, co-edited with Wayne L. Alloway and John G. Lacey. Eugene, OR: Cascade Books, 2010.

21. *From Rome to Beijing: Symposia on Robert Jewett's Commentary on Romans*, edited by K. K. Yeo. Lincoln, NE: Kairos Studies, 2013.

22. *Romans: A Short Commentary*. Minneapolis: Fortress, 2013.

23. *The Corinthian Correspondence: Redaction, Rhetoric and History*, with Frank Witt Hughes. Washington, DC: Fortress Academic/Lexington, 2021.

Editorial Projects

1. Editor of *Christology and Exegesis: New Approaches,* issue of *Semeia: An Experimental Journal for Biblical Criticism* 30 (1984), assisted by associate editors, L. W. Hurtado and P. R. Kiefert.

2. Co-editor with D. E. Groh, *The Living Text: Essays in Honor of Ernest W. Saunders.* Washington, DC: University Press of America, 1985.

3. Coeditor of *Common Life in the Early Church: Essays in Honor of Graydon F. Snyder.* Harrisburg, PA: Trinity, 1998.

4. Coeditor with Wayne L. Alloway Jr. and John G. Lacey, *The Bible and the American Future,* lectures presented at the St. Mark's Theological Conference, October 18–20, 2009. Eugene, OR: Cascade Books, 2009.

5. Coeditor with Wayne L. Alloway Jr. and John G. Lacey, *The Shame Factor: How Shame Shapes Society,* lectures presented at the St. Mark's Theological Conference October 24–26, 2010. Eugene, OR: Cascade, Books, 2011.

Honorary Volumes

1. *Celebrating Romans: Template for Pauline Theology: Essays in Honor of Robert Jewett.* Edited by Sheila E. McGinn. Grand Rapids: Eerdmans, 2004.

2. *Scripture, Cultures, and Criticism: Interpretive Steps and Critical Issues Raised by Robert Jewett.* Contrapuntal Readings of the Bible in World Christianity. Edited by K. K. Yeo. Eugene, OR: Pickwick Publications, 2022.

Abbreviations

BDAG Walter Bauer, Frederick W. Danker, W. F. Arndt, and F. W. Gingrich. *A Greek-English Lexicon of the New Testament and Other Early Christian Literature.* 3rd ed. Chicago: University of Chicago Press, 2000

CIJ Jean-Baptiste Frey. *Corpus Inscriptionum Judaicarum.* 2 vols. Edited by R. P. Vatican City: Pontificio Ist., 1936–1952

DNTB *Dictionary of New Testament Background.* Edited by Craig A. Evans and Stanley E. Porter. Downers Grove, IL: InterVarsity, 2000

LSJ Henry George Liddell, Robert Scott, and Henry Stuart Jones. *A Greek-English Lexicon.* 9th ed. Oxford. Clarendon, 1996

NTG *Novum Testamentum Graece,* Nestle-Aland. 28th ed. Münster: Institute for New Testament Textual Research, 2012

TDNT *Theological Dictionary of the New Testament.* 10 vols. Edited by Gerhard Kittel and Gerhard Friedrich. Translated by Geoffrey W. Bromiley. Grand Rapids: Eerdmans, 1964–1976

TLNT Ceslas Spicq. *Theological Lexicon of the New Testament.* 3 vols. Translated and edited by James D. Ernest. Peabody, MA: Hendrickson, 1994

Contributors

Frederick Mawusi Amevenku (PhD, Stellenbosch University), senior lecturer and director of graduate studies, Trinity Theological Seminary, Legon-Accra, Ghana. His publications include "Faith Healing in Ghanaian Christianity: An Examination of Attitudes and Practices Based on an Exegesis of James 5:13–18," *Trinity Journal of Church and Theology* 18, no. 4 (September 2015) 87–101; "Contemporary Pro-homosexual Hermeneutics and the Rise of Homophobia in Africa: A Christian Response," *Journal of African Biblical Exegesis* 5 (January 2014) 126–151. Email: fm.amevenku@trinity.edu.gh.

Keith Augustus Burton (PhD, Northwestern University), graduate professor of religion, AdventHealth University. He is the author of *Laying Down the Law* (2013); *The Compassion of the Christ* (2004); and *The Blessing of Africa* (2007). *Christianity Today* recently listed Burton among the twenty-five people who have shaped Black religious thought in the past century. Email: keith.burton@ahu.edu.

Douglas A. Campbell (PhD, University of Toronto), professor of New Testament, The Divinity School, Duke University. He also is the director of the Certificate in Prison Studies at Duke. His publications include *The Quest for Paul's Gospel* (2005); *The Deliverance of God* (2009); *Framing Paul* (2014); and *Pauline Dogmatics* (2020). Email: dcampbell@div.duke.edu.

William S. Campbell (PhD, University of Edinburgh), senior research fellow, Abraham Geiger College, the University of Potsdam Germany. His research focuses on a social-historical approach to Paul, with particular reference to ethnicity, theology, and ethics and the relevance of these for emerging Christian identity. His publications include *Paul and the Creation of Christian Identity* (2008); *The Nations in the Divine Economy: Paul's Covenantal Hermeneutics and Participation in Christ* (2018); and a major publication, *Romans: A Social Identity Commentary* (2022). Email: campbell@geiger.edu.de.

A. Andrew Das (PhD, Union Theological Seminary in Virginia), Niebuhr Distinguished Chair and professor of religious studies at Elmhurst University. He has written or edited nine books, including *Solving the Romans Debate* (2007); *Paul and the Stories of Israel* (2016); and a major commentary on *Galatians* (2014). Email: adas@elmhurst.edu.

Christopher Deacy (PhD, University of Wales), reader in theology and religious studies and head of the department, University of Kent. His works include *Christmas as Religion: Rethinking Santa, the Secular, and the Sacred* (Oxford University Press, 2016); *Screening the Afterlife: Theology, Eschatology and Film* (Routledge, 2012); and *Screen Christologies: Redemption and the Medium of Film* (University of Wales Press, 2001). Email: c.deacy@kent.ac.uk.

Kathy Ehrensperger (PhD, University of Wales), research professor of New Testament in Jewish Perspective, Abraham Geiger College, University of Potsdam. Her works include *Paul and the Dynamics of Power: Communication and Interaction in the Early Christ-Movement* (2007); *Paul at the Crossroads of Cultures: Theologizing in the Space-Between* (2013); and *Searching Paul: Conversations with the Jewish Apostle to the Nations* (2019). Email: kathy.ehrensperger@uni-potsdam.de.

Meng Hun Goh (PhD, Vanderbilt University), assistant professor of New Testament, Taiwan Graduate School of Theology. Recent publications include "'Influenced' or 'Possessed'? An Alternative Interpretation of Luke 1:17b," *Taiwan Journal of Theology* (2021); "The Fellowship of Witnessing: Interpreting 1 John 1:1–10 from the Margin," *Sino-Christian Studies* (2022). Email: menghgoh@gmail.com.

Najeeb T. Haddad (PhD, Loyola University Chicago), assistant professor and chair of religious studies, Notre Dame of Maryland University. His works include *Paul, Politics, and New Creation: Reconsidering Paul and Empire* and "God and New Creation in Galatians, 2 Corinthians, and Romans" in a forthcoming collection, *God in Paul's Letters*. He is a first-generation Arab (Jordanian) American and an Orthodox Christian biblical scholar. Email: nhaddad@ndm.edu.

Kong Hock Hii (PhD, Garrett-Evangelical Theological Seminary) served as New Testament lecturer at Sabah Theological Seminary, Malaysia, from 2007 to 2012. Since 2013, he has served as bishop of Sabah Annual Conference, The Methodist Church in Malaysia. Email: khhii@yahoo.com.

T. Christopher Hoklotubbe (ThD, Harvard University), member of the Choctaw Nation (Oklahoma) and assistant professor of religion, Cornell College (Mount Vernon, Iowa), and the director of graduate studies for NAIITS: An Indigenous Learning Community. He is the author of the award-winning *Civilized Piety* (2017) and is currently researching North American Indigenous interpretations of the Bible. Email: choklotubbe@cornellcollege.edu.

Frank W. Hughes (PhD, Northwestern University), priest-in-residence, Episcopal Church of the Redeemer, Ruston, Louisiana. He is the author of *Early Christian Rhetoric and 2 Thessalonians* (1989) and is co-author, with Robert Jewett, of *The Corinthian Correspondence: Redaction, Rhetoric, and History* (2021). Email: fwhughes54@hotmail.com.

Ellen Jewett (MM, SUNY Stony Brook) has enjoyed a varied career as a violinist, performing in major concerts halls worldwide. She has served on the faculties of McGill University, SUNY Stony Brook, Ithaca College, Ankara University, and is the founder and artistic director of Klasik Keyifler, an NGO and festival in Cappadocia. Ellen Jewett has recorded on labels such as Naxos, Centaur, and Chandos. Website: http://www.ellenjewett.com/; email: ellen@klasikkeyifler.org.

Robert K. Johnston (PhD, Duke University), senior professor of theology and culture, co-director of the Reel Spirituality Institute, Fuller Theological Seminary. His writings include *The Christian at Play* (1983); *Reel Spirituality: Theology and Film in Dialogue* (2006); and *God's Wider Presence* (2016). Email: johnston@fuller.edu.

Brigitte Kahl (Dr. sc. theol., Humboldt University Berlin) is a native of East Germany, where she taught ecumenics and biblical studies. In 1998, she became a professor of New Testament at Union Theological Seminary in New York. Her publications include *Galatians Re-Imagined: Reading with the Eyes of the Vanquished* (2010). Email: bkahl@uts.columbia.edu.

Kar Yong Lim (PhD, Wales University), lecturer in New Testament studies and director of postgraduate studies, Seminari Theoloji Malaysia, Malaysia. His publications include *"The Sufferings of Christ are abundant in Us": A Narrative Dynamics Investigation of Paul's Sufferings in 2 Corinthians* (2009); *Metaphors and Social Identity Formation in Paul's Letters to the Corinthians* (2017). Email: karyong@stm2.edu.my.

Sheila E. McGinn (PhD, Northwestern University), professor of New Testament and Early Christianity, John Carroll University. Recent publications include "Romans," in *The Jerome Biblical Commentary for the Twenty-First Century*; *The Jesus Movement and the World of the Early Church* (2014); and *By Bread Alone: The Bible through the Eyes of the Hungry* (2014). Email: smcginn@jcu.edu.

Aliou Cissé Niang (PhD, Brite Divinity School [TCU]), associate professor of New Testament, Union Theological Seminary. His writings include *Faith and Freedom in Galatia and Senegal* (2009); *A Poetics of Postcolonial Biblical Criticism: God, Human-Nature Relationship, and Negritude* (Cascade Books, 2019); "The Political Ethics of Léopold Sédar Senghor" in *The Palgrave Handbook of African Social Ethics*, edited by Nimi Wariboko and Toyin Falola (Palgrave Macmillan, 2020); "Contested Spaces: Diola Christianity in Rural and Urban Senegal," in *World Christianity, Urbanization, and Identity* (2021). Email: aniang@uts.columbia.edu.

Lallene J. Rector (PhD, Boston University), president emerita, professor of psychology of religion and pastoral psychotherapy, Garrett-Evangelical Theological Seminary. She is a clinically trained pastoral psychotherapist and psychoanalyst. Her works include "Developmental Aspects of the Twinship Selfobject Need and Religious Experience" in *Progress in Self Psychology: How Responsive Should We Be?*, edited by Arnold Goldberg, Vol. 16: 257–75; "Mystical Experience as an Expression of the Idealizing Selfobject Need" in *Progress in Self Psychology: The Narcissistic Patient Revisited*, edited by Arnold Goldberg, Vol. 17: 179–95. E-mail: lallene.rector@garrett.edu.

Zakali Shohe (DTh, Trinity Theological College, Singapore under ATESEA Theological Union), research fellow under Alexander von Humboldt Stiftung, Germany. She has authored *Acceptance Motif in Paul: Revisiting Romans 15:7–13* (2016) and *Redefining Relationships in Romans: A Socio-Historical and Political Reading* (2020). She has contributed chapters to several monographs and written articles in periodicals and is the co-editor of *Theology In-Context* (2010). Email: shohezakali@yahoo.com.

Aída Besançon Spencer (PhD, Southern Baptist Theological Seminary), senior professor of New Testament, Gordon-Conwell Theological Seminary. She has written numerous works, including *Paul's Literary Style* and *Beyond the Curse*. Born and reared in Santo Domingo, Dominican Republic, she is a Presbyterian minister who has served as an educator, founding pastor of an organization, and community organizer. Email: aspencer@gcts.edu.

K. K. Yeo (PhD, Northwestern University), Harry R. Kendall Professor of New Testament at Garrett-Evangelical Theological Seminary and affiliate professor at the Department of Asian Languages and Cultures at Northwestern University. He is an elected member of the Society of New Testament Studies (since 1998), a Lilly Scholar (1999), and Henry Luce Scholar (2003). He is the author of many books, including *What Has Jerusalem to Do with Beijing?* (2018); he is editor of *The Oxford Handbook of the Bible in China* (2021). Email: kkyeo@garrett.edu.

Part I

Scripture, Paul, and Ancient Cultures

1

Beyond the Acts-Based Approach to Pauline Biography

Douglas A. Campbell

Abstract

THE INTERPRETATION OF PAUL'S letters in the modern era takes place historically, in conversation with their original circumstances, which presupposes a detailed biography of Paul's life. But most interpreters presuppose a biography based on a literal reading of Acts that treats the life of Paul told there as correct in every detail and in the correct sequence. Paul's letters are then inserted into this framework. Robert Jewett demonstrated that this approach generates insuperable difficulties in terms of dating and "compression" and must be abandoned for a biography that begins with the letters, evaluating the Acts data in light of the events and sequences attested there—an approach pioneered originally by John Knox and then furthered by works like Jewett's own important analysis.[1]

Overview

Most modern interpreters of Paul generate their readings of his letters in conversation with their original contexts, which presupposes a reconstruction of the apostle's biography that tells us where he was and what he was doing when he wrote them, not to mention who he was writing to and why. Crafting the right biography of Paul can be a complex matter, however. But, as a handful of scholars such as Robert Jewett have repeatedly pointed out, this task is usually undertaken by way of shortcut, that is, by relying on a

---

1. Jewett, *Chronology*.

reading of the book of Acts in fairly literal terms. (The episodes concerning Paul's life are assumed to be true *and* the sequence in which the book of Acts recounts them.) The letters are simply inserted into Acts' story of Paul as they seem to fit. This story of Paul will probably be familiar to most readers since any Bibles with maps in the back usually reproduce this outline directly, along with most NT introductions. But is this straightforward, Acts-based approach to Paul's life reliable?

Unfortunately, as scholars like Robert Jewett have shown, when we place all our interpretative weight on this framework, and on its key date that locks it in place, we find that they give way. In order to appreciate these difficulties, however, we must first trace out the basic outline of Paul's apostolic career as Acts, read in a strictly linear fashion, describes it.

Outline

In brief: Acts begins its account of the early church in Jerusalem, and Paul begins his story there too. But his story really starts in earnest after his dramatic call *en route* to Damascus, which in view of its importance is described by Acts three times.[2] Paul's mission is then orchestrated in Acts by a series of "missionary journeys"; he circles out through unevangelized provinces and cities in the northeastern Roman Empire, planting churches and then back to Jerusalem, before being arrested there on his fifth visit. However, his first visit to Jerusalem takes place very quickly after his call. So the missionary journeys only become a prominent feature after his second visit to Jerusalem. Three journeys then take place before his final fifth visit (so before visits three, four, and five). This final visit introduces a long narrative of imprisonments and trials, which transport Paul, in the most ironic of circumstances, to Rome, where the story ends with the apostle anticipating a fatal trial before the emperor. Here is the outline:

- Call on the road to Damascus
- JV1 (first visit to Jerusalem)
- (Ministry in Syrian Antioch)
- JV2
- First missionary journey to Cyprus, Galatia, and Pamphylia
- JV3
- Second missionary journey to Macedonia, Achaia, and Asia

2. Acts 9:1–8; 22:6–11; 26:12–18.

- JV4
- Third missionary journey to Asia
- JV5: arrest in Jerusalem
- Long series of imprisonments and trials, including a journey to Rome and final detention there

Until the modern period, a strictly sequential use of this story as a biographical framework for Paul actually posed insuperable difficulties largely because of the data found in Paul's letter to the Galatians, although pre-Renaissance interpreters were not usually especially interested in strict, if not critical, historical reconstruction. So the following challenges were not always noted.

In ancient Greek, the word "Galatians" basically means "Gauls" or "Celts" (3:1). Moreover, in the eponymous letter's opening arguments, Paul supplies an unusually detailed account of his relationship with Jerusalem, including specific time intervals between two visits there. After his call, Paul visited Jerusalem "in the third year," and then again, on a visit that clearly included an important consultation, "in the fourteenth year." Ancient interpreters referred the letter's Gallic recipients to the ethnic group known to inhabit a region in what is today central Turkey, a migration of Gauls having taken place there centuries earlier. They knew further that, as Acts describes things, Paul could only have traveled through this area at the beginning of his *second* missionary journey when he traveled from Syria to Europe (see bullet seven above). However, by this point in the Acts narrative, Paul has already visited Jerusalem *three* times, while his letter only speaks, very clearly, of two (see bullets 2, 4, and 6). So Acts simply has to be mistaken, at least in strictly sequential historical terms. Hence, in a distant anticipation of much modern scholarly work on the Gospels, ancient authors concluded that the narrative of Acts was not in a strict sequence and may even have included episodic doublets, and they proceeded to work biographically in a more haphazard manner (which many of them were already doing anyway).

Vindication?

This problem was potentially resolved in the modern period, however, by the work of W. Ramsay who, in the late 1800s, discovered that a Roman province called "Galatia" had been formed in 25 BCE. The kingdom of Galatia was bequeathed posthumously by its ruler, King Amyntas, to the Roman emperor, Augustus. But Augustus also incorporated a series of colonies lying to the south of the ethnic kingdom into his new province, including some of the very cities Acts describes Paul visiting during his first missionary journey. And, at this moment, it becomes plausible to suggest that Paul's letter to the Galatians was written earlier in his career, after the first missionary journey, when only two visits to Jerusalem had been made according to Acts. Galatians 2:1–10 then provides an insider's account of the visit mentioned vestigially in Acts 11:27–30 and does not describe the conference of Acts 15:1–29. A straightforward *coordination* between Galatians and Acts now becomes possible.

But this still leaves the challenge posed by the long time intervals Paul enumerates in Galatians between his first two visits to Jerusalem—the issue that Robert Jewett aptly names the problem of "compression," which we will discuss further momentarily.[3] His missionary journeys do not begin in Acts until after his second Jerusalem visit, so is it really plausible to suppose that he remained in Damascus after his call—an interval Acts describes as "many days" (9:23)—for up to three years, and then stayed for up to fourteen years working only in Tarsus and Syrian Antioch before beginning the far-flung missionary journeys that so characterized his subsequent career? A strict harmonization between Acts and the letters entails this biography.

Two key pieces of evidence arguably come to Acts' support here in relation to the story it tells about Paul's mission in Corinth.

Acts notes a series of distinctive events during Paul's mission in that important Achaian commercial center (18:1b–18a). Among other things, on arriving, Paul meets Prisca and Aquila, who have "just" been forced to leave Rome because of some executive decree by the emperor Claudius (18:2–3). And, at some point during the mission, Paul is tried in front of a governor called Gallio (who famously refuses to take part in a case that he adjudges to be nothing more than a nasty squabble within the Jewish community; see 18:12–17). Acts states, in addition, that Paul worked in Corinth for eighteen months (18:11). Arguably, two key external markers now allow scholars to pinpoint these events, thereby ultimately vindicating Acts' testimony impressively.

The first key marker derives from the discovery in 1905 of an inscription at Delphi that mentions L. Annaeus Gallio. In its final reconstructed form, achieved in 1967, nine coordinated fragments determine that Gallio was the governor of Achaia at a time when Claudius was acclaimed as imperator for the twenty-sixth time, which probably denotes a date in 51 CE.[4] Governorships were exercised from July 1, normally for one year, so

---

3. Jewett, *Chronology*, 64–75.

4. The inscription's complex details are discussed concisely by Jerome Murphy-O'Connor, *Paul: A Critical Life*, 15–22.

it follows that Paul could have been tried by Gallio anywhere from July 1, 51 CE through the early months of 52. (Gallio left his appointment early, taking a sea voyage to address an illness as attested in a letter written by his brother, Seneca [*Ep.* 104.1].) This inscription vindicates the veracity of the Gallio episode in Acts directly, and also creates a tight chronological window for Paul's mission in Corinth; his time there must overlap with a period extending just from mid-51 to early 52 CE.

Complementing this marker is data from various ancient historians attesting to an action by the emperor Claudius against the Jews living in Rome. Acts states that Paul met Aquila and Priscilla on his first arrival in Corinth because an imperial edict promulgated by Claudius had forced the couple to leave Rome (18:2), thereby dating Paul's Corinthian mission to this event. And a Claudian action against the Jews in Rome is also attested by Suetonius, Dio Cassius, and Orosius.

Suetonius and Orosius speak of an "expulsion" of the Jews from Rome, although both sources are cryptic and a little garbled. Most importantly, Orosius states that this took place during Claudius's *ninth* year. Since this year basically equates to 49 CE, and Acts speaks of a mission by Paul in Corinth lasting eighteen months (18:11), we are clearly in—or almost in— the same chronological window as the governorship before Gallio attested from mid-51 CE, Orosius supplying the second all-important marker for this coordination.

The coordination is tight, but it works if Paul arrives at the very end of Claudius's ninth regnal year, in early January 50 CE. An eighteen-month-long ministry as detailed by Acts then takes him through—just—to the arrival of Gallio by July 1, 51 CE. If Paul's trial was undertaken immediately, then this evidence does fit together. Indeed, it can be claimed that this is an unusually impressive set of chronological correlations for a set of ancient sources, and it has been enough to convince many scholars that Acts is "telling it like it is." In particular, this happy conjunction arguably validates Acts' episodic *and* sequential veracity. The long-time intervals that Galatians specifies between Paul's first and second visits to Jerusalem can be accommodated after the founding events for the Jesus movement, along with the additional events that have to fit into this period.

We are on reasonably safe ground supposing that the Easter events took place in 30 CE, plus or minus three years. We must allow time for the early church to grow to the point that Paul persecutes it just prior to his dramatic call. We must then add around sixteen years for the Galatian intervals. After these have elapsed—perhaps in mid-48 CE—Paul must undertake his first missionary journey through Cyprus, Pamphylia, and Galatia (Acts 13– 14), his third visit to Jerusalem, and then undertake his second missionary journey as far as Corinth. This is a lot of time and activity, so the "fit" before an arrival in Corinth in early 50 CE is quite tight, but it is doable with a little bit of biographical nip and tuck as necessary.

Career

The broader trajectory of Paul's life can now be filled in around this key cluster of data points. His missionary journey to what is now Europe must have begun mid-way through Claudius's reign, in the late 40s CE, after the long pause detailed by Galatians in and around Syrian Antioch through the late 30s and early 40s. But after his journeys began, they proceeded apace. Calculating forward from a Corinthian mission in 50–51 CE, scholars suppose that on his third missionary journey, which began shortly thereafter, following his fourth Jerusalem visit, Paul spent two years and some months in Ephesus evangelizing Asia, presumably from late 51 CE through early 54 CE, after which he began his final fateful journey to Jerusalem. This was conspicuously circuitous, passing through Macedonia and Achaia and back again, Paul leaving Corinth for the last time only in the spring of 55 CE.[5] Nero has meanwhile become emperor after the death of Claudius in October 54 CE.

Paul's missionary journeys ended when he circled back to Jerusalem on this fifth visit, was arrested there, and was incarcerated in Caesarea. He languished under the governorship of Felix from mid-55 through late 56 CE, since Acts speaks of a "two-year" detention. The newly-arrived and vastly more competent governor Festus then tried Paul who, fearing the outcome of the case, appealed famously to the emperor. Paul's voyage to Rome and sojourn on Malta consequently fall through the winter of 56–57 CE, and his incarceration in Rome, also for "two years," would have lasted until at least mid-58 CE and possibly into early 59 CE.

With this framework in place, we can turn to the letters and ask where they best belong.

Placing the Letters

Some of Paul's letters must now fit into a certain location in this schema, while other locations tempt interpreters to place them there.

---

5. Paul's reference to Athens only denotes where he was when he dispatched Timothy, not where he is at time of writing; 2 Cor 1:19 references the ongoing work of the full mission team after Timothy and Silas have arrived from Thessalonica in Corinth, not Paul's immediate arrival; and so on.

Galatians, as we have already seen, is the earliest letter extant from Paul and must be placed after Jerusalem visit #2 and the first missionary journey but before Jerusalem visit #3. This seems to be roughly two full years earlier than Paul's arrival in Corinth, so this framework suggests its composition in 47 CE.

Romans fits much later in the sequence, in the spring of 55 CE, during Paul's final stay in Corinth as he anticipates what will turn out to be his final visit to Jerusalem. It follows that he wrote 1 and 2 Corinthians in the previous year, 54 CE, since these three letters are mutually involved with the collection of a great sum of money for the Jerusalem congregation.

First Thessalonians seems to reflect an early stage in that congregation's development and so to belong to Paul's first journey through the area, around 49 CE, although Acts creates a conundrum here. The letter implies that it was written from Athens (3:1). Paul is clearly sending Timothy back and forth to the fledgling congregation while he waits with Silas in Athens for news (1:1; 3:2–6). However, Acts takes pains to place Paul in Athens alone, only sending Silas and Timothy on from Thessalonica and Berea to link up with him after he has moved on from Athens to Corinth (17:13–15; 18:5). This data has led to some explanatory ingenuity if the letter is located, as Acts now necessitates, in Corinth.

If 2 Thessalonians is deemed authentic, it should be placed in this period as well. Strictly speaking, it is only "second" because it is shorter in length. It could therefore easily have been written before 1 Thessalonians. However, most Acts-based interpreters seem to prefer its placement in second position, after that letter, if they accept that it is genuine.

Setting aside the Pastorals for the time being, Paul's four remaining letters were written from prison, and long incarcerations are now evident in Caesarea and Rome. Unsurprisingly, scholars are often tempted to fill these with some letter writing.

In particular, Paul speaks in Philippians 1:13 of the gospel spreading through the *praetōrion*, which could be read as a reference to the emperor's Praetorian Guard, stationed in the main in Rome. And in 4:22, he sends greetings "especially from those of Caesar's Household," which refers either, literally, to members of the emperor's close family or, more plausibly (as suggested by Lightfoot) to members of the vast imperial bureaucracy, which was also centered in, although by no means limited to, Rome. Classicists tend to refer to this sprawling patronage network as "Caesar's Household." Hence this data almost begs interpreters to place Philippians during Paul's imprisonment in Rome, the center of imperial power, not to mention the scene of many a toga-clad Hollywood epic that biblical scholars probably watched in their youth. A two-year incarceration overcomes the travel challenges this scenario faces.[6] (Unfortunately, both of the key interpretative judgments underlying this location will ultimately prove inaccurate.)

Ephesians, Colossians, and Philemon clearly belong together, if they are authentic, although no data point specifically toward Rome. Hence, scholars can take their pick of locations because Paul himself attests to frequent trials—which imply imprisonments—well before Acts places him in a detention (2 Cor 11:25). Scholars nevertheless usually place these letters in Rome, or less frequently in Caesarea, although some suggest an imprisonment during Paul's long ministry in Ephesus. Second Corinthians 1:8–9 attests to some terrible trial during this mission, even using a fragment of judicial language to describe it: "we ourselves bore within ourselves the sentence of death . . ." (v. 9).[7] Nevertheless, all three options for these imprisonments are clearly suggested by the Acts-based approach.

Table 1.1: An Acts-Based Biography
of Paul's Life and Letters

Acts		Paul's Movements	Date	Letter Placement
I. 1:1—8:40		The early church grows in Jerusalem, Judea, and Samaria.	Absent	
II. 9:1–30 (anticipated by 8:1, 3)		Paul is called *en route* from Jerusalem to Damascus, then returns to Jerusalem briefly and goes to Tarsus (Cilicia).	Jerusalem Damascus Jerusalem (visit #1) Cilicia (Tarsus)	Up to three years in Damascus
III. 9:31—11:18		Peter takes a missionary journey through coastal Judea and back to Jerusalem. The first overt pagan, Cornelius, converts.	Absent	

---

6. The letter envisages multiple journeys between Paul's place of incarceration and Philippi. However, the most expeditious journey by sea from Rome to Philippi could have taken as little as seventeen days, so each separate communication presupposes just over a month of travel. Scheidel and Meeks, "The Stanford Geospatial Network Model of the Roman World."

7. All quotations from the biblical text are my own translation.

Acts		Paul's Movements	Date	Letter Placement
IV. 11:19–30	Paul and Barnabas go to Syrian Antioch, where the disciples are first called Christians. They travel to Jerusalem with money to alleviate the effects of a famine.	Syria (Antioch) Jerusalem (visit #2)	Up to fourteen years in Syrian Antioch	
V. 12:1–24	Peter is imprisoned but miraculously escapes.	Absent		
VI. 12:25—14:28	Paul's first missionary journey takes place, with Barnabas, through Cyprus, Pamphylia, and Galatia, and then back to Antioch.	Cyprus Pamphylia Galatia		ca. 47: Galatians
VII. 15:1–35	A great council in Jerusalem decides the terms of pagan inclusion in the messianic Jewish community.	Jerusalem (visit #3)		
VIII. 15:36—18:22	Paul's second missionary journey, with Silas, takes place through Galatia to Macedonia, Achaia, and briefly to Asia.	Macedonia Achaia Asia (briefly) Jerusalem (visit #4)	January 50: arrival in Corinth; mid 51: trial before Gallio in Corinth; mid 51: Jerusalem visit #4	50: 1 Thessalonians 2 Thessalonians*

Acts		Paul's Movements	Date	Letter Placement
IX. 18:23—21:17	Paul's third missionary journey takes place, primarily concentrating on Asia, then returning to Jerusalem circuitously through his other Aegean mission fields.	Asia Macedonia (briefly) Achaia (three months) Macedonia (briefly) Asia (coastal) Jerusalem (visit #5)	Late 51–early 54: arrival in Ephesus; early 54–early 55: final journey around the Aegean to Jerusalem; early-mid 55: Jerusalem visit #5	("Ephesians"* Colossians* Philemon) 54: 1 Corinthians 2 Corinthians 55: Romans
X. 21:17—26:32	Paul is arrested, tried, and imprisoned in Jerusalem and Caesarea.	Jerusalem (visit #5 continued) Caesarea	Mid 55–late 56: incarceration under Felix late 56: trial before Festus	("Ephesians"* Colossians* Philemon)
XI. 27:1—28:31	Paul undertakes a dramatic voyage to Rome, surviving a shipwreck *en route*. After wintering on Malta, his detention continues in Rome.	Malta Rome	Late 56–early 57: voyage to Rome; winter on Malta early 57–mid 58/early 59: Roman incarceration	Philippians "Ephesians"* Colossians* Philemon

* denotes widely-argued pseudonymity

Problems with the Usual Approach

Despite the dominance of the Acts-based approach within modern Pauline interpretation, however, we need to face the unpleasant fact that the framework contains serious problems, and few scholars have grasped and articulated these better than Robert Jewett.

One such problem, which he was well aware of, is the fragility of its key chronological cluster. Although the Gallio datum is firm, the assertion that Claudius expelled the Jews from Rome at some point in 49 CE, allowing Paul to meet the migrating Prisca and Aquila during his first mission in Corinth, eighteen months before his trial in 51 CE, as Acts says, is implausible. (It would follow that Acts is conflating events from separate visits, which is not uncommon in ancient biographies and biographical histories that tend to group events by topic.)

The Acts-based biography rests largely on the attestation of Orosius, who was a notoriously bad historian and wrote long after the critical event in question. (His *Historiae Adversus Paganos* was written ca. 416 CE.) His incompetence is evident in the key datum that the Acts-based biography relies on:

> Josephus reports, "In his ninth year the Jews were expelled by Claudius from the city." But Suetonius, who speaks as follows, influences me more: "Claudius expelled from Rome the Jews constantly rioting at the instigation of Christ." (*Historiae Adversus Paganos* 7.6.15–16)

No such quotation can be found in Josephus, whose works are extant, calling Orosius's chronological claim immediately into question. That a Claudian expulsion of the Jews from Rome even took place rests now on the witness of Suetonius, who is Orosius's only obvious source. (The all-important second infinitive in Acts 18:2 itself is ambiguous; the verb could denote purpose or result.)

Suetonius was much closer to the events in question (his work, *The Twelve Caesars*, was written in 121 CE), but his information is both compact and garbled: "Since the Jews constantly made disturbances at the instigation of *Chrestus*, he [the emperor Claudius] expelled them from Rome" (*Claudius*, 25.4). That a messianic agitator was directly causing problems at Rome during the reign of Claudius is clearly false, while other doubts about the accuracy of this statement can be raised. Hence, it is significant that Dio Cassius, writing his massive *Roman History* through the early 200s, deliberately nuances this scenario:

> As for the Jews, who had again increased so greatly that by reason of their multitude it would have been hard without raising a tumult to bar them from the city [of Rome], he [Claudius] did not drive them out, but ordered them, while continuing their traditional mode of life, not to hold meetings. (*Roman History* 60.6.6)

Dio states here that the Jews were *not* expelled by Claudius, although many of the pious, forbidden from praying or learning Torah in their synagogues, would have left following the withdrawal of their right to associate, perhaps creating the impression of an expulsion. Two further observations suggest that Dio's account is more plausible than Suetonius's (that is, apart from the considerable superiority of Dio as a historian over Suetonius in general terms).

First, Dio is well aware of an earlier expulsion of the Jews from Rome by Tiberius and knows that the later Claudian action was both different and milder. The earlier expulsion undoubtedly took place and was so traumatic that other ancient historians besides Suetonius and Dio note it. Tacitus and Josephus provide details, and it even left an imprint on Tertullian.[8] But these other historians are all silent concerning any later expulsion by Claudius, suggesting that the rather sensational Suetonius could be confusing a softer Claudian judgment with the earlier Tiberian action—and he is, after all, describing it in just one sentence. He is not supplying legal or political nuance as Dio is. It is doubtful that a full-fledged Claudian expulsion ever took place.

Second, Dio provides a plausible account of what Claudius did do to the Jews in Rome, joining hands again with data from other ancient historians in a way that Suetonius and Orosius do not, although connecting here especially with Philo.[9]

The Jews experienced a terrible crisis during the reign of Gaius, first in relation to emperor worship in general, the tensions being especially acute in Alexandria, and then with his particular plan to install an enormous cult statue of himself in the temple in Jerusalem. Gaius's assassination halted this incendiary policy, but Claudius still had to address the lingering disruptions, and his firm admonitions to the citizens in Alexandria are extant. The data in Dio suggests that he took an even firmer step in Rome itself, withdrawing the Jews' right to associate. This was a standard Roman response to perceived urban disorder, although it was much less aggressive—and much more enforceable—than an expulsion. Moreover, Dio places this Claudian action right where it should be, after the assassination of Gaius and the new emperor's accession, in 41 CE. (No such crisis necessitating the far more dramatic step of a Jewish expulsion is evident in 49 CE.[10])

The data in Dio opens up another, more plausible date and rationale for the arrival of Prisca and Aquila in Corinth, in 41 CE, and basically

---

8. These ancient data are referenced and discussed by Murphy-O'Connor (*Paul: A Critical Life*, 9–15), although he reaches slightly different conclusions than Jewett and I do.

9. See Philo's *On the Embassy to Gaius*, esp. §§ 156–57 (in *The Works of Philo*, 771). Philo himself does not mention Tiberius's expulsion, probably for obvious reasons. His overt agenda is to portray Gaius as deviating from the standard Julio-Claudian policy enacted by wise rulers. See also his *Flaccus*, passim (in *The Works of Philo*, 725–41).

10. Slightly offsetting this evidence in Dio is the absence of his account of Claudius's ninth year. But although we don't possess the source, his comment in 60.6.6 does not actually make sense if he wrote later of a Jewish expulsion.

torpedoes the Acts-based biography—although the alternative date fits neatly into an epistolary approach, thereby vindicating Acts' episodic reliability. There was a Claudian action against the Jews in Rome, and Prisca and Aquila did arrive in Corinth because of it. But it was their pious response to the withdrawal of their right to associate and the resulting abrogation of synagogue worship that led to their decision to leave the city in 41 CE, as Claudius sought to calm the Jewish tumult still eddying at Rome after the horrors of the reign of Gaius.

If the chronological centerpiece for an Acts-based biography proves to be unstable, can we point to other problems? Another that Robert Jewett also pointed to is worth briefly mentioning.

Compression

The time intervals Paul specifies in Galatians between his first and second visits to Jerusalem—2.x and 13.x years respectively—must fit before the fixed cluster of markers that Acts-based biographers appeal to in relation to Paul's mission in Corinth. And many events take place in the book of Acts after Paul's second visit to Jerusalem but before his arrival in Corinth in 18:1: the first missionary journey, the all-important third Jerusalem visit with its conference, and most of the action in the second missionary journey occur in this interval. A very simple problem arises at this moment. These events just cannot all fit into this space, generating the problem Robert Jewett referred to as "compression."[11]

Calculating backwards from the Corinthian markers, we generate the following chronology:

1. July 51 CE: Trial before Gallio in Corinth (18:12–17)
2. January 50 CE: Arrival in Corinth
3. Second missionary journey as far as Corinth (15:36–18:11)
4. Jerusalem visit #3 (15:1–35)
5. Composition of Galatians
6. First missionary journey (Acts 12:25–14:28)
7. Jerusalem visit #2 (11:27–30)
8. Interval of 13.x years (by implication, in and around Antioch; 11:19–26)

---

11. See Jewett, *Chronology*, 64–75.

9. Jerusalem visit #1 (9:26–30)

10. Interval of 2.x years (by implication, in and around Damascus; see Acts 9:23)

11. Call near Damascus (9:1–25; cf. 2 Cor 11:32–33)

The difficulty should be apparent. If we subtract 15.x+x years from early 50, we end up in 34 CE, and we are now perilously close to the time period when Jesus was probably crucified. (The usual dates suggested are 30, 33, and 34 CE.) But we have only gotten as far as Paul's second visit to Jerusalem! We have not yet included *any* of the other events in Paul's life that lie outside these time periods but need to happen in this space as well, notably, his first missionary journey, his third visit to Jerusalem, and his second missionary journey as far as Corinth, which included a great deal of travel. Moreover, the second journey planted congregations in Philippi, Thessalonica, Berea, and Athens, before the mission in Corinth, which surely took some time. Neither have we included the events that must unfold after the Easter events but before Paul's call. As it stands then, this framework does not really work. As Robert Jewett observes, a problem of chronic "compression" is generated. This biographical framework has Paul doing very little—being strangely immobile mainly in Syrian Antioch—for around sixteen years (so Acts 11:19–30), after which he suddenly springs to life and does most of the things that Acts writes about him in an astonishingly short period of time. And, in fact, it is too short.

It is possible to ease the pressure here a little by reinterpreting Paul's numerical language, reading his Galatian intervals "concurrently" or some such. This resolves at least some of the compression by reducing the time period before his second Jerusalem visit to 13.x years after his call. Things are still tight, but at least they become vaguely workable. But at bottom, this is to make recourse to fuzzy math. There is no indication in the text of Paul's letter that these are anything but specifications of the time intervals elapsing between the events he is talking about, which are different and suggest adding them together for the purposes of biography. (And the epistolary chronology will ultimately determine that the intervals are as they appear, namely, consecutive.)

Conclusion

Many other concerns about an Acts-based biography of Paul could be raised.[12] But these are the two key issues, both of which were clearly explained by Robert Jewett. So, ideally, enough has been said here to clear the way for students of Paul to realize that they must set their faces against any easy approach to Paul's biography in terms of the book of Acts. We must consider instead the harder, steeper climb to a Pauline biography that begins with the letters—a letter-based approach—which Robert Jewett was such an important advocate for.

Bibliography

(* For Further Reading)

*Campbell, Douglas A. *Framing Paul: An Epistolary Biography*. Grand Rapids: Eerdmans, 2014.
Dio Cassius. *Roman History*. 9 vols. Translated by Herbert B. Foster and Earnest Cary. Loeb Classical Library. Cambridge: Harvard University Press, 1914.
*Jewett, Robert. *A Chronology of Paul's Life*. Minneapolis: Fortress, 1979.
Josephus. *Jewish Antiquities*. 9 vols. Translated by H. St. J. Thackeray and Ralph Marcus. Loeb Classical Library. Cambridge: Harvard University Press, 2001.
*Knox, John. *Chapters in a Life of Paul*. Rev. ed. London: SCM, 1987 (1950).
*Murphy-O'Connor, Jerome. *Paul: A Critical Life*. Oxford: Oxford University Press, 1996.
Orosius. *Seven Books of History Against the Pagans*. Translated by A. T. Fear. Liverpool: Liverpool University Press, 2010.
Philo. "Flaccus." In *The Works of Philo*, translated by C. D. Yonge, 725–41. New updated ed. Peabody, MA: Hendrickson, 1993.
———. "On the Embassy to Gaius." In *The Works of Philo*, translated by C. D. Yonge, 757–90. New updated ed. Peabody, MA: Hendrickson, 1993.
Scheidel, Walter, and Elijah Meeks. "The Stanford Geospatial Network Model of the Roman World." Orbis.Stanford.edu. http://orbis.stanford.edu/.
Seneca. *Letters from a Stoic*. Translated by Robin Campbell. London: Penguin, 2004.
Suetonius. *The Twelve Caesars*. Rev. ed. Translated by Robert Graves. London: Penguin, 2007 (1957).

---

12. For example, the multiplication of events surrounding the Judaizing crisis is odd. Paul ends up making three visits to Jerusalem instead of one to address the issue, with the key events seeming to repeat themselves a little too closely on each of those occasions. We could also note the carelessness and/or vagueness of many statements in Acts; for example, a period in Damascus we know from Paul lasted two years and several months is referred to as "many days." Acts also contains a number of basic factual bloopers (see Luke 2:1–2; 3:2; Acts 5:36–37; 21:39).

Study Questions

1. How does the usual approach to reconstructing the life of Paul work? (Recall that this is important because it provides the key background information against which often we read his letters, allowing us to calculate when they were written, what was going on his life as he was writing them, and even sometimes to whom he was writing.)

2. What is the key dating cluster in this approach that is often touted as its greatest triumph but turns out to be one of its greatest weaknesses?

3. What is the problem of "compression," which suggests abandoning this whole approach to reconstructing Paul's life and to placing and interpreting his letters in these terms?

2

Robert Jewett and the Corinthian Correspondence

FRANK W. HUGHES

Abstract

THIS ESSAY DETAILS A central problem of the interpretation of 1 and 2 Corinthians: the question of the literary integrity of those two New Testament letters, along with the solution proposed by Robert Jewett and me. This solution involves a partition theory of both 1 and 2 Corinthians. Also involved in the interpretation of (especially) 1 Corinthians is the question of whether the opponents of Paul were "full blown" Gnostics or proto-Gnostics.

Introduction

One of the biggest problems in the New Testament is the question of whether 1 and 2 Corinthians are integral letters, or whether there are several letters embedded in either or both. Paul rakes the Corinthians over the coals for the first four chapters of 1 Corinthians for their lack of unity, and yet in 1 Corinthians 11:18, Paul does not fully believe that the Corinthians were divided into factions; in 11:19, Paul even suggests that divisions are actually necessary to find out who the genuine people are. In the opening chapters of 2 Corinthians, Paul says that he wrote a letter "out of anguish of heart and with many tears" (2:4)[1] to deal with the break that had happened between Paul himself and the Corinthians, and that, after the congregation's repentance, the break seems now to have been healed. Yet in 2 Corinthians 10:1—13:13, Paul writes

---

1. All quotations from the biblical text are my own translation.

a sarcastic letter attacking the Corinthians. Since in 2 Corinthians 1:1—2:13, Paul wrote to confirm the reconciliation that had taken place between the Corinthians and himself, one should ask why Paul would then write material that could only serve to inflame the relationship once more. Is it likely that 2 Corinthians 1:1—2:13 could be in the same actual letter as 2 Corinthians 10:1—13:13? Scholars who partition 2 Corinthians say "no." Thus, the question of the literary integrity of 1 and 2 Corinthians is a problem that has remained for over a century of scholarship.

Robert Jewett's involvement with the Corinthian correspondence, including the issue of the integrity of both 1 and 2 Corinthians, goes back to his Tübingen dissertation from 1966. In *Paul's Anthropological Terms*,[2] Jewett took the position that both 1 and 2 Corinthians were not integral letters: several letters from Paul to Corinth were embedded in the letters we know in the New Testament.

Schmithals's Gnostic Thesis and Partition Theory

Jewett was sympathetic to what Walter Schmithals had argued in the book translated as *Gnosticism in Corinth*,[3] both including his reconstruction of multiple Corinthian letters embedded within 1 and 2 Corinthians and also Schmithals's argument with respect to Gnosticism. In *Paul's Anthropological Terms*, Jewett reviewed Schmithals's partition theory of the Corinthian correspondence, basically accepting the six-letter partition theory involving both 1 and 2 Corinthians. Predictably 1 Corinthians 11 was included in Schmithals's Epistle A, and 2 Corinthians 1:1-2:13 + 7:5—8:24 constituted Epistle F.[4] This meant that 1 Corinthians 11:2-34 presupposes a time in which Paul was not too concerned about the division in the Corinthian church, about which he has heard but does not fully believe. One must contrast this with Schmithals's Epistle B, including 1 Corinthians 1:1—6:11, where Paul had received a detailed report from "those of Chloe," which he obviously fully believed (1 Cor 1:11–15). So Schmithals, who was far from the first scholar to partition 1 and 2 Corinthians, showed at length the differences in the stages of the human situation to which the apostle Paul was responding by letter. Thus, Paul wrote letters to the same Corinthian church, but at different times, based on his increasing level of knowledge of what was happening in that congregation.

2. Jewett, *Paul's Anthropological Terms*.
3. Schmithals, *Gnosticism in Corinth*.
4. Schmithals, *Gnosticism in Corinth*, 100–101n30.

Rudolf Bultmann and Ernst Käsemann had argued that the problem in the Corinthian church was best explained by the hypothesis that the Corinthian problem was Gnosticism. In *Paul's Anthropological Terms*, however, Jewett had a more critical and nuanced attitude toward the identification of Gnosticism as the Corinthian problem. Jewett argued that Käsemann's and Bultmann's identifications of the Corinthians as Gnostics "were doomed from the outset."[5] Jewett was positive about Dieter Georgi's identification of the opponents of Paul as "wandering charismatic preachers."[6] Jewett wrote, "Georgi makes a good case from parallels in the Hellenistic culture that this triumphant apostolic existence was thought of as an expression of being a Hellenistic 'divine man.'"[7]

Jewett insisted on the need for modern readers to distinguish among the theologies of Paul, the "divine man" missionaries who came into Corinth, and members and factions of the Corinthian congregation itself.[8] Jewett accepted Schmithals's thesis about Gnosticism *in part*, noting that other scholars had differentiated among the four parties mentioned in 1 Corinthians 1:12. Schmithals held that the "Christ-party" were Gnostics, and that a major part of the conflict within the Corinthian congregation was a conflict between the Christ-party and those of the other factions. Jewett argued that features of the Corinthian congregation were consistent with a type of Gnosticism. He wrote, "The Gnostics, by virtue of their possession of the wisdom and spirit, believed they had a divine power (1 Cor 8:9; 9:4–6) and freedom (1 Cor 9:1) which expressed itself in the motto *"panta moi exestin"* (1 Cor 6:12; 10:23)."[9] Jewett concluded, "In summary, the main opponents of Paul within the Corinthian congregation itself were radical enthusiasts who can be termed Gnostics because of their belief in salvation through *sophia/gnōsis* and because of their consistently dualistic world view."[10]

In order to make any partition theory fully believable, one needs to state plausible reasons for the differences between the reconstructed original forms of Paul's letters to the Corinthians and the forms in which we have them as 1 and 2 Corinthians. This Jewett did in 1978 in his article, "The Redaction of I Corinthians and the Trajectory of the Pauline School."[11] The article argued Jewett's partition theory of 1 Corinthians, making a proposal

---

5. Jewett, *Paul's Anthropological Terms*, 28.
6. Jewett, *Paul's Anthropological Terms*, 28. See Georgi, *Opponents of Paul*.
7. Jewett, *Paul's Anthropological Terms*, 29.
8. Jewett, *Paul's Anthropological Terms*, 27–29.
9. Jewett, *Paul's Anthropological Terms*, 39.
10. Jewett, *Paul's Anthropological Terms*, 40.
11. Jewett, "Redaction of I Corinthians."

concerning why and how redaction of several of the original Corinthian letters was done in order to produce 1 Corinthians. Jewett referred to his work in this article as "redaction criticism," analogous with redaction criticism of the synoptic gospels.

Redaction Hypothesis

Drawing on Günther Bornkamm's famous article,[12] in which there was a "frame letter" into which different fragments of authentic Pauline letters were inserted, based on particular redactional motives, to form 2 Corinthians, Jewett in the article proposed that there was a frame letter and redaction that took place, which resulted in the creation of 1 Corinthians. Why was this redaction done? In Jewett's words:

> My thesis is that the insertion of segments into the frame letter as well as the provision of several interpolations reveal a conflict in the place of origin, probably Ephesus, concerning charismatic authority. Gnostic or enthusiastic proponents of the earlier pattern of pneumatic leadership, who probably cited passages from an original Pauline letter in support of their position, are countered by redactional juxtapositions with elements from other Pauline letters that were marked by commands and rules. The redaction of 1 Corinthians can thus be seen as a step in the direction of apostolic legitimacy as expressed in the later Pastoral Epistles.[13]

The frame letter of 1 Corinthians (Jewett's Letter C) had material in it that would have been highly useful by those who were Gnostics. This letter argued that there were some Jesus-believers who had spiritual wisdom, and there were others who did not. The redaction that created 1 Corinthians out of several authentic Pauline letters was intended to take the original frame letter of 1 Corinthians, Letter C, out of the hands of those who would have interpreted some of Paul's original letters to Corinthian Jesus-believers to argue in favor of Gnostic ways of understanding the identities of members of the church. Jewett, in 1978, continued to understand the opponents of Paul in Corinth as Gnostics, and he also understood the opponents of the redactors who produced the canonical 1 Corinthians as Gnostics.

In 1977, *The Nag Hammadi Library in English* was published by James M. Robinson as general editor, followed by revised editions appearing in

---

12. Bornkamm, "Vorgeschichte."
13. Jewett, "Redaction of I Corinthians," 391.

1981, 1988, and 1996.[14] During the 1980s and 1990s, there was a growing awareness among scholars of the complexity of Gnosticism and the multiple Gnostic systems of thought and belief. By the time Jewett and I started actively writing our book, he was describing the Corinthian opponents of Paul as "proto-Gnostics" rather than Gnostics. It would not be surprising if he were influenced by the appearance in English of Hans Conzelmann's commentary on 1 Corinthians in 1975 with its thoughtful assessment of theories of the identity of the Corinthian opponents of Paul. Conzelmann wrote: "There are also isolated traces of the beginnings of the formation of what later presented itself as 'Gnosticism,' that is, Gnosticism *in statu nascendi*. The Corinthians could be described as proto-Gnostics."[15] This balanced view was the view we adopted in our book. We agreed with Conzelmann that it is possible to distinguish between "full blown" Gnosticism on the one hand, as represented by what Irenaeus of Lyons wrote against and as found in the Nag Hammadi documents, and proto-Gnosticism on the other hand.

Rhetorical Criticism

In the 1980s, several scholars got involved in rhetorical criticism of Pauline letters, including Jewett. Pauline letters, as well as other letters in the Pauline corpus, were analyzed according to precepts of Greek and Roman rhetoric. In 1980, Jewett began work on his large Romans commentary, which appeared in 2006. In 1979, the commentary on Galatians by Hans Dieter Betz had appeared. Jewett called that commentary "a quantum leap" in the study of Pauline letters. Jewett had always taken form criticism of letters pioneered by Paul Schubert very seriously.[16] He was highly interested in the structure of letters and other aspects of the study of letters that could help modern readers understand what Paul was doing as he wrote letters to congregations.[17] Jewett's article, "Romans as an Ambassadorial Letter," was a first foray into connecting form criticism and the study of types of letters with Paul's ministry activities.[18] He was very interested in rhetorical criticism of Paul's letters. By the fall of 1980, Jewett was actively learning about rhetoric and epistolary types, and he started developing his theory of Romans as a rhetorical letter. He agreed with Betz that Galatians was a letter

14. Robinson, ed., *Nag Hammadi Library in English*.
15. Conzelmann, *1 Corinthians*, 115.
16. Schubert, *Form and Function of the Pauline Thanksgivings*.
17. Betz, *Galatians*.
18. Jewett, "Romans as an Ambassadorial Letter."

written in judicial rhetoric, and he was moving toward a firm understanding of Romans as a letter written in epideictic rhetoric.

The reason for Jewett's development of rhetorical criticism was that his scholarship on Paul was deeply historically centered. Because Jewett always asked historical questions about Paul, and frequently couched questions about the literary phenomena in Paul's letters in historical terms, it was natural for Jewett to be acutely attuned to everything he could find about how Paul most likely composed his letters. After he asked *how* Paul's letters were written, Jewett invariably moved to the question of *why*. It was always supremely important why Paul wrote the letters he did: Jewett wanted to use any kind of analysis of Paul's letters to help him answer historical questions about Paul and his activities in churches. Since Paul was writing letters in particular ways to congregations, his letter writing was a historical phenomenon. It was precisely as a historical critic that Jewett approached rhetorical criticism. This was his approach in his large Romans commentary, which appeared in 2006.[19] The analysis of persuasion techniques Paul was using in his letters mattered, along with the identification of the particular matters concerning which Paul was doing persuasion—matters that included both Paul's theology and also practical problems of mission strategy.[20]

In 1993, Jewett published a new article, "Paul's Dialogue with the Corinthians . . . and Us." This article, written for working pastors and preachers, shows its readers further development of Jewett's understanding of the Corinthian correspondence. Over the course of his entire career, Jewett worked to understand and explain the situational character of each of the letters of Paul. Concerning the Corinthian letters, Jewett wrote:

> One of the hazards of the lectionary system is that it rips passages out of their contexts and invites treatment of the text as independent, abstract, dogmatic statements. I propose in this study to recontextualize each of the paragraphs to allow an imaginative portrayal of their original relevance in real life situations in the early church. This can provide raw material for more vivid sermonizing that gives attention to the story behind the text, including the other half of the conversation with the Corinthians to which Paul is responding. This could provide the basis for provocative comparisons with other stories and conversations in contemporary life.[21]

19. Jewett, *Romans: A Commentary*.

20. For further information on rhetorical criticism as it developed in the 1980s and beyond, see Hughes, "George Kennedy's Contribution."

21. Jewett, "Paul's Dialogue with the Corinthians," 89.

In this article, Jewett advocated that there were seven original letters and letter-fragments in 1 and 2 Corinthians.[22] He showed how several of the seven original Corinthian letters were parts of the interactions Paul had with the Corinthian Jesus-believers. On the basis of this historical reconstruction, he offered commentary on the 1 Corinthians readings in *The Revised Common Lectionary* for the Second through the Sixth Sundays after the Epiphany in Year B.[23] So for Jewett, the reconstruction of multiple Corinthian letters did *not* result in a tearing apart of the Corinthian correspondence but in a responsible "recontextualization" of various segments of the Corinthian dialogue with Paul.

What were these contexts? These letters in their chronological sequence can be summarized as follows. Letter A is incomplete, but it includes a *probatio* with two parts. Letter B lacks an epistolary prescript, and yet we found that the most difficult section of all, 2 Corinthians 6:14—7:1, comes into focus when we interpret it as part of the *exordium* of Letter B, which includes the material against immorality along with Paul's detailed refutation of those who deny the resurrection. Letter C, the "frame letter" standing behind the canonical 1 Corinthians, is a complete letter, with a three-part *probatio* and a striking *peroratio* in 1 Corinthians 13:1-13. Letter D, 2 Corinthians 8:1-24, is a fragment of a letter Paul wrote to encourage the Corinthians to collect money for the offering for fellow believers in Jerusalem. It followed Letter C closely in time. Letter C was a plea for unity, and it appears that Paul asked the congregation to raise the money thereafter in Letter D, thinking that his plea for unity in Letter C would have been successful.

By the time Paul wrote Letter E, he now understood that he must defend himself and prosecute his opponents. This he does in a measured way in 2 Corinthians 2:14—6:13 + 7:2-4, still proclaiming in the *peroratio* of this letter his love for the Corinthian congregation. After he wrote Letter E, Paul made his painful second visit to Corinth. Paul and his apostleship were rejected in Paul's presence. Paul then wrote Letter F. After Letter F was read to the Corinthians, the congregation, or perhaps the major portion of it, realized that a serious turnaround was necessary. They did indeed repent, and they punished the evildoer, apparently a ringleader of the opposition to Paul. Then Paul wrote Letter G, 2 Corinthians 1:1—2:13 + 7:5-16, the letter that uses the well-known topics of consolation to help effect fully a reconciliation between the Corinthian congregation and Paul. Paul in 2 Corinthians 2:6-11 tells the Corinthian congregation that the evildoer has now been punished enough, and that they should welcome this person back into the fellowship

22. Jewett, "Paul's Dialogue with the Corinthians," 91-92.
23. *Revised Common Lectionary*, 43-44.

of the church. Letter H, 2 Corinthians 9:1–15, is a fragment of yet another fundraising letter, written to the churches of Achaia rather than to Corinth; the circumstance of this letter is different from that of Letter D.

There are several problematic passages in the Corinthian correspondence. One of them is 1 Corinthians 14:33b–36. Jewett dealt with the practical historical results of the literary question of Pauline authorship of these verses in an essay, "The Sexual Liberation of Paul and His Churches." It illustrates Jewett's view of what happened to Paul's theological legacy in practical church tradition.[24] Jewett argued that Paul himself supported the equality of women and men in the missionary work in which he was engaged as an apostle. Citing 1 Corinthians 16:19, he held Prisca, who is mentioned first, along her husband Aquila, to be close missionary colleagues of Paul. Later in Romans 16:3–4, he refers to Prisca and Aquila as "co-workers." Jewett stated about them, "It is clear that they are not in any sense subordinate to Paul."[25] Jewett went on to argue that "[t]he capstone in this evolution toward 'equality-in-principle' between male and female in the church is 1 Cor. 11."[26] Jewett went on to trace Paul's movement toward consistent equality in 1 Corinthians 6:12–20 and 7:1.[27] Jewett regarded 1 Corinthians 14:33b–36 as an interpolation with "non-Pauline content."[28] Jewett regarded the Pastoral Epistles as pseudonymous and as evidence that the Pauline school moved away from Paul's own ideas. Thus, in Jewett's words:

> The reduction of the female role to housekeeping duties and the concern that prominent female leaders might look scandalous in the Greco-Roman world are characteristic here. This is the capstone of a subordinate definition of the feminine role that came to hold sway through most of Christian history.[29]

While I was a doctoral student in 1982–1984, Jewett continued to develop his understanding of the Corinthian letters. In discussions about the Corinthian letters, it became clear to us that it was possible to try to understand the resulting reconstructed letters and letter-fragments as documents of Paul's rhetoric, and so to approach the reconstructed letters and letter-fragments using rhetorical criticism. Focusing not on the small figures of rhetoric (which come under style) but on invention and arrangement, I

---

24. Jewett, "The Sexual Liberation of Paul and His Churches."
25. Jewett, "The Sexual Liberation of Paul and His Churches," 46.
26. Jewett, "The Sexual Liberation of Paul and His Churches," 49.
27. Jewett, "The Sexual Liberation of Paul and His Churches," 50.
28. Jewett, "The Sexual Liberation of Paul and His Churches," 54–56.
29. Jewett, "The Sexual Liberation of Paul and His Churches," 57.

began creating rhetorical analyses of various reconstructed Corinthian letters. What especially caught our attention was that Letter C is a beautifully organized letter with a three-part *probatio* and a marvelous *peroratio* in 1 Corinthians 13 that demonstrated both the function of recapitulation and an appeal to the emotions. We both discerned careful crafting by Paul of the recapitulation of the argument of Letter C in 1 Corinthians 13. Notably, the matters that were recapitulated in 1 Corinthians 13 were the parts of 1 Corinthians that were in Letter C, and not the parts that were from other letters, in Jewett's partition theory. I produced another rhetorical analysis of 2 Corinthians 2:14—6:13 + 7:2-4 and found that a particular early verse in that letter, which we now call Letter E, had a *partitio* that gave an indication in that letter of the parts of the *probatio* that would follow.[30] It also had *narratio* broken up into parts inserted into parts of the *probatio*, which was advised in Pseudo-Aristotle's *Rhetorica ad Alexandrum*, a most important source for ancient teaching on deliberative rhetoric. In early 1985, I analyzed the earliest letter-fragment in the Corinthian sequence, 1 Corinthians 11:2-34. The letter of reconciliation, as we then called it, 2 Corinthians 1:1—2:13 + 7:5—8:24 (as we then understood 2 Cor 8:1-24), we found to be a finely crafted deliberative letter. With Jewett's full encouragement and criticism, I found that Jewett's partition theory resulted in seven letters and letter-fragments that could well be understood as documents of rhetoric. Of course, they were not speeches, but letters. Nonetheless, with Jewett's and my growing knowledge of ancient rhetoric, we could perceive and describe the rhetorical coherence in each of these letters and letter-fragments. If these analyses were correct, the same Paul wrote letters with strong points of contact with all three *genera* of rhetoric: epideictic, deliberative, and judicial.

One might ask, what did Aristotle, Demosthenes, Cicero, and Quintilian have to do with Pauline letters? These handbooks of rhetoric, along with speeches and letters of Demosthenes, showed Jewett and me a great deal about a significant part of the intellectual and public atmosphere into which the followers of Jesus would create letters and other writings designed to persuade other Jesus-believers to do and to believe various things. Jewett's perception was that the Corinthian letters, as reconstructed, demonstrated Paul's growing awareness of the extent of the conflict between himself and Corinthian Jesus-believers. In Letter A, which included most of 1 Corinthians 11, Paul knew little or believed little about the extent of the Corinthian problem, and so he responded accordingly. As we read and interpreted Letters B through F, we could see Paul's understanding of the Corinthian church growing greater, at the same time that portions of the congregation

---

30. Hughes, "Rhetorical Criticism and the Corinthian Correspondence."

in Corinth were in the process of rejecting Paul and his teaching.[31] At the beginning of the severe Letter F, Paul noted that his opponents classified his letters as "weighty and strong," very much in contrast with Paul's appearance, in 2 Corinthians 10:10. We take Paul's quotation of his opponents at his word here. This means that Paul's opponents understood Paul's letters to be persuasive, while Paul's physical appearance was that of weakness. Paul accepted this charge in order to lambast his opponents in Letter F. When we could see the historical sequence of the multiple Corinthian letters in our reconstruction, the rhetorical character of these letters demonstrated the robustly situational character of Paul's letters.

Because of his research in the Corinthian letters over the years Jewett changed his mind about a number of things. The most difficult passage of the Corinthian correspondence for Jewett and me to place was 1 Corinthians 9:1–18. We were both convinced that it did not make sense where it stood in the canonical form of 1 Corinthians. Yet, when it was placed in the middle of the severe letter of 2 Corinthians 10:1—13:13, it made rhetorical sense as part of the "foolish discourse." Paul argued for the right to financial support for himself—and then he nobly refused this support from the Corinthian church. Manifestly, this was a foolish thing to do, and so it made great sense in Letter F. After years of consideration of where 1 Corinthians 9:1–18 fit best in Letter F, Jewett settled on its location, with my assent, between 2 Corinthians 11:9 and 11:10, though for many years it was between 11:11 and 11:12, and later it was between 12:13 and 12:14. All these possibilities were carefully evaluated.

Another change of mind concerned 2 Corinthians 8 and 9. It was not until 2011 that Jewett read the commentary by Calvin J. Roetzel[32] and the article by Margaret M. Mitchell[33] that argued that 2 Corinthians 8 was considerably earlier than the "letter of consolation" that was the next-to-last letter in the historical sequence in Jewett's partition theory. Jewett and I became convinced they were right. So the Jewett-Hughes partition theory now embraced eight letters and letter-fragments, referred to as Corinthian Letters A through H. This is the partition theory that we adopted in our jointly-authored book.

In Pauline scholarship, the partitioning of 2 Corinthians is now conventional. The partitioning of 1 Corinthians is not. Yet the partitioning of any Pauline letter needs to be based on the identification of rough or awkward transitions from one passage to another. This is easy to do in 2 Corinthians. After much discussion about how to strengthen the case for partitioning 1 Corinthians, Jewett decided to identify all the rough

---

31. Hughes, "Paul and Traditions of Greco-Roman Rhetoric."
32. Roetzel, *2 Corinthians*.
33. Mitchell, "Paul's Letters to Corinth."

transitions he found. I concurred with this list. Jewett then proceeded to write chapter 3 of our book, which explained in detail why each of these transitions were rough. In chapter 4 of the book, Jewett took his literary analysis of the rough transitions in 1 Corinthians and did redaction criticism, showing the likelihood of the redaction and the historical reasons the redactors would have wanted to do what they did.

Jewett's Parkinson's Disease, in the last five years of his life, if not longer, made it extremely difficult for him to write. He had already been unable to use a computer mouse when he wrote his large Romans commentary. In the last several years before his death, it was impossible for him to use a computer keyboard, so that he was forced to craft the last chapter of our book, "The Publication of 1 and 2 Corinthians: From Scroll to Codex," using dictation software. Yet this chapter, written solely by Jewett, nonetheless has a crispness Jewett's readers will recognize. In agreement with Harry Y. Gamble's *Books and Readers in the Early Church*,[34] Jewett argued that there must have been an event in the history of Jesus-believing communities that caused the shift from papyrus scrolls to the codex, the technical term for a bound book. This event, Gamble argued, was the publication of the Pauline corpus.[35] Jewett took this argument one step further: he argued that the fact that there were no copies on papyrus scrolls in existence meant that there must have been an effort to destroy all copies of Paul's letters that were found on scrolls: "There must have been many such documents in circulation within decades of Paul's founding missions. An extremely urgent need must have been felt by the second- and third-generation congregations to search out and destroy every copy of Paul's letters in scroll form."[36] This rationale, Jewett argued, was the effort by those who redacted the Corinthian correspondence into the canonical form of 1 and 2 Corinthians, to take letters like the frame letter of 1 Corinthians, which we identify as Letter C, which had chapters in it that said that spiritual people had wisdom and unspiritual people did not. These chapters would have been extremely useful to proto-Gnostics in Pauline congregations. The redaction into the canonical form of 1 Corinthians served to take these evidently dangerous chapters and render them relatively harmless, so that proto-Gnostics could not claim that the apostle was on their side or that they got their ideas from Paul's own letters.

Thus, the struggle in Pauline congregations between proto-gnostics and those who opposed them, most likely in the late first or early second century, is not only the best historical explanation for the redaction that produced the canonical 1 Corinthians but also is the best explanation for why copies on papyrus scrolls disappeared. Jewett argued:

34. Gamble, *Books and Readers*.
35. Gamble, *Books and Readers*, 62–63.
36. Hughes and Jewett, *Corinthian Correspondence*, 258–59.

The redaction of the letters to Corinth and Rome in the struggle against early heresy among Jesus-believers required a publication in redacted form that would replace the most dangerous Pauline letters that were being employed by teachers perceived to be heretics. The redacted letters needed to be published in a form that would not allow further large-scale editing, which the choice of codex automatically accomplished by being written on both sides of the page.[37]

Thus, our book provides an explanation not only of the literary phenomena of the redactions of 1 and 2 Corinthians but also the reasons for it. The final form of our partition theory of Corinthians is as follows:

Table 2.1: Partition Theory of Corinthians

Corinthian letters and fragments	Equivalents in the canonical 1 and 2 Corinthians
A	1 Cor 11:2, 17–34a + 1 Cor 11:3–16 + 1 Cor 16:1–4 + 1 Cor 11:34b
B	2 Cor 6:14—7:1 + 1 Cor 6:12–20 + 1 Cor 9:24—10:22 + 1 Cor 15:1–58 + 1 Cor 16:13–24
C	1 Cor 1:1—6:11 + 1 Cor 7:1—8:13 + 1 Cor 9:19–23 + 1 Cor 10:23—11:1 + 1 Cor 12:1–31a + 1 Cor 14:1c–33a + 1 Cor 14:37–40 + 1 Cor 12:31b—13:13 + 1 Cor 16:5–12
D	2 Cor 8:1–24
E	2 Cor 2:14—6:13 + 2 Cor 7:2–4
F	2 Cor 10:1—11:9 + 1 Cor 9:1–18 + 2 Cor 11:10—13:10
G	2 Cor 1:1—2:13 + 7:5–16 + 13:11–13
H	2 Cor 9:1–15

Conclusion

Jewett's publications on the Corinthian letters illustrate the range of his scholarly concerns about the interpretation of these letters. Foremost among his concerns was the question of how many Corinthian letters Paul

---

37. Hughes and Jewett, *Corinthian Correspondence*, 259.

wrote and sent; this concern is inextricably linked to what Paul thought he was doing when he wrote these letters.

In Jewett's long career, his many writings generally focused on biblical texts and how they should best be interpreted. In 1988, when he was awarded the Harry R. Kendall chair of New Testament Interpretation at Garrett-Evangelical, I opined that Jewett's writing was all about the application of modern methods of study to particular biblical texts, and the dialogue between modern biblical studies and the historical and contemporary world. Books like *Paul The Apostle to America* made that interpretive concern quite explicit, not least through their titles and subtitles.[38] Yet it would be a mistake not to recognize that Jewett's fully scholarly works—such as his large Romans commentary, both parts of his dissertation (both *A Chronology of Paul's Life* and *Paul's Anthropological Terms*), and the Corinthian book—also had deep hermeneutical significance and revealed Jewett's undying concern for the pastoral implications of his innovative exegesis. These concerns were the result of Jewett's profound respect for the historical and theological significance of the situational character of all biblical texts, and especially Paul's letters, in their contexts. The goal of all sorts of exegetical work on Paul's letters was to understand Paul in his situational contexts. Our new book will allow readers of Paul to see connections between Paul and the contexts of people like us. This work is the necessary antidote to the belief held by some, in Jewett's memorable words, that Paul's theology was "zapped into him all at once on the road to Damascus."

Our jointly-authored book was the final publication by Robert Jewett. It is a fitting conclusion to his extremely productive career as a highly esteemed teacher, a pastor and preacher, a creative scholar, a faithful friend, a tireless researcher, and a writer whose works could not only inform but also surprise and delight, as they will continue to do.

Bibliography

(* For Further Reading)

Betz, Hans Dieter. *Galatians: A Commentary on Paul's Letter to the Churches in Galatia.* Hermeneia. Philadelphia: Fortress, 1979.
*Bornkamm, Günther. "Die Vorgeschichte des sogenannten zweiten Korintherbriefes." In *Sitzungsberichte der Heidelberger Akademie der Wissenschaften, Philosophische-historische Klasse,* 7–36. 2nd Abhandlung. Heidelberg: Winter, 1961.
Consultation on Common Texts. *The Revised Common Lectionary.* Nashville: Abingdon, 1992.
Conzelmann, Hans. *1 Corinthians: A Commentary on the First Epistle to the Corinthians.* Translated by James W. Leitch. Hermeneia. Minneapolis: Fortress, 1988.

38. Jewett, *Paul the Apostle to America.*

*Donfried, Karl P., and Johannes Beutler. *The Thessalonians Debate: Methodological Discord or Methodological Synthesis?* Grand Rapids: Eerdmans, 2000.
Gamble, Harry Y. *Books and Readers in the Early Church: A History of Early Christian Texts.* New Haven: Yale University Press, 1995.
*Georgi, Dieter. *The Opponents of Paul in Second Corinthians: A Study of Religious Propaganda in Late Antiquity.* Philadelphia: Fortress, 1986.
Hughes, Frank W. "George Kennedy's Contribution to Rhetorical Criticism of the Pauline Letters." In *Words Well Spoken: George Kennedy's Rhetoric of the New Testament,* edited by C. Clifton Black and Duane F. Watson, 125–37. Studies in Rhetoric and Religion 8. Waco, TX: Baylor University Press, 2008.
———. "Paul and Traditions of Greco-Roman Rhetoric." In *Paul and Ancient Rhetoric: Theory and Practice in the Hellenistic Context,* edited by Stanley E. Porter and Bryan R. Dyer, 86–95. New York: Cambridge University Press, 2015.
———. "Rhetorical Criticism and the Corinthian Correspondence." In *The Rhetorical Analysis of Scripture: Essays from the 1995 London Conference,* edited by Stanley E. Porter and Thomas H. Olbricht, 336–50. JSNTSup 146. Sheffield: JSOT, 1997.
Hughes, Frank W., and Robert Jewett. *The Corinthian Correspondence: Redaction, Rhetoric, and History.* Lanham, MD: Lexington/Fortress Academic, 2021.
Jewett, Robert. *A Chronology of Paul's Life.* Philadelphia: Fortress, 1979.
———. *Paul The Apostle to America: Cultural Trends and Pauline Scholarship.* Louisville: Westminster John Knox, 1994.
———. *Paul's Anthropological Terms: A Study of their Use in Conflict Settings.* Arbeiten zur Geschichte des antiken Judentums und des Urchristentums 10. Leiden: Brill, 1971.
———. "Paul's Dialogue with the Corinthians . . . and Us." *Quarterly Review* 13 (1993) 89–112.
———. "The Redaction of I Corinthians and the Trajectory of the Pauline School." *Journal of American Academy of Religion Supplement* 46 (1978) 389–444.
———. "Review of Walter Schmithals, *Gnosticism in Corinth* and *Paul and the Gnostics.*" *Journal of Biblical Literature* 93 (1974) 630–32.
———. *Romans: A Commentary.* Hermeneia. Minneapolis: Fortress, 2007.
———. "Romans as an Ambassadorial Letter." *Interpretation* 36 (1982) 5–20.
———. "The Sexual Liberation of Paul and His Churches." In *Paul the Apostle to America: Cultural Trends and Pauline Scholarship,* 45–58. Louisville: Westminster John Knox, 1994.
*Kennedy, George A. *New Testament Interpretation through Rhetorical Criticism.* Chapel Hill: University of North Carolina Press, 1984.
*Martin, Troy W., ed. *Genealogies of New Testament Rhetorical Criticism.* Minneapolis: Fortress, 2014.
Mitchell, Margaret M. "Paul's Letters to Corinth: The Interpretive Intertwining of Literary and Historical Reconstruction." In *Urban Religion in Roman Corinth: Interdisciplinary Approaches,* edited by Daniel N. Schowalter and Steven J. Friesen, 307–38. Cambridge: Harvard University Press, 2005.
*Porter, Stanley E., and Bryan R. Dyer. *Paul and Ancient Rhetoric: Theory and Practice in the Hellenistic Context.* Cambridge: Cambridge University Press, 2016.
Robinson, James M., ed. *The Nag Hammadi Library in English: The Definitive New Translation of the Gnostic Scriptures, Complete in One Volume.* 4th rev. ed. Leiden: Brill, 1996.

Roetzel, Calvin J. *2 Corinthians*. Abingdon New Testament Commentaries. Nashville: Abingdon, 2007.

*Schenk, Wolfgang. "Der 1. Korintherbrief als Briefsammlung." *Zeitschrift für die neutestamentliche Wissenschaft und die Kunde der älteren Kirche* 60 (1969) 219–43.

*Schmithals, Walter. *Gnosticism in Corinth: An Investigation of the Letters to the Corinthians*. Translated by John E. Steely. Nashville: Abingdon, 1971.

———. "Die Korintherbriefe als Briefsammlung." *Zeitschrift für die Neutestamentliche Wissenschaft und die Kunde der älteren Kirche* 64 (1973) 263–88.

Schubert, Paul. *Form and Function of the Pauline Thanksgivings*. Beihefte zur Zeitschrift für die neutestamentliche Wissenschaft und die Kunde der älteren Kirche 20. Berlin: Töpelmann, 1939.

Study Questions

1. Do you think that partition theories of the Corinthian correspondence are more or less likely than theories that hold that 1 and/or 2 Corinthians are integral letters? Why or why not?

2. Does your understanding the situation of each Pauline letter in its literary and historical contexts help you understand the theology of Paul as a whole?

3. How relevant are contextual interpretations of Paul's letters to historical issues such as slavery or contemporary issues such as the rights and roles of women?

3

A Question of Perception

Food Debates in Corinth

Kathy Ehrensperger

Abstract

TABLE FELLOWSHIP IS THE heart of the early Christ movement. Robert Jewett has emphasized the importance of this practice in the formation of its identity and ethos. Based on his important research, the debates about food in Corinth are seen as debates about how to avoid idolatry. Jewish ways of negotiating this issue in a dominating pagan environment contribute to understanding Paul's specific advice to his gentile addressees. In this contribution to a volume that honors the work and legacy of Robert Jewett, I would like to explore some of the questions Paul addresses in 1 Corinthians that concerned these communal meals.

Introduction

That communal meals were a decisive and identity-shaping practice in the early Christ movement has been highlighted by Robert Jewett in many of his publications.[1] Whether in tenement meeting rooms, in outdoor spaces, or in parts of grand houses, by coming together to share a meal, Christ followers provided support for each other at the physical as well as the spiritual level. In the context of shared meals, social interaction took place and contributed to the working out of the implications of being part of this movement in terms of everyday life. At shared meals especially, the

---

1. Jewett, "Are There Allusions to the Love Feast in Rom 3:8–10?," 265–78. Jewett, *Romans: A Commentary*, 829–73.

non-Jews who had joined the movement learned life in Christ, praying, singing, and honoring God as the God of all creation. Robert Jewett noted the importance of this shared practice, which is an often-overlooked aspect shared also between Paul and the Gospels.[2] In this contribution to a volume that honors the work and legacy of Robert Jewett, I would like to explore some of the questions which Paul addresses in 1 Corinthians which concerned these communal meals.

It should not surprise us that, with the central role that the coming together for meals played, also key questions and some controversial discussions emerged on these occasions. I am presenting my arguments from the presupposition that Paul remained rooted in his Jewish tradition, and that the Christ movement did initially not emerge in opposition to Judaism but as part of and as a variety within the diversity of Jewish traditions of the Second Temple Period. Paul understands himself as called to proclaim the gospel to the non-Jewish nations and thus, in his letters, addresses specifically non-Jewish Christ followers, providing teaching and guidance for their new life in Christ.[3]

At Corinth

In 1 Corinthians 8, 10:14–22 and 10:26–11:1, Paul addresses specific questions that must have emerged in the context of shared meals. These passages all involve questions of venue and menu, namely where it was appropriate to eat, particularly when eating out, and what was appropriate to eat as a Christ follower. The decisive factor driving these debates were not the ingredients of a meal but how one could avoid participation in idolatry in a context permeated with the worshipping of numerous so-called deities. How could one know where and when to participate in social activities and where and when to avoid them? What were the criteria for respective decisions?

In his discussions concerning venues and menus, that is, eating options in the Christ-movement, Paul refers several times to perception (*syneidēsis*) as the decisive parameter for such decisions. The issues arise in particular when meat is involved in the discussion. Interestingly, the question is not sorted with reference to the food on the table or in the marketplace. The fact that the meat on the table might not stem from an "allowed" animal or might not be slaughtered according to respective rules of the Torah does not play any part in this discussion. This clearly indicates that there are no Jewish kashrut issues concerning food at stake in these passages. Reference is

2. Cf. Ehrensperger, "At the Table," 531–50, now also in my *Searching Paul*, 91–109.
3. For a more detailed argument about this, see my *Searching Paul*, 11–14, 181–94.

made to something that is not on the table. Interestingly, also the issue often considered to be the most significant—that is, table fellowship between Jews and non-Jews—is not in view at all. Where table fellowship is in view, as in 1 Corinthians 10:14–22, the question centers not on Jews and non-Jews but on whether those who have turned from idols to the "living God" (1 Thess 1:9) can continue to share a table with "demons." Table fellowship between people who are different is presupposed in 1 Corinthians 10:26–11:1, where it is considered "normal" that a Christ-follower might be invited to the house of a pagan, and that he/she would accept the invitation. The host in this case cannot be Jewish, since the issue that might cause a problem in such a situation is food that had been involved in sacrificial activities. A Christ-follower in a Jewish house could assume that everything was done in accordance with what was required when one worshipped the God of Israel exclusively. In the fourth passage in 1 Corinthians, where table fellowship is in view, namely 11:17–34, the issue is not with whom to share a table, but to share the table properly when celebrating the Lord's supper—that is, in a way that does not humiliate any brother or sister. The social relations here concern people of different social classes. Neither the food on the table nor the fellowship between Jews and non-Jews is under debate in these cases. The only discussion of table fellowship that involves Jews and non-Jews emerges in Galatians 2:11–14, where it is unclear what the actual issue was. Potentially, it had more to do with the venue than the menu.[4]

Even in the extended discussions in 1 Corinthians, where food is actually mentioned, it is not the question of which food can be consumed that needs to be solved in Paul's view. Although the debate involves questions concerning meat (1 Cor 10:23–11:1), Paul argues that rather than the food involved, it is actually the perception of the other that is decisive for the course of action to be taken. How what one does is perceived by others, in what light one's practice is seen by others, is the criterion for eating or not eating.

The term *syneidēsis* plays an important role here. Traditional translations refer to this as "conscience." This implies that what Paul might have been concerned about is some inner dimension of the soul, something introspective. The term, however, refers to something outward. *Syneidesis* can be linked either to *eidos,* in which case, it has something to do with outward appearance or perception, that is, something that is seen. If the term is seen as more closely related to *eidēsis,* which is mostly translated as knowledge,[5] not much is changed, as what is seen is what might or can be known. Thus,

---

4. Fredriksen, *Paul the Pagans' Apostle*, 96–99.
5. E.g., Philo, *Plant.* 36; *Migr.* 42.

Paul is not concerned with how the inner self or soul of someone might discern the practices of Christ-followers, but how such practice is perceived by either a brother or sister within the movement (1 Corinthians 8) or how it is perceived by outsiders, that is, pagans (1 Cor 10:23–31).

On Temple Meals

In the case of 1 Corinthians 8, the perception of the behavior of a Christ-follower by a fellow brother or sister is in view. Keeping in mind that Paul addresses non-Jews in his letters,[6] he discusses in 1 Corinthians 8 a question most likely raised by non-Jewish Christ-followers in Corinth as he introduces the issue with *peri de* (8:1), indicating that he now replies to something most likely addressed in a letter sent to him. The issue concerned is whether, for a Christ-follower, it would be possible or not to participate in a temple meal. It seems at first sight astonishing that such a question would be raised at all. Paul would certainly have already made it clear that following Christ meant that they would honor the one God exclusively. This would have been basic initial teaching in Christ, one would assume. Why then does this question emerge in the first place?

We have to bear in mind that what was certainly clear and straightforward in theory was less clear in practice. What actually did constitute idolatry—that is, worshipping and serving a deity other than the One God—was, if not a matter of debate, at least in practice an issue of blurred boundaries among some Jews living in the diaspora.[7] A Jewish inscription from Gorgippa at the Bosporus dated 41 CE (*CIJ* 690) refers to the manumission of a slave, with what seems to be a clear reference to the One God (*theōi hypistōi pantakratori eulogētōi*—"to God the most high, almighty, blessed"), but what follows is a polytheistic juridical formula (*hypo Dia, Gēn, Helion*—"under Zeus, Earth, Sun"). The dedication notes that it is made in the *proseuchē*, which has been demonstrated as being an exclusively Jewish term.[8] There is further inscriptional evidence that Jews did visit temples of other deities, as for example, from near the temple of Pan in Edfu in Upper Egypt (dated between the second and first century BCE). Although the inscriptions do not suggest worshipping activities of the Jews named there, it is noteworthy that they placed their dedication

---

6. See William S. Campbell's contribution to this volume.

7. Cf. Horrell, "Idol Food, Idolatry and Ethics in Paul," 124–25.

8. See Horbury and David, *Jewish Inscriptions of Graeco-Roman Egypt*, 14; and Frey, *Corpus Inscriptionum Judaicarum* [*CIJ*].

of thanksgiving within the compound of another deity.[9] When it comes to the manumission of slaves, Jews in the diaspora seem to have adopted the recognized practice that manumission required a deity acting as a broker, and the actual manumission was a handover of the slave to the deity. An inscription from Delphi (*CIJ* 711, 119 BCE) mentions that someone called *Ioudaios* sold his slave Amuntas to Apollo, a sale that should be actualized upon the death of the *Ioudaios*. Whether these examples provide a glimpse into exceptional or common practices among diaspora Jews is difficult to assess. But they clearly indicate that at least, in some instances, the boundaries between what was considered faithful adherence to the traditions of the ancestors, including exclusive loyalty to the one God, and idolatry were blurred. The boundary between what was considered idol worship and merely shared common practice may have been a matter of local and, possibly, individual perception.

Such variations in the perceptions of these boundaries could have contributed significantly to the problems Paul feels he needs to address in his letter. So, he specifically replies to what seems to have been a specific question *peri tēs brōseōs oun tōn eidōlothytōn*—"concerning the food that had been involved in idol sacrifices."[10] He shares their view, that actually idols do not exist, and there is no God but one. He further agrees that there are many so-called deities and lords, which may be seen as gods and accepted as lords. But he insists that for them—now in Christ—there is only one. For them, he is the creator of heaven and earth, they have one Lord only and through this Lord only they actually exist—as Christ following assembly (8:4-6). Paul confirms that this is so, this is the accurate understanding for those who had responded to the call of God in Christ. But it is not at all clear for all who responded to this call. In verse 7, we have evidence that Paul is addressing non-Jews: they are those who, in their former lives, used to consider idols as deities. It is in relation to them, that is, to those whose perception is not clear but "weak," that the question of eating or not eating at the temple should be decided. But why could those who see things clearly, like Paul, those who have knowledge, why could they not participate in a temple meal? Interestingly, Paul does not argue that this is impossible because this would constitute idolatry. He does not accuse those who have "knowledge" of committing idolatry by participating in a temple meal. So, one could conclude that, in principle, it is possible to participate in such a meal and enjoy the meat served on such

---

9. Horbury and David, *Jewish Inscriptions of Graeco-Roman Egypt*, 14, and Frey, *Corpus Inscriptionum Judaicarum* [CIJ], 211–12.

10. All quotations from the biblical text are my own translation.

an occasion. But despite agreeing with this argument in principle, Paul emphasizes that this is absolutely impossible.

These temple feasts were public occasions. A Christ-follower would be seen by others, whether Christ-followers or pagan neighbors, as participating in a pagan festival. The non-Jewish Christ-follower may be very clear in his own perception (*syneidēsis*), that this is not idol food, since those to whom a sacrifice is offered are only so-called deities and, in that sense, do not exist (they are demons and should not be worshipped). But others may perceive this activity in a different light. Especially another non-Jewish Christ follower could be led to think that such participation expresses the reverence of a pagan deity and thus, since his perception was weak, would conclude that worshipping another deity alongside the God of Israel was an actual option for a Christ follower (1 Cor 8:12). By participating in a temple meal with such a perception however, this weaker brother or sister would commit idolatry. For a Christ follower, this would have devastating effects, in Paul's view. As Paul notes in 1 Corinthians 8:7 "and their perception/knowledge being weak, (they) would be tainted (by idolatry)" (*kai hē syneidēsis autōn asthenēs ousa molynetai*). To encourage another person to come to wrong conclusions and to thereby get involved in idolatry means to sin against the brother or sister. Interestingly, it is not the idolatrous behavior to which the brother is wrongly encouraged that is considered sin here, according to Paul's argument; instead, it is the misleading behavior that causes this wrong perception that is sin. This means that it is not the perception of the "strong" or knowledgeable Christ follower that is the decisive criterion for assessing which practice or behavior is appropriate in Christ, but the perception (*syneidēsis*) of the weaker brother or sister is decisive for participating or not participating at a temple meal.[11]

The Question of Provenance

Paul's arguments in 1 Corinthians 10:23–11:1 are very similar, although the situations concerned are different. In chapter 8 (and 10:14–22), there is no doubt that the food involved had been involved in sacrificial activities for a so-called deity (although Paul emphasizes that the knowledgeable Christ followers' perspective would classify such food as offered to demons). However, the problem is not the food, that is, the menu, but the venue where the food is consumed. The venue is seen as the reason

---

11. A similar argument is made in Romans 14, where also the perception of the "weaker" brother is the criterion for eating or not eating meat. See William S. Campbell's contribution to this volume.

participation in the meal is not an option, since the context of the meal, not the meal as such, can give the impression of participation in worshipping another deity. The situations envisaged in 10:23—11:1 are different. Whether or not the food is to be considered as consecrated to so-called deities is a matter of discernment in each of these cases. These cases resemble those in later Rabbinical literature, which discuss so-called food or objects of doubtful provenance.[12] There could be no doubt concerning the provenance of meat served at a temple meal.

But this is not the only place in the first century one could encounter the problem, and meat would be on the menu. And it is here the question of provenance comes into play. In numerous situations, it is not clear beyond doubt from where the meat originated. Paul turns to such cases in 10:23—11:1. The question is what a Christ follower should do when he does not know the status of food in a pagan dominated environment. Paul's short answer is "do not ask." This seems arbitrary, turning a blind eye, but it actually is coherent with the argument in chapter 8.

It is presupposed by Paul, that Christ followers would go to the market (*macellum*) to buy meat or would accept an invitation by a pagan neighbor to share a meal. This indicates that a social interaction with pagan neighbors was taken for granted, as it was actually for Jews in the diaspora. Christ followers should not self-isolate, inasmuch as Jews in the diaspora did not self-isolate. The pagan environment did not prohibit social and economic interaction.[13] However, one needed to know how to interact with these neighbors, and here the non-Jewish Christ followers were in need of education. As noted, Jews had centuries of experience in living in these environments as minorities and had developed numerous ways to negotiate the boundaries between their own exclusive loyalty to the one God and idolatry.

In a still predominantly pagan context, it remained an issue for Jews also in rabbinical times to negotiate this boundary. An entire tractate in the Mishna, Avodah Zarah, is dealing with these.[14] Thus, in Avodah Zarah 4:2-3, there is a debate about items that are found around a statue of Mercure, the god of travelers and traders. Such statues were often placed at a crossroads, and travelers dedicated rows of stones or food there in honor of the god. In the Mishnah, the debate concerns the criteria by which one can discern whether something that is found near the statue has been dedicated to the deity or not. Rabbi Yishmael says: three stones near the statue are

---

12. Tomson, *Paul and the Jewish Law*, 208–20.

13. Fredriksen and Irshai, "Include Me Out," 117–32.

14. Although the Mishnah, of course, was compiled at the end of the second/beginning of the third century, it can be assumed that trajectories of older traditions are included in this collection. See, e.g., Stemberger, "Dating Rabbinic Traditions," 231–45.

prohibited, two stones are allowed and thus can be used. And the sages say: what seems to belong to the statue is not allowed, what does not seem to belong to the statue is allowed. Thus, coins and clothes are allowed; however, grapes, corn wreaths, wine, oil or flour, or anything that could be offered on an altar, is not allowed. Three stones in a row most likely are a sign of intention, two stones could be there just by chance. How something is perceived does not depend on the object as such but on the perception of the pagan (not the Jewish) person. The intention can only be discerned in relation to signs, not something inherent to the objects.

A similar argument is presented in the story of Rabban Gamaliel, who visits a Roman bath with a statue of the goddess Aphrodite. The reason for this not constituting a problem is presented in Avodah Zarah 3:4: That which pagans treat as a deity is prohibited, that which they do not treat as a deity is allowed. The statue in the bath is not being worshipped since this can only happen in the precincts of a temple. This means the statue can be perceived to be an ornament; hence, Rabban Gamaliel can visit the bath without any problem. Only actual acts of worship, such as offerings, are considered to be idolatry. This enabled Jews to negotiate everyday life in a pagan context without transgressing the first commandment.

The need for discernment involved debates and required guidance among Jews, and it is thus not a surprise at all that the new non-Jewish Christ followers had questions concerning this as well. Paul's arguments and guidance is part of these Jewish debates and guidance on how to discern what constitutes idolatry and what does not. Only, he does this for the assemblies of non-Jewish Christ followers he had founded.

Paul's reference to the *syneidēsis* of either the shop-keeper or the host is consistent with rabbinical argumentation, as seen above, and clearly points to the heart of the problem: the past involvement in pagan cultic rituals does not relate to the nature of the food itself. Moreover, this is also consistent with Greek and Roman perceptions of what is going on in the context of a sacrificial process. A sacrifice consisted of a range of ritual activities that included purification, public procession including dance and music, the dedication of an animal and/or frugal substances, the killing and, significantly, the offering of the "material" to the deity through burning their share (the *exta*, the noble parts, that is, the *vitalia*—vital organs).[15] The animal was rendered sacred in this process; this means dedicated to the deity, and it thereby was transmitted into the possession of the deity. In this status of sacredness, no human being could have a share in what belonged to the deity.

---

15. Rüpke, *Religion of the Romans*, 144; Eberhardt, *Ritual and Metaphor*, 29–30; Scheid, "Sacrifices for Gods and Ancestors," 263–72n267.

Normally, it was then consumed by the deity in the form of smoke. The parts of the animals that were not meant for consumption by the deity, however, had to be released through a ritual act and be given back to humans for consumption—hence the sacrificial process involved a ritual of profanation. The deity released thereby some of the meat from their possession as a gift for human consumption. It was transferred from the status of sacred back to the status of profane. So, although the meat that could be bought in the marketplace had in most cases been involved in a sacrificial act, it was not sacred meat, technically not even in the perception of pagans. It had to be profane in order to be consumable. This is most likely behind the view that such meat could also be eaten by those who exclusively worshipped the God of Israel, whether in and through Christ or not.

It remains what it is—food emerging from God's good creation—hence, God is the only one who should be addressed in thankfulness before consuming the meal. The food as such is not inherently affected or contaminated by the ritual in which it was involved; hence, it can be consumed in a non-sacrificial context, provided the blessing over the food is offered to the one God. But when declared as food that had been involved in polytheistic cultic rituals, then consumption is excluded for Christ followers, whether they are Jews or from the nations.

Paul is careful to clarify that this knowledge, of course, does not change the perception of the food for the Christ follower (for whom idols do not exist, but are at the most, lesser demons which, as a result of confusion, are worshipped as deities) but would affect the perception of the Christ follower by the shop-keeper or the host. Although the food as such still is not the problem, the awareness of the shop keeper/host changes the situation decisively. The Christ follower, in buying or eating food that had been explicitly declared to be idol food, would be seen as buying or eating it in full awareness of this, and hence consenting to the respective cult practice. To be seen as participating in or consenting to a cult by eating food that had been declared as offered to a deity is the decisive step that constitutes the crossing of the boundary to idolatry. The argument here is actually coherent with the argument in chapters 8 and 10:14-22: *to be seen* as participating causes others, "weaker" brothers/sisters or polytheistic shopkeepers and hosts, to mistakenly consider such practice as acceptable for Christ followers.

Conclusion

The confusion in the perception others draw from this or that behavior causes the problem. Thus, not the intention of the practitioner but the effects of his/her activity, are decisive here. For an individual to knowingly participate in such practices, at the temple table or in more private contexts, would have implications for the well-being and holiness of the community. In the first instance, the public temple context as outlined above, this is an insider issue because a brother/sister would be harmed;[16] in the second instance, this is an insider/outsider issue because non-Christ-followers, non-Jewish or Jewish, would get a distorted view of the *ekklēsia* as not exclusively devoted to loyalty to the one God only. The *ekklēsia* is called to live in all aspects of their lives to the honor and glory of God. Like in Greek and Roman cults, the key aspect of the communicative act of sacrifice is to honor the deity as the giver of life and well-being. For polytheists, this implied honoring numerous deities who were responsible for diverse aspects of life and well-being. For Jews, and now also for Christ followers from the nations, such honor was due only to the God of Israel. It is this exclusive loyalty that matters most as Paul summarizes, *Eite oun esthiete eite pinete eite ti poieite, panta eis doxan theou poieite.* ("So whether you eat or drink, or whatever you do, do all to the glory of God"; 10:31). The guiding parameter in relation to *exestin* is the *doxa theou* ("glory of God"). The members of the *ekklēsia theou* ("church of God") have to negotiate what exactly this entails within the cultural contexts in which they live. This includes aspects of Greek and Roman and other ways of life that do not challenge the *doxa theou* ("glory of God") and the exclusive loyalty demanded of Christ followers. Hence, the liberty of the Christ followers in the contexts assumed here is not constrained by the shop-keeper or host, as Paul notes, "Why should my liberty be subject to the judgement of someone else's consciousness?" (10:29). The limitation of freedom is set by the *doxa theou*. The concern in this passage in the end is not the shop-keeper or host but the *doxa theou*. Relationships to outsiders are important inasmuch as they impinge on this central concern (10:32–33). The concern for the other, who in this passage is an outsider, has to be seen not as a self-standing ethical concern but as clearly rooted in the concern for the *doxa theou*. The shopkeeper and host are primarily relevant for their perception of the *ekklēsia*. The community should be seen as honoring the *doxa theou* in holiness in all their activities, that is, in their entire lives. The template to follow (not copy) is Christ himself.[17] Responding to the call in which they were called implied to embody the message of the gospel with their entire lives. In Romans 12, this is referred to as the *logiken latereia*; in 1 Corinthians 10:31, it is referred to as honoring God. This is not some abstract confession to which one consents, but it is lived in

---

16. This is also the key aspect in Romans 14. See my "Called to be Saints," 90–109.
17. Cf. Ehrensperger, *Paul and the Dynamics of Power*, 137–54.

embodied lives in relation to those with whom Christ followers share their lives, close and more distant, whether in Christ or not. This is what it means to imitate Christ.

Bibliography

(* For Further Reading)

Eberhardt, Christian A. *Ritual and Metaphor: Sacrifice in the Bible*. Resources for Biblical Studies 68. Atlanta: Society of Biblical Literature, 2011.
* Ehrensperger, Kathy. "At the Table: Common Ground between Paul and the Historical Jesus." In *Jesus Research: The Second Princeton–Prague Symposium on Jesus*, edited by James H. Charlesworth, 531–50. Grand Rapids: Eerdmans, 2014. Now also in Ehrensperger, *Searching Paul: Conversations with the Jewish Apostle to the Nations. Collected Essays*, 91–109. Wissenschaftliche Untersuchungen zum Neuen Testament 429. Tübingen: Mohr Siebeck, 2019.
———. "'Called to be Saints': The Identity Shaping Dimension of Paul's Priestly Discourse in Romans." In *Reading Paul in Context: Explorations in Identity Formation, Essays in Honour of William S. Campbell*, edited by J. Brian Tucker, Kathy Ehrensperger, 90–109. Library of New Testament Studies 428. London: T. & T. Clark, 2013.
———. *Paul and the Dynamics of Power: Communication and Interaction in the Early Christ-Movement*. Library of New Testament Studies 325. London: T. & T. Clark, 2007/09.
———. *Searching Paul: Conversations with the Jewish Apostle to the Nations. Collected Essays*. Wissenschaftliche Untersuchungen zum Neuen Testament 429. Tübingen: Mohr Siebeck, 2019.
Fredriksen, Paula. *Paul the Pagans' Apostle*. New Haven: Yale University Press, 2017.
*Fredriksen, Paula, and Oded Irshai. "Include Me Out: Tertullian, the Rabbis and the Graeco-Roman City." In *L'identité à travers l'éthique: Nouvelles perspectives sur la formation des identités collectives dans le monde greco-romain*, edited by Katell Berthelot et al., 117–32. Turnhout: Brepols, 2015.
Frey, Jean-Baptiste. *Corpus Inscriptionum Judaicarum*. 2 vols. Edited by R. P. Vatican City: Pontificio Ist., 1936–1952.
Horbury, William, and Noy David. *Jewish Inscriptions of Graeco-Roman Egypt: With an Index of the Jewish Inscriptions of Egypt and Cyrenaica*. Cambridge: Cambridge University Press, 1992.
Horrell, David. "Idol Food, Idolatry and Ethics in Paul." In *Idolatry: False Worship in the Bible, Early Judaism and Christianity*, edited by Stephen C. Barton, 124–25. T&T Clark Theology. London: T. & T. Clark, 2007.
Jewett, Robert. "Are There Allusions to the Love Feast in Rom 3:8–10?" In *Common Life in the Early Church: Essays Honoring Graydon F. Snyder*, edited by Julian V. Hills et al., 265–78. Valley Forge, PA: Trinity, 1998.
*———. *Romans: A Commentary*. Hermeneia. Minneapolis: Fortress, 2007.
Rüpke, Jörg. *Religion of the Romans*. Translated and edited by Richard Gordon. Cambridge: Polity, 2007.

Scheid, John. "Sacrifices for Gods and Ancestors." In *A Companion to Roman Religion*, edited by Jörg Rüpke, 263–72. Blackwell Companions to the Ancient World. Malden, MA: Blackwell, 2007.

Stemberger, Günther. "Dating Rabbinic Traditions." In *Judaica Minora: Geschichte und Literatur des rabbinischen Judentums*, 231–45. Texts and Studies in Ancient Judaism. Tübingen: Mohr Siebeck, 2010.

Tomson, Peter. *Paul and the Jewish Law: Halakha in the Letters of the Apostle to the Gentiles*. Compendia rerum Iudaicarum ad Novum Testamentum. Section 3, Jewish Traditions in Early Christian Literature 1. Minneapolis: Fortress, 1990.

Study Questions

1. In what ways is the context relevant for understanding the problem with meat in Corinth?

2. In what sense are the problems addressed by Paul in Romans 14 similar and different from those in Corinth?

3. Why does Paul spend so much time and space in this letter about issues concerned with the table?

4

The Good Citizen

A Philological Analysis of *Politeuō* in Philippians 1:27 and 3:17—4:1

NAJEEB T. HADDAD

Abstract

PAUL'S USE OF THE noun *politeuesthe* in Philippians 1:27 and *politeuma* in Philippians 3:20 has seen its fair share of scholarship. This essay will seek to develop portions of Jewett's "Conflicting Movements in the Early Church as Reflected in Philippians"[1] by introducing the reader to philological biblical interpretation, a method championed by Jewett in his *Paul's Anthropological Terms* and Romans commentary. Then, by analyzing Philippians 1:27 and 3:17—4:1, this essay will help the reader better appreciate the wider socio-historical, Greco-Roman, and Hellenistic Jewish context of Paul's use of these two terms.

Introduction

Biblical philological criticism, in the narrow sense, is a study of biblical languages (Hebrew, Aramaic, Coptic, Greek, etc.): vocabulary, grammar, syntax, along with the historical origin of those words. More specifically, biblical philology is regarded as "historical linguistics," which is a diachronic study of how a language undergoes change over a period.[2] Sheldon Pollock defines it as "the discipline of making sense of texts that only real command

---

1. Jewett, "Conflicting Movements in the Early Church as Reflected in Philippians."
2. Brown, "Biblical Philology," 295.

of language and real care for interpretation make possible."[3] It may also concentrate on the manuscript tradition centering on why vocabulary, grammar, and syntax are modified across the different documents.[4] For Pollock, philology is concerned with authorial intent, reception history, and contemporary interpretation.[5] The biblical scholar depends on philological studies to offer a better exegetical reading of the sacred scriptures.

In 1971, Robert Jewett, of blessed memory, published a revised version of his doctoral dissertation, *Paul's Anthropological Terms: A Study of Their Use in Conflict Settings*. In this work, Jewett offers a philological and theological study of Paul's anthropological terms. He recognized the insufficiency of a purely lexical method since it often results in the abstraction of the term from its context, both literarily and historically. Jewett, rather, approaches Paul's anthropological vocabulary by considering the different literary and historical contexts of the texts. This philological biblical method employed was not new to the guild; however, his approach was more refined when compared to earlier scholarship.[6]

Jewett's approach is summarized in three steps. First, "the approach will be to take account of the literary context of the sentence, the paragraph, and the letter as whole." In part, step one is the acquisition of insights from biblical commentaries to take account of grammatical structures, as well as using form-critical studies to help determine "the character and role of the setting in which the term is found." Second, the term is analyzed within the historical context of the document. Considering Paul, it is important to ask *when* and from *where* the letter was written, *to whom* was the letter addressed, *why* the letter was being written, and *what* was the nature of the letter? These questions will better allow the investigator to understand the character of Paul's letter and help reconstruct the historical situation behind the letter. The final step of Jewett's method is to relate the specific term to Paul's linguistic horizon, particularly Paul's Hellenistic Jewish and Greco-Roman political, rhetorical, and philosophical milieu.[7] This final step seems most daunting, yet biblical commentaries that focus on grammar and syntax will grant the investigator a tremendous advantage.[8]

---

3. Pollock, "Philology and Freedom," 15.
4. On the history of philological criticism in the humanities, especially among biblical scholars, see Turner, "Biblical Philology," 357–80.
5. Pollock, "Philology in Three Dimensions," 401.
6. For example, see Barr, *Semantics*. Cf. Jewett, *Paul's Anthropological Terms*, 7.
7. Jewett, *Paul's Anthropological Terms*, 7–8.
8. For example, see Jewett, *Romans: A Commentary*.

Using Jewett's philological method, this essay will explore Paul's use of the noun *politeuma* and its cognate *politeuesthe* in Philippians 1:27 and 3:20. First, this essay will outline the historical place of Philippi in the first century CE, as well as the circumstances of the letter. Then I shall briefly examine the history of research, evaluating the literary context of both Philippians 1:27 and 3:20. Finally, Philippians 1:27 and 3:20 will be analyzed considering the historical situation of the Philippian believers and Paul's Hellenistic Judaism. One will notice how the situation of Philippian believers affects the language Paul incorporates into this letter. Moreover, Paul adapts and transforms *politeuesthe/politeuma* according to his Hellenistic Jewish worldview alongside his gospel.

Politeuma and Paul's Letter to the Philippians

Historical and Literary Issues

The former Hellenistic city of Philippi became a Roman colony in 42 BCE, in the aftermath of Marc Antony and Octavian's battle against partisans of the Republic, Cassius, and Brutus (assassins of Julius Caesar).[9] Antony settled veterans of the war in this territory, securing a strategic position on the Egnatian Way. The colony was founded again, under a new political constitution in 30 BCE, by Octavian when he settled Roman citizens there. Even though the city was politically Roman, it remained culturally Greek.[10]

Philippi was an elite-dominated, military colony. For almost three centuries, from 42 BCE to the third-century CE, the same elite group retained power. However, all the Roman citizens of Philippi did not belong to the dominant group. Moreover, the Romans only made up a fraction of the population. Cédric Brélaz notes:

> As shown by many inscriptions, a very high percentage of the population of Philippi in the first century CE . . . was made up of Greek and Thracians. Although they had lost much of their land to the creation of the colony in 42 BCE, the local population of the former Greek city of Philippi was allowed to stay in the territory of the new community as foreign residents, or *incolae*, as they were called in Latin.[11]

---

9. I am indebted to Cédric Brélaz, whose work on first-century Philippi I closely follow. See Brélaz, "First-Century Philippi," 153–88.

10. Fee, *Paul's Letter*, 25–26.

11. Brélaz, "First-Century Philippi," 162.

Even though the native residents no longer enjoyed certain civic rights, they were still considered a part of the colony. It is likely that the native Greek/Thracian inhabitants, along with a minority of Jews, if any, made up the first community of Christ believers in Philippi.[12]

Many commentators agree that Paul wrote Philippians. The integrity (unity) of the letter, rather, is challenged. Is it a single letter or a composite of several? An argument for or against the integrity of the letter will not be rehearsed here.[13] However, I shall assume the unity of the letter, as did Jewett, for several reasons: the earliest manuscript traditions do not indicate a partition;[14] no external evidence exists for a literary reconstruction of several letters into one; editorial revisions attempt to alleviate, not aggravate, literary problems and inconsistencies.[15] Moreover, as Jewett and others have shown, despite the abrupt transitions of the letter (e.g., 3:1–2), the theme(s) of the letter is unified, and there are no significant signs of division beyond conjecture.[16]

Another important literary question is Paul's physical location when he wrote this letter. Internal evidence suggests Paul wrote the letter while imprisoned (Phil 1:7, 13, 14). Traditionally, it is suggested that Paul wrote while imprisoned in Rome (60–62 CE). Others have suggested Corinth (50 CE), Ephesus (54–55 CE), or Caesarea (57–59 CE).[17] In keeping with recent trends, I will assume an Ephesian provenance (54–55 CE), as Jewett previously suggested.[18] Though this essay will assume an Ephesian provenance, it is important to observe a caution highlighted by Moisés Silva; "[the letter's provenance] remains little more than a theory, and any exegetical conclusions that lean heavily on it must be regarded as methodologically weak or even invalid."[19]

---

12. Brélaz, "Outside the City Gate," 123–40.

13. On the integrity of Philippians, see, e.g., Jewett, "Epistolary Thanksgiving," 40–53; Reed, "Philippians 3:1," 63–90; Hawthorne and Martin, *Philippians*, xxx–xxxiv; Reumann 3.20–21, *Philippians*, 8–13; Silva, *Philippians*, 12–14.

14. See Chester Beatty Papyrus 46; "Reading the Papyri: P46/The Pauline Epistles," University of Michigan Papyrus Collection, https://apps.lib.umich.edu/reading/Paul/index.html.

15. Silva, *Philippians*, 12–13.

16. For a more detailed argument in support of the literary integrity of Philippians, see Hawthorne and Martin, *Philippians*, xxx–xxxiv. On the unity of theme(s), see Jewett, "Epistolary Thanksgiving," 40–53.

17. For an evaluation of the arguments on provenance, see Hawthorne and Martin, *Philippians*, xl–l.

18. Jewett, *Paul's Anthropological Terms*, 21–22.

19. Silva, *Philippians*, 7.

One final literary question is the occasion of Paul's writing to the Philippians. Part of the difficulty answering this question arises from the different topics that are brought up in this letter.[20] Several scholars have proposed a singularity of purpose in the letter, including Ernst Lohmeyer, J. A. Motyer, Paul A. Holloway, John Paul Heil, and Mark A. Jennings.[21] I am convinced by the argument set forth by Jennings, who says that Paul's letter is deliberative; the sole purpose is to persuade the Philippian believers to maintain "its exclusive partnership with him and his gospel mission."[22] Paul's is urging the Philippians to accept his gospel mission and keep it until the parousia (Phil 2:16). Jennings further notes that Paul's deliberative argument runs on three essential principles. First, is the notion of *koinōnia*; mutuality and reciprocity are essential to Paul's gospel, and a break from Paul will not fare well for believers "on the day of Christ" (Phil 2:16). Second, the rivals of Paul are those who reject Paul and his gospel. To join the rivals is a break of *koinōnia*. Finally, the letter concerns finances. Jennings says, "The Philippians' spiritual commitment to him and the advancement of the gospel is not to be separated from their obligations to aid [Paul] in his ministry."[23] Yet, with these three tenets in mind, we can better appreciate Paul's attempt at maintaining communion with the Philippian Christ believers.

History of Research

The verb *politeuō*, which derives from the word *polis* (a "city" or "city-state"), first appears in Philippians 1:27a. It is a *hapax legomenon* in the undisputed letters of Paul. The verb is commonly used by Greco-Roman authors and has the connotation to "live in the *polis* as a free citizen." But in Philippians 1:27a, the verb is rendered in the middle present imperative, second-person plural *politeuesthe*. The LSJ defines the medial form *politeuomai* as one who "takes an active part in the affairs of the *polis*"; hence, to "live as a free person."[24] However, a simple lexical definition, in this instance, does not clarify how the verb can be understood within the larger context of this letter. First, it is likely that the great majority, if not all, of the Philippian Christ believers were Greek/Thracian, non-citizens of the Roman colony.[25] The

---

20. Hawthorne and Martin, *Philippians*, lvii–lviii; cf. Jennings, *Price of Partnership*, 2.

21. Lohmeyer, *Der Brief an die Philipper*; Motyer, *The Message of Philippians*; Holloway, *Consolation in Philippians*; Heil, *Philippians*; Jennings, *Price of Partnership*.

22. Jennings, *Price of Partnership*, 4.

23. Jennings, *Price of Partnership*, 4–6.

24. LSJ, 9th ed. (1996), s.v. "*politeuomai*."

25. Fowl, *Philippians*, 61.

NRSV translates *politeuesthe* as "manner of living"; however, the meaning of *politeuesthe* becomes lost in translation: "Only, live your life in a manner worthy of the gospel of Christ" (*Monon axiōs tou euangeliou tou Christou politeuesthe*).[26] If Paul is directing the Philippian community to live a life that is consistent with their faith, why does he not use vocabulary that is extensively employed in his letters, like *peripateō, zaō,* or *prassō*?[27] Such a translation, unfortunately, seems to miss the larger metaphor.

In R. R. Brewer's classical lexical study of *politeuomai*, he argued that "conduct relative to some law of life—political, moral, social, or religious—is signified."[28] However, Brewer overpoliticizes *politeuomai*, overlooking Paul's own Hellenistic Jewish milieu. E. C. Miller challenges Brewer's overt Greco-Roman understanding using Hellenistic Jewish literature, including the LXX and Acts, to help illuminate Philippians 1:27.[29]

For Miller, *politeuesthe* is related to the Jews' covenant relationship with God shown in obedience to the Torah.[30] He further suggests that the term is used to exhort "the congregation at Philippi to hold fast its identity as the new Israel, free from the obligations of the old Law, Torah."[31] There are three examples I wish to highlight from Miller's article. First, in 1–4 Maccabees, *politeuesthai* is used to connote the communal and distinct life of Jews whom God has set apart from the gentiles. The passage in 2 Maccabees 6:1 reads, "Not long after this, the king sent an Athenian senator to compel the Jews to forsake the laws of their ancestors and *no longer to live by the laws of God*" (*tois tou theou nomos mē politeuesthai*) (NRSV).[32] Notice how the medial verb *politeuesthai* does not mean to live "any" manner of life, but one within the bounds of the "law of God." In a similar fashion, Philo of Alexandria employs the verb *politeuontai* (present, indicative, middle, third-person plural) in his *On the Confusion of Tongues*[33] to describe the heavenly region where the wise ones' citizenship lies (*men ton ouranion chōron en hō politeuontai*). The Philonic use resembles the Greco-Roman use; however, it is adapted to Philo's diasporic Jewish thinking. Finally, Josephus in *The Life*[34] uses the imperative

---

26. New Testament Greek text is from the NA28 (*Novum Testamentum Graece*, Nestle-Aland, 28th ed.).

27. Cf. Fee, *Paul's Letter*, 161; Jennings, *Price of Partnership*, 78n23.

28. Brewer, "The Meaning of *Politeuesthe*," 80.

29. Miller, "Politeuesthe in Philippians 1:27," 86–92.

30. Cf. Hawthorne and Martin, *Philippians*, 69.

31. Miller, "Politeuesthe in Philippians 1:27," 94.

32. LXX Greek text is from A. Rahlfs.

33. Philo, *On the Confusion of Tongues* 78, LCL.

34. Josephus, *The Life* 1.12, LCL.

politeuesthai in similar fashion to the Maccabean corpus and carries the connotation of living a life in accordance with the Torah of God: "I began to *govern my life* by the rules of the Pharisees" (*arxamēn politeuesthai tē farisaiōn airesei katakolouthōn*). These and other examples lead Miller to understand Paul's use of *politeuesthai* as a way of life dedicated to Christ, since Christ replaces the centrality of the Torah in Paul's gospel.

Miller's approach is not without criticism. His theological contrasts between a Hellenistic Jewish and "Christian" understanding of *politeuesthai* often goes beyond the evidence in Philippians. Timothy C. Geoffrion observes this weakness, especially regarding references to the church as the "new Israel," or the contrast between the Torah and the "new law which is the Gospel."[35] However, Geoffrion's conclusion is strikingly similar to Miller's. As Jennings notes, "Geoffrion's separation of 'heavenly citizenship' from Miller's 'new (eschatological) Israel' turns out to be a distinction without a cause."[36] Yet, Miller's approach is worth further consideration.

To best capture Paul's background, one must duly consider how Paul was working within the framework of the Hellenistic Jewish speculative tradition. If we take, for example, the Prologue to the Gospel of John, 1:1–18, one will readily notice the author's indebtedness not only to the Jewish wisdom tradition but also to Hellenistic Judaism.[37] Though the author of the Prologue and, for example, Philo, are both within the Hellenistic Jewish speculative tradition, they do differ from one another. As Thomas H. Tobin demonstrates, John drew upon these sources and worked within the Hellenistic Jewish tradition not only adopting certain ideas, which can be seen in Philo, but also adapting ideas to fit his community's belief in Christ. This is most especially seen in the Prologue's identification of the Word (*Logos*) of God incarnate in Jesus of Nazareth (John 1:14).[38]

In the same way, Paul adopted certain modes of thinking that were commonplace in Hellenistic Jewish thinking yet appropriated and transformed it for use within his own belief system. Neither does this notion disqualify Paul as a Hellenistic Jew nor does it confirm him to be a "Christian" in any contemporary sense. Rather, Paul was one among many Hellenistic Jews who wrote from within this speculative tradition. For example, in "The Importance of Hellenistic Judaism for the Study of Paul's Ethics," Tobin analyzed how the practice of virtue and the Mosaic law are interpreted in

---

35. Geoffrion, *Rhetorical Purpose*, 48.
36. Cf. Jennings, *Price of Partnership*, 81.
37. See Tobin, "Prologue of John," 252–69.
38. Cf. Haddad, "Paul the Hellenistic Jew," 86–100; Tobin, "Prologue of John," 268–69.

Hellenistic Jewish literature, such as the Letter of Aristaeus, 4 Maccabees, Philo, and Josephus.[39] In each instance, Tobin notes how "Observance of the Mosaic law led to the practice of virtues and avoidance of vices that they shared with their fellow citizens . . . in all this the goal was to redescribe the value of observing the law and not to offer an alternative to its observance."[40] Drawing similarities to Paul, Tobin further demonstrates how Paul was aware of Hellenistic Jewish interpretations on the observance of the law but appropriates the tradition in the service of his gospel. For example, in 1 Corinthians 9:8–12, Paul interprets Deuteronomy 25:4, "You shall not muzzle an ox while it is treading out the grain" (NRSV) to refer to human conduct rather than animal rights.[41] If we were to summarize Paul's place within the Hellenistic Jewish tradition, we can say:

> Paul understood that faith in Christ releases believers from observation of the Mosaic law (cf. Gal 5:1). The basic principle of the Christian life, says Paul, is "faith working through love," empowered by the Spirit of God (Gal 5:5–6). Therefore, for Paul, the observance of the Mosaic law was not a way for Christ believers to live in a manner worthy of the gospel (Phil 1:27). Instead, believers are exhorted to directly practice virtues, avoiding vice, without reference to the law (i.e., Gal 5:1—6:10, and, to a lesser extent Rom 7:7–25).[42]

Taking all this information into account, *politeuesthe* is consistent with Hellenistic Jewish thought, as Miller noted, about Israel's fidelity toward God and the Torah. In a sense, it is the rejection of all things that are outside the realm of the God of Israel and God's law. However, when Paul incorporates *politeuesthe*, he nuances the term and its cognate, considering the non-citizen status of the Philippian Christ believers and offering them a way to fulfill the divine mandates of Christ—the direct practice of virtue over vice. At the heart of Philippians is a call to unity, as the heavenly community of God, by fulfilling the mandates of the gospel of Christ that Paul preaches to them.

---

39. Tobin, "Importance of Hellenistic Judaism," 147–65.

40. Tobin, "Importance of Hellenistic Judaism," 159.

41. Tobin, "Importance of Hellenistic Judaism," 160. See the parallels between Rom 7:7–25 and Philo's *On the Special Laws* 4.78.

42. Haddad, "Paul the Hellenistic Jew," 97.

Exegesis: Philippians 1:27 and Philippians 3:17—4:1

The imperative *politeuesthe* in Philippians 1:27 is a direct call to the Philippian believers to live out their faith in Christ by practicing virtue over vice. Paul retains the semantic meaning of the verb: "citizens of the *polis* are compelled to participate in the civic life for the good of state." Likewise, believers are obligated to live their lives practicing virtue over vice as they belong to a unique citizenship that is both now and not yet. It is a citizenship recognized among the body of believers and one that exists in heaven (3:20). Notice as well that *politeuesthe* is calling the community to remain in their faith. Philippians 1:27 reads, "Only, live your life in a manner worthy of the gospel of Christ [*Monon axiōs tou euangeliou tou Christou politeuesthe*], so that, whether I come and see you or am absent and hear about you, I will know that you are standing firm (*stēkete*) in one spirit, striving side by side with one mind for the faith of the gospel" (NRSV). *Politeuesthe* is a call to a consistent way of living, despite Paul's own presence or absence. It is a call to a covenantal relationship, governing their action according to the manner of living according to their new *politeuma* or commonwealth. It is one reason Paul says in Philippians 3:20 that their *politeuma* is in heaven.

Moreover, he calls the Philippians to *stēkete en heni penumati* or "stand firm in one spirit" (*stēkete* is the present active indicative verb, second-person plural formed from the perfect tense of *histanai* [from *histēmi*]). The verb is figuratively used and often appears in Paul's hortatory sections of his letters, for Christ believers to "stand firm" in their faith (1 Cor 16:3; Gal 5:1; Phil 4:1; 1 Thess 3:8. Cf. 2 Thess 2:15).[43] Paul does not directly mention who the opponents of the Philippian believers are. Ultimately, whether it is a specific group or groups of opponents, Paul's ultimate concern is that the believers embrace Paul's gospel, remaining one with him.[44] This notion is further evidenced when Paul mentions the *koinonia pneumatos* ("fellowship in the spirit") in Philippians 2:1. In and by the spirit, they are united with one another in Christ, with Christ, and with Paul.[45] This "citizen-like" behavior and "standing firm" in unity with Christ (and Paul) is further emphasized in Philippians 3:17—4:1.

The passage in Philippians 2:1—4:3 forms part of the conclusion of the *probatio*, or rhetorical proofs, of the letter.[46] Here, Paul provides the

---

43. Geoffrion (*Rhetorical Purpose*, 24) suggests that this verb has military overtones. However, the verb *stēkō* does not carry this sense in the first century ce. Cf. Jennings, *Price of Partnership*, 84n46.

44. Jennings, *Price of Partnership*, 83.

45. Haddad, *Paul, Politics, and New Creation*, 158.

46. On Paul's use of rhetoric in general, see Betz, *Galatians*. On Paul's use of

Philippian Christ believers good reasons to take up the initial call to "live your life in a manner worthy of the gospel of Christ." In Philippians 3:17—4:1, which forms part of the conclusion of the *probatio*, Paul encourages them to "stand firm in the Lord" (*stēkete en kyriou*). Notice the recurrence of two words in this passage that calls our attention back to Philippians 1:27: *politeuma* (nominative neuter singular noun) and *stēkete*. The passage in 3:17—4:1 is considered to bring 1:27 to a conclusion. Once again, Paul is calling the Philippian believers to remain one with him, not only by using the imperative *stēkete* but also by calling them to become imitators of him (*Summimētai mou ginesthe*) (Phil 3:17). By becoming imitators of Paul, they will ultimately fulfill the mandate *monon axiōs tou euangeliou tou Christou politeuesthe* (Phil 1:27). Likewise, if they become imitators of Paul and fulfill their obligation to consistently live, as do citizens of a *polis*, according to the gospel Paul preached to them, they will inherit eternal life (Phil 3:21).

In Philippians 3:20–21, Paul suggests that the Philippian believers' *politeuma* is in heaven, and at the parousia, Christ will "transform the body" (*metaschēmatisei to sōma*).[47] Considering that a large part of the community was likely non-citizens, Kathy Ehrensperger notes "the assertion that they too are part of and actively participate in a civic community seems in tune with the lack of such possibilities for Greeks and Thracians in the Roman social and symbolic universe of the city."[48] They are to practice their *citizenship* now (Phil 1:27) in order that they may more fully participate in their heavenly city at *the end*. This notion of heavenly citizenship is a concept found in Philo.[49] The wise men, says Philo, realize that they will only find their citizenship in heaven:

> Their souls are never colonists leaving heaven for a new home . . . To them the heavenly region, where their citizenship (*politeuontai*) lies, is their native land; the earthly region in which they became sojourners is a foreign country.[50]

As Wendy Cotter notes, "all Christians have become 'foreigners' since their true home city is heaven."[51] This notion must have been easy to accept for

---

rhetoric in Philippians, especially the *probatio*, see Witherington, *Paul's Letter to the Philippians*, 110–13.

47. On transformation in Paul's eschatological soteriology, especially as it relates to Paul's new creation theology, see Haddad, "God and New Creation."

48. Ehrensperger, "Rooted in Heaven," 74.

49. This similarity does not imply that Paul read Philo's work. Rather, it is to demonstrate that both were part of the larger Hellenistic Jewish speculative tradition.

50. Philo, *On the Confusion of Tongues* 77–78, LCL.

51. Cotter, "Our *Politeuma*," 104. I am convinced by Cotter's argument regarding

the natives of Philippi (Greeks and Thracians) who were considered foreigners in their own home. However, living as citizens of heaven in the now, they will inherit the fullness of that citizenship (rights and privileges) in "the end" (*to telos*) (cf. Phil 3:19). In following Paul's example, the believers are assured of their communal place among the people of God.[52]

Final Remarks

A philological biblical method allows the investigator to critically examine and analyze the literary and historical context of a particular passage and book. Considering the examination of *politeuma* and *politeuesthe* in Paul's letter to the Philippians, a philological approach allows one to discover the contours of Paul's thought. This task has been accomplished not only by reading and evaluating previous scholarly hypotheses, but also by contextualizing Paul within his broader Greco-Roman environment and, more narrowly, his Hellenistic Judaism.

However, there are certain limitations with language. It can be difficult to confirm a meaning, especially when analyzing an ancient text. Because certain definitions are malleable, especially when attempting to convey meanings from ancient/koine Greek into English, one is often limited in their ability to define certain words. For example, a difficulty not addressed in this essay, purposely done so, is how to translate *politeuesthe* and *politeuma* in Philippians 1:17 and 3:20 respectively. Some translators, such as Hawthorne and Martin, translate *politeuesthe* in 1:27 as "show yourselves to be good citizens."[53] Yet, this English translation misses Paul's intention—applying more of a civic understanding. Therefore, the philological investigator and historical critic must be aware of such limitations and always proceed with caution.

Bibliography

(* For Further Reading)

Barr, James. *The Semantics of the Biblical Languages*. Oxford: Oxford University Press, 1961.
Betz, Hans Dieter. *Galatians: A Commentary on Paul's Letter to the Churches in Galatia*. Hermeneia. Philadelphia: Fortress, 1979.

---

ancient associations and the Philippian believers' view of their community in light of Paul's gospel. See Cotter, "Our *Politeuma*," 92–104.

52. Jennings, *Price of Partnership*, 147.
53. Hawthorne and Martin, *Philippians*, 68.

Brélaz, Cédric. "First-Century Philippi." In *The First Urban Churches 4: Roman Philippi*. Writings in the Greco-Roman World Supplements 13, edited by James R. Harrison and L. L. Welborn, 153–88. Atlanta: SBL, 2018.

———. "'Outside the City Gate': Center and Periphery in Paul's Preaching in Philippi." In *The Urban World and the First Christians*, edited by Steve Walton, Paul R. Trebilco, and David W. J. Gill, 123–40. Grand Rapids: Eerdmans, 2017.

Brewer, Raymond R. "The Meaning of *Politeuesthe* in Philippians 1:27." *Journal of Biblical Literature* 73 (1973) 76–83.

Brown, Schuyler. "Biblical Philology, Linguistics and the Problem of Method." *Heythorp Journal* 20 (1979) 295–98.

*Cotter, Wendy. "Our *Politeuma* is in Heaven: The Meaning of Philippians 3:17–21." In *Origins in Method—Towards a New Understanding of Christianity: Essays in Honour of John C. Hurd*, edited by Bradley H. McLean, 92–104. Journal for the Study of the New Testament Supplements 86. Sheffield: Sheffield Academic, 1993

Ehrensperger, Kathy. "Rooted in Heaven and Resident in Philippi, but no *ekklēsia*?" In *The First Urban Churches 4: Roman Philippi*, edited by James R. Harrison and L. L. Welborn, 63–78. Writings in the Greco-Roman World Supplements 13. Atlanta: Society of Biblical Literature, 2018.

Fee, Gordon. *Paul's Letter to the Philippians*. New International Commentary on the New Testament. Grand Rapids: Eerdmans, 1995.

Fowl, Stephen E. *Philippians*. Two Horizons New Testament Commentary. Grand Rapids: Eerdmans, 2005.

Geoffrion, Timothy C. *The Rhetorical Purpose and the Political Military Character of Philippians: A Call to Stand Firm*. Lewiston, NY: Mellen Biblical, 1993.

Haddad, Najeeb T. "God and New Creation in Galatians, 2 Corinthians, and Romans." In *God in Paul's Letters*. Catholic Biblical Quarterly Imprints. Washington, DC: Catholic Biblical Association, forthcoming.

———. "Paul the Hellenistic Jew: The Contributions of Thomas H. Tobin, SJ, to New Testament Scholarship." *Biblical Research* 66 (2021) 86–100.

———. *Paul, Politics, and New Creation: Reconsidering Paul and Empire*. Lanham, MD: Lexington/Fortress Academic, 2021.

*Harrison, James R., and L. L. Welborn, eds. *The First Urban Churches 4: Roman Philippi*. Writings From the Greco-Roman World Supplement Series 14. Atlanta: Society of Biblical Literature, 2018.

*Hawthorne, Gerald F., and Ralph P. Martin. *Philippians*. 2nd edition. World Biblical Commentary 43. Grand Rapids: Zondervan, 2004.

Heil, John Paul. *Philippians: Let Us Rejoice in Being Conformed to Christ*. Early Christianity and Its Literature 3. Atlanta: Society of Biblical Literature, 2010.

Holloway, Paul. *Consolation in Philippians: Philosophical Resources and Rhetorical Strategy*. Society for New Testament Studies Monograph Series 112. Cambridge: Cambridge University Press, 2001.

*Jennings, Mark A. *The Price of Partnership in the Letter of Paul to the Philippians: "Make My Joy Complete."* London: Bloomsbury T. & T. Clark, 2018.

Jewett, Robert. "Conflicting Movements in the Early Church as Reflected in Philippians." *Novum Testamentum* 12 (1970) 362–90. https://doi.org/10.2307/1559934.

———. "The Epistolary Thanksgiving and the Integrity of Philippians." *Novum Testamentum* 12 (1970) 40–53.

*———. *Paul's Anthropological Terms: A Study of Their Use in Conflict Settings*. Arbeiten zur Geschichte des antiken Judentums und des Urchristentums 10. Leiden: Brill, 1971.

*———. *Romans: A Commentary*. Hermeneia. Minneapolis: Fortress, 2007.
Josephus. Translated by H. St. J. Thackeray et al. 10 vols. Loeb Classical Library. Cambridge: Harvard University Press, 1926–65.
Liddell, Henry George, Robert Scott, and Henry Stuart Jones. *A Greek-English Lexicon* [LSJ]. 9th ed. Oxford: Clarendon, 1996.
Lohmeyer, Ernst. *Der Brief an die Philipper*. 9th ed. Kritisch-exegetischer Kommentar über das Neue Testament 9/1. Göttingen: Vandenhoeck & Ruprecht, 1953.
Miller, Ernest C. "*Politeuesthe* in Philippians 1:27: Some Philological and Thematic Observations." *Journal for the Study of New Testament* 15 (1982) 86–96.
Motyer, John A. *The Message of Philippians: Jesus Our Joy*. The Bible Speaks Today. Downers Grove, IL: InterVarsity, 1984.
Philo. *On the Confusion of Tongues*. Translated by F. H. Colson, G. H. Whitaker, and R. Marcus. 12 vols. Loeb Classical Library. Cambridge: Harvard University Press, 1929–62.
Pollock, Sheldon. "Philology and Freedom." *Philological Encounters* 1 (2016) 4–30.
———. "Philology in Three Dimensions." *Postmedieval* 5 (2014) 398–413.
"Reading the Papyri: P46/The Pauline Epistles." University of Michigan Papyrus Collection. https://apps.lib.umich.edu/reading/Paul/index.html.
Reed, Jefferey T. "Philippians 3:1 and the Epistolary Hesitation Formula: The Literary Integrity of Philippians, Again." *Journal of Biblical Literature* 115 (1996) 63–90.
Reumann, John. "Philippians 3.20–21: A Hymnic Fragment?" *New Testament Studies* 30 (1986) 593–609.
*Silva, Moisés. *Philippians*. 2nd ed. Baker Exegetical Commentary on the New Testament. Grand Rapids: Baker, 2005.
*Tobin, Thomas H. "The Importance of Hellenistic Judaism for the Study of Paul's Ethics." In *Early Christian Ethics in Interaction with Jewish and Greco-Roman Contexts*, edited by Jan Willem van Henten and Joseph Verheyden, 147–65. Studies in Theology and Religion 17. Leiden: Brill, 2013.
———. "The Prologue of John and Hellenistic Jewish Speculation." *Catholic Biblical Quarterly* 52 (1990) 252–69.
Turner, James. "Biblical Philology." In *Philology: The Forgotten Origins of the Modern Humanities*, 357–67. Princeton: Princeton University Press, 2014.
Witherington, Ben III. *Paul's Letter to the Philippians: A Socio-Rhetorical Commentary*. Grand Rapids: Eerdmans, 2011.

Study Questions

1. Define "philological criticism" and describe both the strengths and limitations of this biblical method.

2. How would you choose to translate the imperative verb *politeuesthe* in Philippians 1:27? Explain why you chose this translation?

3. Would you consider incorporating philological criticism in your future studies? Why or why not?

5

Human Trafficking in Romans 1:18–32

Sheila E. McGinn

Abstract

THE CONTEMPORARY ANTI-GAY READING of Romans 1:18–32 ignores Paul's rhetorical agenda in his missive to the communities of believers in the imperial capital and violates a fundamental ethical standard for biblical interpretation. A careful linguistic and social-contextual reading of Paul's language in this passage overturns that reading and illustrates that Paul was condemning practices associated with pornographic spectacles and other types of human trafficking, not loving relationships between consenting adults.

Introduction

In recent years, a section of Romans 1:18–32 has become a "bludgeon text" in relation to LGBTQ+ issues. But the contemporary "anti-gay" reading of Romans 1:18–32 mistakes Paul's agenda in this letter to the imperial capital. Contextualizing Paul's remarks against his own cultural context as a Jewish subject of the Roman Empire *ca.* CE 58 challenges the contemporary oppressive use of the text. If we view Romans in light of widespread rumors about the imperial city in the late 50s, we see that Paul was condemning practices associated with human trafficking, not loving relationships between consenting adults.

This topic would have been dear to the heart of Bob Jewett, who took seriously the cultural contextualization both of the New Testament texts and of the contemporary appropriations of those texts. Starting with his dissertation work on the polemical context of Paul's vocabulary, later published as *Paul's Anthropological Terms: A Study of Their Use in Conflict Settings*, and continuing with his early monographs on *The Captain America Complex* and *Jesus Against the Rapture*, which focused more on the contemporary misreading of NT texts, Jewett persistently engaged the sacred texts and their contemporary contexts with a critical eye. Nor was this a passing phase in his scholarship; *au contraire*, as we can see from his treatment of *Christian Tolerance: Paul's Message to the Modern Church*, such works as *Paul the Apostle to America*, *Saint Paul at the Movies*, and his magisterial Hermeneia commentary on Romans, this focus on cultural engagement with and appropriation of the biblical texts formed a foundation for all of Professor Jewett's work. This essay is intended to further that engagement by addressing an often misunderstood and misused passage in Paul's letter "to all God's beloved in Rome" (Rom 1:7).[1]

The kind of social-historical approach to Romans taken in this essay contextualizes the letter in Paul's and his audience's own time and place. The "world behind the text" shapes the background against which the letter should be understood *now*, precisely because that is the backdrop against which it would have been understood *then*. Paul's message has significance for modern audiences, but we simply cannot access Paul's message without doing the work of situating his essay in his own socio-cultural and historical context. Failing that, we see "darkly, as in a mirror," our own preconceptions rather than Paul's message. Without such contextualization, the biblical text, rather than providing the locus for revelatory encounter, is reduced to an echo chamber of contemporary assumptions and ideologies. Noncontextual readings, therefore, violate hermeneutical ethics by presenting as "God's word" interpretations based on eisegesis of the readers' ideological investments rather than exegesis of biblical texts. Contextualizing the biblical texts in their own social-cultural and historical situations, on the other hand, allows the word to speak and continue to challenge contemporary readers as it challenged the original audiences.

Literary Context of Romans 1:18–32

Paul's letter to the Roman churches is divided into three major doctrinal sections: 1:18–4:25, 5:1–8:39, and 9–11. In the opening section of Romans 1:18–4:25, Paul affirms the impartiality of divine justice and the salvation of Jews and gentiles, expositing the character of divine justice and exploring how this justice of God (*dikaiosynē Theou*) works for the salvation of the entire cosmos, including the people of Israel and the gentile nations.

---

1. Elements of this essay were briefly explored in McGinn, "Romans," 1528–87.

The opening pericope (1:18–32) of this first argumentative section segues from the broad theme of God's justice and salvation of all believers to reprise the detrimental effects of false worship, correlating impiety (*asebeia*) and injustice (*adikia*), a rejection of God's justice (*dikaiosynē*). Those who oppose God are not only impious; they suppress the truth by such injustice (1:18); thus, they are subject to the divine wrath (*orgē*) being revealed (*apokalyptō*) in Paul's time.[2]

Presenting a notion of what has been called natural revelation, Paul claims that the invisible God is revealed in the created world, which displays God's attributes (1:19–20). While the Jewish people have the advantage of the revealed word in the Torah and the Prophets, this additional modality of revelation by analogy from creature to Creator means that no human has any excuse for denying the divine reality or for idolizing any reality other than the true God.

However, in spite of the ubiquity of the divine presence in the created realm, some humans persist in their denial—not merely of God's existence but, more importantly, their obligation to glorify and give thanks (*eucharisteō*) to God—instead relying on the futile calculations of hearts devoid of understanding (1:21–23). On the basic biblical principle that one becomes conformed to the image of the deity one worships, Paul unfolds what results from worshiping false deities rather than the true God whose creative hand is evident in every aspect of the world God has fashioned.

> [24]Therefore God handed them over (*paredōken*) in the lusts (*epithymias*) of their hearts to impurity (*akatharsian*), to the dishonoring (*atimazethai*) of their bodies among themselves, [25]because they exchanged the truth about God for a lie and worshiped (*esebasthēsan*) and served (*elatreusan*) the creature rather than the Creator . . . (1:24–25).[3]

Wider Biblical Context of Romans 1:18–32

Paul's critique here exhibits typical features of earlier biblical diatribes against paganism (e.g., Isa 9:16–20; Wis 3–14). The allegation that pagans have "exchanged the truth of God for a lie" (v. 25) may serve as an oblique reference to the "fall" scenario in Genesis 3, where the "temptation" concerning "the

---

2. This apocalyptic language conveys that Paul views his audience as living in the time of fulfillment of the divine plan.

3. Unless otherwise noted, all quotations from the biblical text are my own translation.

knowledge of good and evil" entails arrogating to human beings the ability to decide what will be named as good or evil, regardless of divine justice or truth.[4] As Ben Sira's reflection on Genesis 2–3 insists, humans are created with the full knowledge of good and evil; such wisdom is "poured forth" on all the created world.[5] The human decision to go against divine justice derives not from ignorance but from an impious disobedience that rejects the appropriate human stance of "fear of the Lord" and thereby cuts off the sinner from divine wisdom (Sir 1:11–30).

Roman Cultural Context of Romans 1:18–32

We must keep in mind, however, that Paul is not engaged in a library debate with a generic audience about a stereotypical pagan mistake. Paul is writing to Christ-believers in the capital city of the Roman Empire, whose inscriptions and coinage proclaim the ruler to be "worshipful" (*Augustus*) "son of God" (*divi filius*). More immediately, however, Paul's audience would recognize the language of the imperial cult, the honoring of the "worshipful" (*sebastos*) Caesar, who arrogates to himself and his "divine" forbears the worship (*latreia*) that is due to God alone.

> [26]For this reason God gave them up (*paredōken*) to degrading passions (*pathē atimias*). Their women exchanged natural intercourse (*tēn physikēn chrēsin*) for unnatural (*tēn para physin*), [27]and in the same way also the men, giving up natural intercourse (*tēn physikēn chrēsin*) with women, were consumed with passion for one another. Men committed shameless acts with men and received in their own persons the due penalty for their error.
>
> [28]And since they did not see fit to acknowledge God, God gave them up (*paredōken*) to a debased mind (*eis adokimon noun*) and to things that should not be done. [29]They were filled with every kind of wickedness (*adikia*), evil, covetousness, malice. Full of envy, murder, strife, deceit, craftiness, they are gossips, [30]slanderers, God-haters, insolent, haughty, boastful, inventors of evil, rebellious toward parents, [31]foolish, faithless, heartless, ruthless. [32]They know God's decree (*to dikaiōma*), that those who practice such things deserve to die—yet they not only do them (*auta poiousin*) but even applaud (*alla kai syneudokousin*) others who practice them (Rom 1:26–32; NRSV).[6]

---

4. See Clark, "A Legal Background," passim.
5. Sir 1:9; see Berg, "Ben Sira," passim.
6. The verb *syneudokeō* also appears in Acts 22:20, in which Paul is depicted as

The repetition of *paredōken* in verses 26 and 28 reinforces the notion that, while God alone is worthy of worship, God has the authority to "hand over" recalcitrant humans to the control of other forces.[7] New Testament usage of this term tends to have punitive connotations—e.g., Paul and the canonical gospels use this same term to refer to the "handing over" of Jesus to the Roman authorities to be crucified (Rom 8:32; Mark 3:19, 15:15; Matt 27:26; Luke 23:25; John 19:16)—but more broadly it means to "entrust" or give an object into someone's custody (as, e.g., Matt 25:14; John 19:30; Acts 6:14). The Torah was entrusted to Israel by God through Moses, and the Spirit of Jesus was entrusted to those at the foot of the cross. This is no punishment, but in fact a matter of gift. Is such a trust a permanent disposition? One assumes, with respect to the Torah and the Spirit, that this would be the case. When *paradidōmi* is used in the punitive sense, however, there is no indication that such custody will be a permanent reality. The "handing over" comprises a corrective measure that allows the subjects to "bottom out," recognize the error of their ways, and turn back to God.

The *topos* of "idolatry = moral debasement" would be reinforced in Paul's mind by rumors about behavior in the imperial household over recent decades. Just a quick reprise may suffice to convey what would come to mind when Paul—and his Roman audience—thought of ruling-class Roman mores. The Emperor Tiberius (who reigned CE 14–37) was noted for lascivious and pedophilic behavior, especially in his later period after retiring to Capri.[8] Gaius "Caligula" (CE 37–41) was said to have engaged in incest with all his sisters and prostituted them to his political supporters.[9] Claudius (CE 41–54) had a reputation for cruelty, due in part to his fondness for gladiatorial games.[10] Married four times, Claudius was repeatedly cuckolded by his third wife, Valeria Messalina (*ca.* CE 17–48), who was infamous for her voracious sexual drive and promiscuous behavior. Juvenal (*Satire* VI:114–135) characterizes Messalina as sneaking out of the imperial palace at night to act as a whore, while Pliny the Elder rather gleefully claims that she set an all-night duel with a prostitute to see which of them could

---

"approving" the stoning of Stephen: "'And while the blood of your witness Stephen was shed, I myself was standing by, approving and keeping the coats of those who killed him'" (Acts 22:20; NRSV). Such "approval" implies active facilitation of the action, not mere casual observation.

7. Compare Acts 7:42–43, where the figure of Stephen speaks of God "handing over" idolatrous Israelites "to worship the host of heaven," including such foreign deities as Moloch and Remphan.

8. Suetonius, *Life of Tiberius* 43–45.

9. Suetonius, *Life of Caligula* 24.

10. Suetonius, *Life of Claudius* 34.

have sex with the most partners—which duel Messalina won by chalking up twenty-five liaisons.[11] While at least some of these accusations against Messalina may comprise later politically motivated smear tactics, the Roman Senate's *damnatio memoriæ* after her execution for treason indicates that she was infamous even at the time.[12]

The reader must take Paul's objections about the Roman environment with a grain of salt; he has no first-hand knowledge of the situation. Paul is reflecting provincial views of Rome as a den of iniquity, and his objections about immoral behavior comprise standard rhetorical *topoi*—in this case, stock complaints against false religion. Would Paul know all these details about the Roman imperial household? Not likely, but the reputation of the city of Rome as a cesspool of vice, particularly of sexual immorality, seems to have been rampant, and not only in the Jewish world. The explicit sexual imagery on mosaics, pottery, and other artwork of the period certainly would be shocking to Jewish sensibilities, even among diaspora Jews who may have taken the prohibition of images rather more loosely than those in Judea.[13] And Paul's Roman audience could hardly be unaware of rumors of the "goings on" in the imperial palace, such that even a hint at profligate behavior would recall the kinds of scandalous gossip enshrined in the histories of Pliny the Elder (CE 23–79), Suetonius (*ca.* CE 69–*ca.* 122), and the satires of Juvenal (*ca.* CE 55–*ca.* 138).

Romans 1:18–32 and Philo's Perspective on Spectacles

Looking more closely at the language of "applause" (v. 32) raises an additional question concerning the context of such behaviors as those Paul lists here. Evidence from Philo of Alexandria's discussion of theatrical performances provides some illumination for this question. Philo's perspective on public performances—whether musical performances, athletic events, or theatrical events—is almost univocally negative. As Jeff Jay points out, Philo views music, pantomimes, and mimes as effeminate,[14] while sporting events (purportedly hosted in honor of Zeus or some other deity) are far from

11. Pliny the Elder, *Natural History* X.
12. Varner, "Portraits, Plots, and Politics," 64.
13. The synagogue at Dura-Europos in eastern Syria provides a well-known, though late (mid-third century), example of iconographic elements in diaspora Jewish art. For a recent discussion of the significance of the iconography in its Roman-Syrian cultural context, see Stern, "Mapping Devotion in Roman Dura Europos"; also see Moormann, "The Murals of the Synagogue at Dura Europos."
14. Philo, *De Agricultura* 35; cited in Jay, "The Problem of the Theater in Early Judaism," 223.

sacred "because victors in events like boxing and pankration receive crowns and applause for violence that is otherwise liable to punishment when it is inflicted outside theater walls."[15] Popular acclaim for events such as these illustrate a fundamental disordering of the human mind that subordinates the rational faculty (*nous*) to irrational senses, which is a relationship contrary to nature. Those who frequent theatrical events gorge themselves on sensory input rather than cultivating the rational mind; thus, theatrical performances illustrate a licentiousness that overturns life at its most basic level.[16] Jay summarizes: "The shows turn men into women, crown injustice and violence with victory laurels, and nourish the senses, thereby empowering their usurpation of *nous* as the rightful guide of life."[17]

For Philo, theatrical culture erodes social life well beyond the theatrical performances themselves, corrupting other civic affairs because they foster a widespread practice of deception and falsehood. "Theatrics invade the law courts, council chambers and theaters alike because in all these places the men who practice deception are, Philo writes, 'like those who put fine theatrical masks over the most shameful faces expecting not to get caught by the audience.'"[18] In other words, all types of spectacles—theatrical performances, sporting events, musical performances—promote ways of being human that are contrary to nature. Nevertheless audiences, Jewish and gentile, willingly attend these spectacles and applaud the participants.

Romans 1:18–32 and Human Trafficking

Flavius Josephus contributes another set of details to reframe Paul's remarks in this section of Romans 1. While we know that Jews in various cities of the empire did participate in theatrical events and similar spectacles, both as members of the audience and as performers,[19] Josephus recognizes yet another more troubling role in the spectacles when Jews "performed"

---

15. Jay, "The Problem of the Theater in Early Judaism," 223; citing Philo, *De Agricultura* 113–21.

16. Philo, *De Agricultura* 35; cited in Jay, "The Problem of the Theater in Early Judaism," 223.

17. Jay, "The Problem of the Theater in Early Judaism," 223–24.

18. Jay, "The Problem of the Theater in Early Judaism," 224; citing Philo, *De mutatione nominum* 198.

19. Jay, "The Problem of the Theater in Early Judaism," 234; citing the edict of Julius Caesar granting seats to Hyrcanus and other Jewish dignitaries. See "The Problem of the Theater in Early Judaism," 235, for a discussion of Roman Antioch under the Emperor Gaius. Jay, "The Problem of the Theater in Early Judaism," 237, citing Josephus, *Vita* 16 on Aliturus, the mime-actor who was a favorite of Nero and Poppaea.

under duress. Alexandrian Jews "were led in procession to the theater for crucifixion during the pogrom of 38."[20] After Paul's time, in the early 70s, this practice of displaying Jews as trophies for public execution was repeated in Rome and elsewhere to celebrate the Roman victory over Judea. Based on the reports of Josephus and other contemporary sources, Jeff Jay argues that Jews were more likely to appear as captives rather than voluntary performers in spectacles—a fact that cannot have enticed Jews to have a positive attitude toward such public events.

The evidence thus indicates that Jewish "performers" in diaspora shows during the first century more often than not . . . [made] forced appearances as captives rather than voluntary performances as actors. Josephus confirms this impression when he writes of Jews' unrelenting loyalty to God's decrees: "Many [Jews] on many occasions have been seen in the theaters enduring prisoners' tortures and all manner of death so as not to emit any word against the laws and the supplemental writings."[21]

It is not clear how extensive it was to see *Jews* executed this way before CE 58, when Paul likely is writing this letter to the Roman house churches, but certainly the public execution of prisoners took place nearly on a daily basis in the city of Rome.

Because the pericope in Romans 1:24–27 has been used as a "clobber text" to denigrate persons with same sex orientation, it is worth reminding the reader that such a use strips the text of its social and historical contexts and brings it to bear on an issue that Paul's own audience would never have imagined or understood. Paul's contemporaries would have been familiar with multiple types of exploitative sexual relationships, including pedophilia, prostitution, and slavery. In each case, such relationships reveal and inscribe abusive power structures; they have nothing to do with loving sexual relationships between consenting adults. Whatever contemporary moral arguments one wants to mount about same-sex relations, it is ethically irresponsible to use this passage in Romans 1 to close off contemporary explorations of the issues.

The more likely background to understanding this text for Paul and the Roman *ecclesia* would have been the infamous parties at the imperial palace outlined above, which included live sexual "entertainment" performed on command by enslaved persons. Particularly given that Paul highlights the fact that others "approve" or "applaud" these behaviors (*syneudokeō* carries a connotation of strong agreement or cooperation), a *Sitz im Leben* of

---

20. Jay, "The Problem of the Theater in Early Judaism," 238; citing Philo, *In Flaccum* 74–80.

21. Jay, "The Problem of the Theater in Early Judaism," 239; citing Josephus, *Contra Apion* I.43.

entertainment or public performance of some type (e.g., a dinner party, theatrical presentation, or other spectacle) is implied.[22] There is no indication that private behavior is in view anywhere in this passage.

In addition, Paul's Roman audience—especially those of Jewish origin but even proselytes from gentile religions—would likely have recognized the biblical tradition behind Paul's metaphorical use of sexuality to talk about religious adherence. Given that "fidelity" serves as a standard *topos* for highlighting the superiority of Israelite religion vs. those of "the [other] nations," whose religious practice comprises "infidelity" or even "promiscuity," we should not infer that any specific situation among the Roman believers gives rise to this brief diatribe on Paul's part. What is important for Paul's argument is to establish the validity of the Jewish religion—which involves worship of the true God—in contrast to pagan worship of multiple false images of God, regardless of how many people might "applaud" those other images and means of worship.

Conclusions on Romans 1:18–32

In summary, Paul uses this opening section of his discussion of salvation in Christ to lay the groundwork for his gospel by establishing its intellectual and moral superiority to paganism. If one becomes conformed to the image of the deity one worships—a proposition that Paul assumes would be accepted *prima facie* by his ancient audience—then one should worship the deity who is living and true, who made human beings and calls them to become their highest selves. For who would want to become less human, more like "dumb" animals, or half-human and half-animal as many pagan idols depict (e.g., the forms of "birds and animals and reptiles" that one sees in Egyptian religious imagery)? This is what happens to humans who deny the foundational revelation of the Creator.

Paul concludes this section with another standard *topos*, a vice list like those common in Greco-Roman culture (Rom 1:29–31).[23] Not an exhaustive set of possibilities of how to violate divine justice, the phrase "every form of wickedness (*adikia*, literally, 'injustice'), evil, greed (*pleonexia*), and

---

22. The emperor Nero was known for his love of mime and music, himself performing in several dramatic recitations. During his reign, mime grew increasingly realistic, including on-stage performance of the behaviors described in the recitation. Harold C. Baldry indicates that "We read of sexual intercourse on the stage, even of executions carried out in reality when a condemned criminal was substituted for the actor" (Baldry, "Theatre and Society," 20).

23. For a brief discussion and select bibliography on the virtue-and-vice-list form, see Harrison, "Virtues and Vices."

malice" (v. 29) serves to evoke other "improper" behaviors (*kathēkonta*, "unfitting things") that are not itemized in the vice list. Note that the sense of what is "fitting" is culturally conditioned and refers to commonly accepted mores rather than a sense of universal, divine law.

The somewhat repetitive series of vices in 1:29–31 seems to cluster into three broad categories: defects of social-political power dynamics (murder, rivalry, treachery, spite, gossip [*psithyristēs*], scandal-mongering, impiety [*theostygeis*]); characteristics of interpersonal power struggles (insolence, haughtiness, boastfulness, rebelliousness toward parents); and destructive economic power dynamics (*adikia, pleonexia*, envy [*phthonou*], heartlessness, mercilessness [*aneleēmosynē*]). It is possible that Paul viewed some of these behaviors as problematic among his Roman ecclesial audience, but it is more likely that these behaviors are highlighted because of how aptly they capture the common stereotypes about behavior in the imperial capital, which would be significantly reinforced by recent events there (including assassination of the two prior emperors).

Given the conventional nature of this type of ethical teaching, it is not surprising that this vice list evinces little particularly "Jewish" or "Christian" sensibilities until we reach 1:31, where those who violate divine wisdom are characterized as "senseless" (*asynetos*, undiscerning), "faithless" (*asynthetos*, covenant-breakers), "heartless" (*astorgos*, devoid of natural family affection), and "ruthless" (*aneleēmonas*, merciless). This last set of traits carries resonances of Micah 6:8, where the fundamental behaviors of the Israelite covenant comprise doing justice (*mishpat*), loving mercy (*chesed*), and walking (*leket*) humbly with God. If one follows the traditional redaction-critical rule that what is changed or repeated reveals the key themes the redactor wanted to emphasize, the third cluster of vices—those with the economic justice focus—are exposed as most important for Paul's purposes in this letter. This reinforces a reading of 1:24–28 as referring not to consensual sex but rather exploitative sexual behaviors that a contemporary audience would characterize as elements of human trafficking.

Social-historical contextualization of this section of Romans thus unveils the gay-bashing use of this passage as an illegitimate form of eisegesis that misuses the scriptural text to justify a "form of wickedness" that Paul rejects in the associated vice list. The social-cultural and literary contexts of the pericope focus on issues of economic exploitation—issues that are blithely ignored by anti-gay readings, which deflect Paul's key issues in this passage and reduce the living word to a dead, and sometimes deadly, letter. A social-historical reading, on the other hand, lets Paul's words speak anew to the present generation of issues equally important to a twenty-first-century audience as they were to those in Paul's original audience: defects of social-political and interpersonal power dynamics (e.g., the kinds of malice and gossip endemic to many contemporary "social-media" environments) and destructive economic power dynamics (e.g., heartless and merciless political and economic structures). This contextual reading challenges contemporary readers to return to the heart of the good news of Jesus and to imagine, with Paul, how to implement that gospel in the concrete world of today, among "all God's beloved" in every place.

Bibliography

(* For Further Reading)

Baldry, Harold C. "Theatre and Society in Greek and Roman Antiquity." In *Drama and Society*, edited by James Redmond, 1–21. Themes in Drama 1. Cambridge, UK: Cambridge University Press, 1979.

Berg, Shane. "Ben Sira, the Genesis Creation Accounts, and the Knowledge of God's Will." *Journal of Biblical Literature* 132 (2013) 139–57.

Clark, W. Malcolm. "A Legal Background to the Yahwist's Use of 'Good and Evil' in Genesis 2–3." *Journal of Biblical Literature* 88 (1969) 266–78.

*Harrison, James R. "Virtues and Vices: New Testament Ethical Exhortation in Its Graeco-Roman Context." *Oxford Bibliographies*. Modified May 24, 2017; https://www.oxfordbibliographies.com/view/document/obo-9780195393361/obo-9780195393361-0236.xml.

Jay, Jeff. "The Problem of the Theater in Early Judaism." *Journal for the Study of Judaism* 44 (2013) 218–53.

Jewett, Robert. *The Captain America Complex: The Dilemma of Zealous Nationalism*. Philadelphia: Westminster, l973.

———. *Christian Tolerance: Paul's Message to the Modern Church*. Philadelphia: Westminster, l982.

———. *Jesus Against the Rapture: Seven Unexpected Prophecies*. Philadelphia: Westminster, l979.

———. *Paul the Apostle to America: Cultural Trends and Pauline Scholarship*. Louisville: Westminster John Knox, 1994.

———. *Paul's Anthropological Terms: A Study of Their Use in Conflict Settings*. Arbeiten zur Geschichte des antiken Judentums und des Urchristentums 10. Leiden: Brill, 1971.

———. *Romans: A Commentary*. Hermeneia. Minneapolis: Fortress, 2007.

———. *Saint Paul at the Movies: The Apostle's Dialogue with American Culture*. Louisville: Westminster John Knox, 1993.

———. *Saint Paul Returns to the Movies: Triumph over Shame*. Grand Rapids: Eerdmans, 1999.

Josephus [Titus Flavius Josephus, *né* Yosef ben Matityahu]. *Contra Apion*. The original Greek edition by B. Niese and the William Whiston English translation are available through Perseus and Project Gutenberg, respectively. See http://www.josephus.org/works.htm for links.

———. *Vita*. The original Greek edition by B. Niese and the William Whiston English translation are available through Perseus and Project Gutenberg, respectively. See http://www.josephus.org/works.htm for links.

*McGinn, Sheila E. "Biblical Violence and Divine Justice: Toward an Ethic of Biblical Interpretation." *Conversations with the Biblical World* 39 (2019 [2020]) 283–93.

———, ed. *Celebrating Romans: A Festschrift in Honor of Robert Jewett*. Grand Rapids: Eerdmans, 2004 [2005].

———. "Galatians 3:26–29 and the Politics of the Spirit." *Proceedings: EGLBS & MWSBL* 13 (1993) 89–101.

*———. "Human Trafficking and the Bible: Linking the Past to the Present. Response to the Panel Discussion." *Conversations with the Biblical World* 36 (2016 [2017]) 245–60.

*———. "Romans." In *The Jerome Biblical Commentary for the Twenty-First Century: Third Fully Revised Edition*, edited by John J. Collins et al., 1528–87. London: T. & T. Clark, 2022.

McGinn, Sheila E., and Megan T. Wilson-Reitz. "2 Thessalonians vs. the *Ataktoi*: A Pauline Critique of 'White-Collar Welfare.'" In *By Bread Alone: The Bible through the Eyes of the Hungry*, edited by Sheila E. McGinn et al., 185–208. Minneapolis: Fortress, 2014.

Moormann, Eric M. "The Murals of the Synagogue at Dura Europos as an Expression of Roman *Koine*." Open Access © 2021 Eric M. Moormann; published by De Gruyter; licensed under the Creative Commons Attribution—Non-Commercial-No Derivatives 4.0 International License; https://doi.org/10.1515/9783110732139-009.

Philo of Alexandria [Philo Judaeus]. *De Agricultura*. English translations of the works of Philo are available at https://www.earlyjewishwritings.com/philo.html.

———. *De mutatione nominum*. English translations of the works of Philo are available at https://www.earlyjewishwritings.com/philo.html.

———. *In Flaccum*. English translations of the works of Philo are available at https://www.earlyjewishwritings.com/philo.html.

Pliny the Elder [Gaius Plinius Secundus]. *Natural History*. The English translations of this six-volume work are available at https://www.gutenberg.org/ebooks/author/50041.

Stern, Karen B. "Mapping Devotion in Roman Dura Europos: A Reconsideration of the Synagogue Ceiling." *American Journal of Archaeology* 114 (July 2010) 473–504. http://www.jstor.org/stable/25684291.

Suetonius [Gaius Suetonius Tranquillus]. *Life of Caligula*. English translations of the fourteen-volume *Lives of the Twelve Caesars* are available at https://www.gutenberg.org/ebooks /author/2024. The volume on Caligula is at https://www.gutenberg.org/ebooks/6389.

———. *Life of Claudius*. English translations of the fourteen-volume *Lives of the Twelve Caesars* are available at https://www.gutenberg.org/ebooks/author/2024. The volume on Claudius is found at https://www.gutenberg.org/ebooks/6390.

———. *Life of Tiberius*. English translations of the fourteen-volume *Lives of the Twelve Caesars* are available at https://www.gutenberg.org/ebooks/author/2024. The volume on Claudius is found at https://www.gutenberg.org/ebooks/6388.

Varner, Eric R. "Portraits, Plots, and Politics: '*Damnatio memoriae*' and the Images of Imperial Women." *Memoirs of the American Academy in Rome* 46 (2001) 41–93.

Study Questions

1. What do you see as the benefits and potential drawbacks of the kind of social-historical contextualized reading McGinn pursues in this essay?

2. Paul's rhetoric in this pericope presents non-Jewish religion as fundamentally defective, leading to "unnatural" and vicious behaviors. Do you agree with Paul's perspective on this point? How so? Do you have ethical concerns about Paul's "us vs. them" type of rhetoric in this section of Romans?

3. If McGinn is right that Paul's redactional work in this section of Romans focuses attention on the third cluster of vices (those with the economic justice focus), what would that mean for how to preach this text? What would be the "take-away" for a contemporary audience close to you?

6

Scripture and Echoes in Romans

Robert Jewett on Midrash and on Adam in Romans 7:7–12

A. Andrew Das

Abstract

ROBERT JEWETT'S ROMANS COMMENTARY offers an excellent starting point for the multidisciplinary study of Paul, including the apostle's use of the Jewish Scriptures and intertextuality. Jewett employs the categories of quotation, echo, and midrash. He tracks patterns of midrashic usage in Romans, but more recent work has questioned whether midrash is a Second Temple category. Jewett's instructive caution is on display in his skepticism about certain echoes; for instance, that Paul is referring to Adam's reception of the as-yet unwritten Torah in the Garden in Romans 7:7–13.

Introduction

For those entering a session on the apostle Paul at the Society of Biblical Literature (SBL), for many years somewhere near the front row and surrounded by beloved friends and students, would be Bob Jewett, clearly engaged. Those nearby could watch the reactions on Jewett's face to gauge the worthiness of the presentation. The more animated the interaction, the better the paper. Reading the late Bob Jewett's commentary on Romans is much like attending those professional sessions years ago. Jewett's command of the literature and multiple disciplines is enviable, and his reactions priceless. His labors are now impacting yet another generation of students and scholars. Writing in his memory is difficult since one so wants to continue to study the reactions on his face, in conversation, and in print. He had so much to offer for those with ears to hear.

Jewett on Method: Paul's Use of the Scriptures

The SBL's Paul and Scripture Seminar (2005–2010) was followed by a seminar on Scripture in 1 Corinthians and then by the Scripture and Paul Seminar (2016–present). The latter sponsored a session in memoriam of Jewett in 2021.[1] A student or colleague could learn much, methodologically, from Jewett's commentary on Paul's use of Scripture. Although he was writing before the conclusion of the original Paul and Scripture Seminar (the commentary was published in 2007), he had anticipated many of their results. Paul opens the Letter to the Romans affirming a gospel derived from "the holy scriptures" (1:2), "written for our instruction that we might have hope" (15:4).[2] Nowhere does Paul quote the Scriptures as extensively.[3] In each instance of scriptural quotation, Jewett carefully reviews whether and, if so, how the apostle rewords the original for the sake of his own context and argument.[4]

Apart from instances of quotation, Jewett often notes echoes of the Scriptures based on shared vocabulary. For instance, in Romans 1:21, Jewett contends that the combination of futility and thoughts derives from LXX Psalm 94:11, even as "senseless" "heart" derives from LXX Psalm 75:5–6.[5] Jewett is even willing to consider a *single* word as a potential echo of the Scriptures, provided the word is distinctive. In his discussion of Romans 8:26, Jewett notes the rarity of the verb "lends assistance" (*synantilambanō*) in the NT (elsewhere only in Luke 10:40). The word is used for a person taking on part of another's labors, but Jewett is drawn to the context of LXX Psalm 89:21. The use of the verb in the context of Yahweh's own assistance of the people of Israel renders Psalm 89:21 a close parallel to Romans 8:26.[6]

---

1. For the published papers from these seminars, see *Scripture, Texts, and Tracings in 1 Corinthians*; *Scripture, Texts, and Tracings in Romans*; and *Scripture, Texts, and Tracings in 2 Corinthians and Philippians*. Currently the seminar is completing its work on Galatians and 1 Thessalonians.

2. Jewett, *Romans: A Commentary*, 25.

3. Jewett draws on the rhetorical method of citation in Stanley, *Arguing*, 9–21, 62–71.

4. But, at the same time, very sensitive to potential textual variants.

5. Jewett, *Romans: A Commentary*, 158.

6. Jewett, *Romans: A Commentary*, 521.

On the other hand, Jewett is pessimistic a few verses later about the popular connection of God's not "sparing" (*pheidomai*) his Son in Romans 8:32 to Abraham's near sacrifice of Isaac, the Aqedah. The problem, he observes, is that "sparing" a life is common in the Septuagint (e.g., 2 Sam 18:5; 21:7, 9) and in the Greco-Roman world (e.g., Dionysius Halicarnassus *Antiq. Rom.* 5.10.7; Diodorus Siculus *Hist.* 13.76.5). "There is nothing unusual about this terminology in a world in which the vanquished often fell to the mercy of victors."[7] Again, the difference between Jewett's acceptance of a Psalm 89:21 echo and his denial of an Aqedah echo is the *strength* of the verbal connection, that Yahweh's "lending assistance" in LXX Psalm 89:21 is *distinctive*. Jewett does not limit himself, however, to the traditional categories of quotation and allusion/echoes.

Midrash in Romans

Jewett employs a less common category for Paul's use of Scripture: midrash. Here he was relying on his old friend and colleague at Garrett-Evangelical Theological Seminary, William Richard Stegner. Stegner's work on Romans appeared in 1984, and Jewett repeatedly returned to it in his commentary, no doubt, because of Jewett's shared concern with the textual features Stegner had noticed.[8] Jewett traces a pattern of explaining a Scriptural text by means of secondary texts with diatribal elements to elicit audience response. In Romans 4:1-25, Paul posits Genesis 15:6 (cited in Rom 4:9, 10, 22, and 23), elaborated on by means of Psalm 31:1, Genesis 17:5, and Genesis 15:5.[9] Even more intricate is Paul's midrash or explanation of Genesis 21:12 in Romans 9 by means of secondary texts with the catchwords "call" and "seed" from Genesis 18:10, 14; 25:23; Malachi 1:2-3; Exodus 33:19; and Exodus 9:16, 26.[10] In Romans 9, Paul also develops the motif of election in Genesis 21:12 by means of secondary texts with the catchwords "call" and "beloved" from Isaiah 29:16; Hosea 2:25; 2:1, and with the catchwords "sons" and "seed" from Isaiah 10:22-23 and Isaiah 1:9.[11] Romans 11:1-6 is both diatribe and midrash with proof texts from 1 Samuel 12:22/ Psalm 94:24 that "God has not rejected his people," supported by citations

---

7. Jewett, *Romans: A Commentary*, 537. For a similarly negative conclusion, see Das, "Israel's Exodus."

8. Stegner, "Romans 9.6-29—A Midrash," 37-52.

9. Jewett, *Romans: A Commentary*, 27.

10. One need not point to later midrashim. Catchwords was a common method of interpretation at Qumran; Brooke, *Dead Sea Scrolls*, 65.

11. Jewett, *Romans: A Commentary*, 27.

from 1 Kings 19:10 and 18 to show that the remnant is saved by grace alone. Romans 11:7–10 is a midrash with citations from Deuteronomy 29:4 and Psalm 68:23 on the source of Israel's obtuseness.[12]

Jacob Neusner defines midrash rather broadly as Jewish interpretation of sacred, canonical texts, but more specifically in the forms of paraphrase, prophecy, or parable—including Qumran pesharim, the retellings of Scripture in Pseudo-Philo, the *Genesis Apocryphon*, and *Jubilees* in the Second Temple period.[13] Whereas Neusner traces the existence of midrash into the Second Temple period, most scholars now believe that midrash did not emerge until well after 70 CE and the rise of the rabbis, most likely at the time of the Amoraim as a response to early Christian appropriation of the Hebrew Bible.[14] Jewett did not draw in his commentary on the SBL Midrash sessions (we may have missed him in those near-front rows), but the Jewish scholars represented there also trace the development of midrashic patterns of thought to a later time, after 70 CE and the shift from a temple-centered to a text-centered religion. David Aaron concludes about the precedents for rabbinic interpretative techniques: "While there is no reason to doubt that common methods of argument had long since been standardized, formalization of these exegetical rules does not appear prior to the Sifra's introductory passage. This suggests an early third-century origin . . . there is no evidence of formalized rhetorical practices prior to the Rabbinic period."[15] The Sifra's listings of Ishmael's principles is a composite of several sources, and Hillel's principles are not articulated consistently across the versions. The listings of interpretive principles thus appear to be later literary creations designed to

---

12. Jewett, *Romans: A Commentary*, 27.

13. Neusner, *What Is Midrash?* 8–10; on the definition, following Porton, "Defining Midrash," 62. See, however, his later "Midrash, Definitions of."

14. Teugels and Ulmer ("Introduction," i) identify midrash as a "particular mode of interpreting the Hebrew Bible that was developed by the rabbis of late antiquity in the Land of Israel." Although there are earlier precedents for it, "certain characteristic features of *midrash* developed at specific times and in specific contexts" (Teugels and Ulmer, "Introduction," ii). So also Lim ("Origins and Emergence," 611), despite the parallels for exegetical techniques at earlier points. After developing a set of identifying features of midrashic exegesis (see pp. 3–4), Philip S. Alexander concludes: "In the light of this definition is it possible to identify midrash outside Rabbinic literature? I am inclined to say, No: midrash is best confined to early Rabbinic Bible exegesis. The differences I perceive between the Rabbinic and the non-Rabbinic texts are more important than their similarities"; "Midrash and the Gospels," 11. Matthew Goldstone, for instance, disagrees with those who find an embrace of multivocality as a defining feature of midrash as opposed to earlier forms of biblical interpretation: the midrashim *explicitly eliminate* interpretive possibilities but Second Temple interpreters only implicitly; "Towards a New Understanding," 72–73, 85.

15. Aaron, "Language and Midrash," 401.

support rabbinic techniques. In fact, neither the traditions ascribed to Hillel nor to Ishmael employ the majority of their supposed exegetical principles, most of which appear rabbinized.[16] The hermeneutical rules, whether Hillel's seven, thirteen, or thirty-two, do not correspond to the later midrashic forms of exegesis: "If midrash is a game and the various lists of middot are the rules, then it must be said that the rule-books bear little relationship to the game as actually played."[17]

Second Temple literature—whether Josephus's writings, Jubilees, the Genesis Apocryphon, or even the Qumran pesher—takes a very different approach to language than rabbinic midrash, which assumes that the full meaning of the Torah lies *behind* the surface of the words to be discovered via the rabbinic methods of exegesis.[18] With Instone-Brewer:

> The methods actually used in pre-70 CE Rabbinic Judaism are very different from the lists of *middot* or "rules" of hermeneutics compiled in classical Rabbinic literature. Only a few of these *middot* are found in traditions before the destruction, and there are many others that are not named in any of the ancient lists.[19]

Siegert defines Hellenistic Jewish "midrash" very broadly and yet concludes that "their many particularities do not recur in Rabbinic texts."[20] Despite partial Hellenistic Greek precursors to later rabbinic midrash, "If by midrash we mean free commentary on biblical texts through narrative expansion, quotation of masters of the past, and diverse forms of reasoning, there is no Jewish text written in Greek that is in every respect midrashic."[21] Jewett wants the focus to remain on the textual features on display, in this case, the use of catchwords and secondary texts in the interpretation of Scripture. Stegner, relying on Borgen, remains a helpful starting point in identifying specific parallels in Philo.[22]

---

16. Porton, "Midrash, Definitions of," 527; Porton, "Hermeneutics, A Critical Approach."

17. Alexander, "Midrash and the Gospels," 9; so also Lim, *Holy Scripture*, 128–29. Kern-Ulmer ("Hermeneutics" 268–92, esp. 268–72) represents the more optimistic minority position on the dating of the Hillel and Ishmael traditions.

18. Aaron, "Language and Midrash," 403, 410–11.

19. Instone-Brewer, "Hermeneutics, Theology of," 292–93

20. Siegert, "Hellenistic Jewish Midrash," 199; for instance, Hellenistic authors never quote others by name and yet may write under their own names; it is the reverse in later rabbinic literature, 200; see the comparisons throughout, e.g., 248.

21. Siegert, "Hellenistic Jewish Midrash," 199.

22. Stegner, "Romans 9.6–29," 38 and 50n6; Borgen (*Bread from Heaven*, 51–98) had noted instances in which the midrashim, Philo, and New Testament authors interpret a biblical text by catchwords and by juxtaposing subordinate texts.

The Qumran pesharim serve as a case study—and warning—against too quickly assuming continuity. Some have spoken of "midrash pesher" at Qumran.[23] After considering the proposed parallels between the Qumran scrolls, the later midrash, and the New Testament, George Brooks concludes that "The interpretative differences are as numerous as the similarities."[24] "Where should the continuities and discontinuities be located?... Is 'midrash' a suitable term for use by either Qumranologists or Neutestamentlers?"[25] Or with Maurya Horgan:

> When the pesharim and certain midrashic writings are compared, their respective historical contexts are often neglected. Seeking to illuminate the pesharim, all of which were written before AD 70, by pointing to similar elements in rabbinic writings dating from the second century AD is taking the cart before the horse... The term "midrash" is neither a useful nor an informative term by which to characterize the pesharim.[26]

The techniques of pesherite exegesis, including the seven middot of Hillel, are not distinctive but shared by Hellenistic rhetoricians and jurisprudence.[27] Timothy Lim concludes:

> Given these considerations, it would seem best to leave this genre out of consideration of pesherite exegesis. At most, it may be said that the pesharim are midrashic, in the general and non-specific meaning of the word. In other words, while it is undeniable that some of the techniques found in the Midrashim also appear in the pesharim, these exegetical features are not exclusively found in them nor is recognition of their similarities sufficient to allow a simple equation of the one genre with the other.[28]

Jewett's use of the category is a reminder that more work is needed to identify the distinguishing features of Jewish interpretation at each stage over time, and one must still navigate the pre-/post-70 CE changes and

---

23. E.g., Ellis, *Prophecy and Hermeneutic*, 154.

24. Brooke, *Dead Sea Scrolls*, 94. The New Testament and Qumran are simply both eschatological forms of first-century Judaism.

25. Brooke, *Dead Sea Scrolls*, 69.

26. Horgan, *Pesharim*, 252.

27. Daube, "Rabbinic Methods."

28. Lim, *Holy Scripture*, 129.

characteristics.²⁹ More work cataloging Second Temple parallels to rabbinic midrashic interpretive techniques is in order.

Romans 7:7–12: The Garden of Eden?

Jewett's sober and cautious critical instincts repeatedly serve him well throughout the Romans commentary. He was not one to jump quickly on a scholarly bandwagon or to entertain a fad. Many Romans specialists, for instance, are optimistic that Paul is alluding to Adam in Romans 7:7-12. Ernst Käsemann in his Romans commentary quipped, "There is nothing in the passage which does not fit Adam, and everything fits Adam alone."³⁰ Romans 7:9 says, "I was once alive apart from the law." Such a description would not match the situation of humanity before the arrival of the law since no one after Adam was "living" in its theological sense prior to and apart from the law (thus Rom 5:12-19). For Käsemann, then, Romans 7:9 expresses the words of Adam reflecting on his experience in the garden prior to the command not to eat of the tree. Note that Paul shifts from speaking of the law (*nomos*) at this point to a "command" (*entolē*). He had been living apart from and before a command had been given to him. Once that command had been given to Adam, not eating from the one tree would preserve life, even as the command of Romans 7:10 is for the sake of life (*eis zōēn*). Eve then experienced desire in Genesis 3:6 for the fruit of the tree after the serpent "deceived" her (Gen 3:13: *apatan*) even as the personified sin "deceived" the "I" in Romans 7:11 (*exapatan*; cf. 2 Cor 11:3; 1 Tim 2:14.). "I died" would be Adam's description of his experience after violating the command (Gen 2:17; 3:3, 19).³¹

Jewett granted "potential allusions" to the garden of Eden but remained skeptical nonetheless.³² Paul has been describing in Romans 7:7-12 an "I" who desires to do what is good but produces evil instead. Jewett

---

29. There were, however, precursors to rabbinic midrashim: Targum/Aramaic Bible, direct, simple interpretations of the scriptural sense, haggadic expansion, and halakhic midrash that posited one verse to help explain another; Schiffman, "Dead Sea Scrolls," 40–54. As Lim put it: "Mention 'midrash' nowadays and a whole set of objections immediately come to mind. It has been overused to such an extent that it has come to mean little more than a sexy synonym for exegesis"; "Origins and Emergence of Midrash," 611.

30. Käsemann, *Commentary on Romans*, 196. See the fuller explication of this position in Lyonnet, "L'historie"; also Theissen, *Psychological Aspects*, 202–11.

31. Many find the echoes of Adam (and Eve) persuasive; e.g., Adams, "Paul's Story of God and Creation," 27–28; Hofius, *Paulusstudien II*, 104–54.

32. Jewett, *Romans: A Commentary*, 442.

explains that this feature is foreign to the Adam story in Genesis or in later Jewish literature.[33] Surveys of Second Temple narrations of the Adamic accounts are missing this element.[34] Allusions to Adam in Romans 7:7-12 are therefore unlikely.

Several additional considerations reinforce Jewett's skepticism. Paul has been forthright in referring to Adam earlier in Romans (5:12-19) and elsewhere (1 Cor 15:45)—as well as to Eve (1 Cor 11:7-9; 2 Cor 11:3)—but Paul makes no reference in Romans 7:7-11 to Adam, Eve, the serpent, or the tree with its fruit. The key players in Genesis remain unmentioned. Further, the plot points Paul highlights elsewhere from Genesis 1-3 are at odds with what he is stressing in Romans 7:7-12: *Eve* was deceived and not Adam (2 Cor 11:3; cf. 1 Tim 2:14), and Adam was by no means powerless to resist sin and thus was held responsible for the entry of sin into the world (Rom 5:12-19).[35]

Paul's governing question for the remainder of Romans 7: Is the law sin? (Rom 7:7). Romans 7:7-12 must relate, then, to the law of Moses. Perhaps Paul is alluding to a tradition in which Adam was entrusted the law of Moses in an as-yet unwritten form. Adam encountered in the "command" the law of Moses. In agreement with the thesis question of Romans 7:7, Paul refers to the commandment in Moses's Decalogue not to covet (*ouk epithymēs*), to which he will return in Romans 13:9 when discussing the Decalogue again.[36] One would expect parallels for an Adamic/Torah connection elsewhere in Second Temple Judaism.

Unfortunately, evidence that Adam was entrusted with the Torah of Moses in an as-yet unwritten form is rather weak in the Second Temple period (cf. the much later Tg. Neof. 1 on Gen 2:15; 3:9, 22, or b. Sanh. 56b).[37] Peter Stuhlmacher traces just such a connection to the Life of Adam and Eve (32 + 37); Josephus, *Ant.* 1:41-47; 4 Ezra 3:7; 7:11; and Philo *Leg. All.* 1.90-97.[38] None of these texts, however, can bear the weight. Josephus—as also 4 Ezra 3:7 and 7:11—explains the "commandment of God" merely as an injunction against touching the tree. Nothing is said of Moses's Torah. Philo characteristically allegorizes the command regarding the tree, but he never

---

33. Jewett, *Romans: A Commentary*, 442.

34. E.g., Lichtenberger, *Das Ich Adams*, 205-41.

35. Gundry, "Moral Frustration," 231-32.

36. Moo, "Israel and Paul in Romans 7:7-12," 123. Jervis goes so far as to conclude that the reference to the Mosaic "commandment" disqualifies Adamic references in 7:7-12 ("Sin's Use of the Obedience of Faith," 193-96, 206-7).

37. Contra Lyonnet, "L'historie," 137-38; Wedderburn, "Adam in Paul's Letter," 420.

38. Stuhlmacher, *Paul's Letter to the Romans*, 107. Note the late date of Hofius's examples (*Paulusstudien II*, 115n44), all rabbinic.

implies that the entire law had been entrusted to Adam. The Septuagint, for that matter, did not employ the "desire"/"covet" word group (*epithymia*) in Genesis 3. The later rabbis made a more limited claim, interpreting the command in the garden in terms of the tenth commandment (b. Sabb. 145b–146a; Yebam. 103b; Abod. Zar. 22b). Some Second Temple Jews may likewise have fused the command not to eat with not coveting or desiring (Apoc. Mos. 19.3; Apoc. Abr. 23.1–14; Philo, *QG* 1.47–48 and perhaps *Opif.* 56 §§157–60; *Leg.* 2.18 §§72, 74).[39] Fourth Ezra 7:11 speaks of desire in relation to Genesis 3:5–6 (but *not epithymia*).[40] After surveying the evidence in favor of this connection, Ziesler immediately qualifies that "The evidence is not extensive, and for reasons of geography as well as dating, we cannot be sure that Paul used or even knew this tradition."[41]

As for the claims that Adam and Eve were in possession of the law or that the command in the garden could be equated with the tenth commandment—if these traditions could be securely dated to the first century and were known to Paul, the apostle would not have agreed with them. In Romans 5:13–14, the era from Adam to Moses was "*before* the law." The law entered *between* Adam and Christ (Rom 5:20). In Galatians 3:17, Moses's law came 430 years *after* the promise to Abraham. Theissen, despite favoring a connection between Adam and the law, was forced to concede "that retrojection of the law into paradise contradicts [Paul's] theological interests."[42] Paul is sketching a problem of a personified sin leading *to* desire in Romans 7:7–12 (esp. 7:8), but any allusion to desire in the garden would be working in the *reverse*: desire producing sin.[43] Thus, unlike Paul, the author of the *Apocalypse of Moses* (19.3) describes the serpent sprinkling on the fruit the evil poison of desire (ἐπιθυμία), the root of all sin. An allusion to Adam in Romans 7:7–12 would be contrary to Paul's description of the law elsewhere.

Further problems plague an "Adam"/"I" identification:

1. If the "I" of Romans 7:7–12 is alluding to Adam, then, the Adamic "I" serves as a *representative* figure for what *all* humanity now experiences, but the description of being "apart from the law" matches Adam only as an *individual*.

---

39. Ziesler, "Tenth Commandment," 47; Theissen, *Psychological Aspects*, 204–6, and Wedderburn, "Adam in Paul's Letter," 420–21.

40. Theissen, *Psychological Aspects*, 203n3.

41. Ziesler, "Tenth Commandment," 47.

42. Theissen, *Psychological Aspects*, 203n3.

43. Keck, *Romans*, 183.

2. Paul elsewhere affirms that sin did not exist or dwell in Adam before the fall (Rom 5:12). Paul's choice of verb in Romans 7:9 is therefore inappropriate for the *entry* of sin into the world (*anazaō*; "*revived*"). Paul's choice of verb in 7:9 identifies sin as *already* dwelling within the "I" before springing to life again and impacting his consciousness.[44]

3. God issued the command not to eat *right after* Adam's creation and not after a significant interval (Gen 2:15–17; so also Sir 17:7, 11–12).[45] Adam was never "apart from the law" in the garden for any meaningful period of time.

4. Had Paul intended Adam as the referent of the "I," he would have indicated that more clearly by consistently using "apart from *the commandment*." "The commandment" would be more appropriate for Adam and yet still permit an application by extension to the Mosaic law.

5. The "I" of Romans 7:7–12 remains the same as the "I" in Romans 7:14–25, and nothing in vv. 14–25 alludes to Adam. The inner struggles and emotions of 7:7–25 are not characteristic of Adam's portrayal in Jewish literature.[46]

Significant, unaddressed obstacles therefore stand in the way of identifying allusions to the garden of Eden in Romans 7:7–12 and the experience of the first humans. Paul is best taken as simply developing a topic from Romans 7:1–6, the enslaving character of Moses's law. The law is not sinful, but sin has hijacked the law (7:7). Jewett's skepticism of the allusion is well justified.[47]

---

44. Gundry, "Moral Frustration," 231; Milne, "Romans 7:7–12," 11.

45. Gundry, "Moral Frustration," 231, who added: "If by some trick of the imagination it could be thought there was such an interval, its extreme brevity militates against Paul's making it a discrete period of salvation-history and describing life during it with an imperfect tense, which implies some duration of action (*ezōn*)."

46. Gundry, "Moral Frustration," 229. Sin in Romans 7:7–25 is depicted in terms of "inner processes" whereas Adam was tempted from without; Theissen, *Psychological Aspects*, 203.

47. Jewett (*Romans: A Commentary*, 442) was also skeptical, even more so, of an allusion to Israel's experience at Mt. Sinai. For more on this, see Das, *Solving the Romans Debate*, 219–21. For a plea for a more rigorous methodology in detecting such allusions, see Das, *Paul and the Stories of Israel*.

Conclusion

Jewett's Romans commentary is a helpful starting point for research on any number of topics, including his probing of Paul's use of Scripture. Jewett was willing to explore new categories, such as midrash, and yet was careful not to jump too quickly onto bandwagons. He did not leave matters at the level of abstraction on midrash but provided a detailed examination of the structure and patterns in Paul's use of the Scriptures: whether introductory formula ("he said"), the use of catchwords, or the use of secondary scriptural texts to explain a primary one. His critical eye recognized pitfalls in the Adam proposals for Romans 7:7–12. One may part ways from Jewett, but only with very good reason.[48]

Bibliography

(* For Further Reading)

Aaron, David H. "Language and Midrash." In *Encyclopedia of Midrash: Biblical Interpretation in Formative Judaism*, edited by Jacob Neusner and Alan J. Avery-Peck, 1:400–411. 2 vols. Leiden: Brill, 2004.

Adams, Edward. "Paul's Story of God and Creation: The Story of How God Fulfils His Purposes in Creation." In *Narrative Dynamics in Paul: A Critical Assessment*, edited by Bruce W. Longenecker, 19–43. Louisville: Westminster John Knox, 2002.

Alexander, Philip S. "Midrash and the Gospels." In *Synoptic Studies: The Ampleforth Conferences of 1982 and 1983*, edited by Christopher M. Tuckett, 1–19. Journal for the Study of the New Testament Supplements 7. Sheffield: Sheffield Academic, 1984.

Belleville, Linda, and A. Andrew Das, eds. *Scripture, Texts, and Tracings in Romans*. Lanham, MD: Lexington/Fortress Academic, 2021.

Belleville, Linda, and B. J. Oropeza, eds. *Scripture, Texts, and Tracings in 1 Corinthians*. Lanham, MD: Lexington/Fortress Academic, 2019.

Borgen, Peder. *Bread from Heaven: An Exegetical Study of the Concept of Manna in Gospel of John and the Writings of Philo*. Novum Testamentum Supplements 10. Leiden: Brill, 1965.

Brooke, George J. *The Dead Sea Scrolls and the New Testament*. Minneapolis: Fortress, 2005.

Das, A. Andrew. "Israel's Exodus Outside Paul's Corinthian Correspondence." In *Paul and Moses: The Exodus and Sinai Traditions in the Letters of Paul*, edited by Florian Wilk, 53–66. Studies in Education and Religion in Ancient and Pre-Modern History in the Mediterranean and Its Environs 11. Tübingen: Mohr Siebeck, 2020.

*———. *Paul and the Stories of Israel: Grand Thematic Narratives in Galatians*. Minneapolis: Fortress, 2016.

---

48. On Jewett's use of Isa 66:19 in Rom 15:24, 28, see Das, "Paul of Tarshish." Ideally, the rationale for the rare departure is sufficient. Jewett's is a high bar.

———. "Paul of Tarshish: Isaiah 66.19 and the Spanish Mission of Romans 15.24, 28." *New Testament Studies* 54 (2008) 60–73.

*———. *Solving the Romans Debate*. Minneapolis: Fortress, 2007.

Das, A. Andrew, and B. J. Oropeza, eds. *Scripture, Texts, and Tracings in 2 Corinthians and Philippians*. Lanham, MD: Lexington/Fortress Academic, 2022.

Daube, David. "Rabbinic Methods of Interpretation and Hellenistic Rhetoric." *Hebrew Union College Annual* 22 (1949) 239–64.

Ellis, E. Earle. *Prophecy and Hermeneutic in Early Christianity*. Grand Rapids: Eerdmans, 1978.

Goldstone, Matthew. "Towards a New Understanding of the Defining Features of Rabbinic *Midrash*." In *Torah is a Hidden Treasure: Proceedings of the Midrash Section, Society of Biblical Literature Volume 8*, edited by W. David Nelson and Rivka Ulmer, 71–98. Judaism in Context 22. Piscataway, NJ: Gorgias, 2019.

Gundry, Robert H. "The Moral Frustration of Paul Before His Conversion: Sexual Lust in Romans 7:7–25." In *Pauline Studies: Essays Presented to Professor F. F. Bruce on His 70th Birthday*, edited by Donald A. Hagner and Murray J. Harris, 228–45. Grand Rapids: Eerdmans, 1980.

Hofius, Otfried. *Paulusstudien II*. Wissenschaftliche Untersuchungen zum Neuen Testament 143. Tübingen: Mohr Siebeck, 2002.

Horgan, Maurya P. *Pesharim: Qumran Interpretations of Biblical Books*. Catholic Biblical Quarterly Monograph Series 8. Washington, DC: Catholic Biblical Association of America, 1979.

Instone-Brewer, David. "Hermeneutics, Theology of." In *Encyclopedia of Midrash: Biblical Interpretation in Formative Judaism*, edited by Jacob Neusner and Alan J. Avery-Peck, 1:292–316. 2 vols. Leiden: Brill, 2004.

*Jewett, Robert. *Romans: A Commentary*. Hermeneia. Minneapolis: Fortress, 2007.

Käsemann, Ernst. *Commentary on Romans*. Translated by Geoffrey W. Bromiley. Grand Rapids: Eerdmans, 1980.

Keck, Leander E. *Romans*. Abingdon New Testament Commentaries. Nashville: Abingdon, 2005.

Kern-Ulmer, Rivka. "Hermeneutics, Techniques of Rabbinic Exegesis." In *Encyclopedia of Midrash: Biblical Interpretation in Formative Judaism*, edited by Jacob Neusner and Alan J. Avery-Peck, 1:268–92. 2 vols. Leiden: Brill, 2004.

Lichtenberger, Hermann. *Das Ich Adams und das Ich der Menschheit: Studien zum Menschenbild in Römer 7*. Wissenschaftliche Untersuchungen zum Neuen Testament 164. Tübingen; Mohr Siebeck, 2004.

Lim, Timothy H. *Holy Scripture in the Qumran Commentaries and Pauline Letters*. Oxford: Oxford University Press, 1997.

———. "Origins and Emergence of Midrash in Relation to the Hebrew Bible." In vol. 2 of *Encyclopedia of Midrash: Biblical Interpretation in Formative Judaism* edited by Jacob Neusner and Alan J. Avery-Peck, 595–612. 2 vols. Leiden: Brill, 2004.

Lyonnet, S. "L'historie du salut selon le chapitre VII de l'épitre aux Romains." *Biblica* 43 (1962) 117–51.

Milne, D. J. W. "Romans 7:7–12, Paul's Pre-Conversion Experience." *Reformed Theological Review* 43 (1984) 9–17.

Moo, Douglas J. "Israel and the Paul in Romans 7:7–12." *New Testament Studies* 32 (1986) 122–35.

Neusner, Jacob. *What Is Midrash? and A Midrash Reader*. South Florida Studies in the History of Judaism 106. Atlanta: Scholars, 1994.

*Neusner, Jacob, and Alan J. Avery-Peck, eds. *Encyclopedia of Midrash: Biblical Interpretation in Formative Judaism*. 2 vols. Leiden: Brill, 2004.

Porton, Gary G. "Defining Midrash." In vol. 1 of *The Study of Ancient Judaism*, edited by Jacob Neusner, 55–92. New York: Ktav, 1981.

———. "Hermeneutics, A Critical Approach." In *Encyclopedia of Midrash: Biblical Interpretation in Formative Judaism* edited by Jacob Neusner and Alan J. Avery-Peck, 1:250–68. 2 vols. Leiden: Brill, 2004.

———. "Midrash, Definitions of." In *Encyclopedia of Midrash: Biblical Interpretation in Formative Judaism*, edited by Jacob Neusner and Alan J. Avery-Peck, 1:520–34. 2 vols. Leiden: Brill, 2004.

Schiffman, Lawrence H. "Dead Sea Scrolls, Biblical Interpretation in." In *Encyclopedia of Midrash: Biblical Interpretation in Formative Judaism*, edited by Jacob Neusner and Alan J. Avery-Peck, 1:40–54. 2 vols. Leiden: Brill, 2004.

Siegert, Folker. "Hellenistic Jewish Midrash." In *Encyclopedia of Midrash: Biblical Interpretation in Formative Judaism*, edited by Jacob Neusner and Alan J. Avery-Peck, 1:199–250. 2 vols. Leiden: Brill, 2004.

Stanley, Christopher D. *Arguing with Scripture: The Rhetoric of Quotations in the Letters of Paul*. New York: T. & T. Clark, 2004.

*Stegner, William Richard. "Romans 9.6–29—A Midrash." *Journal for the Study of the New Testament* 22 (1984) 37–52.

Stuhlmacher, Peter. *Paul's Letter to the Romans: A Commentary*. Translated by Scott J. Hafemann. Louisville: Westminster John Knox, 1994.

Teugels, Lieve, and Rivka Ulmer. "Introduction." In *Midrash and the Exegetical Mind: Proceedings of the 2008 and 2009 SBL Midrash Sessions*, edited by Lieve Teugels and Rivka Ulmer, i–v. Judaism in Context 10. Piscataway, NJ: Gorgias, 2010.

Theissen, Gerd. *Psychological Aspects of Pauline Theology*. Translated by John P. Galvin. Philadelphia: Fortress, 1987.

Wedderburn, A. J. M. "Adam in Paul's Letter to the Romans." In *Studia Biblica 1978: III*, edited by E. A. Livingstone, 413–30. Journal for the Study of the New Testament 11. Sheffield: JSOT, 1980.

Ziesler, J. A. "The Role of the Tenth Commandment in Romans 7." *Journal for the Study of the New Testament* 33 (1988) 41–56.

Study Questions

1. According to Robert Jewett and his colleague, William Stegner, what are the distinguishing features of midrash in Romans?

2. What Second Temple (pre-70 CE) precedents are there for later rabbinic midrash, and how strong are those connections?

3. What evidence is there, pro and con, for allusions to Adam in Romans 7:7–13?

7

The Measure of Strength in Romans 14:1–15:6

Paul's Redefinition

WILLIAM S. CAMPBELL

Abstract

IN THE DECADE OF the 1990s, a group of scholars that included Robert Jewett and myself devoted attention to placing Paul in historical context, especially in Romans. This emphasis has continued and flourished, but one area that has proved resistant has been the location of Romans in some meaningful relation to the culture and ethos of Rome itself as the center of the empire. This remains an under-researched area, partly because Paul had never visited Rome. A careful study of Paul's forms of argumentation in Romans reveals that he was well informed about issues current in Rome at the time of writing and able to respond to them. I will consider Paul's teaching in Romans 14:1–15:6 as a redefinition of "strength" and in relation to its function within the letter. I will seek to answer the question whether this section concludes the paraenesis of the letter and, if so, how 15:7–13 both concludes and relates to all that precedes it.

Introduction

I will consider Romans primarily from a social-historical perspective, eclectically drawing on other approaches where helpful, building on the research summarized in the *Romans Debate* and effectively exemplified in Jewett's Romans Commentary in the Hermeneia Series, both of which have had the effect of leading to a fresh attempt to view the letter historically and contextually as presenting a coherent argumentation addressing the Roman context.[1] I view Paul's statements in his letters as particular, contextually related statements, rather than as only theological proclamation.

The Addressees in Romans: *Ethnē* in Christ

At the commencement of his letter, in 1:5–6 and 1:13–15, Paul distinguishes the Romans as *ethnē*, i.e., non-Jewish. Paul describes his own appointment through "our Lord Jesus Christ through whom we have received grace and apostleship to bring about the obedient hearing of faith among all the *ethnē* for the sake of his name, *including yourselves* . . ." (1:4b–6).[2] In 1:13–15, he continues, "But I do not want you to be ignorant, brothers and sisters: I have often intended to come to you . . . in order that I might harvest some fruit *among you just as (I have) among the rest of the ethnē.*" There is again no mention of Jews as is reflected also even in 11:13, "Now *I am speaking to you ethnē* . . . ," where he goes on to describe these addressees as "a wild olive shoot" which would exclude Jews, "the natural branches" (11:17–21). That Paul could operate along ethnic lines is demonstrated by his reference to *ethnē* in 15:16–18, describing himself as *leitourgos* ("minister") to the *ethnē*, and passing on thanks from "all the *ekklēsiai* of the *ethnē*" in 16:4 to Aquila and Prisca. Paul was no stranger to ethnic issues, especially inter ethnic disputes—for example, Galatians 2:11–15—but his stance was not one of "for there is no (ethnic) distinction" but rather "for there is no discrimination."[3]

For some scholars, the Jewish content of the argument and the discussion of, or reference to, actual Jews, Paul's *syngeneia* ("kin"; 9:3) might suggest that Jews may be among the audience addressed in Romans. This remains only a presupposition; there is no explicit textual support. The careful reading of Romans, especially chapters 4, 7 and 9–11, points only to a gentile audience which, unsurprisingly continues in chapters 14–15. Jewish or related issues do not demand Jews *among the addressees,* and audience cannot confidently be derived or identified from content alone. This is not because Paul is careless where ethnic references or labels are concerned. Quite the opposite is true. Grammatical and rhetorical clues are highly relevant. Rafael Rodriguez has demonstrated at length that Paul in Romans is careful to differentiate himself as Jewish by referring to his gentile addressees in the second person plural, thereby at certain points excluding himself, a Jewish

---

1. Donfried, *Romans Debate*, 103.

2. Unless otherwise noted, all quotations from the biblical text are my own translation.

3. Cf. Campbell, *Nations*, 129–52.

apostle. By a careful use of pronouns singular and plural, Paul can indicate the points at which he is in complete solidarity with his addressees, and those others where he clearly excludes himself from the plural "you" that includes them.[4] So too in 14:1–15:6; no Jews are addressed but rather only issues concerning non-Jews that may parallel or reflect similar discussions among Jewish groups.[5] And this suggests that it is not an *ethnic issue as such* that here differentiates the stances between the differing "groups."

The "Weak" and the "Strong"

In the Roman context, wherever Christ-followers assembled, in a house or in a tenement dwelling setting or possibly both or other,[6] there were disputed issues threatening to cause serious division among the gentile Christ-followers. Had this not been the case, it would have been offensive for Paul to warn against it. Differing practices were being followed among the *ethnē* in Christ concerning eating meat, drinking wine, and observing days, but this had led to the question: whose conscience should be determinative? We discern the labels of "weak" and, with refocusing, also of the "strong" in chapter 15 as those emanating from among the Romans themselves, rather than from Paul's choice of terminology. In order to enter meaningfully into the debate, Paul had to use recognizable labels for the disputants in order to make a contribution that would be intelligible to his audience.[7] "Weak" is hardly complimentary but Paul, though he does not include himself in the category, offers no criticism of it.[8]

These labels need not indicate that the Roman *ethnē* were divided into two distinct groups. That there existed among them an "us-and-them" othering tendency seems indicated, but not with great precision. It seems that Paul's strategy, even where he differentiates, is not to intensify this tendency. Thus in 14:1, where he begins with the call to welcome "the weak," Paul differentiates in his paraenesis, clearly indicated in his concern that "the weak" should be welcomed, but not in order to quarrel over differing convictions.

Paul's parenesis in chapters 14:1–15:6 aims to challenge the self-styled "strong" among the Christ-followers "to bear with" (*bastazein*), accommodate the "weak." Pressure is put on these "strong" because they have the freedom to

---

4. Cf. Rodriguez's study, which focused on chapters 5–8, but is valid also throughout Romans ("Romans 5–8").

5. Cf. also Campbell, *Romans. A Social-Identity Commentary* on this passage.

6. Possibly not even in, but near, a building.

7. Jewett, *Romans: A Commentary*, 836.

8. Rodriguez, "Romans 5–8," 264.

change their behavior pattern to accommodate "the weak" without damaging their own integrity. The verb *proslambanō* (14:1, 15:7) has the technical sense of "welcome someone" into one's home or circle of acquaintances, accept with an open heart.[9] Nonacceptance of a brother or sister is ruled out by the cited example of Christ, who has welcomed all who respond to his call (15:7). Paul's strongest support for his argument for mutual acceptance comes in 14:10b, "for we will all stand before the judgement seat of God." We acknowledge the strength of the "household" nuances of the term "to welcome," and that it could reflect the context of a common meal in a home (though not necessarily a house).[10] Throughout chapter 14, the "self-styled strong" are only negatively identified in their destructive effect upon "the weak." They are depicted in their failure to carry the "weak," in not abstaining from anything that acts as a hindrance, in not walking in love of the other. "The weak," on the other hand, have convictions that they feel demand abstinence from anything that may cause them to stumble and may result in their ruin if forced to yield to the power of "the strong" (14:21–23).

It is only from 15:1 that Paul will include himself along with a group labelled "the strong." This means that, until this point, Paul does not acknowledge that he shares the stance of these so-called "strong." We label as self-designated "strong" that "group" implied in Paul's paraenesis in chapter 14 who despise or injure "the weak." Paul does not refer to anyone as "strong" in chapter 14. There is an implicit critique of "the strong" in Paul's not declaring himself as willing to be included in this category label until 15:1. Thus, he does not include himself in their self-understanding as "strong," as reflected in their uncaring treatment of "the weak" which he (Paul) opposes in chapter 14. By the time he reaches 15:1, Paul has expressed his views on how and how not to treat "the weak" and thus revised the received designation implied in chapter 14—to what we might term "the redefined strong"—in such a way that he can include himself in the description from 15:1.

The Inversion of Roman Imperial Influence

It appears that this label, "the strong," was being used by some among the *ethnē* in Christ to denote a sense of superiority. This is expressed in the attitude of those who eat something and others who do not which leads to

---

9. Fitzmyer, *Romans*, 689. Donfried notes that the verb "to welcome" is used to address someone who is not already in intimate communion with the one addressed; *Romans Debate* 110; cf. also Esler, *Romans*, 347–48.

10. Jewett, *Romans: A Commentary*, 972; Adams, *Meeting Places*, 43–44.

the former despising the latter. The verbal form, *exoutheneō* ("to despise"), is referring to the scornful rejection of another from a position of perceived superiority, often in an intergroup context.[11] This may indicate the influence of Roman imperial attitudes toward weakness generally, an ethos favoring "strength." Thus James Harrison, commenting upon Seneca's condemnation of the Jewish people, notes how "victory" ideology totally shaped the Roman perception of the world.[12] But, in Paul's perspective, "the weak" must be included among those welcomed, whatever their weakness involves.

Even though "the weak" may be weak, their faith is still valid. "The one thing Paul does demand from "the weak" is the recognition that *other* believers can act otherwise . . ."[13] Paul's use of the term "weak" may in fact be an indicator of his critique of the Roman ethos of strength, which regarded non-Roman cultural patterns as "weak."[14] The Roman public in their imperial context were accustomed to view "strength" as an indicator of honor, and "weakness" (w)as a term of contempt.[15] Thus, there would be an incentive to seek to belong to a category indicating "strength" in the contemporary social *value scale* that included the public acclaim for military and athletic prowess, and the celebratory victory parades after successful military campaigns. This is the Roman ethos that is potentially influencing the "so-called strong" among Paul's addressees as demonstrated in their tendency to despise those whom they perceived and labelled as "weak." The sharing of some common patterns of eating, drinking, and celebration of days with Jews may have assisted those fearing to eat meat possibly sacrificed to idols. It may also have alienated those *ethnē* in Christ, who, like Paul, would eat meat in the right context, and who may have reacted against what they perceived as unjustified limitations on their gentile "freedom" in Christ (idols do not exist and have no power).

What extends the power and effect of this Roman self-perception of "strength" is that it may incite or encourage a devaluation of Jews and Judaism in light of their inclusion in the category of the subdued nations. For diverse reasons, particularly the (temporary) expulsion of some Jews, this perception could have found expression in Rome at this time. It could include, as we have noted earlier, the view that those who are not victorious have been deserted by their gods and that the gods of the victors were

11. Esler, *Romans*, 350.
12. Harrison, *Reading Romans*, 326.
13. Barclay, *Gift*, 514.
14. Rodriguez, *Call Yourself a Jew*, 267.
15. Reasoner, *Strong*, 58–62; Jewett, *Romans: A Commentary*, 835.

more powerful.[16] In any case, it encouraged a gentile ethos of superiority over Jews. Even though we have found no evidence for the presence of Jews or Jewish Christ-followers in Romans 14, the vocabulary associated with Jewish patterns in public life is present (e.g., idolatry, pollution, stumbling, and blaspheming). This indicates some discussion of, and possibly the existence of, both shared and disputed values by the *ethnē* in Christ with Jews concerning issues in the wider community. It could be that those who share patterns of behavior in relation to idolatry and things sacrificed to idols were despised by those who thought themselves superior.

But it is the Lord who enables (*dynatei*) the weak to stand (14:4). *We note here the resonance with the dynatoi of 15:1* (cf. also 1:16, 11:23). Thus, the standing of "the weak" is established firmly at the outset of the conversation because the Lord is with them to empower them. "The weak" by themselves would remain "weak," but since the Lord has accepted them and is with them, they have access to divine power (cf. 1:16). However, there is no suggestion here that "the weak" should be accepted temporarily on condition that they become more "enlightened" or more conforming. *They are not viewed as being only a temporary phenomenon.* This is further elaborated in 14:5–12, where the emphasis is also on the presence of the Lord in the discussion, alongside the focus on all being fully convinced in their mind (14:5b). Those who observe certain days as special do so "in honor of the Lord," but so also those who do not, as well as those who eat or abstain from specific foods; in that sense, all give thanks to God, whose presence and whose law must be taken into account as the norm through Christ in all decisions concerning idolatry, even for the *ethnē*.

The "strong" are called to "bear the weak," and to accept them, not merely as a temporary measure but as they are, since God has welcomed these without discrimination.[17] In opposition to the Roman cultural pattern, Paul reverses the normal structure of obligation of "the weak" being obligated to submit to "the strong."[18] In contrast, the "strong" are here obligated to bear with the weaknesses of "the weak" and not to please themselves. This is a redefinition of what constitutes strength: not to "lord it over" others, not to despise as would be the demonstration of strength according to Roman elite ideology, but rather the opposite. Strength means to provide support, empower, care for, and respect the other.

---

16. After the fall of Jerusalem to Titus, outsiders inferred that the god of the Jews had been defeated by the gods of Rome; cf. Fredriksen, "Divinity, Ethnicity, Identity," 107–108.

17. Cf. Donfried, *Romans Debate*.

18. Jewett, *Romans: A Commentary*, 877.

An Associate Holy Community and the Limitation of "Freedom" (Rom 14:13–23)

Commentators have noted Paul's mildness of tone and inclusive attitude in Romans 14–15, but this should not obscure his seriousness—here he is dealing with vital issues that may hinder, even destroy, both a brother or sister's faith and the persons themselves. This is indicated by the effect of causing the other to "stumble." Paul sees that *broma* ("food") may cause "the ruin" of the other; *lypeitai*, translated as "being injured" here bears the connotation of causing grief or suffering. In 14:15, this is followed by the second person singular imperative, *mē apollue*, from the verb *apolluō* denoting more devastating harm.

This could indicate kashrut-related issues, especially if pork were involved and if Jews were among the addressees. But, given Paul's clear address of this letter to non-Jews, the more likely issue is the perception of food involved in idolatry. Indeed, the term *koinos* used by Paul in 14:14 sheds light on this. Rather than *koinos* being the equivalent of "impure" (*akathartos*), it has been demonstrated that the term took on a specific meaning in Greek Jewish literature referring to all that did not conform to Jewish ways of life. It does not replicate a specific Hebrew term but developed in the diaspora of the Second Temple period, where Jews had to negotiate the boundaries to their host cultures.[19] *Koinos* refers to that which is common among non-Jewish peoples. This can be food such as pork, or it can even generally relate to non-Jews and their way of life, which is decisively shaped by their worshipping of their gods,[20] characterized by Paul as confusion (1:18–32). If meat and wine were under discussion as an issue concerning kashrut rules, it would be relevant only for Jews; hence a majority of interpretations assume that Paul also addressed Jews in Romans.[21] But since he is here addressing non-Jews, kashrut cannot be directly relevant.[22] What is relevant, however, is the risk of perceived idolatry, a real issue for *ethnē* in Christ, in their unavoidable contacts with other groups at the street corners, markets, and public spaces in their locality.

Since meat and wine production involved dedications to the gods, these could be considered as contaminated by these practices. To avoid any risk of being involved in idolatrous behavior, some *ethnē* in Christ may have avoided meat altogether, eating only vegetarian as some Jews also did. There

---

19. Cf. Eschner, *Essen*, 91–92.
20. Cf. Eschner, *Essen*, 95.
21. For a good discussion of these issues, see Ehrensperger, "Called," 90–109.
22. Kashrut laws only apply to Jews.

may be a deliberate exaggeration in Paul's diatribal style, in that it is unlikely that some believed in eating anything and, similarly, in the reference to eating only *lachana*, i.e., vegetable leaves (14:2).

Such avoidance may be significant since gentile Christ followers most likely were former God-fearers. Not only this, but the Roman context was a context in which Jews were numerous, and in which there had been a long-term Jewish and non-Jewish interaction. Even in the centuries prior to the coming of Christ, Jews had developed well considered ways of positive social interaction on their terms. Debates among Jews concerning what may be eaten would not have been confined to inner-Jewish debates and, in any case, these included God-fearers and proselytes. But even apart from such shared history, non-Jewish Christ-followers needed to consider such issues as the consumption of food in such a way as to avoid contamination with idolatry. Since meals are at the center of piety in antiquity, gentile Christ-followers probably followed similar guidelines for the avoidance of idolatry as were common among Jews. In this, the commonality with Jews is greater by far than the ethnic commonality shared with their pagan neighbors. So, although Romans addresses only *ethnē* in Christ, the addressees live in the streets of Rome inhabited by a wide diversity of people (and their practices) whom they encounter every day. The *ethnē*, in drawing attention to themselves by refusal to sacrifice, could easily become targets of local resentments and anxieties. Some of these "neighbors" might be hostile; thus, stereotyping, misrepresentation, and opposition might be common, and possibly may have been considered justified against those who were putting the entire community at risk by insulting the gods in not participating in sacrificial activities.

If some Christ-followers were not sure, that is, if they were "weak in faith" and thought that meat and wine were contaminated (by idolatry), then they would be harmed in being pressured to eat and drink against their conscience. It is their perception that is decisive for what is "good" for them, not some abstract principle that might theoretically be legitimate. What is *koinos*, is *koinos* for the one who considers it *koinos*; it is not based on some natural quality (14:20). For the one who perceives the food to be eaten as *koinos*, it is for them the same as committing idolatry and thus, for Paul, indicates sin. Idolatrous gentiles, that is those "apart from the law," are doomed to perish (Rom 2:12). Conscientious gentile Christ-followers, in response to Paul's teaching on idolatry and all that follows from it, might consider themselves polluted by idolatry. To push a brother or a sister in that direction causes serious harm to them but also to the community as a whole.[23] As Ehrensperger states:

> The issue of food only comes into play in relation to the main concern of holiness. The food that the "weak" gentiles wish to abstain from eating could cause the stumbling of a brother or sister. To act in a way that harms the brother or sister constitutes an immoral deed, and the impurity that is associated with such a deed, classified as sin, thus threatens to profane the holy community, that is, it threatens to "blaspheme your good" (14:16).[24]

In Paul's view, this stumbling exists not only as a limited perception of certain people but also it becomes a cause of sin for the entire community, which would be broken by such behavior and weakened in its solidarity.[25] The communal aspect of injuring a brother or sister further illustrates the seriousness with which Paul viewed such an action.

Thus, instead of listing which things may be eaten or drunk, Paul states what behavior is permissible and what is prohibited. Paul is adamant, he knows and not only so, but he is convinced in the Lord Jesus that nothing is *koinos* in itself (14:14). This, then, is not only his own personal understanding, but normal Jewish perception, such as categories set out in the Torah specifying Israel's identity as a holy people belonging to God. Now this also applies to *ethnē* in Christ. They, having turned from the Roman gods and their associated practices, need to know who they now are and how this identity should be expressed. Core, of course, is exclusive trust in the one God, and as significant as this, care for the brother and sister.

Paul calls the Romans "beloved" even though they are not Jews (1:7; 12:19). We note that already in chapter 8 many of the descriptors of Israel as God's people appear first in the description of *ethnē* in Christ and are then repeated concerning Jews in chapter 9. Paul is thus seeking to transform these non-Jews into a holy people, not as a replacement for Israel, but as an associate people *representing the nations alongside God's people Israel.* They do have a distinct identity as those from the nations who follow Christ, their elder brother (8:29), the Messiah of Israel. They neither take over Israel's identity and role, nor do they replace these. Although the Torah is Israel's peculiar possession, it is also not without relevance for non-Jews who are similarly called to serve Israel's God and to identify, in a (gentile) pattern of life, with his (Torah) guidance for living. So even though *ethnē* in Christ are called "apart from the law," the law has abiding relevance in how it relates to non-Jews

---

23. Cf. Ehrensperger, "Called," 105.
24. Cf. 2 Cor 6:16–18 as identity descriptions now also for non-Jews in Christ.
25. Cf. Ehrensperger, "Called," 90–109.

who also worship the God of Israel, hence, the continuing significance of the avoidance of idolatry and the recurrence of the vocabulary of holiness. When the issue of idolatry is in question, Christ-following Jews and *ethnē* in Christ would find themselves in unison with other unpersuaded Jews in opposition to all forms of idolatry or appearances of such.

Romans 14:17–23:
Walking in Love, The Way of the Kingdom

Intrinsically connected to this exclusive loyalty to the one God is what Paul refers to as *kata agapen peripateis* ("walking in love"), i.e., a life guided by love of the other, the individual as a member of a holy people. We must note and keep in our focus that in 13:8–10, Paul has interpreted love as the fulfilling of the law, so this does *not* indicate, though he regards all things as *kathara* ("pure"), that Paul from this stance regards the law as somehow annulled or *passé*; rather, the one who loves his neighbor is the evidence of the law being fulfilled.[26] Thus, for the *ethnē*, living by love through the Spirit is their equivalent of doing the will of God, their "good." It seems that by the language of "your good," Paul may be indicating how the *ethnē* may adapt the language of holiness in Christ in relation to idolatry in a context where such issues are under discussion.

According to Paul, the "polluting" factor for the holy communities of those in Christ is the effect of some of the group's behavior on the brother, which instead of building up (14:19),[27] injures the other (14:15). For a non-Jew, to lose the support of other Christ-followers and to be damaged by their opposition or lack of support would leave such a person isolated and confused. If unable or unwilling to return to their former pagan way of life, and not finding acceptance and peace or joy with those in Christ, this is destruction of a very serious kind. Behavior is never purely one's own private business as an individual, but a community-oriented issue, and it is this extra-individual dimension that confirms its holiness or lack of it.

It is out of this concern that Paul calls upon those in Christ not, for the sake of food, to destroy the work of God (14:20). Paul's solution is abstinence from such food or drink that causes others to fall. It is "good" (*kalon*) to live thus, but "it is "wrong" (*kakon*) for you to eat meat or drink wine that makes a brother or sister "stumble" (14:21, cf. 1:32). This is not to demand that "the

---

26. MacMurray, *Sacrifice*, 188–93.

27. The language of building or construction can be taken as evidence for house building; it belongs to this linguistic context, but for more, see Adams, *Meeting Places*, 43–44.

self-styled strong" who despise "the weak" or cause them to stumble (with whom Paul does not identify) should give up their own conscientious principles of how to live according to Christ, but in those circumstances where there is a real risk of ruining or destroying the "weaker" ones, one ought to abstain from consuming what gives cause for offence. Each can rightly hold on to their own convictions, but they retain these between themselves and God (14:22) and must not allow them to become a cause of stumbling for the other. God's blessing is on those who are not self-incriminated "by what they approve" (14:22). We take this to refer to the outcome of acting out their own convictions in a given situation. On the other hand, if some have conscientious concerns about the consumption of certain food or drink, but nevertheless proceed to consume this, they are self-judged, not because of the nature of what is consumed but because they did not act in accordance with their faith. Paul's norm for behavior is "whatever is not by faith is sin" (14:23). One's faith can be a guide as to what is good.

Strength as Paul understands it, instead of risking or causing the destruction of the weaker brother or sister, means to follow the call to mutual upbuilding in love and respect as the characteristic criterion of the kingdom of God. Paul uses this theme sparingly, but whenever it occurs, it denotes something of significance. Here we have a broad definition of the kingdom in a neat summary of its nature and effects, which has *a wider horizon than the household*. Rather than engaging in negative conflicts about what one should eat or drink, Christ-followers should pursue what makes for righteousness and peace, "for the kingdom of God is not food and drink, but rather righteousness and peace and joy in the Holy Spirit" (14:17). Righteousness is noted first, but immediately followed by "peace and joy through the Holy Spirit." The unity of the Spirit is very high on Paul's list of priorities and indicates his continuing concern that these newly founded communities of Christ-followers do not live in competitive conflict with one another but become communities of mutual support in which they can grow together not in competition but in solidarity and (together) realize the goals of the kingdom, righteousness, peace and joy in the Holy Spirit. Starting from small beginnings, they cannot afford to lose any one of their members because of the destruction wrought by some who confuse, and thus cause the ruin of, one "on behalf of whom Christ died" (14:15). But those who live by this pattern of loving "the weak" will be acceptable to God and should have human approval (14:18).[28] Not only this, Paul does not overrule but actually legitimates diversity of opinion and practice as in keeping with the pattern of Christ who has welcomed all of them.

---

28. Jewett, *Romans: A Commentary*, 877.

Strength Redefined: Romans 15:1–6

Continuity in subject matter is demonstrated by the term "weak" in 15:1. A major theme is presented as a focus for the paraenesis in 15:2, "pleasing God and others." Following the example of Christ, whom Paul proclaims as one who did not please himself, they must "please their neighbor" in self-denial of their own freedom and thereby empower those who are "weak," enabling them to stand, rather than fall. Each must please the neighbor, "for the good" (*to agathon*) not only of the neighbor but of everyone, i.e., the upbuilding of the "community." The great exemplar for this is Christ, who did not please himself, and Scripture is cited in evidence that he voluntarily denied himself for the sake of others (15:3). The importance Paul attaches to his call to mutual acceptance and welcoming one another is demonstrated by his use of the example of Christ himself as the basis for his paraenesis.

What follows in 15:4–5 appears to be an argument that the Scriptures were meant for *ethnē* in Christ (cf. 4:23–25) and not only for Jews.[29] Paul is pointing out to the *ethnē* in Christ that the Scriptures are part of the Jewish symbolic universe into which they have been adopted. To belong to Christ even as non-Jews signifies a link with the people of Israel and their traditions.

Chapter 15 begins almost as a repetition of 14:1. Here Paul, significantly, includes himself in the "we who are strong" (v. 1). Thus "we, the strong," i.e., *hoi dynatoi*, ought to put up with or "bear" the weaknesses of "the weak," pointing to the reason for the label "weak." Not only are "the weak" more fully referenced, but the identity of "the strong" is explicitly specified. They are those who are now called upon to carry the weaknesses of "the weak." The call to bear or carry (*bastazein*), the weaknesses of "the weak" links back directly to 11:18, which was a high point of Paul's warning against the unwarranted proud self-understanding of the Romans, "If you do boast, remember it is not you who bears (*bastazeis*) the root but the root that bears you." This call to carry "the weak" must necessarily apply to the entire community. In 14:15 and 20, Paul has explicitly taken the side of "the weak" in ruling that it is wrong to cause someone to fall by what one practices, so we must be careful not to misinterpret the significance of Paul's inclusion among "the strong" in 15:1. This has led us to question the designation of *hoi dynatoi* as an opposing group to "the weak." "The weak" are clearly so designated more than once in chapter 14 as, for example, 14:1, whereas "strong ones," *hoi dynatoi*, are only so designated as the subject of the first verse in 15:1 and otherwise do not appear.

---

29. Jewett, *Romans: A Commentary*, 881–82.

Our presuppositions might lead us to read back Paul's self-identification as being among the *hoi dynatoi* in 15:1 into the previous chapter, something Paul did not do. Thus, if it might be assumed that some of the Christ-followers in chapter 14 were behaving selfishly and trying to force their "strong" opinions on those who are weak, even to the point of risking their destruction, then we cannot label these as *hoi dynatoi*, "the strong" with whom Paul explicitly identifies only at 15:1. Paul would not associate himself with a group whose behavior he explicitly repudiates.[30]

What is notable in chapter 15:1–6 is that *Paul not only includes himself among "the strong," but he now also supplies a positive description of "strong" identity*. We would not even have known the label "strong" if, like the Romans, we had still been waiting to hear the conclusion of Paul's references to "the weak" after chapter 14 in 15:1–6. "The strong" are not defined negatively in opposition to "the weak," as in binary groupings, but are here defined as those who care enough for the well-being of "the weak" that they are willing and able to adjust their patterns of behavior for the benefit of these. They are sufficiently concerned about the upbuilding of the community that they refuse to endanger "the work of God" that these weak "gentiles" represent. It seems that here in 15:1, Paul slightly adjusts his description to indicate clearly in direct address *his own view*, that the proper definition of "strong" people is not those who seek to exert force upon the ones who are weak in order to overpower them, but rather "the strong" are those who, like him, seek to empower weaker brothers and sisters by holding them up and by avoiding, or abstaining from, what causes them injury.

The goal of such a pattern of life is to enable all "to live in harmony with one another in accordance with the self-giving of Christ (14:5) so that "together you may with one voice glorify the God and Father of our Lord Jesus Christ" (15:6). If Paul's advice is taken, as he hopes it will, it will bring harmony and unity in keeping with the acceptance of "the weak" and thus of ongoing diversity.

Locating 14:1—15:6 within Romans

Our chosen text is bounded by chapter 13 on the one hand and 15:14–33 on the other. We found that the topic dealt with can be summed up by the repeated theme "welcome one another" in 14:1 and 15:7. But although 14:1—15:13 has a coherent theme and is itself clearly separated from the topic of Paul's future travel plans, etc. in 15:14–33, we wish to conclude by differentiating 15:7–13 from the content of 14:1—15:6. The information

---

30. Cf. Ehrensperger, "Paul," 88–90.

concerning Paul's future plans in 15:14–33 does not constitute an adequate conclusion to the preceding theological discourse of the letter. An appropriate conclusion is in fact provided in 15:7–13, which acts as conclusion both for the issue of "the weak and the strong" in 14:1—15:6 and also for the argumentation of the entire letter. What is the rationale for distinguishing verses 7–13 as this conclusion?

Romans 15:7–8 introduces a christological argument that in some respects replicates the theme of Paul's genealogy of Christ in the introduction in 1:1–6. In 15:7, Paul refers to "the Christ" as the one who has welcomed the *ethnē*. The powerful argument here is that "the Christ" did not please himself (15:3–6) and is thus the recommended role model for the Romans. Paul then tells the Romans to remember this gracious activity of Christ in his becoming a "*diakonos* of the circumcision" to maintain the faithfulness of God. Christ's action resulted in two outcomes: (1) in making good (actualizing) the promises given to the patriarchs; and (2) by giving the *ethnē* cause to glorify God for his mercy. Since Paul in our reading is addressing only the *ethnē* in Christ at Rome, we might have anticipated that Paul would have limited his statement to the outcome only for the *ethnē*, but here the outcome for the Jewish people is also, even primarily, stressed. The stress is upon a dual outcome of Christ's activity, one that binds him to both Jews and the *ethnē* in Christ. Thus 15:7 states, "accept one another therefore just as Christ accepted you, for the glory of God." This verse represents both a repetition, but also an expansion, of 14:1 in that here the ultimate aim is "the glory of God," and there is added content introduced by the description of Christ's activity as having an enormous outcome, not for the addressed *ethnē* only but for both Jews and *ethnē*.

This outcome is demonstrated in the exhortation coined in the second of four biblical citations in verses 8–12 (which have the function of adding support for the mutual acceptance of 15:7). The second citation, "Rejoice, O nations with his people" (15:10) is a universalizing or at least an expansion of Paul's call for mutual acceptance. The *meta* ("with") denotes two distinct ethnic entities, the nations and Israel, not only the *ethnē* as in chapters 1:1—15:6. After 15:7, Paul widens the horizons of his call to the *ethnē* in Christ at Rome. Not only are they to accept "the weak" among themselves, but they are to praise God "with his people Israel."

Now, for the first time, Israel is included within the horizon of the guidance given to *ethnē* in Christ. But neither Israel nor individual Jews are addressed; it is the *ethnē* in Christ who are advised concerning their relation to Israel. Paul does not single out Jewish Christ-followers as such at this point; here, they are presumed as part of Israel.

If the scope of Paul's guidance had been limited to *ethnē* in Rome as denoted in Romans 14:1—15:6, then we would be limited to regarding the problem of "the weak" and "the strong" as the concluding issue addressed in the letter. In previous readings, where the tension here was ascribed to ethnic issues between Jews and the *ethnē* in Christ, it could, with some latitude, be thus perceived. But the added input concerning the Christ, and the expansion of the effect of his service as *diakonos* to include in its scope both the *ethnē* and the Jewish people, supported by four significant scriptural citations, seems unwarranted as a response to only local issues. If, however, we recognize that Paul has expanded the horizon of his parenesis to call for reconciliation with the Jewish people, then the magnitude of this challenge warrants the implementation of all the support Paul utilizes. To be clear about our exegesis at this point: just as Paul does not fully identify with "the strong" until 15:1, and thus the content of 15:1–6 cannot be read back into chapter 14, so too what succeeds 15:6 in 15:7–13 must not be simply presumed for 15:1–6 but must be given the weight it deserves as an appropriate conclusion. This conclusion is timely in that it is coherent with very recent research, which gives added significance to Romans 9–11 and to 15:7–13 as together forming the culmination of Paul's argumentation concerning Israel and the *ethnē*. From a social and cultural perspective, the *ethnē* in Christ as an associate people will be stronger if they can live in difference from, but in acceptance of, Israel as the historic people of God.

Bibliography

(* For Further Reading)

Adams, Edward. *The Earliest Christian Meeting Places: Almost Exclusively Houses?* Library of New Testament Studies 450. London: Bloomsbury T. & T. Clark, 2013.
Barclay, John M. G. *Paul and the Gift*. Grand Rapids: Eerdmans, 2015.
Campbell, William S. *The Nations in the Divine Economy: Paul's Covenantal Hermeneutics and Participation in Christ*. Lanham, MD: Lexington/Fortress Academic 2018.
*———. Romans. *A Social-Identity Commentary*. London: T. & T. Clark, 2022.
Donfried, Karl P. ed. *The Romans Debate*. Rev. and exp. ed. Grand Rapids: Baker Academic, 1977, 1991, 2011.
*Ehrensperger, Kathy. "'Called to Be Saints,' The Identity-Shaping Dimension of Paul's Priestly Discourse in Romans." In *Reading Paul in Context: Explorations in Identity Formation—Essays in Honour of William S. Campbell*, edited by Kathy Ehrensperger and J. Brian Tucker, 90–109. Library of New Testament Studies 428. London: Bloomsbury 2010.
———. "Paul, Emasculated Apostle or Manly Man? Gendered Aspects of Cultural Translation." In *Searching Paul: Conversations with the Jewish Apostle to the*

Nations, 73–90. Wissenschaftliche Untersuchungen zum Neuen Testament 429. Tübingen: Mohr Siebeck, 2019.

Eschner, Christine. *Essen im antiken Judentum und Urchristentum: Diskurse zur sozialen Bedeutung von Tischgemeinschaft, Speiseverboten, und Reinheitsvorschriften.* Ancient Judaism and Early Christianity 108. Leiden: Brill, 2019.

Esler, Philip F. *Conflict and Identity in Romans: The Social Setting of Paul's Letter.* Minneapolis: Fortress 2003.

Fitzmyer, Joseph A. *Romans: A New Translation with Introduction and Commentary.* Anchor Bible 33. New York: Doubleday 1993.

*Fredriksen, Paula. "Divinity, Ethnicity, Identity: 'Religion' as a Political Category in Christian Antiquity." In *Comprehending Antisemitism through the Ages: A Historical Perspective*, 101–20. Berlin: De Gruyter Open Access, 2021.

Harrison, James R. *Reading Romans with Roman Eyes: Studies on the Social Perspective of Paul.* Paul in Critical Contexts. Lanham, MD: Lexington/Fortress Academic 2020.

Jewett, Robert. *Romans: A Commentary.* Hermeneia. Minneapolis: Fortress, 2007.

MacMurray, Patrick. *Sacrifice, Brotherhood, and the Body: Abraham and the Nations in Romans.* Lanham, MD: Lexington/Fortress Academic 2021.

*Reasoner, Mark. *The Strong and the Weak: Romans 14:1—15:13 in Context.* Society of New Testament Studies Monograph Series 103. Cambridge: Cambridge University Press, 1999.

Rodriguez, Rafael. *If You Call Yourself a Jew: Reappraising Paul's Letter to the Romans.* Eugene, OR: Cascade Books, 2014.

———. "Romans 5–8 in Light of Paul's Dialogue with a Gentile Who 'Calls Himself a Jew.'" In *The So-Called Jew in Paul's Letter to the Romans*, edited by Rafael Rodriguez and Matthew Thiessen, 101–31. Minneapolis: Fortress, 2016.

Study Questions

1. In what ways does Paul show familiarity with the situation at Rome to which he writes?

2. Paul addresses gentiles in Romans but in a context where Jews appear to be also listening in. Discuss with reference to ethnic issues.

3. "Paul inverts the meanings of the labels 'strong' and 'weak' in Romans 14–15 in the light of Christ 'who did not please himself.'" Is this claim a fitting conclusion to Romans?

Part II

Pauline Theology and Interdisciplinary Study

8

To Imagine Otherwise

Interpreting Romans 7:14–25 from the
Perspective of Scriptural Criticism

Meng Hun Goh

Abstract

THIS ESSAY USES SCRIPTURAL criticism to highlight the textual, hermeneutical, and contextual choices interpreters make in their interpretation of Romans 7:14–25, which can be identified as primarily individual-centered (highlighting one's inability to fulfill the law), community-centered (highlighting the inability of a distorted value and system to achieve goodness), or other-centered (highlighting the absolutization of anything good that can turn it into evil). This foregrounding of choices underscores the ethics of interpretation and promotes dialogues and learning from each other without co-opting the other.

> When one surveys recent books written by Americans for the scholarly audience, a lack of interest in culturally indigenous interpretation remains typical. But the orientation of many Pauline scholars is departing from European paradigms and prejudices, and is making significant advances against traditional biases about Paul...[1]

---

1. Jewett, *Paul the Apostle to America*, 23–24.

Introduction

Jewett's words in the epigraph may surprise some American readers in the United States because today we do not lack biblical interpretations that are in dialogue with the US contexts. But can "culturally indigenous interpretation[s]" be considered scholarly? Yes, of course! If we are always already embodied and shaped by our social locations,[2] how can our exegesis be without presuppositions?[3] Our interpretation is inevitably a "fusion of horizons"[4] between the text and how we interpret it from our context.[5] And if some traditional interpretations of Paul are not without "European paradigms and prejudices," then it is only scholarly to examine our contexts and presupposed worldviews. Thus Jewett exhorted US biblical scholars to develop their own interpretive logic and orientation, rather than just following those set by the European academy.

This emphasis on engaging the context from which one interprets the biblical texts is well noted in Jewett's *The Captain America Complex, Christian Tolerance, Saint Paul at the Movies, Paul the Apostle to America, Saint Paul Returns to the Movies, Captain America and the Crusade Against Evil, Mission and Menace*, etc. (see bibliography). In these works, Jewett's persistent critiques of zealotry for honor acquisition in the US context are evident in his biblical exegesis. In his commentary on Romans, as Jewett made known (1) his contextual concern (e.g., fanaticism, imperial

---

2. See Merleau-Ponty, *Phenomenology of Perception*; Segovia and Tolbert, eds., *Reading from This Place*, vols. 1–2.

3. Bultmann, "Is Exegesis without Presuppositions Possible?" 289–96. Yeo further notes: "At best the 'exegesis/eisegesis' concern might be a construct that assumes a scholar can transcend his culture and detach himself from his own time and place, yet be able to become immersed in the past and know it with certainty. At worst, the 'exegesis/eisegesis' differentiation is a scholarly fear of living in partial knowledge, the insecurity of shared ownership of any text, or the alienation of self from the network of texts with which we all work." Yeo, *Musing with Confucius and Paul*, 54.

4. Gadamer writes: "A person who is trying to understand a text is always projecting. He projects a meaning for the text as a whole as soon as some initial meaning emerges in the text. Again, the initial meaning emerges only because he is reading the text with particular expectations in regard to a certain meaning. Working out this foreprojection, which is constantly revised in terms of what emerges as he penetrates into the meaning, is understanding what is there." Gadamer, *Truth and Method*, 269.

5. Bal further argues: "Texts by definition being semiotic constructs, necessitating the active participation of readers or listeners for their existence, the textual object is dynamic, unstable, elusive . . . It is naive to believe that we can analyze without interpreting, that we can work and live without lending meaning to the world around us." Bal, *Murder and Difference*, 135–36.

ideology)[6] and (2) the hermeneutical framework (e.g., honor and shame),[7] we see that (3) his choice of exegetical approach (e.g., rhetorical analysis focusing on how to effectively persuade a particular audience)[8] most helpfully addresses his contextual concern and complements his hermeneutical framework. This tripolar integrated relationship in interpretation—of context, hermeneutics or worldview, and biblical text—is what scriptural criticism aims to foreground.

What Is Scriptural Criticism?

Scriptural criticism makes explicit the interwoven relationship between the three modes of existence—i.e., "aspects of the believer-reader's existence" as Cristina Grenholm and Daniel Patte explicate in terms of individual-centered (autonomy), community-centered (relationality), or other-centered (heteronomy)[9]—and the three poles of subject matters that are analyzed (i.e., text, contextual concern, and hermeneutical framework)[10] in our interpretation.

The word "scriptural" acknowledges that the biblical texts are a Word-to-live-by for believers in their everyday lives. Scripture is not just an object to be analyzed, it is also a subject addressing and transforming believers. In the words of Sandra Schneiders, Scripture is not only "a human text that

---

6. For instance, the first sentence of the "Preface" of Jewett's commentary: "That Romans was a missionary document aimed at overcoming the premises of imperial honor was first suggested by a missionary to Africa in 1863." Jewett, *Romans: A Commentary*, xv. Elsewhere Jewett writes: "The hypothesis developed in my commentary is that Paul depicts himself as the person prior to his conversion, a zealous fanatic who obeyed the Jewish law perfectly but with such eagerness to achieve honor that he produced evil results." Jewett, *Romans: A Short Commentary*, 99.

7. For example, Jewett wrote: "In the shameful cross, Christ overturned the honor system that dominated the Greco-Roman and Jewish worlds, resulting in discrimination and exploitation of barbarians as well as in poisoning the relations between the congregations in Rome." Jewett, *Romans: A Commentary*, 1.

8. For instance, Jewett wrote: "In the effort to follow Paul's attempt to persuade and transform the Roman congregations, one should bring to bear all of the available historical and cultural information." Jewett, *Romans: A Commentary*, 1.

9. Grenholm and Patte, "Overture," 35.

10. Hence, in the ten volumes of the *Romans through History and Cultures Series* that demonstrate the practice of scriptural criticism, readers will notice such bold-typed letters as "A" (Analytical Frames), "H" (Hermeneutical Frames), "C" (Contextual Frames), and sometimes "I" (Interplay of Frames) to indicate the interpretive pole that is at work in the process of interpretation. Grenholm and Patte, *Romans through History and Cultures*.

manifests all the traits of such an artifact and must be dealt with accordingly," it also "mediate[s] the believer's encounter with God" in the present.[11]

How is such encounter perceived as critical to biblical interpretation? If "the study of scripture raises questions of an interrelation between time and eternity, of humanity's historically participating in transcendence, of a link between the human and the divine,"[12] then the modes of existence should not be overlooked in exegesis, in particular if honor and shame are the "core"[13] or even "pivotal"[14] values that undergird the ancient Mediterranean worldview. If "[h]onour felt becomes honour claimed and honour claimed becomes honour paid,"[15] as Julian Pitt-Rivers stresses, then we need to note that even though honor is a collective value, it can still be perceived in terms of individual-centered (honor claimed), or community-centered (honor paid), or other-centered (honor felt).

This observation foregrounds several key points highlighted by scriptural criticism. First, the felt or religious dimension of honor, prominent in my Chinese Malaysian cultural value, is often neglected in biblical studies. Likewise, if shame can be perceived as a "double movement" of "both subjectification and desubjectification"[16] (that is, a subject exists as nonsubject), then it can be viewed as "associated with one's sense of self in its most singular sense, with what makes one a unique individual."[17] But this bodily felt (not just ideological) dimension of shame, just like the (heteronomous) religious perception,[18] is seldom explored in biblical studies.

Second, if honor can be experienced, perceived, and explained in terms of individual-centered, community-centered, or other-centered, then we

---

11. Schneiders, *The Revelatory Text*, xviii.

12. Smith, *What Is Scripture?*, 22. Patte notes that since interpretations "affect readers in their life contexts . . . critical biblical studies needs to account for faith-interpretations [in particular if faith can be broadly conceived as one's 'ultimate concern,' as Paul Tillich puts it], simply because they are themselves interpretations, and that there is no meaningful interpretation of a text without a life-centered pragmatic dimension . . ." Patte, "Critical Biblical Studies From A Semiotics Perspective," 18.

13. Plevnik, "Honor/Shame," 89.

14. Malina, *The New Testament World*, 27–57; Malina and Neyrey, "Honor and Shame in Luke-Acts," 25–66. For nuances on understanding honor and shame in the biblical texts, see deSilva, *Despising Shame*, 24; Downing, "'Honor among Exegetes,'" 53–73; Lawrence, "'For truly, I tell you, they have received their reward' (Matt 6:2)," 687–702.

15. Pitt-Rivers, "Honour and Social Status," 22; Pitt-Rivers, *The Fate of Shechem*, 2; Pitt-Rivers, "Honor," 503.

16. Agamben, *Remnants of Auschwitz*, 106.

17. Oliver, *The Colonization of Psychic Space*, 119.

18. Lancaster, "Scriptural Criticism and Religious Perception," 271–83.

need to discern which mode of existence we privilege (whether consciously or not) in our interpretation. To discern such a choice making, we need to read *with* other interpretations instead of disregarding and even co-opting their "interpretive line of reasoning," as Patte has recently shown.[19]

Third, choice making means responsibility and accountability.[20] In spelling out the textual, hermeneutical, and contextual choices in our interpretation, many may think that it is too personal, risky, and vulnerable. But if interpretation can bring life or death to its recipients, should there not be a genuine conversation between the interpreter and the audience? A juxtaposition of interpretations of a distinctive interpretive line of reasoning (of individual-centered, community-centered, or other-centered) can make us aware of our limitation and unintentional message.[21]

Fourth, it is not true that anything goes. If how we perceive the world and the text affects how we make choices, then our interpretation is always contextual; it is not universally valid. Grenholm and Patte stress that while all interpretations are "[exegetically] legitimate and [hermeneutically] plausible until proven otherwise,"[22] their validity and value must be assessed in each context. It is when interpreters do not assume responsibility for their interpretation that "truly 'anything goes!'"[23]

Fifth, as our context and social location affect our hermeneutical and textual choices, we need to flesh out, in both the text and our context, the root problem that lies behind the problems. We need to analyze whether the fundamental problem is a wrong/lack of knowledge, wrong/lack of will, wrong/lack of ability, wrong/lack of vision, wrong ideology, etc.[24] Such analysis can help us address the problems effectively. For Grenholm and Patte, such identification of root problem and the corresponding role of Scripture

---

19. Patte, *Romans*.

20. Patte, *Ethics of Biblical Interpretation*.

21. From the perspective of semiotics, unintentional message or surplus of meaning teaches us that intentional message or "what the author meant" is "only one of the several significant dimensions of a discourse, and not necessarily the most important." Patte, "A Western Biblical Scholar *Reading* Romans *with* Greek Fathers and Eastern Orthodox Biblical Scholars," 209–12.

22. Grenholm and Patte, "Encore," 2, 11, 13. Also, see the conversation between Patte and Jewett: Patte, "A Response to Robert Jewett's Hermeneia Commentary on Romans," 153–67; Jewett, "Response to Washington Colleagues," 177–86.

23. Grenholm and Patte, "Encore," 14.

24. Grenholm and Patte, "Overture," 38–39; for more details, see Patte, et al., *The Gospel of Matthew*, 19–42; Patte, *The Challenge of Discipleship*; Patte, *Discipleship According to the Sermon of the Mount*.

to tackle the problems is embodied by responsible preachers; otherwise, their sermons would hardly engage their audience.²⁵

Admittedly "the term 'scriptural criticism' will evoke a legalistic and authoritarian view of Scripture often associated with its designations as Canon and as inerrant Word of God."²⁶ However, the discipline of "criticism" makes scriptural criticism "an interpretive practice that acknowledges that critical analytical biblical studies are part of a broader investigation that encompasses both the religious and critical dimensions of biblical interpretation."²⁷

With this review of scriptural criticism from a multiracial, multireligious, and multicultural Chinese Malaysian background, the importance of identifying distinctive interpretive lines of reasoning in interpretation readily comes to the fore on the issues of power relations and positions in "race"/"ethnic groups," religions, cultures, gender, etc. Having taught at a Presbyterian seminary in Taiwan (island) for the past six years, I find such identification particularly helpful to a society that prides itself for democracy but is aggravated by social media that is unabashedly ideologically-driven. Besides the spread of "fake news" or "alternative facts," exacerbated by a year-round election culture, manipulative media framing and cyberbullying have been running amok for years—targeting opponents, resulting in suicide and the ruin of reputation by the so-called "cyber army" or "cyber warrior."²⁸ Engaging Romans 7:14–25 from this context, I present three textually legitimate and hermeneutically plausible interpretations from the individual-centered, community-centered, and other-centered perspectives to see how each interpretation may shed light on my context, and vice versa.

An Individual-Centered Interpretation of Romans 7:14–25

The following interpretation is individual-centered because it focuses on an individual's proper knowledge of the law and sin.²⁹ Rudolf Bultmann writes, "'I' and 'I,' self and self, are at war with each other . . . is the essence of human

25. Grenholm and Patte, "Overture," 3, 8, 12–14.
26. Grenholm and Patte, "Overture," 3.
27. Grenholm and Patte, "Overture," 3.
28. For example, see https://www.cw.com.tw/article/5094849; https://www.thestar.com.my/aseanplus/aseanplus-news/2020/10/26/nearly-half-of-taiwan-teens-involved-in-cyberbullying (accessed September 24, 2021).
29. For example, Schnelle writes: "Sin and law appear as trans-individual powers that are at work in individual events and circumstances." Schnelle, *Apostle Paul*, 335.

existence under sin"[30] as an individual seeks to realize their own selfhood.[31] Here, an autonomous "I" is assumed. But what is the root problem that prevents one from fulfilling the law? For many scholars, the answer is clear: "I am of the flesh, sold into slavery under sin" (7:14).[32]

But who is this "I" under sin?—"Pre-Christian" Paul or the "Christian" Paul (since 7:7–13 is cast in past tense, while 7:14–25 in the present tense)?[33] Adam? A fictive or typical unregenerate or regenerate person? etc.[34] If "I" refers to the "Christian" Paul, then how does one account for 6:2, which speaks of believers who died to sin and are no longer living it (cf. 6:14, 22, etc.)? And how does the law put the "I" into a deeper trouble?[35] Did Paul not say in Philippians 3:6 that he is blameless according to the righteousness of the law? Was Paul referring to his pre-Christian perspective? Or was it common in ancient Judaism to claim blamelessness without "infer[ring] that the law had been kept?"[36] Or was Paul confessing an ongoing struggle between "in the flesh" and "in the spirit," as the Qumran *Hodayot* (*Thanksgiving Hymns*) show?[37]

Given this division of the self and of the law[38] (or two laws: law of God vs. law of sin, or law of mind vs. another law), we can say that the struggle makes us recognize the limit of our knowledge and will. As Karl Barth puts it, struggles make one "shattered on God, without the possibility of forgetting Him" and, as such, needing God's grace.[39] We should know that the self

---

30. Bultmann, *Theology of the New Testament*, I.245.

31. For Barth, when "Men *hold the truth imprisoned in unrighteousness*, they have lost themselves." Sin takes place when "[s]tretching out to reach what they are not, men encounter what they are, and they are thereby fenced in and shut out." Barth, *The Epistle to the Romans*, 244, 248.

32. Moo, *The Epistle to the Romans*, 454; also, Ridderbos, *Paul*, 130; Fitzmyer, *Romans*, 473.

33. Moo, *The Epistle to the Romans*, 448; also Bultmann, *Theology of the New Testament*, I.247.

34. Moo, *The Epistle to the Romans*, 445–47; Fitzmyer, *Romans*, 463–65. Highlighting the eschatological tension, Dunn thinks that 7:24 clearly speaks of Paul the Christian. Dunn, *Romans 1-8*, 410.

35. While law has various meanings, Moo argues that the law in Romans 7 refers to the Mosaic law. Moo, *The Epistle to the Romans*, 428; Bultmann, *Theology of the New Testament*, I.250; Leenhardt, *The Epistle to the Romans*, 177; Fitzmyer, *Romans*, 456; contra Schnelle, *Apostle Paul*, 337–38.

36. Thielman, *From Plight to Solution*, 110.

37. Seifrid, "The Subject of Romans 7:14–25"; also, Thurén, "Romans 7 Derhetorized"; Timmins, *Romans 7 and Christian Identity*.

38. Dunn argues that "both the 'I' and the 'law' [are] divided between the two ages of Adam and Christ in a period when these two ages overlap." Dunn, *Romans 1-8*, 377.

39. Barth, *The Epistle to the Romans*, 270.

and the current law are not reliable, lest we "fall into the dangerous habit of thinking that our laws, or rules, can be the source of true holiness."[40] Such unreliability should not lead to the banality of evil.

A Community-Centered Interpretation of Romans 7:14–25

As Eugene TeSelle and R. Ward Holder point out that Augustine's and John Calvin's interpretations of Romans 7 are directly tied to their contextual concerns,[41] we see Jewett's concern for fanaticism in dialogue with Paul's "preconversion" zealotism, where the "I" is in/disformed by her/his habitus.[42] Hence, "[w]hat Paul describes in Romans 7 is not a failure to fulfill the law [contra the individual-centered interpretation] . . . but rather the inability of such violent legalism to achieve the good."[43]

Referring to the *Discourses of Epictetus* (e.g., 1.12), Jewett agrees with Stanley Stowers that the "I" in Romans 7 is like a diatribal "speech-in-character" (*prosōpopoiia*) rhetoric.[44] As such, the dilemma of "what I will, I do not do, and I do what I hate" not only points to "pre-Christian" Paul's "sin of legalistic zealotism."[45] It also refers to, as Stowers argues, the gentile Godfearers "caught between two cultures."[46] Consequently, they are disoriented. Worse, the "I" is fragmented to begin with, as W. E. B. Du Bois's "double consciousness" tells us: "One feels his twoness—an American, a Negro; two souls, two thoughts, two unreconciled strivings; two warring ideals in one dark body, whose dogged strength alone keeps it from being torn asunder."[47] Or, in the words of Frantz Fanon, "The presence of the Negroes beside the whites is in a way an insurance policy on humanness."[48] That is, not only do Black people have to suppress who they are, what they will, and

---

40. Moo, *Encountering the Book of Romans*, 110.

41. TeSelle, "Exploring the Inner Conflict," 111–46; Holder, "Calvin's Hermeneutic and Tradition," 98–119.

42. Bourdieu defines habitus as "systems of durable, transposable dispositions, structured structures predisposed to function as structuring structures." Bourdieu, *The Logic of Practice*, 53.

43. Jewett, *Romans: A Short Commentary*, 99.

44. Stowers, *A Rereading of Romans*, 258–84. Stowers defines speech-in-character as "a rhetorical and literary technique in which the speaker or writer produces speech that represents not himself or herself but another person or type of character" (16–17).

45. Jewett, *Romans: A Short Commentary*, 104.

46. Stowers, *A Rereading of Romans*, 278.

47. Du Bois, *The Souls of Black Folk*, 3.

48. Fanon, *Black Skin, White Masks*, 98.

perform according to the social norm (hence they hate what they do), their caught-in-betweenness is even universalized and becomes a source of white people's assurance and identification.

This ideological critique underscores the root problem that lies with vision and systemic evil. That is, sin in terms of zealotism can turn an honorable pursuit into a deadly endeavor, or sin in terms of social structure can force people to behave in a certain way, despite their unwillingness. Here, the crucifixion of our Lord Jesus Christ can problematize the existing value system since what is honorable was abused as despicable and shameful!

An Other-Centered Interpretation of Romans 7:14–25

If the "'I' is a composite of various elements that defy a single identification,"[49] since it can embody gentile, Jewish, and Christian experiences, then the law—which, according to Giorgio Agamben has the etymological meaning of "to divide, to attribute parts"[50]—should make manifest these various elements. But if sin is against the law, and the law can be summed up as "do not desire" (7:7),[51] then sin in desiring would be against the division by the law. Whatever sin acquires, it would want to categorize it into a totality.[52] When the "I" is always caught in between "God and antigod powers" (such as sin and death),[53] "I" is alerted to the power that demands its allegiance.

This root problem of totalization, for Patte, is what sin seeks to do in asserting itself and turning what is partial and incomplete into absolute and final.[54] Sin, as such, is more than personal guilt and social shaming. It is an overwhelming power in which whatever is good and holy, once absolutized, can become evil, as if there is no more goodness, or goodness cannot be understood otherwise, but must be interpreted according to the logic of totality.

Hence, in contact with the law, sin "as the power of and reality of covetousness, is both stimulated and unmasked by the law as the divine

---

49. Dodd, *Paul's Paradigmatic 'I,'* 230.
50. Agamben, *The Time That Remains*, 47.
51. For example, Moo, *The Epistle to the Romans*, 435–36.
52. Or as Byrne puts it: "Righteous living—and the hope of salvation which it entails—is possible not despite the removal of the law but because of it." Byrne, *Romans*, 209.
53. Gaventa, "The Shape of the 'I,'" 91.
54. Patte, *Paul's Faith and the Power of the Gospel*, 263–77.

commandment."[55] That is, facing the law of God, sin is stimulated to have Jesus Christ our Lord crucified, but as Patte points out, the resurrection of Jesus Christ by God then unmasks the sin of totality for what it is, to foreground how the law is distorted into a self-serving system.[56] As sin is within us (7:17, 20), and our inner being rejoices together with the law of God (7:22), sin seeks to "con-fuse" them together. But for Paul, through God's intervention, we can discern how the law of God distorted into the law of sin when it crucified Jesus (7:25)!

Conclusion

Just as Jewett adapted European Pauline scholarship "for the American scene,"[57] scriptural criticism argues that the value of an interpretation hinges on its constructive engagement with the context. Because interpretation does matter, the ethics of interpretation and the foregrounding of our textual, hermeneutical, and contextual choices become critical to mutual learning. In a society rife with political-party's ideology, Taiwan's Christians need to see how toxic media framing is also caused by systemic evil. Because for individuals raised in a certain ideology, even if they do not want to hurt others, their ideology justifies the harm by portraying others as evil. The cross and resurrection of Jesus, however, problematize a "we" vs. "them" dichotomy and challenge any totalization that marginalizes others. Indeed, as Christ the abject becomes the deliverer, we are alerted to how the justice of God has been manifested outside the law and yet witnessed by the law and the prophets (3:21).

Bibliography

(* For Further Reading)

Agamben, Giorgio. *Remnants of Auschwitz: The Witness and the Archive.* Translated by Daniel Heller-Roazen. New York: Zone, 1999.
———. *The Time That Remains: A Commentary on the Letter to the Romans.* Translated by Patricia Dailey. Stanford: Stanford University Press, 2005.
Bal, Mieke. *Murder and Difference: Gender, Genre, and Scholarship on Sisera's Death.* Translated by Matthew Gumpert. Bloomington: Indiana University Press, 1988.
Barth, Karl. *The Epistle to the Romans.* 6th ed. Translated by Edwyn C. Hoskyns. London: Oxford University Press, 1968.

---

55. Käsemann, *Commentary on Romans*, 193.
56. Patte, *Paul's Faith and the Power of the Gospel*, 281–86.
57. Jewett, *Paul the Apostle to America*, 12.

Bourdieu, Pierre. *The Logic of Practice*. Translated by Richard Nice. Stanford, CA: Stanford University Press, 1990.
Bultmann, Rudolf. "Is Exegesis without Presuppositions Possible?" In *Existence and Faith: Shorter Writings of Rudolf Bultmann*, translated by Schubert M. Ogden, 289–96. New York: Meridian, 1960.
———. *Theology of the New Testament*. 2 vols. Translated by Kendrick Grobel. 1951, 1955. Reprint, Waco, TX: Baylor University Press, 2007.
Byrne, Brendan. *Romans*. Sacra Pagina 6. Collegeville, MN: Liturgical, 1996.
deSilva, David A. *Despising Shame: Honor Discourse and Community Maintenance in the Epistle to the Hebrews*. Rev. ed. Studies in Biblical Literature 21. Atlanta: Society of Biblical Literature, 2008.
Dodd, Brian. *Paul's Paradigmatic 'I': Personal Example as Literary Strategy*. Journal for the Study of the New Testament Supplements 177. Sheffield: Sheffield Academic, 1999.
Downing, F. Gerald. "'Honor' among Exegetes." *Catholic Biblical Quarterly* 61 (1999) 53–73.
Du Bois, W. E. B. *The Souls of Black Folk*. New York: Bantam Classic, 2005.
Dunn, James D. G. *Romans 1–8*. Word Biblical Commentary 38A. Dallas: Word, 1988.
Fanon, Frantz. *Black Skin, White Masks*. Translated by Charles Lam Markmann. Forewords by Ziauddin Saddar and Homi K. Bhabha. London: Pluto, 2008.
Fitzmyer, Joseph A. *Romans*. Anchor Bible Commentary. New York: Doubleday, 1992.
Gaca, Kathy, L. L. Welborn, Daniel Patte, Eugene TeSelle, Cristina Grenholm, Kathy Ehrensperger, Vasile Mihoc, Khiok-Khng Yeo et al. *Romans through History and Cultures Series*. 10 vols. London: T. & T. Clark/Bloomsbury, 2002–2013.
Gadamer, Hans-Georg. *Truth and Method*. 2nd rev. ed. Translation revised by Joel Weinsheimer and Donald G. Marshall. New York: Continuum, 2004.
Gaventa, Beverly Roberts. "The Shape of the 'I': The Psalter, the Gospel, and the Speaker in Romans 7." In *Apocalyptic Paul: Cosmos and Anthropos in Romans 5–8*, edited by Beverly Roberts Gaventa, 77–91. Waco, TX: Baylor University Press, 2013.
*Grenholm, Cristina, and Daniel Patte. "Encore: Playing Scriptural Criticism on Romans in Multiple Keys." In *Modern Interpretations of Romans: Tracking Their Hermeneutical/Theological Trajectory*, edited by Daniel Patte and Cristina Gren-holm, 1–32. Romans through History and Cultures Series 10. New York: Bloomsbury T. & T. Clark, 2013.
———, eds. *Romans through History and Cultures: Receptions and Critical Interpretations*. 10 vols. London: Bloomsbury/T. & T. Clark, 2000–2013.
*———. "Overture: Receptions, Critical Interpretations, and Scriptural Criticism." In *Reading Israel in Romans: Legitimacy and Plausibility of Divergent Interpretations*, edited by Cristina Grenholm and Daniel Patte, 1–54. Harrisburg, PA: Trinity, 2000.
Holder, R. Ward. "Calvin's Hermeneutic and Tradition: An Augustinian Reception of Romans 7." In *Reformation Readings of Romans*, edited by Kathy Ehrensperger and R. Ward Holder, 98–119. Romans through History and Cultures Series 8. New York: T. & T. Clark, 2008.
Jewett, Robert. *Captain America and the Crusade against Evil: The Dilemma of Zealous Nationalism*. Grand Rapids: Eerdmans, 2003.
———. *The Captain America Complex: The Dilemma of Zealous Nationalism*. Philadelphia: Westminster, 1973.

———. *Christian Tolerance: Paul's Message to the Modern Church*. Philadelphia: Westminster, 1982.
———. *Mission and Menace: Four Centuries of American Religious Zeal*. Minneapolis: Fortress, 2008.
———. *Paul the Apostle to America: Cultural Trends and Pauline Scholarship*. Louisville: Westminster John Knox, 1994.
———. "Response to Washington Colleagues." In *From Rome to Beijing: Symposia on Robert Jewett's Commentary on Romans*, edited by K. K. Yeo, 177–86. Lincoln, NE: Kairos Studies, 2012.
*———. *Romans: A Commentary*. Hermeneia. Minneapolis: Fortress, 2007.
———. *Romans: A Short Commentary*. Minneapolis: Fortress, 2013.
———. *Saint Paul at the Movies: The Apostle's Dialogue with American Culture*. Louisville: Westminster John Knox, 1993.
———. *Saint Paul Returns to the Movies: Triumph over Shame*. Grand Rapids: Eerdmans, 1999.
Käsemann, Ernst. *Commentary on Romans*. Translated and edited by Geoffrey W. Bromiley. Grand Rapids: Eerdmans, 1980.
Lancaster, Sarah Heaner. "Scriptural Criticism and Religious Perception." In *Gender, Tradition and Romans: Shared Ground, Uncertain Borders*, edited by Cristina Grenholm and Daniel Patte, 271–83. New York: T. & T. Clark, 2005.
Lawrence, Louise Joy. "'For truly, I tell you, they have received their reward' (Matt 6:2): Investigating Honor Precedence and Honor Virtue." *Catholic Biblical Quarterly* 64 (2002) 687–702.
Leenhardt, Franz J. *The Epistle to the Romans: A Commentary*. Translated by Harold Knight. London: Lutterworth, 1961.
Malina, Bruce J. *The New Testament World: Insights from Cultural Anthropology*. 3rd ed. Louisville: Westminster John Knox, 2001.
Malina, Bruce J., and Jerome H. Neyrey. "Honor and Shame in Luke-Acts: Pivotal Values of the Mediterranean World." In *The Social World of Luke-Acts: Models for Interpretation*, edited by Jerome H. Neyrey, 25–66. Peabody, MA: Hendrickson, 1991.
Merleau-Ponty, Maurice. *Phenomenology of Perception*. Translated by Collin Smith. London: Routledge, 2002.
Moo, Douglas J. *Encountering the Book of Romans: A Theological Survey*. 2nd ed. Grand Rapids: Baker Academic, 2014.
———. *The Epistle to the Romans*. Grand Rapids: Eerdmans, 1996.
Oliver, Kelly. *The Colonization of Psychic Space: A Psychoanalytic Social Theory of Oppression*. Minneapolis: University of Minnesota Press, 2004.
Patte, Daniel. *The Challenge of Discipleship: A Critical Study of the Sermon on the Mount as Scripture*. Harrisburg, PA: Trinity, 1999.
———. "Critical Biblical Studies from A Semiotics Perspective." In *Thinking in Signs: Semiotics and Biblical Studies . . . Thirty Years Later*, edited by Daniel Patte, 3–26. *Semeia* 81. Atlanta: Scholars, 1998.
———. *Discipleship according to the Sermon on the Mount: Four Legitimate Readings, Four Plausible Views of Discipleship, and Their Relative Value*. Valley Forge, PA: Trinity, 1996.
*———. *Ethics of Biblical Interpretation: A Reevaluation*. Louisville: Westminster John Knox, 1995.

———. *Paul's Faith and the Power of the Gospel: A Structural Introduction to the Pauline Letters*. Philadelphia: Fortress, 1983. Reprint, Eugene, OR: Wipf & Stock, 2016.

———. "A Response to Robert Jewett's Hermeneia Commentary on Romans." In *From Rome to Beijing: Symposia on Robert Jewett's Commentary on Romans*, edited by K. K. Yeo, 153–67. Lincoln, NE: Kairos Studies, 2012.

*———. *Romans: Three Exegetical Interpretations and the History of Reception*. Vol. 1: *Romans 1:1–32*. New York: T. & T. Clark, 2018.

———. "A Western Biblical Scholar *Reading* Romans *with* Greek Fathers and Eastern Orthodox Biblical Scholars." In *Greek Patristic and Eastern Orthodox Interpretations of Romans*, edited by Daniel Patte and Vasile Mihoc, 203–22. Romans through History and Cultures Series 9. New York: Bloomsbury T. & T. Clark, 2013.

Patte, Daniel, Monya A. Stubbs, Justin Ukpong, and Revelation E. Velunta. *The Gospel of Matthew: A Contextual Introduction for Group Study*. Nashville: Abingdon, 2003.

Pitt-Rivers, Julian. *The Fate of Shechem or The Politics of Sex: Essays in the Anthropology of the Mediterranean*. London: Cambridge University Press, 1977.

———. "Honor." In *International Encyclopedia of the Social Sciences*, edited by David L. Sills, 6:503–11. New York: Macmillan, 1968.

———. "Honour and Social Status." In *Honour and Shame: The Values of Mediterranean Society*, edited by John G. Peristiany, 19–77. Chicago: University of Chicago Press, 1966.

Plevnik, Joseph. "Honor/Shame." In *Handbook of Biblical Social Values*, edited by John J. Pilch and Bruce J. Malina, 89–95. 3rd ed. Matrix 10. Eugene, OR: Cascade Books, 2016.

Ridderbos, Herman. *Paul: An Outline of His Theology*. Translated by John Richard De Witt. Grand Rapids: Eerdmans, 1975.

Schneiders, Sandra M. *The Revelatory Text: Interpreting the New Testament as Sacred Scripture*. 2nd ed. Collegeville, MN: Liturgical, 1999.

Schnelle, Udo. *Apostle Paul: His Life and Theology*. Translated by M. Eugene Boring. Grand Rapids: Baker Academic, 2005.

Segovia, Fernando F., and Mary Ann Tolbert, eds. *Reading from This Place*. Vol. 1: *Social Location and Biblical Interpretation in the United States*. Minneapolis: Fortress, 1995.

———, eds. *Reading from This Place*. Vol. 2, *Social Location and Biblical Interpretation in Global Perspective*. Minneapolis: Fortress, 1995.

Seifrid, Mark A. "The Subject of Romans 7:14–25." *Novum Testamentum* 34 (1992) 313–33.

Smith, Wilfred Cantwell. *What Is Scripture? A Comparative Approach*. Minneapolis: Fortress, 1993.

Stowers, Stanley K. *A Rereading of Romans: Justice, Jews, and Gentiles*. New Haven: Yale University Press, 1994.

TeSelle, Eugene. "Exploring the Inner Conflict: Augustine's Sermons on Romans 7 and 8." In *Engaging Augustine on Romans: Self, Context, and Theology in Interpretation*, edited by Daniel Patte and Eugene TeSelle, 111–46. Harrisburg, PA: Trinity, 2002.

Thielman, Frank. *From Plight to Solution: A Jewish Framework for Understanding Paul's View of the Law in Galatians and Romans*. Novum Testamentum Supplements 61. Leiden: Brill, 1989.

Thurén, Lauri. "Romans 7 Derhetorized." In *Rhetorical Criticism and The Bible*, edited by Stanley E. Porter and Dennis L. Stamps, 420–40. Journal for the Study of the New Testament Supplements 195. London: Sheffield Academic, 2002.

Timmins, Will N. *Romans 7 and Christian Identity: A Study of the 'I' in Its Literary Context*. Society for New Testament Studies Monograph Series 117. Cambridge: Cambridge University Press, 2017.

Yeo, K. K. *Musing with Confucius and Paul: Toward a Christian Chinese Theology*. Eugene, OR: Cascade Books, 2008.

Study Questions

1. What are the three modes of existence and three poles of analysis foregrounded by scriptural criticism?

2. What are the five main points highlighted by scriptural criticism in this essay?

3. What are the root problems and corresponding solutions proposed by the individual-centered, community-centered, and other-centered interpretations?

9

Shame and Honor Systems in the Book of Romans

A Psychological Analysis of the Struggle for Superiority Within and Between the Roman Tenement and House Churches

Lallene J. Rector

Abstract

A Kohutian psychoanalytic perspective is employed to illuminate psychological dynamics in the honor and shame system dominating early Roman tenement and house churches. Their mutual shaming of each other and competitive struggle for superiority is understood as disturbance in the mirroring selfobject need with its attendant emotional vulnerabilities to shame. The suggestion is offered that Paul's antidote, "the agape" or love feast, functions as a cultural selfobject with potentially transformational impact on these struggles.

Introduction

This essay is a study in applied psychoanalysis. It explores a Kohutian interpretation of the struggle for superiority in the Roman house and tenement churches, i.e., the struggle between Jewish and gentile Christian converts addressed in the book of Romans.[1] Such appeals to and enactments of

---

1. Given the limitations of time, space, and the fact that the essay author is not a biblical scholar, this exploration will grant, *without argument*, the historical, biblical, and cultural analyses of Dr. Robert Jewett.

superiority are understood as the effort to protect factions within those congregations from experiencing the painful affect or emotion of shame. The psychology of the self, originally developed by Heinz Kohut,[2] is offered as a heuristic device for understanding how certain aspects of psychological and theological anthropologies, or views of human nature, may be illustrated in the Romans text.

Based on the findings of Robert Jewett's later textual, historical, and cultural analyses of the book of Romans,[3] it is argued that the disturbance or psychological injuries in the basic selfobject need for "mirroring"[4] are at the core of the competitive struggle for superiority within these churches. The experiences of understanding, recognition, and admiration contribute to strengthening self-esteem, and thus reduce the need for appeal to a more exclusive status. Because these needs are also shaped by the cultural context in which they are experienced, the psychology of the self can expand our understanding of the impact on those living within such an honor/shame system.

Mindful of the larger cultural context of honor/shame and the ensuing claims to superiority, Jewett interprets Paul's reference to "the agape" in Romans 13:10 as a transformative meal: "The agape does no evil to the neighbor; therefore the agape is law's fulfillment."[5] Jewett explains that this fulfillment of the law is the *love feast*, which now demands followers to love one another rather than meeting the daily and many disparate demands of the old law. "Here enemies are welcomed to the Lord's table where they are transformed rather than annihilated."[6] As a *positive* theory about the human self's inescapable narcissistic needs for psychological sustenance and reliable self-esteem, the psychology of the self illuminates both the Roman house and tenement churches' competitive dynamics and Paul's remedy of the love feast.

---

2. Heinz Kohut (1913–1981), born in Austria and raised in Vienna, fled Nazi Germany in 1939 within months of Sigmund Freud's escape to London. Kohut arrived in Chicago, Illinois, in early 1940 via London. He joined the Institute for Psychoanalysis of Chicago, where he became a nationally recognized scholar and clinician. During the last decade of his life and based upon his clinical experience, Kohut advanced a new theoretical perspective on narcissism and its developmental trajectories through life. The utilization of empathy became the centerpiece of clinical investigation and treatment. Kohut called his theory the "psychology of the self." During his life, the theory was extended and continues to be elaborated by other clinicians and scholars.

3. Jewett, *Romans: A Short Commentary*; and Jewett, *Romans: A Commentary*.

4. Kohut, *Analysis of the Self*.

5. Jewett's translation in Jewett, *Romans: A Short Commentary*, 246.

6. Jewett, *Romans: A Short Commentary*, 182.

The essay concludes with the suggestion that the love feast itself functions as a "cultural selfobject,"[7] meeting certain psychological needs of the self and resulting in transformative effects in both individual and group-church lives. It seems to be Paul's antidote to the search for superiority of one group over another. In addition, the love feast was potentially a counter-cultural force in the broader honor/shame systems of Rome. As such, if widely revived in current Christian practices, the love feast might also serve as a transformative force in today's church and beyond. Several questions for further consideration and discussion are offered.

Methodology Limitations

The psychology of the self is culturally bound, as are all theories, and was extrapolated from clinical experience primarily with Caucasian patients. Kohut was Austrian, originally trained in ego psychology, and developed his theory in latter part of the twentieth century. Years of psychoanalytic practice and astute clinical observation led him to the conclusion that a group of his patients were experiencing difficulties that simply could not be effectively addressed by ego psychology. In response, he developed a new psychoanalytic theory to better address what he called the "narcissistic disorders."[8]

It was not until later in his life that Kohut became interested in how the psychology of the self might enhance the theoretical understanding of group dynamics. Because the theory was initially based on the clinical data of individual psychoanalyses, its application to groups began as a nascent discussion of the self and the group in 1978 and resulted in a paper five years later, "The Self and the Group: A Tentative Exploration in Applied Self Psychology."[9] In it, Dr. Mark Gehrie, a trained anthropologist and psychoanalyst, addressed methodological issues in applied psychoanalytic studies in his discussion of a clinical case with a second-generation Japanese-American. Cultural dynamics were prominent in the patient's personality and stimulated further study of the implications for cultural

---

7. Kohut, "Self Psychology and the Sciences of Man." The concept was hinted at in the paper and will be explicated later in this essay.

8. Kohut, *Analysis of the Self, Restoration of the Self,* and *How Does Analysis Cure?*

9. Gehrie, "The Self and the Group: A Tentative Exploration in Applied Self Psychology." In 1978, Dr. Mark J. Gehrie, former colleague of Heinz Kohut at the Institute for Psychoanalysis of Chicago, was requested by Kohut to "look into" the matter of a group self. This referenced paper was the result of Kohut's request and eventually became a touch point for the concept of the "cultural selfobject." (Private conversation with Dr. Gehrie, October 9, 2021).

dimensions in psychological experiences. During Kohut's life and following his death, the theory was extended and continues to be elaborated by other clinicians and scholars in the concept of a "cultural selfobject."[10] The meaning and application of these terms and their relevance to the study of Romans are discussed below following a brief review of Jewett's major observations and conclusions regarding Paul's response to the superiority dynamic within and between the Roman churches.

The Christian Situation in Rome

Jewett's lifetime devotion to the book of Romans resulted in unique attention to the honor and shame system in Roman culture. He investigated the impact of this larger cultural dynamic for Paul's particular audience in Rome and the way the honor/shame dialectic was manifested in the difficulties of the house and tenement churches. In each congregation, the different groups of Jews and gentiles were engaged in intense competition with each other. They cast accusations back and forth about how the opposite group was failing to embody honor. In addition, there was social shaming on both sides related to the perceived weaknesses of each other. Also replicated were the discriminatory attitudes toward the Jews in the broader Roman culture. The categories of the "the weak" and the "strong" (Rom 14:1—15:13) emerged and were probably initiated by the gentiles.

In these disputes, the Jews were predominantly regarded as the weak ones for continuing to follow and be concerned with dietary laws, holy days, and circumcision. And, in turn:

> According to 14:1—15:7, the "weak" are judging their competitors for failing to live up to kosher food laws and to celebrate Christ on designated holy days. While the "strong" criticized their opponents for lacking freedom from the law. The very names they applied to each other, "weak/strong," "circumcised/uncircumcised" were honorific on differing scales of honor held by these groups . . . to accuse each other of dishonor entailed mutual damnation with each side claiming divine approbation for themselves and divine wrath against their opponents.[11]

In Roman society, gentiles were in the majority, and though Christianity in Rome began with Jewish converts, the Jews remained the minority in

---

10. Sheppard, *Self, Culture, and Others in Womanist Practical Theology*, 114–15; and Lee, *Selves In-Between: Offering Care and Forging Bonds with Difference*, 27–29.

11. Jewett, *Romans: A Short Commentary*, 188.

the churches as the number of gentile Christian converts increased. Noting the diversity of Paul's audience, Jewett observed:

> The ethnic diversity of the Roman congregations encouraged a continuation of a combative tendency that was present throughout the culture. Despite their comparatively low status, the house and tenement churches in Rome were engaged in fierce competition with one another for superior honor.[12]

It is evident that competition for superiority must necessarily have included mutual shaming of each other since pointing out the flaws and failings of another lifts the esteem of the accuser, while the accused is often left with feelings of shame.

Superiority Struggles Observed

Jewett carefully identified several realms wherein these claims of superiority were being made. The following chart briefly captures Jewett's categories of difference and/or similarity as they are manifested in demographic variables, leadership styles, and partisan commitments.

Table 9.1: Roman Churches

Tenement Churches	House Churches
Demographics: Populated largely by "the underclass" Christians with meager financial resources. Meetings were typically held at ground-level shops in tenement buildings and would have included immigrant members.	*Demographics*: Populated by more affluent Christians who could afford to rent appealing venues for the church meetings, as well as provide the food eaten at the love feast. Members might also have included immigrants.
Theological Issues: The members' boasting about keeping law, food constraints, and observing holy days indicated they did not fully understand that God's grace was given to all faithful persons.	*Theological Issues*: The members' boasting about freedom from the law and more liberal views also indicated *they* did not fully understand God's grace was given to *all* faithful persons.

---

12. Jewett, *Romans: A Short Commentary*, 188.

Tenement Churches	House Churches
Leadership Styles: Focused on egalitarian, shared leadership. No one assumed the authority to be the leader or host based on economic status. Leadership was shared.	*Leadership Styles*: Jewett introduces the term "love-patriarchalism" as the form of leadership. The leader hosted the venue, the dinner, and enjoyed the authority that comes from more *resources*.
Partisanship: Strife and religious zealousness were present; partly cultural, partly Jewish.	*Partisanship*: Strife and religious zealousness were present; partly cultural, partly Jewish.

Overview of the Psychology of the Self

Heinz Kohut's psychology of the self is a complex theory replete with difficult technical language that is challenging, as well as provocative, for the layperson. He posited three basic psychological needs, "selfobject" needs, and a developmental line of narcissism across life that was manifested in each of these needs. The concept of selfobject described the nature of these needs and was defined as that aspect of a psychological function provided from outside the self but experienced as if it were part of the self, hence the lack of a hyphen in the term. As a selfobject need matures developmentally, satisfaction of the need can be met by internalized capacities and/or those that have been abstracted beyond the literal provision from an external source, for example, ideals and values.

Narcissism is popularly thought of as an obnoxious, extreme self-centeredness that is often expressed in a sense of entitlement and demands for attention. While some earlier developmental forms of narcissism do manifest in these ways, *at all ages*, Kohut did not regard narcissism as inherently negative or as a character flaw. By virtue of being human, we are inescapably self-interested. It is a central feature of Kohut's psychological anthropology.

In self psychology, empathy plays a central role in healthy emotional development as well as in the clinical situation where narcissistic needs may emerge in the transference to the therapist. It is the capacity of the observer/listener to put themselves inside the experience of another person and to convey that understanding back to the other, engaging in this back-and-forth communication until the other person feels understood. The experience of empathy includes the "mirroring" experience of feeling recognized, understood, and accepted. These empathic experiences help to develop self-esteem and equilibrium in the face of inevitable disappointment and/or unempathic responses.

Positive developmental movement requires empathic-enough responses along the way. If the joys and disappointments of life are met with empathy, the child slowly begins to internalize their own capacity for empathy with self and others, moving from a developmentally appropriate self-centered stage to a more "mature" point in development. For Kohut, experiencing empathy was the emotional oxygen required for the well-being of the self and necessary for the mature transformation of narcissism into the qualities of wisdom, humor, acceptance of finitude, creativity, and empathy.[13]

As noted above, Kohut describes a developmental trajectory for narcissism moving from "archaic," early developmental expressions to more mature expressions. This is the case for each of the three basic needs of the self: idealization, twinship, and mirroring.

Idealization is associated with a specific aspect of the self, the repository of ideals and values. The developmental trajectory here traces the shift from early forms of idealization that are manifested in the assumption and expectations that the idealized other is perfect. For the child, this will likely begin with an experience of a parent as all-knowing, or in bragging to others that, "My mother/father is "the most . . ." this or "the best . . ." that. When the idealized other invariably disappoints, then an empathic response is critical for helping the child learn to manage these disappointments without becoming cynical, depressed, or concluding later as an adult that there is nothing worth giving oneself to, and/or no worthy purpose.

Twinship is the need for experiences of alikeness that, in their earliest form, reassure us we are a human being among other human beings. As emotional and psychological development continue, the self will seek those who are experienced as more specifically like us in some important feature. For example, we may have experiences of being with others who are all Christians like we are, or experiences that we are all Black men in a certain setting, or we that we all go to the same church, or that we all survived the earthquake, etc.

These "twinship" experiences provide a foundation for the sense of belonging. At the mature end of this developmental line, we can live comfortably with difference and feel a fundamental sense of belonging by virtue of sensing ourselves to be human among other human beings. However, the need for more specific experiences of alikeness continues throughout life and function as places of emotional respite for us. The need to be with

13. Kohut, "Forms and Transformations of Narcissism," 243–72.

others like us in certain ways is to be supported. If development of this need goes awry, then persons may become not only anxious in the face of difference, but even extremely fearful of others perceived as significantly different. Sometimes this extreme fear erupts in violence against the other based on a need to feel safe from the felt danger of such differences.

Mirroring, as noted above, is closely associated with the grandiose part of the self. The early developmental expressions are seen in attention seeking, confirmation, compliments, admiration, or overt self-centeredness. More mature forms can be seen in reliable self-esteem and the recognition that while one is unique, one is not always the best, the first, or the winner. There is an acceptance that oneself cannot be the center of attention all the time, nor can one expect to be exempt from anything that once felt "beneath" one. The mirroring selfobject need is closely affiliated with the affect of shame when one's grandiosity, sense of great specialness, or inflated ideas of one's capacities are revealed in an unkind or critical way. See the chart below.

Table 9.2: The Grandiose Self: The Developmental Trajectory of the Mirroring Selfobject Need

"Archaic" or "Early" Developmental Manifestations	Optimal Empathic Frustration and/or Traumatic Empathic Responses		Mature Developmental Manifestations
• In early development, experience is processed through the self, hence the "self-centeredness" of a child: wanting to be the first, the only one, or the best. • Empathy can take the form of literal mirroring. • *Seeing* disappointment, or the excitement of new skills can be expressed in verbal or physical ways: (clapping hands, joy on the caregivers' face, etc.).	<u>Optimal</u> Caregivers admire and celebrate accomplishments with an attempt to match the emotional tenor of the moment, e.g., "Wow, look at you!" or "I know you are disappointed about . . ."	<u>Traumatic</u> Critical responses about the child's efforts or seeking recognition and admiration—such as "don't show off; we don't brag"—can be experienced as shaming, and the child learns to hide "grandiose" expressions of self, e.g., "look at me."	In contrast to early development, "mature" mirroring needs are met through external expressions of appreciation, or compliments, or a nodding in agreement, a smile of approval or delight, hand on the shoulder. The self has internalized a realistic sense of one's abilities, uniqueness, and a reliable sense of self-esteem.

The intense affect of social or personal shame evokes a need for protection against the pain of it. Superiority is often the unconscious defensive response. A child learns quickly that one way to combat this pain is to adopt an *offensive* response by denigrating the other. This response is informed by what may remain unconscious, i.e., the feeling or belief that, "I *am* the superior one." A similar response to the mutual shaming between the tenement and house churches may well have been at play in Rome.

Another means of protection against the revelation of shame both within oneself and/or from external sources is the development of an unconscious false humility. It can hide one's grandiosity or inflated sense of self and thus protects against being accused of thinking too highly of oneself, yet another source of shame. It is not clear that false humility is at play in the Roman churches, but it is very common in religious communities.

The Development of Cultural Selfobject Concept

As noted above, Kohut eventually started to think about a group self and its relation to the leader. Freud before him had already taken up the subject of how psychoanalytic concepts could be applied to group behavior.[14] He posited the notion that a group member could unconsciously allow a loved leader to stand in for their own ego-ideal, the realm of the mind that is the seat of ideals and the sense of how one wants to be as a person. Other group members were also engaged in a similar dynamic, all looking to the leader to be the repository or each member's ego-ideals. Freud observed that while members of a group envy each other, their shared desire to have equal standing protected them against the possibility that another member would dominate the group. This dynamic bound them together in their idealization of the leader. Freud also asserted that the dynamic "stems from the original wish to be ruled by one person: the leader."[15] The members' ongoing relation to the group depended on this shared dimension in their experience of the leader.

In a 1978 paper, Kohut considered at length the German group self and its relationship to Hitler.[16] He describes how the cohesion of a group is established through identification with the leader and with fellow members of the group. The formation of a group and the sustaining of it over time could take two different forms:

14. Freud, *Group Psychology and Analysis of the Ego*.
15. Freud, *Group Psychology and Analysis of the Ego*, 121.
16. Kohut, "Self Psychology and the Sciences of Man."

> . . . on the one hand, sudden, gross, archaic essentially unstable identifications, . . . require the presence of the leader in order to be maintained and disappear *in toto* when he disappears (or becomes unidealizable *via* a failure); and on the other hand, slowly acquired, increasingly mature internal changes, corresponding to transmuted internalization in analysis, that will ultimately remain, even when the leader disappears, psychically or psychologically.[17]

Put more simply, Kohut is describing the differences between a group whose members have developed the capacity to internalize and make part of themselves the shared ideals that are currently binding a group together, in contrast to a group whose "togetherness" depends solely on the literal presence of the leader. Each member of the former group has been able to establish stable internalizations of the shared group ideals, and thus can continue together as a group even if the leader dies or ceases to be part of that group.

Gehrie extended these perspectives in an analysis of the phenomenon of *leaderless* groups as seen in people's sense of belonging and how this was experienced in culturally based groups of alikeness or in the increasing extension of significant emotional ties beyond the family.[18] The introduction of groups whose cohesion is based on a culturally shared experience of belonging and of compelling ideals that bind the group together beyond the physical presence of a leader points to the concept of cultural selfobjects.

Unlike Freud, Kohut was open to the possibility of more salutary psychological benefits of religion. He observed that religion and other cultural manifestations like art, literature, and music, could also be experienced as providing the essential psychological functions for the self: 1) mirroring and the sense of being known, understood and accepted; 2) twinship or belonging based on a sense of alikeness; and 3) ideals that inspired a sense of purpose worth giving oneself to.[19] Sheppard and Lee both address, respectively, the role of cultural selfobject needs potentially being met in being in the experience of alikeness and shared ideals in groups, e.g., Black women/lesbian Black women, or in Korean religious groups.[20]

---

17. Kohut, "Self Psychology and the Sciences of Man," 83.

18. Gehrie, "The Self and the Group: A Tentative Exploration in Applied Self Psychology."

19. See Rector, "The Function of Early Selfobject Experiences in Gendered Representations of God" for a brief discussion of Kohut's views on religion.

20. Sheppard, *Self, Culture, and Womanist Practical Theology*; and Lee, *Selves In-Between: Offering Care and Forging Bonds with Difference.*

The Love Feast and Its "Radical New Form of Mutual Acceptance" as a Cultural Selfobject

Following Paul in the book of Romans, Jewett argued that the combination of the love feast, together with its new form of mutual acceptance, had transformative power. As such, it could function as an antidote to the struggle for superiority and the shaming of each other in the Roman churches. It can be posited that from a psychology of the self perspective, the powerful force of the love feast as described in Romans functioned as a cultural selfobject. The meal provided a psychological container for experience within a Christian group of persons who, regardless of ethnic, theological, or class differences, were called to share a sense of belonging with and to each other based on the ideals of their Christian faith, ideals that had been embodied in the life, ministry, and resurrection of Jesus Christ. The psychological significance of Jesus, their earthly teacher and leader in the flesh, would have been sufficiently internalized so that the group could continue beyond his death, and in fact has to this day. Jesus was the ultimate selfobject. With him, they felt understood (mirroring); they belonged with and to him as human beings via God's incarnation (twinship); and they were infused with an inspired purpose to love one another and to share the good news of the gospel (idealization).

The love feast recognized that behind and beyond the physical group host and facilitator, Jesus was the *real* leader, who though unseen, was present, resurrected in the Spirit. He was inviting his followers to transcend their narcissistic behaviors. He called them, through Paul, to leave behind their expressions of shaming the other and to leave behind their claims of superiority in order to "put on Christ" (Rom 13:14) in expressions of genuine love for one another.

Before concluding, a remaining question must be posed. In light of the stubborn persistence of our "inescapable" human narcissism, is it possible that both Paul and Jewett are too optimistic about the transformational impact of mutual acceptance and the love feast? A strictly *psychological* anthropology might suggest this is, indeed, the case. Wishful thinking, for human beings also are inescapably vulnerable. And as such, we are often given to the means of psychological protection that hurt others. Thus, the cycle of narcissistic injuries seems to continue. Nevertheless, even as Paul acknowledges that "all have sinned and fallen short . . ." (Rom 3:23), Christians are called to believe in the promise, the "ideal," that we can be set free by *God's* ("mirroring") acceptance (Rom 3:24).

This essay has argued that the psychology of the self with its 1) developmental understanding of selfobject needs; 2) the central role of empathy in emotional development; and 3) the importance of emotional and psychological maturation resulting in acceptance of the self's capacities, skills, and talents, as well as limitations, contributes to an expanded understanding of certain aspects of the shame/honor dialectic in the Roman house and tenement churches.

The goal in our human development, and perhaps also in "our going on to perfection"[21] as Christians is to be able to accept the realities of who we are as selves, recognizing what our capacities, skills, and talents are and are not, to discover we can belong in many different ways, but most deeply that we belong because we are human beings among other human beings; and finally, that there are things, purposes, values, and commitments worth our devotion. Experiences of shame and claims to superiority are but manifestations of the need for continuing in the lifelong journey of becoming whole selves.

Bibliography

(* For Further Reading)

Freud, Sigmund. *Group Psychology and Analysis of the Ego* (1921). In *The Standard Edition of the Complete Psychological Works of Sigmund Freud*, Vol. 18, 69–143. London: Hogarth, 1955.

Gehrie, Mark J. "The Self and the Group: A Tentative Exploration in Applied Self Psychology." In *Advances in Self Psychology*, edited by Arnold Goldberg, 367–82. New York: International Universities, 1983.

Jewett, Robert. *Paul's Anthropological Studies: A Study of Their Use in Conflict Settings.* Leiden: Brill, 1971.

*———. *Romans: A Commentary.* Hermeneia. Minneapolis: Fortress, 2007.

———. *Romans: A Short Commentary.* Minneapolis: Fortress, 2013.

*Kohut, Heinz. *The Analysis of the Self: A Systematic Approach to the Psychoanalytic Treatment of Narcissistic Personality Disorders.* New York: International Universities, 1971.

———. "Forms and Transformations of Narcissism." *Journal of the American Psychoanalytic Association* 14 (1966) 243–72.

———. *How Does Analysis Cure?* Edited by Arnold Goldberg with collaboration of Paul Stepansky. Chicago: University of Chicago Press, 1984.

*———. *The Restoration of the Self.* New York: International Universities, 1977.

———. "Self Psychology and the Sciences of Man" (1978). In *Self Psychology and the Humanities: Reflections on a New Psychoanalytic Approach*, edited with an introduction by Charles B. Strozier, 73–94. New York: Norton, 1985.

Lee, AHyun. *Selves In-Between: Offering Care and Forging Bonds with Difference.* Nashville: New Room, 2021.

21. Wesley, "Christian Perfection."

*Rector, Lallene. "The Function of Early Selfobject Experiences in Gendered Representations of God." In *Progress in Self Psychology: Basic Ideas Reconsidered*, edited by Arnold Goldberg, Vol. 12: 249–68. Hillsdale, NJ: Analytic, 1996.

Sheppard, Phillis Isabella. *Self, Culture, and Others in Womanist Practical Theology*. Black Religion/Womanist Thought/Social Justice. New York: Palgrave Macmillan, 2011.

Wesley, John. "Christian Perfection." In *John Wesley's Sermons: An Anthology*, edited by Albert C. Outler and Richard P. Heitzenrater, 64–69. Nashville: Abingdon, 1991.

Study Questions

1. In honor of Dr. Jewett's clear commitment to consider contemporary implications of his analysis, how might *we* respond to these questions:

    a. How are we to live as a result of his analysis?

    b. What might the implications be for the world, for our lives together as human beings, and as members of Christian communities?

    c. Might there be a new form of the "love feast?"

2. Given Kohut's psychological anthropology and its defining element of an inescapable self-interest, were Paul and Dr. Jewett too optimistic about the transformative power of the "love feast"?

10

A Metaphorical Interpretation of *Charis* and *Charisma* in Romans 12

A Cultural-Critical Understanding of "Gift"

K. K. Yeo

Abstract

THE ESSAY EXPLORES THE use of metaphorical analysis of the Greek word *charis(ma)* in Romans 12 (engaging with Jewett's Commentary) as a way to enable a cross-cultural rhetorical interpretation of the theology of "gift" in Greco-Roman and Chinese cultures. The essay will show how both content (gift/honoring, etc.) and method (metaphor, language) can serve as a conduit between—and robust theological reception across—the two civilizations.

Introduction: From Figure of Speech to Interanimation of Predication

The apostle Paul and Robert Jewett are twins to me. From the apostle Paul and from Robert Jewett, my *doktorvater*, I learned the power of language and rhetoric, the significance of cultures, and the sacred task of a culturally critical biblical interpretation. The role of metaphor, or the use of metaphorical language, is the gold testing stone of biblical interpretation.

Metaphor, as a figure of speech, describes and creates reality. Aristotle sees the substitution, comparison, and transference nature of metaphor: "Metaphor consists in giving the thing a name that belongs to something else; the transference being either from genus to species, or from species to genus, or from species to species, or on grounds of analogy" (*Poet.* 1457b).[1] Yet, metaphor is more than a figure of speech; it is in Janet Soskice's view

1. Aristotle, *Rhetoric, Poetics*, 251–52.

"a figurative 'speaking about' that generates new perspective."[2] I. A. Richards also extends the word/name function of metaphor to its omnipresent principle in human cognition (speech and thought); thus, metaphor is a matter of predication or a mental apparatus that involves the *interanimation* of thoughts whereby a "vehicle" from one domain of meaning acts upon a subject called "tenor" of another domain.[3] Similarly, Max Black highlights the *interaction* of this principal subject ("tenor" in Richards) and subsidiary subject ("vehicle" in Richards) and associated commonplaces ("grounding" in Richards).[4] Language works metaphorically; as Ricoeur points out, this "is more" meaning of metaphor is "a calculated error, which brings together things that do not go together . . . it causes a new hitherto unnoticed relation of meaning to spring up between the terms that previous systems of classification had ignored or not allowed . . . A metaphor tells us something *new* about reality."[5] Thus, cross-domain mapping and projection of meaning from one frame to another generate new meaning.[6] In short, language is metaphorical and therefore a metaphor has "is, is not, is more" meanings.

Interpretive Steps and Proofs: *Charis* and *Charisma* as Gift

Contexts: Cultural Understandings of Gift

The English word "gift" is used to translate two Greek words in the Bible,[7] and the wordplay of *charis* (grace/gift) and *charisma* (charismatic gift) in Romans 12 by Paul could be read by using the metaphor of "gift."[8]

2. Soskice, *Metaphor and Religious Language*, 15, 66.

3. Richards, *Philosophy of Rhetoric*, 93, 108–109.

4. Black, "Metaphor," 63–82, "More about Metaphor," 431–57.

5. Ricoeur, *Interpretation Theory*, 51–53 (emphasis mine); cf. his *Rule of Metaphor*, 230, 248 on the duality of reference: "It was and it was not."

6. See de Mendoza, Ruiz, and Peña, "Conceptual Interaction," 254–80, who called this "Combined Input Hypothesis."

7. See Louw and Nida, *Greek-English Lexicon Semantic Domains*, on various "gift" words in the Bible: (1) offering gift (*dōron*; Luke 21:4) [6.142] or present (*dōron, dōrēma, dōrean, dōrophoria*, Acts 2:38, Rom 15:31, 2 Thess 3:8 [57.84–85]; (2) a promised gift or offering to God (*korban*, Mark 7:11–12, a loan word from Hebrew) [53.22]; (3) collection gift/fund (*logeia*, 1 Cor 16:2) [57.66]; (4) give/gift (*didōmi, dotēs, dosis*, Phil 4:15, 17) [57.71, 57–73]; (5) prize or reward (*brabeion* (1 Cor 9:24) [57.120]; (6) gain as a possession (*klēronomos*, Matt 5:5, Rom 8:17) [57.131–135]; (7) generous gift or abundance (*adrotēs*, 2 Cor 8:20) [59.60]; (8) charismatic gifts (*charisma*, Rom 12: 3, 6) [57.102–103]; (8) gracious gift (*charis*, Rom 1:11, 6:23; 1 Cor 16:3) [57.102–103]. In the book of Romans, the word *charis* is used twenty-four times (1:5, 7; 3:24; 4:4, 16; 5:2, 15 [2x], 17, 20, 21; 6:1, 14, 15, 17; 7:25; 11:5, 6 [3x]; 12:3, 6; 15:15; 16:20).

8. Brockhaus, *Charisma*, 200. Taken from Jewett, *Romans: A Commentary*, 745. For

The origin of the concept of "gift" is ambiguous, as various cultural understandings of gift below, taken from Mauss and Horner, show.[9] Classical Greek *dōtinē* has the idea of return-gift or reciprocity. Latin and Greek *dosis* (from which English "dose" derives) carries both nuances of gift and poison (so German). And Latin *hostia* has the notion of hospitality (later found also in Germanic and Slavic societies). In northern India, "a gift (*dan*) involves the transfer of 'inauspiciousness' from giver to recipient."[10] French *donner* may be traced to Hittite *dô* or *dâ*, meaning "to give" or "to take respectively." In Chinese, the word *li* can mean "rite" or "gift," perhaps because ritual ceremony always involves presentation of gifts. And *li* is about the humanizing process in Confucian tradition, as gifting is ingrained in that culture that speaks of one's obligation to gift others in making both parties human (similar to Emmanuel Levinas' thesis).[11] Mauss asserts that some cultures believe a gift has a spirit; thus a gift cannot be possessed by any owner and therefore it needs to be passed along.[12] Yet in ancient Chinese culture, Mauss recounts how a gift is bound to the original owner.[13] Mauss also notices the surplus nature of gift-economy in ancient cultures, similar to Marion's "donating intuition" ("being given" in Husserl phenomenology as in the word *Gegebenheit*) understanding of gift.[14]

Method Applied Multiculturally: Semantic of Gift in Romans 12

This essay uses metaphor and its semantic domain, as found in Lakoff and Johnson's cognitive linguistics theory, to explain Romans 12.[15] Universal experiences do not necessarily lead to universal metaphors that express

---

a detailed study about grace and gift on Paul, see Barclay, *Paul and the Gift*.

9. Horner, *Rethinking God as Gift*, 9–11; Mauss, *The Gift*, 81.

10. Horner, *Rethinking God as Gift*, 10.

11. See Yeo, *Musing with Confucius and Paul*, chaps. 3–4; Levinas, *Otherwise Than Being*.

12. Mauss, *The Gift*, 22.

13. Mauss, *The Gift*, 81.

14. Marion, *Reduction and Donation*, 241, 305 (whose understanding of gift is not determined by being but by the new phenomenological horizon of the call). See the debate between Derrida and Marion on "donation" and "Gegebenheit" in Marion, "On the Gift," 56–78. See also Mauss, *The Gift*, discussion on 78–79.

15. Lakoff and Johnson, "Conceptual Metaphor in Everyday Language," 286–325, and *Metaphors We Live By*. See also Lakoff's extended theory in "The Contemporary Theory of Metaphor," 202–51.

the same figurative meaning.[16] A cognitive linguistic approach that takes cultural nuances and different linguistic cognitions into consideration becomes necessary and prudent. Moreover, since any language regarding God and gift is metaphorical, Derrida, in his discussion of gift, thinks that "the proper Name is never proper because it never makes present."[17] His dialogue partner, Marion, however, qualifies that, "By theology of absence . . . we mean not the non-presence of God, but the fact that the name that God is given, the name which gives God . . . serves to shield God from presence . . . and offers him precisely as an exception to presence."[18]

Grace understood through the vehicle "gift" could be established as a metonymy (substitute for the name of an attribute). Yet, the "is more" tenor of the "gift" metaphor is based on surplus and transcendence, as Marion explains that thought and predication are overwhelmed by excess, the "saturated phenomenon."[19] Gift as a metaphor indicates that we the language users are named and renamed by language all the time; as Marion writes, "The Name—it has to be dwelt in without saying it, but by *letting it say, name and call us*. The Name is not said, it calls."[20]

Indeed, the contextual exegesis of the words *charis* and *charisma* in Romans 12 shows that *charis* means "beauty, joy, and favor or kindness."[21] A grace is a divine gift that is a delight to behold. In many ancient societies, including the Sanskrit word *rah, ratih* carries the meaning of one's present that gives pleasure to another person.[22] The nuances of favor, kindness, and goodwill in the word "grace" are rooted in the Greco-Roman benefaction culture that is ingrained with the ethos of reciprocity; "a chain of obligation that makes equal demand on both the benefactor and the beneficiary."[23]

The literary context of Romans 12:6–8, as found in the outline of Romans chapters 12 and 13, spells out the vocation for the church based on God's mercies and the imitation of Christ, in order that the church's gifts can: 1) build up the Christian community (12:3–13 and 15–16); 2) edify life of the society (12:18–21); and 3) even transform the state (13:1–7). Jewett sees that this section of moral exhortation, 12:1—15:13, "sustains the missional

---

16. Kövecse, *Metaphor in Culture*, 131–160, on conceptual metaphors and their linguistic expression in different languages.
17. Marion, "In the Name," 45 (Derrida's response to Marion).
18. Marion, "In the Name," 37.
19. Marion, "On the Gift," 56.
20. Marion, "In the Name," 37 (emphasis mine).
21. Okorie, "Benefaction in Galatians," 1; Barclay, *Paul and the Gift*, 24–31.
22. Mauss, *The Gift*, 64.
23. Okorie, "Benefaction in Galatians," 3.

imperative of the letters as a whole,"[24] aiming to call Roman believers to cooperate with Paul in the gospel work so that all (Jews and gentiles) will be set right with God and one another, and all nations will be brought to proper worship of this God of grace (15:9-11).[25] Verses 4 through 5 deal with the charismatic gifts as the proper self-understanding, while verses 6-8 describe the exercise of these charismatic gifts as the transformative mission to the world—seen in the structure outline of chapters 12-13:

A—12:1-2: **Calling** based on God's mercies (and grace)

   B—12:3-13: Genuine <u>love (of being church)</u> and God's gifts

      C—12:14-21: Christian life and its impact on *social life*

      C'—13:1-7: Christian life and its transformation of *political life*

   B'—13:8-10: <u>Love</u> one another (<u>church</u>)

A'—13:11-14: **Living the call** by putting on Jesus

Paul knows that humanity cannot save itself (Romans 1-4), but the good news of Jesus is that everyone can receive the Spirit of God when they participate in the dying and rising with Christ (Rom 6-8; 1 Cor 12:12-13). The reception of God's Spirit has no room for pride and prejudice, for the Spirit is God's powerful presence gifted to believers, so that they can serve the body of Christ, the society, and the state. The word *charis* appears in Romans 12:3, according to Jewett, indicating Paul's charismatic authority in the gospel vocation, the same grace that is also given to the Roman congregations.[26]

To give a Christian vision to a society (vv. 4-5), Paul in verses 6-8 lists randomly without hierarchical structure (unlike 1 Cor 12-14: "first apostles, second prophets, third teachers...") the seven gifts of the Spirit—seven as the symbol of totality[27] in how God will transform a community via the democratic giving and cooperative working of these gifts in and through the Roman house churches—as each individual is given the grace of God (3:24; 5:2, 15, 17; 6:14; 12:6) and particular charismatic gift(s) (12:5-6):

1. The gift of **prophecy** in "analogy/ratio of faith" is mainly about forthtelling rather than foretelling, i.e., a critical teaching and bold preaching to warrant changes for a better future aligned with kingdom values.

---

24. Jewett, *Romans: A Commentary*, 724.
25. Jewett, *Romans: A Commentary*, 725.
26. Jewett, *Romans: A Commentary*, 738.
27. Regnstorf, "*hepta ktl.*," *TDNT* 2:628-633.

The gift of giving revelation (e.g., mystery of gentile mission and Israel's salvation, as in 11:25–26) and interpreting divine oracles (e.g., preaching and use of OT throughout Romans) for early Christians is mainly "pastoral rather than esoteric."[28] He who shares this gift will exercise it according to his ratio of faith and as the community weighs and tests (1 Cor 14:29; 1 Thess 5:19–22) the prophecy.[29]

2. The gift of **service** is a gift, according to Jewett, that provides a wide range of in-between services such as serving meals, contributing funds, meeting others' daily needs—without the implication of "menial subordination."[30] This gift serves to overcome a culture that is occupied with narcissistic individualism and self-absorbed freedom.

3. The gift of **teaching**, in early Christianity, is about expounding Christian tradition (Gal 1:12; 2 Thess 2:15; Col 2:7; Rom 6:17), interpreting Scripture (Rom 2:21), and communicating "general paraenesis (1 Cor 4:17; Col 1:28; 2:6–7; 3:16)."[31] The person exercising this gift needs the courage and wisdom to speak the truth rather than remain tone deaf to people crying out for God's justice and mercy in the neighborhood.

4. The gift of **exhortation** is offering medicinal and uplifting suggestions to "care of the souls," inclusive of one's "psychological, social, and intellectual needs" such as "the bereaved, the dying, the exiled, and the victims of injustice or misfortune."[32]

5. The gift of **philanthropy** is about sharing material or resources with dedication, or in Jewett's translation, "simplicity" or "purity of heart,"[33] rather than living in greed or accepting the cultural dogma of fear and lack.

6. The gift of **leadership** with diligence refers to visionary, thoughtful, and empowering presiders. Jewett points out that Paul uses a bland term, *ho proistamenos* ("presider," "pastoral supervisor," or even "administrator"), rather than technical ones like "bishop," "elder," or "patron."[34] Jewett explains that the giftedness of an administrator is

---

28. Jewett, *Romans: A Commentary*, 746.
29. Jewett, *Romans: A Commentary*, 747.
30. Jewett, *Romans: A Commentary*, 749.
31. Jewett, *Romans: A Commentary*, 750.
32. Jewett, *Romans: A Commentary*, 750.
33. Jewett, *Romans: A Commentary*, 752. See 2 Cor 11:3; Col 3:22.
34. Jewett, *Romans: A Commentary*, 752.

his or her "bureaucratic conscientiousness, efficiency, honest effort, goodwill, and vigor."[35]

7. The gift of cheerful **mercy** refers to the joy and empathy that glue the community together within and without in a society that is torn apart. The opposite of this gift is "merciless"; Jewett explains that the word is used in Romans 1:31, signaling "the reprobate mind."[36]

There are more than seven gifts of the Spirit (as different lists are given in 1 Cor 12–14 and Eph 4:11-12). All charismatic gifts have their origin in the mercies of God, and God has given *complete* charismatic gifts to the church for the world.

Cultural Critique: Paul's Understanding of "Gift" in the Greco-Roman Context

Paul's discourse about grace and gifts are part of the economic language that aims to offer a cultural critique of moving readers conceptually from debt, obligation, dependence to freedom, mutuality, and community. For example, the Roman patron-client culture on gift and gifting is based on merit, for gifts are earned, and generosity is measured by what one can produce. This exchange-economic reduces generosity to self-gain. Countering the Roman patronage and benefaction system of "selfish calculation . . . haughtiness,"[37] Paul exhorts followers of Christ to serve and share (12:7).

The gifts of the Spirit are not about virtues of self-cultivation; they are not about human achievement, as most Greco-Roman moral philosophies teach. Believers cannot earn a gift, but they can share it and use it to multiply its blessings to others. Paul's idea of gift is based on "God's mercies" (9:15, 18, 23; 11:30–31; 12:1; 15:9) that drive the following points against conventional ethics.

1. God's "given grace" (12:3) is over against charismatic boasting of exercising gifts of the Spirit for one's own glorification. Grace is a gift and not earned; so also apostolic vocation and *charisma* (charismatic gifts) that are all subsumed "under the structure of divine gift."[38]

---

35. Jewett, *Romans: A Commentary*, 753.
36. Jewett, *Romans: A Commentary*, 753.
37. Jewett, *Romans: A Commentary*, 752–53. See also Barclay, *Paul and the Gift*, 35–39.
38. Jewett, *Romans: A Commentary*, 738.

2. Paul is an advocate of "not high-minded" against the spiritual (12:3) and racial superiority (11:20, 25 specifically of gentile Christians over Jewish Christians) and super-heroism such as that of tyrants.

3. Paul teaches "sober-mindedness according to the measuring rod of faith" over against coercion and homogenization. Jewett sees Paul's sober-mindedness language as paralleling that of "mature civility and submission to law" of the Greek democracies (against oligarchy).[39] The word *metron* can mean measuring rod or the boundary of faith, i.e., one's made proper (right-wising) relationship with God (based on grace alone) that moderates one to accept one's limit (sinners fallen short of God's glory; Rom 3:23),[40] and "the norm that each person is provided in the appropriation of the grace of God, . . . a measuring rod that allows for differentiation."[41]

Grace, or gifts from God, have the same source but are given and received differently to individuals; thus, soberminded persons respect such differences, just as a body has different members that have different uses (12:4–5). The gifts of the Spirit are called *charismata*, rather than *pneumatika* as of 1 Corinthians 12:1–31 perhaps, as Jewett observes, to shift away "from the more spectacularly ecstatic manifestations such as glossolalia [of *pneumatika*] to the [*charismata's*] sober expressions of congregational leadership."[42]

Solidarity of a Christian assembly (*ekklēsia*) does not succumb to homogeneity; unity honors differences. Paul's theological critique targets the socio-political body of Roman society that is either highly segregated or homogenous. With regards to the charismatic gifts, Paul's emphases are: "each one" (*hekastos*, v. 3); "individually" (*to de kath heis*, v. 5); "one body" (*heni sōma*, v. 5) and "in Christ" (v. 5, *en Christōi*); "members one of another" (*allēlōn melē*, v. 5); "different" (*diaphora*, v. 6). The metaphorical "is" and "is not" work in the interanimation of God's bountiful grace and abundant mercy with gifts, as God's grace and mercy temper and reinforce charismatic gifts in the body of Christ, thus overcoming "the binary oppositions of served and servant, privileged and needy, insider and outsider. Excess directed toward mutuality undermines hierarchy."[43]

---

39. Jewett, *Romans: A Commentary*, 740.
40. Jewett, *Romans: A Commentary*, 740–41.
41. Jewett, *Romans: A Commentary*, 742.
42. Jewett, *Romans: A Commentary*, 745.
43. Webb, *The Gifting God*, 151.

Then the interplay of *charis* and *charisma* words, as well as the intertwining of grace and gift in Romans 12, is countercultural, demonstrating the "is more" meaning of the "gift" metaphor. While I do not agree with Jewett's exegesis of "the agape meal is law's fulfillment" in Romans 13:8 and his exegetical connecting of the Romans 12 charismatic gifts to the first-century Christian love feast,[44] I do think a theological understanding of the *agape* meal can explain gift- or *theos*-economy against exchange- or empire-economy. Exchange economy is based on lack that encourages greed in keeping one's gift, whereas Pauline economy is subversive in that it is based on: (1) God's grace that is surplus and unconditional; (2) God's mercies that promote thankful and reciprocal sharing; and (3) God's love that is relational and spontaneous in mutual honoring. This is "a theo-economics of giving, in which generosity is funded by an excess God . . . God gives abundantly, in order to create more giving, the goal of which is a mutuality born of excess but directed toward equality and justice."[45]

John Milbank proposes that the Christian *agape* has transformed the gift exchange but does not suppress gifting's social nature.[46] Celebratory, affective, spontaneous, and reciprocal natures of the Christian grace and gifts are the "is more" metaphorical meaning and are transformative for exchange-economy, which is based on zero-sum thinking. Theos-economy is based on surplus and gratuity in which sharing of divine gifts builds up the divine-human relationship as well as human-human relations.

Our World Today: Paul's Theology of Gift and the Economy of Grace

Contemporary philosophical debate about the metaphor of gift has greatly expanded the linguistic and cultural understanding of the vehicle, the tenor, and power of their interanimation for the production of meaning. For Paul, giving based on unconditional grace liberates one to give freely and cheerfully, creating a community's response-ability and spontaneity to be loving and generous without expecting any returns to oneself. Let me recapitulate a few markers or tenors of Paul's theology of gift below.

First, justice (*dikaiosynē*, or often less powerfully translated as "righteousness" in English) is conditioned by love that reorders a community, whether that community be the church, a society, or a nation. The modern

---

44. Jewett, *Romans: A Commentary*, 748, 751, 762, 777, 805, 807, 814–15; and Yeo, "Paul's Way of *Renren* in Romans 13:1–10," 473–77.

45. Webb, *The Gifting God*, 9.

46. Milbank, "Can a Gift Be Given?" 131.

discourse about justice and rights often overemphasizes actions, behavior and duty, to the point of leaving aside the formation of a person and the community. Justice and right are *not* only legal injunctions or prohibitions ("Thou shalt not . . .") and requirements ("do justly"). When Jesus teaches "love one another" as "the new commandment" (John 13:30)—which Paul also quotes in Romans 13:9–10—this *commandment* has its continuity with Leviticus 19:18 (the old commandment) in the necessity of "loving other" but also goes beyond (the "is more" of metaphor) the duty and legal aspect of loving others. Can love be commanded?—No, except that love is a gift; that is, "the commandment of love . . . is the voice of love itself."[47] Jesus in effect is saying, *to be just* is also essentially to be *a loving person*—be formed by God's love so much so that one just loves to love others. Without love, justice may be restricted to litigation and cold culture; with love and mercy, justice looks toward mutually edifying community and flourishing culture.

If love is the interpersonal relationship that forms *justly* who we are as human beings, and the mutual indebtedness of love is the basis of how we do justice to all people, then Paul says it well in Romans 13:8, "*owe* no one anything except to *love* one another." Love is the eternal "due or debt" one has to others. But how can this Pauline "indebtedness of love" not become trapped in the Nietzschean economy of a vicious cycle of exchange relations, whereby the giver serves the needs of the recipient, who in turn thanks the giver to assert his mastery and degrades the giver to the status of servitude?[48] This gets us to the next marker.

Second, for Paul, only the lubricants of freedom or voluntary reciprocity can make the wheel turn away from the crushing pressure of the Hegelian master-servant dialectic, as even in Christian community, such as in Romans 14 between the "weak and strong" believers, such dialectic could insidiously resurface. Using an economy vehicle, Paul's language of "debt" is neither about a necessary "repayment" to the gift of love one receives nor having an intent of remuneration, Paul's "debt" semantic is in fact a metaphor of critiquing the injustice of the Roman imperial taxation economy (Rom 13:6–8).[49] Though citizens ought to render tax to the empire still, it is the Christian-love "debt" that redefines the cultural economy of "taxation" into unconditional acceptance and honoring of each other by being fully present (the currency) in the household of faith (the mutual

---

47. Levenson, *The Love of God*, 188.
48. See Schrag, *God as Otherwise than Being*, 105.
49. See Jewett's discussion on tax protests and Roman tribute taxation in *Romans: A Commentary*, 798–803.

trust). Compulsion is subverted by voluntary co-participation and contribution of oneself to the whole community (the body).

Paul's understanding of gift is about the caring presence in a body, as embodied by the life of Christ. The ministry of gifting the world with God's encompassing love is modeled after Jesus, whose generosity gift (*charin*) makes him poor for our sake though he was rich (2 Cor 8:5),[50] therefore initiating a new economy that supplies resources for justice and compassion.[51]

The recipient's acknowledgment of gifts from others is not an elevation of one's status, but a thanksgiving response that magnifies the presence of God and his people. A gift giver does not expect a return in the grace-economy. There is no aporia (Derrida),[52] only *fuller re-presence* in the re-membership of the *agapic* event of the Cross. An *agapic* meal exhibits a sharing that expects no return; alms/charity giving needs no acknowledgment. Alms givers have the self-consciousness of thanksgiving out of which comes the moral obligation to be generous because of their fortune for the sake of justice (what is due to) for others.[53]

Third, God alone is the source of all gifts; thus, the rhetoric of his gift of grace and the charismatic gifts is "the rhetoric of excess, the (im)possibility of saying more, doing more, and giving more than exchange encourages or permits . . . The gift is exchange [or rather reciprocated] hyperbolized."[54] God is the giver, and the church is a community of givers who translate all these gifts and the isolated, broken individuals into a larger community reordered by the new economy of kingdom values. Jesus and Paul reject the empire market-economic solution to the problem of scarcity. In terms of basic necessities such as food, Jesus advocates for his disciples to give the crowd more than they need (Mark 5:26), and the disciples are asked to depend on the hospitality of others (Mark 6:8). The kingdom lifestyle of gratitude markedly is contrasted with the greed and anxiety of empire economy. The surplus of God's love and grace does not dissipate in the act of gifting; in fact, it will multiply as gifts are shared and passed along to others. The gifting God is evident in the generous gift; the Holy Spirit, as Paul

---

50. The gift of God, a pure gift of grace, is about God's love for his people, "the Lord set his love (*hašaq*) on you and chose you . . . the smallest (*me'aṭ*) of peoples" (Deut 7:7; also Gen 18:27, 16:8; Ps 22:7)—self-effacement of the Israelites in contrast to the self-aggrandizement of non-Israelite rulers. See Levenson, *The Love of God*, 47.

51. See Webb, *The Gifting God*, 152 regarding Paul's using "economic metaphors for God, calling the gospel a priceless treasure and the Spirit the down payment (1:22) of God's grace."

52. Derrida, *Given Time*, 27–28.

53. Mauss, *The Gift*, 23.

54. Webb, *The Gifting God*, 8.

writes, "God's love has been poured into your hearts through the Holy Spirit that has been given to us (Rom 5:5). The gifting of the Spirit to creation and humanity is the Gift—God's self.

In the Pauline theology of gift, a church community of gifting promotes more givers to engage in gracious acts of giving, and ultimately reorders the world by the growing presence of God, thus living in and with and for one another in equality and solidarity and presence. God's gifts are transcendent; thus, *agape*/love is the "is more" metaphor of all good gifts of God (James 1:17). Against the worldly context of luck, chance, and accident, Paul sees God's re-ordering the world, a sacramental reenactment of God's grace proleptically realized in the "now" (the present), the eschatological banquet. Exercising the gifts of the Holy Spirit is both a loss and a return to the enlarging self, as the church's gifts transform and expand the community and the world.

Conclusion:
Cross-cultural Metaphoric Imagination of Gifting

The gift I received from Dr. Jewett has been the staying power of cross-cultural, intertextual, and interdisciplinary biblical interpretation. Let me conclude with a brief biblical Chinese imagination and reception of gift.

In archaic societies, the ritual of life in the form of gifting is to maintain human solidarity (Mauss's thesis) and make humanity fully human (Confucius's thesis), unity or harmony in diversity. While Confucian and Pauline thought are not the same, they can complement each other. The self does not suffer from denial or lack in gifting from the Pauline perspective; in fact, the self discovers and expands itself in and through its gifting to others. This is the true self, which Confucius calls it *ren ren* ("a loving person" or "fully humane being")—similar to the Pauline notion of setting a proper or right relation with someone else in a covenantal sense (rather than declared as righteous in the forensic sense).[55] Paul's theology goes farther than Confucian anthropology. Yet, Confucian ethics spell out Pauline theology: To be a *ren ren* is to express oneself in loving action and to participate in the holy as the dimension of all truly human existence. To be a *ren ren* is to be courteous, diligent, loyal, brave, and kind (Analects 13:19, 14:5, 17:6)—though different from the charismatic gifts listed in Romans 12—nevertheless as actualized in the ritual of participating in public life. The true and faithful society is one in which human beings treat each other as human (*ren* or humane) or, to be more specific in the Confucian understanding, one in

---

55. See Louw and Nida, *Greek-English Lexicon Semantic Domain*, 34.46.

which life is lived according to the obligations and privileges of *li* (law as rule of life), out of loyalty or love (*zhong, hesed*) and respect (*jing,* honor). As Samuel E. Balentine likewise argues, regarding Jewish and Christian traditions, that "Priestly ministry seeks to build communities of faith in order that communities of faith may *build worlds* where justice, no less than piety, orders life in accord with the Creator's design."[56]

God's gifts to humanity come as both surprise (a call) and task (an imperative). And God's gifts that are "without condition" or "free" do not mean that the gifts are worthless and the recipients are without obligation. Rather, gift/ing is a paradoxical metaphor of realizing the gift of love for its own sake, thus conditioning recipients to be at ease (*wu-wei*, effortlessly) in the reception and further gifting of gifts. Confucius says, "Is *ren* really so far away? No sooner do I desire *ren* than it is here" (Analects 7:30). In other words, the regulation (*jie*) and restrained (*yue*) by *li* (ritualizing) and *yue* (aesthetic delight) describes the *wu-wei* fashion of virtue-cultivation (in this case, "gifting") that is neither forced nor neglected.[57]

To summarize the Pauline thesis in the language of Trinitarian theology, one can say that God (and therefore the people of God) is the Giver (the Father), the Gift/given One (the Son), and the Gifting (the Holy Spirit) who creates and transforms the world through the blessed gifts of the church. Who God is and "God's giving will shape how [the followers of Christ] give to others."[58] God is as God gives, and God gives God's self, the very act of *agape*, which is cruciform and christological. The gift of *agape* to the world subverts the empire logic of domination and violence. Paul describes metaphorically this God's gifting event: "God did not withhold his own Son, but gave him up for us all; will he not with him also give us everything else?" (Rom 8:32).

We shall dearly miss Bob Jewett, a remarkable teacher and a faithful friend, a Christ-like human being whose gift to us has simply been unconditional and graceful, or in one word—his favorite NT word—*agapic*.

Bibliography

(* For Further Reading)

Aristotle. *Rhetoric; Poetics*. Translated by Rhys Roberts and Ingram Bywater. New York: Modern Library, 1984.

---

56. Balentine, *Torah's Vision of Worship*, 176.
57. Slingerland, *Effortless Action*, 70–75.
58. Webb, *The Gifting God*, 4.

Balentine, Samuel E. *Torah's Vision of Worship*. Overtures to Biblical Theology. Minneapolis: Fortress, 1999.
*Barclay, John M. G. *Paul and the Gift*. Grand Rapids: Eerdmans, 2015.
*Black, Max. "Metaphor." In *Philosophical Perspectives as Metaphor*, edited by Mark Johnson, 63–82. Minneapolis: University of Minnesota Press, 1981.
———. "More about Metaphor." *Dialectica* 31 (1977) 431–57.
Brockhaus, Ulrich. *Charisma und Amt. Die paulinische Charismenlehre auf dem Hintergrund der frühchristlichen Gemeindefunktionen*. Wissenschaftliche Taschenbücher 8. Wuppertal: Brockhaus, 1972.
de Mendoza, F. J. Ruiz, and M. S. Peña. "Conceptual Interaction, Cognitive Operations, and Projection Spaces." In *Cognitive Linguistics: Internal Dynamics and Interdisciplinary Interaction*, edited by F. J. Ruiz de Mendoza and M. S. Peña, 254–80. Berlin: Mouton de Gruyter, 2005.
Derrida, Jacques. *Given Time: 1. Counterfeit Money*. Translated by Peggy Kamuf. Chicago: University of Chicago Press, 1992.
*Horner, Robyn. *Rethinking God as Gift: Marion, Derrida, and the Limits of Phenomenology*. Perspectives in Continental Philosophy 19. New York: Fordham University Press, 2001.
*Jewett, Robert. *Romans: A Commentary*. Hermeneia. Minneapolis: Fortress, 2007.
Kövecses, Zoltán. *Metaphor in Culture: Universality and Variation*. Cambridge: Cambridge University Press, 2005.
———. "Recent Developments in Metaphor Theory: Are the New Views Rival Ones?" In *Metaphor and Metonymy Revisited: Beyond the Contemporary Theory of Metaphor*, edited by Francisco Gonzálvez-García et al., 11–25. Amsterdam: Benjamins, 2013.
Lakoff, George. "The Contemporary Theory of Metaphor." In *Metaphor and Thought*, edited by Andrew Ortony, 202–51. 2nd ed. Cambridge: Cambridge University Press, 1993.
Lakoff, George, and Mark Johnson. "Conceptual Metaphor in Everyday Language." In *Philosophical Perspectives on Metaphor*, edited by Mark Johnson, 286–325. Minneapolis: University of Minnesota Press, 1981.
*———. *Metaphors We Live By*. Chicago: The University of Chicago Press, 1993.
Levenson, Jon D. *The Love of God: Divine Gift, Human Gratitude, and Mutual Faithfulness in Judaism*. Princeton: Princeton University Press, 2016.
Levinas, Emmanuel. *Otherwise Than Being or Beyond Essence*. Translated by Alphonso Lingis. The Hague: Nijhoff, 1981.
Louw, Johannes P., Eugene A. Nida. *Greek-English Lexicon of the New Testament Based on Semantic Domains*. 2nd ed. Vol. 1: *Introduction and Domains*; Vol. 2: *Indices*. Minneapolis: Fortress, 1988.
Marion, Jean-Luc. "In the Name: How to Avoid Speaking of 'Negative Theology.'" In *God, the Gift, and Postmodernism*, edited by John D. Caputo and Michael J. Scanlon, 20–53. Bloomington: Indiana University Press, 1999.
*———. "On the Gift: A Discussion between Jacques Derrida and Jean-Luc Marion." In *God, the Gift, and Postmodernism*, edited by John D. Caputo and Michael J. Scanlon, 54–78. Indiana Series in the Philosophy of Religion. Bloomington: Indiana University Press, 1999.
———. *Reduction and Givenness [sic: Donation]: Investigations of Husserl, Heidegger, and Phenomenology*. Translated by Thomas A. Carlson. Evanston, IL: Northwestern University Press, 1998.

Mauss, Marcel. *The Gift: The Form and Reason for Exchange in Archaic Societies*. Translated by Ian Cunnison. London: Routledge, 1990.

Milbank, John. "Can a Gift Be Given?" In *Rethinking Metaphysics*, edited by L. Gregory Jones and Stephen E. Fowl, 119–61. Directions in Modern Theology. Oxford: Blackwell, 1995.

Okorie, Ferdinand Ikenna. "Benefaction in Galatians: An Analysis of Paul's Language of God's Favor in its Greco-Roman Context." PhD diss., Loyola University Chicago, 2018.

Regnstorf, Karl Heinrich. "*hepta ktl.*" *Theological Dictionary of the New Testament* [*TDNT*], edited by Gerhard Kittel, translated by G. W. Bromiley, 2:628–33. 10 vols. Grand Rapids: Eerdmans, 1965.

Richards, I. A. *The Philosophy of Rhetoric*. The Mary Flexner Lectures on the Humanities, 1936. Oxford: Oxford University Press, 1965.

Ricoeur, Paul. *Interpretation Theory: Discourse and the Surplus of Meaning*. Fort Worth: Texas Christian University Press, 1976.

———. *The Rule of Metaphor: Multi-disciplinary Studies of the Creation of Meaning in Language*. Translated by Robert Czerny, with Kathleen McLaughlin and John Costello. London: Routledge & Kegan Paul, 1978.

Schrag, Calvin O. *God as Otherwise Than Being: Toward a Semantics of the Gift*. Northwestern University Studies in Phenomenology & Existential Philosophy. Evanston, IL: Northwestern University Press, 2002.

Slingerland, Edward. *Effortless Action: Wu-wei as Conceptual Metaphor and Spiritual Ideal in Early China*. Oxford: Oxford University Press, 2003.

Soskice, Janet Martin. *Metaphor and Religious Language*. Oxford: Clarendon, 1987.

*Webb, Stephen H. *The Gifting God: A Trinitarian Ethics of Excess*. Oxford: Oxford University Press, 1996.

Yeo, K. K. *Musing with Confucius and Paul: Toward a Chinese Christian Theology*. Eugene, OR: Cascade Books, 2008.

———. "Paul's Way of *Renren* in Romans 13:1–10." In *From Rome to Beijing: Symposia on Robert Jewett's Hermeneia Commentary on Romans*, edited by K. K. Yeo, 469–79. Lincoln, NE: Kairos Studies, 2013.

———. *Rhetorical Interaction in 1 Corinthians 8 and 10: A Formal Analysis With Preliminary Suggestions for a Chinese, Cross-Cultural Hermeneutic*. Biblical Interpretation Series 9. Leiden: Brill, 1995.

Study Questions

1. Why do you think Paul interplays *charis* (grace) and *charisma* (gift) in Romans 12? And what are the implications of this interplay to the believers in Rome?

2. How would your understanding of gift or present help you appreciate Paul's ideas of grace and gifts of the Holy Spirit?

3. How can a biblical understanding of God's grace and gift be helpful to a modern market economy of exchange?

11

The Hermeneutic of Love, Honor, and Hospitality

Redefining Relationships in Romans 12–13

ZAKALI SHOHE

Abstract

THE BELIEVERS' RESPONSIBILITIES AND participation play an important part in the Pauline epistles, especially in Romans. Paul emphasizes the responsibilities of believers, as members of the believing community and of the larger society. Such an emphasis demands a need for redefining relationships. To this end, this essay explores the hermeneutic of love, honor, and hospitality in the context of relationships in Romans 12–13.

Introduction

The idea that believers in Christ continue to belong to the world and participate in the public and private spheres is conspicuous in the Epistle to the Romans, especially the notion of identifying the roles of believers and the restorative approaches to building relationships, which are mentioned in Romans 12–13. The Epistle to the Romans reflects the cultural ethic of honor and the imperial ideologies and, therefore, the need to read behind the text and in between the lines to identify the language and ideology of power. Honor and shame are important socio-political classifications in first-century Rome, and their presence in Paul's letter to the Romans has been underrated. As such, it is important to bear in mind the cultural perspectives in exploring the instructions of Paul in Romans 12–13, as they offer a richer understanding of Paul's exhortations and the gospel about Christ, a point I have also argued in my recent work on Romans.[1] There are also two things in this essay that have continued to be in the background of my thinking; one is Robert Jewett, and the other is the Naga context. In this essay, I am exploring Romans 12–13 so that it is possible to further develop a conversation between Paul and the Naga context.

An important work along this line of interpretation that I am intrigued by is the contribution of Robert Jewett on Paul's Epistle to the Romans.[2] By employing historical-critical approaches, as well as the historical-critical analysis of honor, shame, and the imperial systems in the Greco-Roman world, Jewett extensively analyzes and interprets Paul's Epistle to the Romans. Throughout his work, Jewett demonstrates the eschatological reversal of shame that Paul presents through the gospel of the crucified Christ, in which Jews and gentiles stand on common ground. Jewett highlights the social elements of Paul's gospel to the Roman churches in Romans 12–13. For example, in his interpretation of Romans 12:16, he interprets Paul's exhortation to believers not to be wise in their conceits and to avoid unnecessary superiority as "an expression of the counter-cultural social reality in Christ."[3]

This essay is in line with Jewett in that it explores Romans 12–13 from cultural perspectives of honor. That said, the essay further explores the hermeneutic of love, honor, and hospitality in the context of relationships. Relationships in Roman and Greek society depended on the honor-shame nexus. Giving and receiving honor was an important aspect, and it also determined the place of an individual in society. The honor system also was connected to the practice of gift-giving, which was both public and private.

Likewise, the Naga society, not unlike the Roman time, is confronted by relationships that are defined by social status, honor, and a gift-giving system. Nagaland (a state in northeastern India) is a land of diverse ethnic communities with a varied cultural heritage, traditions, and a community life that plays an important role. In traditional society, the social status and place of the Nagas depended on the ability of a person to provide feasts. These were regarded as "feasts of merit." The feasts were ranked in importance and each feast led to a stage in social ranking.[4] In traditional Naga society, a man did not gain social prestige and status by possessing wealth and accumulating it for his family; he did so only by spending it

---

1. Shohe, *Redefining Relationships in Romans*.
2. Jewett, *Romans: A Commentary*.
3. Jewett, *Romans: A Commentary*, 771.
4. For the feast of merit, refer to Odyuo, "The Various Aspects of Naga Art," 15–16; Luithui, "Naga: A People Struggling for Self-Determination."

for the benefit of the community in return for honor, social prestige, and status.[5] In the present Naga society, the practice of the feast of merit is not explicitly visible, but the hosting of community feasts by well-to-do individuals and families still plays an important part. By hosting such feasts and sharing their wealth with their respective communities, they gain honor and prestige in society. It is not mandatory, but the practice of sharing with the community is tied to honor and status.

As such, within the context of cultural ethics and imperial ideologies, this essay interprets the instructions of Paul in Romans 12–13. First, the essay briefly analyzes the privileged, the honor system, and the reciprocity ethic in the Greco-Roman world. Second, the essay attempts an interpretation of Romans 12–13. Third, it seeks to articulate a hermeneutic that allows for an understanding that takes into account diverse social statuses, cultures, and ethnic people groups.

The Privileged, Honor System, and Reciprocity Ethic in the Greco-Roman World

The Roman law divided society into higher and lower status, i.e., the *honestiores* and *humiliores*.[6] The senators, the equestrians, and the decurions[7] were three elite groups comprised of a small segment of the population of the Roman Empire. Below the elite group were the Plebeians, the free average-working citizens of Rome.[8] At the bottom of Roman society were the slaves. The slaves in Roman law were classified as "speaking tools" (*instrumentum vocale*) that were at the mercy and disposal of the master.[9] Roman society defined the place of its citizens and strangers by rank and status.

Roman society took care to identify social status and legal privileges. The privileged group enjoyed legal privileges. The source of legal privilege was honor and prestige, which in Roman society was *Dignitas*.[10] Status was also visible in their clothing. The visibility of status consciousness was primarily seen in two areas of social life, i.e., the theatres and the public

---

5. Fürer-Haimendorf has done extensive study on some of the tribes in Nagaland (*Naked Nagas*, 101).

6. See Garnsey, *Social Status and Legal Privilege*, 221–22, 235; Garnsey and Saller, *The Roman Empire*, 136. On the rank and social status in Rome, see also Winter, "Roman Law and Society in Romans 12–15," 76–77.

7. See Garnsey and Saller, *The Roman Empire*, 136–37.

8. Winter, "Roman Law and Society in Romans 12–15," 76–77.

9. Garnsey and Saller, *The Roman Empire*, 139.

10. Garnsey, *Social Status and Legal Privilege*, 258–62.

banquets and private dinners.[11] Connected to social status was the honor system that was widely practiced. The cultural values of honor and shame were pivotal in the Mediterranean world.[12] The system of honor was widely operated in Greco-Roman society. An individual was recognized in relation to society or a group, and their place was determined either by honor or by shame within social standards. Honor was desired not only by the rich and powerful, but also by all individuals. It was possible for any individual to make claims to honor; however, its recognition was according to the standards within the community.[13] In Roman society, an individual or the community owed their benefactor gratitude and reciprocity in either material goods or by giving respect and honor.

The honor system also was connected to the practice of gift-giving that was common in the ancient Mediterranean world. The practice of the exchange of gifts is a universal phenomenon indicating a sense of obligation. This practice is exercised both in the public and the private realm. Within the public realm was the practice of civic euergetism or benefaction, which was a Greek system that was inducted into Roman society.[14] The other social system connected to gift-giving was the patronage system commonly practiced in Roman society. In this practice, those from the upper strata of society would develop a patron-client relationship with those from the lower strata of the society.[15] The practice of gift-giving invited reciprocity and encouraged social bonding.

Thus, within the context of the privileged and cultural ethics, this essay interprets Paul's ethical instructions to believers in Romans 12–13.

Interpretation of Romans 12–13

In recent years, there have been a number of studies focusing on reading Paul within the context of the Roman Empire.[16] However, even before recent stud-

11. See Winter, "Roman Law and Society in Romans 12–15," 77–78; Garnsey and Saller, *The Roman Empire*, 139.

12. Crook, "Honor, Shame and Social Status Revisited," 591. For details, see Barton, *Roman Honor*.

13. Oakes, *Reading Romans in Pompeii*, 33. See also to Moxnes, "Honor and Righteousness in Rome," 63.

14. See Elliott, "Patronage and Clientage," 151; Barclay, *Paul and the Gift*, 33–35; Elliott, "Political Paul and the Social Context of Romans 12–13," 4–5.

15. Elliott, "Patronage and Clientage," 148–49.

16. A few works that I had access to are Elliott, *Arrogance of the Nations*; idem, *Liberating Paul*; Horsley, *Paul and the Roman Imperial Order*; idem, *Paul and Empire*; Shohe, *Redefining Relationships in Romans*.

ies on reading Paul within the context of imperial ideology, Adolf Deissmann noted the presence of imperial ideology in Paul's epistles, referring to it as "a silent protest."[17] Yet, today, scholars are not assuming "a silent protest," but are obvious in pointing to the political Roman ideologies, languages, and anti/counter-imperial overtones in Paul's texts.[18] These works read Paul and his gospel about Christ in the context of imperial ideology. Warren Carter moves beyond the interpretation of Romans, especially Romans 12–13, as a political strategy and stresses the need for alternative communities that differ from "the indebtedness and dependency of patron-client relations, from the empire's hierarchy and domination, and the execution of military retaliation."[19] The need for alternative communities is a welcome response to the reality of the Roman establishment and ideology in Pauline writings. However, I agree with Spencer Elliott[20]—his observation that the proposal for alternative communities should not be overemphasized to give the impression that communities were founded specifically as alternatives to Roman establishments *and* his claim that we forget the larger oppositions to the communities of the Mediterranean world.

The over-emphasis on Paul and the imperial system—or the interpretation of Paul within the imperial ideology as the primary purpose of Paul's message in Romans or even in Romans 12–13—can result in a biased interpretation of Paul's ethical instructions. Nevertheless, we cannot deny that Paul framed the life of the community by transforming the system, and also the cultural ethic of honor and shame[21] that existed during his time, by redefining communities and relationships. This was also demonstrated by Jackson Wu, who pointed out the need to be sensitive to portions of Romans and read it with a "new cultural lens."[22] Therefore, in the context of redefining relationships, we will briefly look into three spheres of the believer's life in Romans 12–13: the individual sphere (12:1–2), the community sphere (12:3–13), and the social and civil sphere (12:14–21; 13:1–10).

Individual Sphere: Living, Holy and Acceptable

New Testament exegetes agree that Paul's exhortation to individual believers in Romans 12:1–2 sets the tone for Paul's ethical teachings in Romans

17. Deissmann, *Light from the Ancient East*, 242–78 (quotation from 259).
18. Lopez, *Apostle to the Conquered*, 8.
19. Carter, *Roman Empire and the New Testament*, 21.
20. Elliott, "Political Paul and the Social Context in Romans 12–15," 2.
21. So also Elliott, "Political Paul and the Social Context in Romans 12–15," 2–3.
22. Wu, *Reading Romans with Eastern Eyes*, 5.

12–15.²³ Paul exhorts believers concerning a life acceptable to God. Spiritual renewal and transformation begin with an individual member; transformation is supposed to take root in an individual's inner being by the "renewing of the mind." The Greek word *anakainōsei* (renewing, Rom 12:2) means "becoming new and different" or "renewal" (cf. Col 3:1; Eph 4:23). The cultic and sacrificial ritual was common in the ancient world. Hence, there is a broad consensus that Paul takes up the language of sacrifice from the ancient world, redefines the cultic and sacrificial understanding, and uses it as a metaphor for a believer's relationship with God.²⁴

Three characteristics of sacrifice mentioned in the text are *zōsan* ("living"), *hagian* ("holy"), and *euareston* ("acceptable or well-pleasing") (Rom 12:1). We see a shift from ritual activity in the temple, shrines, or synagogues to a non-ritual relationship of everyday life activities of believers.²⁵ Hence, the attribute "living" fits the shift Paul gives to the ritual language in the understanding of individual beings as living sacrifices. The attribute "holy" as a cultic concept is dedicated to God and his service, while of persons it stands for humans consecrated to God.²⁶ It describes the sacrifice that is not profane, but solely set apart for the glory of God, i.e., believers as living sacrifice. The phrase "pleasing to God" also appears in the LXX (Wis 4:10; 9:10), and it is a *Koine* expression that depicts acting according to divine will.²⁷ Believers as living and holy sacrifices are also expected to be acceptable in the sight of God.

Paul concludes his call to be a living, holy, and acceptable sacrifice with a threefold apposition "good and acceptable and perfect" (Rom 12:2; NRSV). Paul incorporates the threefold apposition from concepts of Greco-Roman and Jewish ethics. However, within the context of Romans 12:1–2, there is a transformative use of Greco-Roman and Jewish concepts.²⁸ The threefold category implies that every ethical category calls for transformation, and

---

23. Käsemann asserts that Romans 12:1–2 provides the main theme (*Commentary on Romans*, 323); Cranfield takes the two verses as the introduction to the whole section (*Critical and Exegetical Commentary*, 595); for Dunn, it is the summary to the whole section (*Romans 9–16*, 707).

24. See, BDAG, 628; Dunn, *Romans 9–16*, 709. For some, Paul follows the tradition in Greek religion, while others explain the language of sacrifice in Romans 12 in line with his Pharisaic background (refer to Jewett, *Romans: A Commentary*, 727.

25. So also Dunn, *Romans 9–16*, 716.

26. As a cultic concept, it is also connected to the city of Jerusalem (2 Esd 21; 1 Macc 2:7; Matt 4:5; 24:15; 27:53; Acts 6:13; 21:28; Rev 11:2). Of persons: e.g., Prophets (Luke 1:70; Acts 3:21; 2 Pet 3:2); John the Baptist (Mark 6:20); Apostles (Eph 3:5); Israel (Isa 62:12); Christians (Rom 1:7; 1 Pet 1:16). BDAG, 9.

27. Foerster, "*Euarestos*," *TDNT*, 1:456–57.

28. Also, Jewett, *Romans: A Commentary*, 734.

the basis for the transformation are the "mercies of God" and the "renewal of the mind" that are revealed in Christ.[29] Paul applies cultic language in presenting believers as living, holy, and acceptable in their relationship with God and with members of the believing community.

Community Sphere: Christ-Believing Community

In Romans 12:3–13, Paul describes the corporate identity of the Christ-believing community. Paul's usage of the virtue *sophronein* ("sober-minded," "think soberly," 12:3) has a classical sense and is close to political usage. Halvor Moxnes suggests that Paul appears comfortable with the Hellenistic use of *sophrosyne* ("soundness of mind," "self-control") in Romans 12. As such, his exhortation to believers not to think highly of themselves is directed to "a total system of relations between individuals of unequal status."[30] In Romans 12:3, it supports the communal meaning, especially when used in connection with the body metaphor in Romans 12:4–5.[31] Paul touches the pride and superior social hierarchy and the privilege that were prevalent in Roman society. As a counter-teaching to the social superiors and inferiors in Roman social hierarchy, Paul uses the metaphor of a body as a single entity with diverse interdependent parts (Rom 12:6–8, 1 Cor 12). Paul reminds Roman believers that their gifts as individuals are not measured according to social hierarchy and status but are measured through faith; he also reminds them that their gifts should be used for building and transforming the community. Although for Roman society, social status defined one's place in society, yet Paul moves beyond social hierarchies and redefines relationships in believers' allegiance to God.

In contrast to the Roman practice of conflict and enmity, Paul exhorts Roman believers in Christ on handling conflicts and adversaries in Romans 12:9–13. He calls for love, to honor one another, and to practice hospitality. Paul addresses the believers in Christ in Rome to honor one another. The Greek word *proēgoumenoi* ("take the lead" or "go ahead," 12:10) means to go before others to show the way. Still, occasionally it is also translated in some versions like Old Latin, Vulgate, Syriac, and Armenian as "outdo." Concerning honor, these versions translate the Greek phrase *tētimē allēlous proēgoumenoi* meaning "outdo one another in showing respect" (12:10).[32]

---

29. Jewett, *Romans: A Commentary*, 735. Other Pauline texts are 1 Cor 1:28; 13:10; 14:20.

30. Moxnes, "Quest for Honor," 222.

31. Moxnes, "Quest for Honor," 221.

32. BDAG, 706. For "outdo," also refer to Moxnes, "Honor and Righteousness in

Thus, Paul in Romans 12:10 is urging believers in Christ to "take the lead" in honoring one another at all times without expecting anything in return. Paul reverses the honor system of Roman society with a call to show honor rather than to expect honor from others,[33] and he departs from the competitive spirit attached with the honor system.[34]

Paul exhorts Roman believers to honor one another in love. He employs the Greek word *philadelphia* ("brotherly love," 12:10) referring to sisterly/brotherly love, a love given without expecting anything in return. Robert Jewett regards it as a genuine love that "manifests itself in the face of congregational conflict and political adversity"[35] In this imperative to the believing community "to take the lead" to honor one another, Paul moves beyond the honor system in Greco-Roman society and redirects honor to the level of taking initiative in love regardless of status. The basis for growing together as a believing community is love. With the use of an attribute of love, i.e., *anypokritos* ("genuine," "un-assumed"; Rom 12:9), Paul calls for sincere love, a love without hypocrisy (cf. 2 Cor 6:6; Rom 13:10; Matt 24:12).

Paul ends his ethical teaching within the community of the believers in Christ with the notion of hospitality. Two Greek words in the New Testament are used for hospitality. One is *philoxenia*,[36] which means "love of a stranger." The Greek word *philo* ("loving," "fond of") is an expression of love, and *xenos* ("foreigner," "outsider") refers to a "stranger" or "someone we have no knowledge of." Accordingly, I would translate it as "love of a stranger." The other Greek word in the New Testament for hospitality is *xenodocheo* ("to receive a stranger"; 1 Tim 5:10). As mentioned earlier, *xenos* means "stranger" and *dechomai* means "receive," "accept," "take with hand" or "embrace." In Romans 12:13, Paul calls believers to "pursue hospitality" by using the Greek words *philoxinian diō kontes* ("given to hospitality"; 12:13).[37] As seen from the two Greek words used for "hospitality" in the New Testament, hospitality is not only being nice to people we know, but also it means making space for strangers and taking by the hand and embracing the Other into our community. Robert Jewett rightly argues that there is no further elaboration on "hospitality to strangers" because the ethic of love is elaborated in Romans 12. So, for Jewett,

---

Rome," 71.

33. So also Oakes, *Reading Romans in Pompeii*, 110; Elliott, "Political Paul and the Social Context of Romans 12–13," 8.

34. Moxnes, "Honor and Righteousness in Rome," 75.

35. Jewett, *Romans: A Commentary*, 760.

36. This word is used in Rom 12:13; 1 Tim 3:2; Titus 1:8; Heb 13:2; 1 Pet 4:9.

37. Generally, *philoxinia* is translated as "hospitality." See Dunn, *Romans 9–16*, 743; Jewett, *Romans: A Commentary*, 765; Fitzmyer, *Romans*, 655.

hospitality is already encompassed in Paul's description of the love ethic.[38] In line with Jewett, I would interpret Paul's call to pursue hospitality in Romans 12:13 within the context of the love ethic as a call to love strangers as if they were siblings in a family.

In the wider Roman culture—where status, wealth, birth, and positions decided one's place in society—Paul calls on the community of believers in Christ by using the metaphor of a body, encouraging sober-thinking and functioning of gifts and responsibilities by practicing love, honor, and hospitality toward one another.

Social and Civil Sphere

The social and civil sphere is indicated in Romans 12:14–21 and 13:1–10. In Romans 12:14–21, Paul addresses Roman believers in their relationship with the wider world. Paul calls for a redefinition of relationships based on harmony and uplifting of one another. Bruce Winter provides an interpretation of Romans 12:14–21 as a counter-cultural response to strife and jealousy in relationships among members within Roman society. Against class and status behaviors and practices, in Romans 12, Paul brings up the will of God for his people and calls believers to the will of God.[39] Believers in Christ are encouraged to bless even those who persecute them (Rom 12:14) and to live peaceably with all by extending good works and hospitality to those outside the boundary of family and community (Rom 12:17–21). Paul's teaching on right living and building relationships with the outside world is broadened in Romans 13:8–10 through the ethic of love.

Paul then specifies his exhortation toward the privileged and the governing authorities in Romans 13:1–7. There are two areas in which the role of the governing authorities is mentioned in Romans 13:1–4: first, they are ordained by God to carry out their responsibilities in keeping law and order; second, they have an obligation to praise those who carry out good works. Paul further outlines the requirements of believers in Christ toward the governing authorities in Romans 13:5–7; to be subject to the governing authorities, for they are ambassadors of God.

Paul sums up the section in Romans 13:7 by laying before his readers a few obligations. The obligations before believers are *phoron* ("tribute"), *telos* ("taxes"), *phobon* ("fear"), and *timēn* ("honor"). Paul exhorts believers to pay tribute to those who are entitled to get tribute. Similarly, in Luke,

---

38. Jewett, *Romans: A Commentary*, 765.

39. Winter, "Roman Law and Society in Romans 12–15," 80–81.

there also are references to paying tribute to Caesar (Luke 20:22; 23:2).[40] Taxes were levied on income, services, and goods, and it was an important source of revenue within the Roman Empire.[41] Fear refers to "fear" or "terror" (1 Pet 3:14). It is also translated as "reverence" and "respect" (Phil 2:12).[42] The Greek word *timē* ("honor"), in the context of selling and buying, means "price" or "value" (Matt 27:9; Acts 4:34; 19:19). It can also mean showing of honor or reverence as an action (Rom 12:10; 1 Tim 6:1) or, as in Romans 13:7, it can refer to the respect one enjoys and honor as a possession (cf. 1 Pet 2:7; 1 Cor 12:24; Rev 4:9).[43] Paul did not want believers in Christ to attract the attention of Roman authorities by denying obligations due to them in the form of tax, honor, tribute, and fear. The Jews, because of their ancestral religion, had special privileges to practice their ancestral customs, which included temple tax to be sent to Jerusalem. Yet, Paul's redefinition of the people of God could no longer claim political privileges.[44] It is therefore likely that Paul brings his teachings on submitting to the official power and governing authorities.

Redefining relationships in individual, communal, social, and civil spheres also helps in understanding Paul's emphasis on the ethical values of love, honor, and hospitality.

The Hermeneutic of Love, Honor, and Hospitality in the Context of Redefining Relationships

It is important at this point to develop a hermeneutic of love, honor, and hospitality because the Pauline community at Rome needed to redefine relationships on the grounds that: it was a community of Jews and gentiles; believers in Christ who were expelled during the time of Claudius had recently returned;[45] the faith community also was existing within the context of Roman imperial ideologies and cultural ethics. Paul calls believers in Christ in Rome to do God's will in a way that moves beyond social status, class, prevalent ideologies, cultures, and ethnic groups. A call to move beyond the prevalent social-cultural

---

40. Other references are 1 Macc 10:31; 11:35; Josephus, *Ant.* 12.141. See BDAG, 811–12.

41. de Ligt, *Fairs and Markets in the Roman Empire*, 169.

42. BDAG, 863–64.

43. BDAG, 817–18.

44. Dunn discusses it in *Romans 9–16*, 769.

45. For details of the historical context of Romans, refer to Shohe, *Acceptance Motif in Paul*.

and political ideologies is grounded in "love, honor and hospitality."[46] It is a call to create "space" for diverse identities and participation that overlaps in the context of community formation.

The social obligations believers in Christ are called to within Roman society or their patron within the social context become subordinate to the pressing debt of love within the believing community.[47] Through the emphasis on the need to practice brotherly/sisterly love, Roman believers in Christ are reminded of the importance of loving God and doing his will and also loving one another and living peaceably among themselves and with the broader society. Paul is referring to a love that transforms and builds up one another, a love that accepts the Other, a love that makes space for the Other, a love that gives without expecting anything in return, and a love that guarantees a peaceful environment (Rom 12:9–10; 13:9–10).

Further, Paul exhorts believers in Christ to take the lead in honoring one another. Believers in any context or situation, when it comes to honor, are to esteem the Other fellow being more highly than himself/herself. In valuing and appreciating one another—regardless of cultural, ethnic, socio-economic, and religious background—we make space for openness to accept one another and build positive and transformative relationships.

Finally, Paul exhorts believers in Christ to practice hospitality. As mentioned earlier, hospitality is not just narrowly understood as feeding someone or giving temporary shelter to someone. Hospitality is not just about being nice; instead, it has a broader connotation. It also includes being just. So, therefore, it calls for the need to listen, appreciate, and acknowledge more openly the critical voices in our midst. It is making space for people we do not know, people outside our families and communities; it is making room for people to be accepted, to feel loved, to stand for their cause; it is embracing these people into our community.

These three motifs—love, honor, and hospitality—are motifs in Paul's exhortation to believers in Christ in the context of redefining relationships. The hermeneutics of love, honor, and hospitality goes beyond the closed exclusive community to include people from all walks of life and social standings. It creates space by moving beyond social hierarchies, social status, and privileges prevalent in Roman society and redefines relationships in terms of believers' common alliance to God.

Early in this essay, I drew parallels between Naga society and Roman society. In that context, it is possible to suggest, albeit provisionally, some of the implications of Paul's hermeneutic for Naga society today, a society

---

46. For discussions on the motif of love, honor, and hospitality, refer to my work, *Redefining Relationships in Romans*, 97–100.

47. Elliott, "Political Paul and the Social Context of Romans 12–13," 10.

in which wealth and status are tied to respect and honor, and divisions continue to exist based on ethnicity.

First, while diversity in Nagaland provides an opportunity to appreciate, respect, and learn from one another, it also has resulted in being overprotective of one's group and identity at the expense of other people groups. Today, instead of celebrating our diversity, there is a tendency to be suspicious among various groups. Different ethnic groups are politically, socially, and economically interdependent. Yet, despite their interdependence, there also is a strong tendency to protect and promote one's tribe. Despite efforts taken in some contexts to build relationships, in general, it continues to remain a challenge for the Nagas in Nagaland. The problem of being divided based on ethnicity continues to exist. By employing the motif of hospitality within the context of the love ethic, Paul reminds believers that in practicing genuine love, relationships are redefined and transformed. He urges believers to pursue hospitality as a call to love strangers. This exhortation of Paul—hospitality rooted in love—also is a call for different ethnic groups in Nagaland to transcend our boundaries, to acknowledge and respect one another, and to create space for openness in our common faith as Christians. The common faith of the Nagas can be an important factor that brings different ethnic groups together and also helps us critically appreciate our differences.

Second, as mentioned earlier, competition for status and honor widely exists in Naga society. A person's place in Naga society is connected to wealth, profession, and family background. As such, honor and respect are also connected to social status and family background. Hence, Paul's call to "take lead" in honoring one another becomes significant. As visible in Paul's exhortation, honor should not be tied to social status; believers in Christ are to esteem the Other more highly than themselves.

Conclusion

Paul articulated the gospel of Christ in ways that were relevant to believers in Rome. The gospel message was designed to help members within the community relate and connect with one another and also connect to the broader society—as the church is also a part of that broader society and not outside it. Thus, as discussed, Paul's gospel emphasizes redefining relationships by considering the wider implications. However, the redefining of relationships cannot take place in isolation; neither it is a passive act nor a one-sided relationship. Rather, it demands obligation to one another. It calls for being careful and mindful of one another. It is a call for living out love, honor, and hospitality.

Bibliography

(* For Further Reading)

Barclay, John M. G. *Paul and the Gift*. Grand Rapids: Eerdmans, 2015.

Barton, Carlin. *Roman Honor: The Fire in the Bones*. Berkeley: University of California Press, 2001.

Bauer, Walter, Frederick W. Danker, W. F. Arndt, and F. W. Gingrich. *A Greek-English Lexicon of the New Testament and Other Early Christian Literature* [BDAG]. 3d ed. Chicago: University of Chicago Press, 2000.

Carter, Warren. *The Roman Empire and the New Testament: An Essential Guide*. Abingdon Essential Guides. Nashville: Abingdon, 2006.

Cranfield, C. E. B. *A Critical and Exegetical Commentary on the Epistle to the Romans*. Vol. 2. International Critical Commentary. Edinburgh: T. & T. Clark, 1979.

Crook, Zeba. "Honor, Shame and Social Status Revisited." *Journal of Biblical Literature* 128 (2009) 591–611.

Deissmann, Adolf. *Light from the Ancient East: The New Testament Illustrated by Recently Discovered Texts of the Graeco-Roman World*. Translated by Lionel R. M. Strachan. 2nd ed. London: Hodder & Stoughton, 1927. Reprint, Eugene, OR: Wipf & Stock, 2004.

de Ligt, L. *Fairs and Markets in the Roman Empire: Economic and Social aspects of Periodic Trade in a Pre-industrial Society*. Dutch Monographs on Ancient History and Archaeology 11. Amsterdam: Gieben, 1993.

Dunn, James D. G. *Romans 9–16*. Word Biblical Commentary 38b. Dallas: Word, 1988.

Elliott, John H. "Patronage and Clientage." In *The Social Sciences and New Testament Interpretation*, edited by Richard L. Rohrbaugh, 144–58. Peabody, MA: Hendrickson, 1996.

*Elliott, Neil. *The Arrogance of the Nations: Reading Romans in the Shadow of Empire*. Paul in Critical Contexts. Minneapolis: Fortress, 2008.

———. *Liberating Paul: The Justice of God and the Politics of the Apostle*. Biblical Seminar 27. Sheffield: Sheffield Academic, 1995. Reprint, Minneapolis: Fortress, 2005.

Elliott, Spencer. "Political Paul and the Social Context of Romans 12–13." Academia.edu. https://www.academia.edu.

Fitzmyer, Joseph A. *Romans: A New Translation with Introduction and Commentary*. Anchor Bible 33. New York: Doubleday, 1993.

Foerster, Werner. "Euarestos." *Theological Dictionary of New Testament*, 1:456–57. 10 vols. Translated by Geoffrey W. Bromiley. Grand Rapids: Eerdmans, 1985.

Foley, Eric. "'Prevenient Grace': The Theological Term for 'Hospitality.'" Dotheword.org. Updated February 29, 2012. https://dotheword.org/2012/02/29/prevenient-grace-the-theological-term-for-hospitality/.

Fürer-Haimendorf, Christoph von. *Naked Nagas: Head-hunters of Assam in Peace and War*. Calcutta: Thacker, Spink, 1962.

Garnsey, Peter. *Social Status and Legal Privilege in the Roman Empire*. Oxford: Clarendon, 1970.

Garnsey, Peter, and Richard Saller. *The Roman Empire: Economy, Society and Culture*. 2nd ed. Oakland: University of California Press, 2015.

Horsley, Richard A. *Paul and Empire: Religion and Power in Roman Imperial Society*. Harrisburg, PA: Trinity, 1997.

———. *Paul and the Roman Imperial Order*. Harrisburg, PA: Trinity, 2004.
*Jewett, Robert. *Romans: A Commentary*. Hermeneia. Minneapolis: Fortress, 2007.
Käsemann, Ernst. *Commentary on Romans*. Translated by G. W. Bromiley. Grand Rapids: Eerdmans, 1980.
Lopez, Davina C. *Apostle to the Conquered: Reimagining Paul's Mission*. Paul in Critical Contexts. Minneapolis: Fortress, 2008.
Luithui, Shimreichon. "Naga: A People Struggling for Self-Determination." International Work Group for Indigenous Affairs. https//:www.iwgia.org/images/publications//naga.pdf.
Moxnes, Halvor. "Honor and Righteousness in Romans." *Journal for the Study of the New Testament* 10 (1988) 61–78.
———. "The Quest for Honor and the Unity of the Community in Romans 12 and in the Orations of Dio Chrysostom." In *Paul in His Hellenistic Context*, edited by Troels Engberg-Pedersen, 203–30. Edinburgh: T. & T. Clark, 2004.
Oakes, Peter. *Reading Romans in Pompeii: Paul's Letter at Ground Level*. Minneapolis: Fortress, 2009.
Odyuo, Iris. "The Various Aspects of Naga Art." *IOSR Journal of Humanities and Social Science* 9/4 (2013) 13–22.
Shohe, Zakali *Acceptance Motif in Paul: Revisiting Romans 15:7–13*. New Testament Studies in Contextual Exegesis 10. Frankfurt: Lang, 2017.
*———. *Redefining Relationships in Romans: A Socio-Historical and Political Reading*. Delhi: Christian World Imprints, 2020.
Winter, Bruce. "Roman Law and Society in Romans 12–15." In *Rome in the Bible and the Early Church*, edited by Peter Oakes, 67–102. Grand Rapids: Baker Academic, 2002.
Wu, Jackson. *Reading Romans with Eastern Eyes: Honor and Shame in Paul's Message and Mission*. Downers Grove, IL: InterVarsity, 2019.

Study Questions

1. Living a right relationship with God and also maintaining a responsible and transforming attitude and behavior toward others within our respective communities and the wider world: How do we balance them, or what should be our yardstick, or can there be a benchmark or a boundary?

2. Hospitality moves beyond the accepted notion of welcoming "strangers" or being nice to the Other in our community." Its wider implication includes a call to "love strangers" and "to be just." How important is it for us today to incorporate this wider connotation of hospitality?

3. Can we consider Paul's message to walk in love, to honor one another, and to practice hospitality as having urgent implications for us and for our present world?

12

Robert Jewett Goes to the Movies

Teaching University Courses on Religion and Film

CHRISTOPHER DEACY

Abstract

THE AIM OF THIS essay is to examine the degree to which Robert Jewett engaged with film as part of his strategy to promote and facilitate a Pauline conversation to a specifically late twentieth-century American audience. After introducing Jewett's methodological framework, the chapter will revisit the ways in which Jewett's work has been utilized by Sara Anson Vaux and other scholars and will assess his legacy and the degree to which Jewett may be considered a pioneering figure.

Introduction

Robert Jewett's two monographs on Saint Paul and film[1]—together with his thesis, with John Shelton Lawrence, on the American Monomyth[2]—have been highly influential in the design, content, and delivery of undergraduate modules on the Bible/theology/religion and film in the US and worldwide. Having used Jewett in my own religion and film teaching at the University of Kent for over fifteen years, I reflect on the ways in which it is profitable to engage with and respond to various facets of Jewett's reading of Paul and how it has shaped one's interpretation of the movies under discussion. The chapter also will revisit the incisive and reciprocal conversation generated in the late 1990s between Jewett and Sara Anson

1. Jewett, *Saint Paul Goes to the Movies* and *Saint Paul Returns to the Movies*.
2. Jewett, *The American Monomyth*.

Vaux on the way in which movie and real-life politically inspired violence, as typified by Clint Eastwood's *Unforgiven* (1992), should be understood, and whether violence can be thought to comprise a dangerous end in itself, as envisaged by Jewett, or a means to a more wholesome, even redemptive, end, as expounded by Vaux. I use the debates that Jewett's thesis has inspired to revisit the way in which Jewett kick-started a dialogue between two or more discrete fields back in the days when the discipline of religion and film had yet to be properly established.

Perspective, Assumption, and Method

Jewett was a pioneering figure. Although, by his own admission, he was not a film theorist or critic, he was someone who was publishing books in the areas of theology and film scholarship at a time when research and teaching in theology, religion, the Bible, and film was in its infancy. Crucially, Jewett was not someone who simply saw film as an opportunity to foster unsophisticated or superficial correlations between theology and popular culture, whereby, as the literature on Christ-figures has demonstrated, Jesus can be isolated and reduced to the norms and vicissitudes of the prevailing culture.[3] Rather, in accordance with the fourth model outlined by H. Richard Niebuhr in his seminal *Christ and Culture*, first published in 1952, there is no need to foster artificial or contrived convergences between theology and culture, and Jewett was adept at emphasizing the dissimilarities and paradoxes at work. Although Jewett was, as we shall see, a reductionistic figure insofar as he was mindful to use films for the degree to which they shed light on some of the same cultural themes and tropes that Paul espoused and wrestled with in his epistles rather than because of some innate value or wisdom films are able to cultivate, Jewett deserves credit for the way in which he was comfortable bringing together popular film with the teachings of Paul. His position was that film can be drawn upon in order to showcase the potential and impact Paul's letters still have the capacity to inculcate in late twentieth century America. Indeed, Jewett could very much be seen as carrying on the tradition espoused by Niebuhr's "Christ and Culture in Paradox" model in that he was inclined to highlight the degree to which a movie's exploration of themes such as justification, shame, honour, grace, love, and righteousness always fell short when juxtaposed and read in the light of the erudite theological deliberations of Saint Paul.

Jewett may not be best known for his engagement with film—and, indeed, when I had the pleasure of meeting him at the American Academy

---

3. See Deacy, "The Pedagogical Challenges of Finding Christ Figures in Film."

of Religion conference in San Diego in 2007, he was clear that the work on film was largely peripheral to his oeuvre—but his use of film was far from random or expedient. As Jewett's research testified, Saint Paul's teaching was shaped more by the popular culture of his day than by any formal religious or educational training. Jewett saw this as fundamental to Paul's understanding of mission, as shown by the time that the apostle used to spend evangelizing in such "secular" locations as the workshop, lecture hall, and street corner. Placing himself "where other people were, to communicate the gospel on their turf,"[4] Jewett hypothesized in *Saint Paul at the Movies* that "Paul would have been a discerning partner in discussing secular movies had they been available in his time," with the issues that they raise and stories they tell "reminiscent of conversations in the workshops where he spent most of his life."[5] Jewett's methodology entailed taking under consideration a common theme he had located in each film with a passage from one of Paul's epistles and using it to supply a commentary, or even a critique, on "the American cultural situation."[6] He was not interested in formulating analogies and parallels, however. Despite his talk of an "interpretive arch, which operates by seeking analogies between ancient and modern texts and situations,"[7] one end of which is anchored in Saint Paul's day, while the other is rooted in contemporary (American) culture, Jewett did not see this as a relationship of equals. Although he stressed the need to treat each film under discussion with respect, and in being interested in what happens when sparks fly between the two arches of the biblical text on the one hand and a film on the other, his basic position was that "the Pauline word is allowed to stand as *primus inter pares*," that is, the "first among equals," since, unlike film, the Bible has "stood the test of time by revealing ultimate truth that has gripped past and current generations with compelling power."[8]

Jewett conceded that films may be "inspired," and he was keen to point out that the Bible should not be an overbearing partner in the hermeneutical dialogue. But this is not a reciprocal relationship for, unlike cinema, "biblical texts have sustained the life and morals of faith communities in circumstances both adverse and happy over several thousand years."[9] The missiological dimension of Jewett's work is apparent in the way that he was seeking to work

4. Jewett, *Saint Paul at the Movies*, 5
5. Jewett, *Saint Paul at the Movies*, 6.
6. Jewett, *Saint Paul at the Movies*, 7.
7. Jewett, *Saint Paul at the Movies*, 9.
8. Jewett, *Saint Paul at the Movies*, 11.
9. Jewett, *Saint Paul at the Movies*, 12.

as an ambassador for Saint Paul in the contemporary world and to undertake what he called "dialogue in a prophetic mode."[10] Films worked for Jewett as modern-day parables that dovetail with the teachings Paul was seeking to address two thousand years ago, and his approach consisted of going beneath what the films are doing on the surface level to discern the underlying message or values they were imparting. Jewett saw himself as being called to this enterprise by "a commitment to pursuing the saving power of the gospel,"[11] venturing into places and spaces where Paul himself would have been prepared to travel. What was good enough for Paul in the first century was good enough for Jewett in the twentieth: "If he refused to make devious discriminations, his followers should do no less."[12]

Jewett's rationale was that the gospel Saint Paul was disseminating was for everyone, regardless of their status, class, social divisions, ethnicity, or position of power in society. Just as Paul wanted to bridge the gaps between different regions and cultures, and thereby become "all things to all people" (1 Cor 9:22), so Jewett was intent on ensuring that Paul's voice can be heard via secular forms of entertainment. At first sight, movies may appear to be an unprofitable means of promulgating Paul's epistles as they are made for profit and, in the eyes of many "highly trained scholars"[13] who are inclined to study books rather than watch movies, they do not require great sophistication in order to be understood. Indeed, as he put it, "self-respecting scholars are understandably reluctant to become 'weak' in order to 'win the weak.'"[14] He was well aware, however, that Paul himself was accustomed to evangelizing in secular environments, such as the workshop or street corner, and he twinned this with the fact that for many Americans today, it is popular culture rather than any formal educational or religious training that shapes them, and which comprises "a primary arena for discovering and debating important moral, cultural, and religious issues."[15] His remit was to "place himself where other people were, to communicate the gospel on their turf,"[16] and Jewett believed that there is an analogy between the kinds of issues that Paul confronted in the first century and the conversations generated by the medium of film. Just as Paul was accustomed to accommodating himself to the audience of the day—so that he was "a Greek

---

10. Jewett, *Saint Paul at the Movies*, 7.
11. Jewett, *Saint Paul at the Movies*, 9.
12. Jewett, *Saint Paul at the Movies*, 12.
13. Jewett, *Saint Paul at the Movies*, 4.
14. Jewett, *Saint Paul at the Movies*, 4.
15. Jewett, *Saint Paul at the Movies*, 5.
16. Jewett, *Saint Paul at the Movies*, 5.

to the Greeks" and "a Jew to the Jews," so Jewett believed that the challenge ahead was to divest so much of Pauline theology of its Eurocentric origins and so enable Paul to become "an American to the Americans."[17] Jewett was explicit: "The potential for Paul's thought for creative interaction with American culture will remain untapped if it does not take account of these formative materials in popular culture."[18]

Interpretive Steps

Having spent a week of focusing on the work of Jewett with my own religion and film students in a module at the University of Kent that has run annually since 2005, what has come to the fore is that Jewett's film analysis was quite different from many other figures who work in the field of theology/religion and film. Other scholars have used Paul in their research, among them Larry Kreitzer[19] and Richard Walsh,[20] but in their cases a more postmodern approach has been applied, whereby we need to be more aware and self-critical of the degree to which we bring our own ideas and influences to the New Testament. According to Kreitzer, "The aim is to listen to the conversation that takes place between biblical texts, great works of literature and cinematic adaptations of those works of literature."[21] Kreitzer takes it for granted that an understanding of the director's intention can contribute to our appreciation of the film they have made. Kreitzer is less beholden than Jewett to setting up a binary between Paul and film, and notes the irony that although for many people today the Bible is "largely viewed as an irrelevancy, a worthless trinket of a bygone era,"[22] it is nevertheless the case that what often underlies a film are biblical images that "seem to lie at an almost subliminal, even mythological, level."[23] Accordingly, for Kreitzer, "inter-disciplinary hermeneutics is a sign of the future."[24]

This is noticeably different from Jewett, who was inclined to see film as an extension of the Pauline missiological agenda. Indeed, Jewett was disinclined to see films as having much to offer in their own right, which is also

---

17. Jewett, *Saint Paul at the Movies*, 7.
18. Jewett, *Saint Paul at the Movies*, 5.
19. See, e.g., Kreitzer, *The New Testament in Fiction and Film*, and *Pauline Images in Fiction and Film*.
20. See, e.g., Walsh, *Finding St. Paul in Film*.
21. Kreitzer, *Pauline Images in Fiction and Film*, 17.
22. Kreitzer, *Pauline Images in Fiction and Film*, 29.
23. Kreitzer, *Pauline Images in Fiction and Film*, 30.
24. Kreitzer, *Pauline Images in Fiction and Film*, 30.

at odds with the work of authors such as Clive Marsh[25] and John Lyden[26] for whom interdisciplinarity plays a more prominent role. Marsh argues, for example, that cinema-going "does not simply fill in the time left by the absence of religion, but actually enables film-watchers to participate in the business of religion."[27] For Lyden, "filmgoers are very involved in their own appropriation of a film, and they do not passively accept whatever it says. They are often highly critical and spend much time discussing films before, during, and after the viewing."[28] The New Testament undergirding was, in contrast, primary for Jewett, and he looked to film to augment the debate that was started two millennia ago rather than to be able to challenge or query anything that Saint Paul himself kick-started. Once it has achieved its purpose, film no longer has anything further to contribute. Together with the interdisciplinary perspectives taught by authors such as Melanie Wright[29] and Robert Johnston,[30] the question could be asked whether Jewett had missed a trick in the overbearing way he engaged with films with which audiences are broadly familiar (such as *Groundhog Day* [Harold Ramis, 1993], *The Shawshank Redemption* [Frank Darabont, 1994] and *Forrest Gump* [Robert Zemeckis, 1994]) but looked at them from the angle of faith.

For Jewett, it was unmistakably the case that Paul's voice always holds sway over our "cultural simplicities."[31] As he wrote in relation to *Unforgiven* (Clint Eastwood, 1992), "When the two models of redemption are held up before us, side by side . . . it should become clear that either choice will eliminate the other,"[32] and so the onus is on us to take sides—and Jewett always chose Paul in relation to whom there is always going to be "a deeper, more divine logic at work."[33] The question is whether film as a medium is being understood on its own merits and whether Jewett's faith-based agenda is limiting the way in which dialogue might be able to accrue.

The task has been to ask whether one should be inclined to want to allow the films to speak on their own terms rather than to rule out from the outset, as Jewett does, that, for example, film could only be of use so

---

25. See, e.g., Marsh, *Cinema and Sentiment*.
26. See, e.g., Lyden, *Film as Religion*.
27. Marsh, *Cinema and Sentiment*, 6.
28. Lyden, *Film as Religion*, 46.
29. See, e.g., Wright, *Religion and Film*.
30. See, e.g., Johnston, *Reel Spirituality*.
31. Jewett, *Saint Paul at the Movies*, 131.
32. Jewett, *Saint Paul at the Movies*, 161.
33. Jewett, *Saint Paul at the Movies*, 131.

long as it points to, and retreats before, the superior insights on display in Paul's epistles.

We see this, for example, in his treatment of *Pale Rider* (Clint Eastwood, 1985), which is one of the case studies I discuss with my students. Jewett thought that Eastwood's Western typifies the way in which many people in society today expect swift vengeance. In its place, Jewett was quick to respond that when it comes to questions of revenge and retaliation, we are usurping God's prerogative, as outlined in Romans 12:19 (ESV)—"Vengeance is mine, I will repay, says the Lord." Such films were, for him, characteristic of trends in the Hebrew Bible that Paul has completed and fulfilled. So, a film like *Pale Rider,* in which we see Eastwood's Preacher—who enters a Californian mining community and saves it from its corporate outlaws—taking the law into his own hands is congruous with the dynamics on display in Numbers 25 with the story of Phinehas the lyncher. Jewett was swift to condemn such waywardness: "The United States has police forces without judicial powers, a court system bound by constitutional restraints, and forms of punishment that often seem awkward and ineffective. Compared with this, who would not prefer the 'miracle' of a Pale Rider?"[34] Jewett was not denying that retributive justice plays a role in Paul's thinking, but this is God's jurisdiction, not ours, and he therefore counselled "patient reliance on the instruments of divine justice."[35] Instead of harboring hatred, Jewett proposed that, in the spirit of Paul in Romans 12:21 ("Do not overcome by evil, but overcome evil with good"; ESV), we should demonstrate concern for our enemy's wellbeing and seek to transform them. Even when we are not sure exactly how to apply Paul's injunctions and wisdom, that does not mean we should look elsewhere, such as to a film, for guidance because Paul still exhibits "a deeper, more divine logic" and has "a deeper understanding of the human psyche"[36] than anything else on offer. We should even, he argued, be thanking Paul for being the exemplar par excellence: "We should find ways to express our gratitude when a system patterned on Paul's ideal of due process of law functions properly."[37]

The same template is on display in Jewett's other film expositions. In the case of *Star Wars* (George Lucas, 1977), for example, Jewett acknowledged that "It involves a ritual reenactment of a story of salvation, comparable to the function of religious rituals studied by anthropologists and theologians,"[38]

---

34. Jewett, *Saint Paul at the Movies*, 123.
35. Jewett, *Saint Paul at the Movies*, 127.
36. Jewett, *Saint Paul at the Movies*, 131.
37. Jewett, *Saint Paul at the Movies*, 132.
38. Jewett, *Saint Paul at the Movies*, 20.

but he felt that the salvation on display fell short. For, whereas, in the film, salvation is achieved by lasers, nuclear torpedoes and spacecraft, and the annihilation of stormtroopers (the American myth of regeneration through violence), for Paul, the means of salvation is the gospel, namely, the good news of God's love. Jewett professed that Paul's gospel does not require the destruction of enemies or in enforcing conformity to a single law but simply entails the message of unconditional love. By contrast, in *Star Wars,* salvation entails the restoration of a hierarchical order of princesses and subjects, warriors and traders, and the "force" is accessible only to select warriors and saints such as Obi Wan Kenobi and the Jedi Knights—the only ones who understand the force and how to use it—with everyone else limited to the role of passive spectator. He was insistent that in the case of Saint Paul, salvation entails the restoration of an egalitarian order that includes male and female, slave and free, Greek and Jew, educated and uneducated, and is based on faith rather than merit or inheritance. There are no passive spectators and no enemies who cannot be reformed. In contrast to *Star Wars,* Paul's gospel is most powerfully experienced when people experience weakness and defeat. So, a clear binary is being set up: whereas in *Star Wars,* one side has to prevail over the other, in Paul's theology, all persons are equal before God, and *everyone* falls short: "For there is no distinction; since all have sinned and fall short of the glory of God" (Rom 3:23; ESV) Jewett argued that the *Star Wars* model is limiting because it is predicated on the notion that "the elimination of the enemy will restore peace and justice."[39] He also felt very strongly that *Star Wars* relies upon the leadership of royalty and the martial instinct of an elite, whereas Paul promoted the resources of the many over the few and so represented a more adequate "gospel."

We also see this dynamic in *The Shawshank Redemption* (Frank Darabont, 1994), which evokes the power of hope and draws on biblical motifs, such as the small rock hidden within the Bible of the corrupt prison Warden in the film. Jewett's approach was to take issue with the way the film concludes, with the innocent person, falsely accused, ultimately being redeemed, retorting that according to Saint Paul, those who have been redeemed are not completely freed from adversity. This is because, as he pointed out with respect to Romans 8:24–25, there is a presupposition of ongoing vulnerability for those who have been redeemed and that "The slaves and former slaves who made up the bulk of the Roman Churches could not entirely overcome exploitation by their masters and patrons."[40] Jewett contrasted this attitude with that of modern American society

---

39. Jewett, *Saint Paul at the Movies,* 27.

40. Jewett, *Saint Paul Returns to the Movies,* 164.

where, he wrote, hope has different connotations: "It is largely the hope of a better tomorrow, when adversity does not overwhelm us. It is essentially the hope for happy endings."[41] He thought that prison escape stories, like *Shawshank*, were part of this trend in the way that they are about escaping from the walls of confinement and finding a second chance by taking on a new identity. Hope and redemption in the context of Paul is, rather, as Jewett saw it, more to do with the overcoming in the present moment of shame "by God's love poured into the heart in the context of the new community."[42] The very individualistic nature of redemption in a film like *The Shawshank Redemption*, where a prisoner manages to outwit the prison authorities and engineers an escape plan by himself, is thus at odds with "the original story of Christ suffering on behalf of prisoners, the ill, the outsiders, the lame, the halt, and the blind."[43] Jewett therefore drew the inescapable conclusion that "A new form of salvation is clearly being offered in this film, one that replaces the intervention of Yahweh at the Exodus and of Christ on the Cross."[44] His critique derives from the way in which what he characterized as secular dispositions have pervaded this and other American movies that are, paradoxically, in conflict with the biblical ethos yet adopt its redemptive language. For Jewett, it is way too narrow and constricting to imagine that a film can be deemed redemptive when it is divorced from the communal bedrock Saint Paul understood, together with one in which "Salvation now comes through the little rock hammer in the hands of an intelligent and determined person who refuses to give up hope in his own capacity to achieve freedom against all the odds."[45]

Rather than set up quite such an explicit dichotomy, other scholars have proposed more dialogical perspectives. A case in point is the fascinating dialogue that took place in the journal *Christianity and Literature* in 1998,[46] when Sara Anson Vaux, who has since authored a book on the ethical vision of the films of Clint Eastwood, took issue with Jewett's critique of Eastwood's Oscar-winning revisionist Western *Unforgiven* (1992). The violence on display in the film was, Jewett claimed, incendiary, inviting audiences to think that problems can be resolved by the power of the gun, and he thought that there is a very small step involved from shooting a corrupt sheriff, as forms the centerpiece of the film's bloody denouement, to "placing

---

41. Jewett, *Saint Paul Returns to the Movies*, 164–65.
42. Jewett, *Saint Paul Returns to the Movies*, 165.
43. Jewett, *Saint Paul Returns to the Movies*, 175.
44. Jewett, *Saint Paul Returns to the Movies*, 180.
45. Jewett, *Saint Paul Returns to the Movies*, 181.
46. See Vaux, "*Unforgiven*."

truck bombs in front of . . . federal buildings."⁴⁷ He was specific, indeed, that the terrorists and militias in today's world are functionally the same as the zealots of the first century. Jewett's argument is a clear one: love and the submission to unjust authorities is far more efficacious, and consonant with the teaching of Paul, than the application of violence. Vaux took a very different approach, seeing *Unforgiven* as a film of "great spiritual richness and great physical beauty that dares to turn ideas about justice upside down; that asks again and again when, if ever, we need to kill; and that insists throughout that as flawed human beings, we *can* and *must* be redeemed by love."⁴⁸ She takes the more nuanced line that Eastwood's bounty-hunter protagonist is neither "blameless hero" nor "seamless villain" but who is "a deeply conflicted person who struggles to carry over his religious convictions into his everyday worlds of work and family."⁴⁹ The film is characterized by the theme of forgiveness, according to Vaux, echoing core Christian themes relating to the thief on the cross in Luke 23 and the woman accused of adultery in John 7. She specifically rejects Jewett's attestation that *Unforgiven* glorifies killing. Paraphrasing Jewett's own language, she writes: "Does it crown a savior on a white horse or in a government-issue cop car who rides into town with guns blazing? The answer is a resounding 'No.'"⁵⁰

The final saloon sequence is redolent in gunfire and violence for sure, but Vaux is more interested in the way in which *Unforgiven* subverts the expectations of the genre and "is heavily qualified by the cinematography of the scene and by nearly two hours of criticism of killing that has preceded it."⁵¹ It is the very deglamorization of violence that pervades this film, which functions as a treatise on death, compassion, virtue, the transformation of an assassin through the love of his late wife, and the attempt to shake off a bloody past: "I seen the error of my ways"; "I ain't like that no more." To this end, *Unforgiven* could be seen as an exploration of renewal and rebirth and a sober commentary on "the price humans pay to continue their battles."⁵² Violence may, for Jewett, have been a barrier toward our ability to deal profitably with questions of justice and vengeance, but Vaux takes Jewett to task for the way in which a film can be violent but not extol it as a virtue. And this is where it is apparent that the debate on violence is seen as being a truncated one if it is restricted to being seen without this

47. Jewett, *Saint Paul Returns to the Movies*, 149.
48. Vaux, *Finding Meaning at the Movies*, 118.
49. Vaux, *The Ethical Vision of Clint Eastwood*, 57.
50. Vaux, *The Ethical Vision of Clint Eastwood*, 58.
51. Vaux, *The Ethical Vision of Clint Eastwood*, 58.
52. Vaux, *The Ethical Vision of Clint Eastwood*, 71.

wider undergirding. For Vaux, indeed, violence could even be construed as a sacrament that celebrates the power of love to heal and restore, thus making it about conversion rather than the glamorization of violence for its own sake. Whereas Jewett saw only a binary between regenerative violence and sacrificial love, Vaux sees the former as a precursor toward the accomplishment of the latter.

Teaching Jewett's pronouncements has thus afforded the opportunity to critique and seek to temper the categorical way in which he was liable to "read" a film, as when he argued while writing about the theme of reaping corruption from the flesh in Galatians 6 that "this is what a film like *Groundhog Day* is all about, even though the filmmakers and actors may not have fully understood these implications themselves."[53] Jewett's expertise on Paul is not in question, but as he himself averred he is not involved in film criticism—"I have neither the talent nor the training."[54] As with his critique of *Unforgiven*, Jewett was predisposed to interpret each of the films under discussion through a pre-established lens in relation to which any (and frankly every) film is going to fall short. And, inevitably, if he is going to read every film through the lens of a body of scholarship with which Jewett, as a Pauline scholar, was an authority, Paul of Tarsus is always going to have the upper hand over Phil Connors of Punxsutawney. In engaging with Jewett, it is important to bring an awareness of the vision and agenda of the author, and whether there are particular challenges that arise when a film is studied from the angle of faith.

Conclusion

In conclusion, Jewett deserves credit for the way he sought to bring together the biblical and the cinematic worlds and to explore ways in which there may be scope to find new ways of channeling the counsel, wisdom, and theology of Saint Paul in an age (late twentieth century) and a milieu (US) where Paul may not otherwise be spoken about to the degree Jewett believes to be so imperative. Jewett saw Paul's teachings as being no less relevant and enduring in the modern world than they were two thousand years ago in the Greco-Roman age. But where Jewett's model does not fully convince is in the degree to which he argues that one of the parties is superior to the other. He may have used the language of dialogue, but it is not a fully reciprocal relationship he envisaged. For Jewett, film was a more lightweight, provisional, and fleeting medium that is beholden to a

---

53. Jewett, *Saint Paul Returns to the Movies*, 92.
54. Jewett, *Saint Paul at the Movies*, 8.

far less resilient secular paradigm, thereby affording them unequal voices. A key question for consideration is whether movies should always be approached cautiously and whether it is wrong to presuppose that a movie can ever have the upper hand in any conversation that might accrue with film. For this reason, Jewett's work might be thought of as unnecessarily self-confined and circumscribed in which film is merely being used for illustrative purposes and not as a medium in its own right. Indeed, the film might be there as a foil for his interpretation of Saint Paul.

For Jewett, it was beyond the pale to countenance the possibility that a film could ever change the way Paul's theology is understood. Implicit in Jewett's methodology was the belief that, if a film deviates from Paul's way of doing things, then the film is deficient. But what Jewett tended not to do was ask why a Pauline paradigm is the only one worth exploring. He would begin and end in the same place—by privileging Paul and not even considering the efficacy of alternative methodological frameworks and approaches. Jewett did not engage with any other works in the field of religion and film—not that admittedly prior to the publication of *Saint Paul at the Movies* in 1993 there were too many in existence, though there were several by the time of his 1999 sequel, *Saint Paul Returns to the Movies*—and for such a pioneering figure, this might perhaps be seen as his Achilles' heel. Rather than presuppose that there is only one monolithic understanding of a film, the challenge to the post-Jewett biblical scholar would be to see whether a re-negotiation between ancient and modern texts could be undertaken and to set aside the notion that there necessarily is an objective or absolute reading of any text. We have already seen work undertaken along these lines in the work of Jeffrey L. Staley who has read intertextually the Gospel of Mark with novels and films, with a view to seeing how a movie can present "an alternative vision of life that challenges traditional cultural values."[55] For George Aichele also, there is much mileage to be accomplished in interpreting the New Testament through the lens of a film instead of simply interpreting a film through the lens of the New Testament. Aichele's approach is to ensure that the meaning of a story is not "locked into its text at the moment of its formation."[56] Larry Kreitzer also proposed this notion of reversing the hermeneutical flow back in 1993, the same year Jewett's first book on Saint Paul and film was published.[57] Rather than elevate one voice in the conversation, Kreitzer's approach has the advantage of ensuring that we continue to have both a greater appreciation of the biblical texts and our

---

55. Staley, "Meeting Patch Again," 226.
56. Aichele, "Foreword," 8.
57. Kreitzer, *The New Testament in Fiction and Film*.

own contemporary cultural worldview, and the direction of travel is, in turn, all the more enriching for being multi-, rather than uni-, directional.

Bibliography

(* For Further Reading)

Aichele, George. "Foreword." In Larry Kreitzer, *Gospel Images in Fiction and Film: On Reversing the Hermeneutical Flow*, 7–10. Biblical Seminar 84. London: Sheffield Academic, 2002.

*Deacy, Christopher. "The Pedagogical Challenges of Finding Christ Figures in Film." In *Teaching Religion and Film*, edited by Gregory J. Watkins, 129–40. Oxford: Oxford University Press, 2008.

*Jewett, Robert. *Saint Paul at the Movies: The Apostle's Dialogue with American Culture*. Louisville: Westminster John Knox, 1993.

———. *Saint Paul Returns to the Movies: Triumph over Shame*. Grand Rapids: Eerdmans, 1999.

Jewett, Robert, and John Shelton Lawrence. *The American Monomyth*. New York: Doubleday, 1977.

*Johnston, Robert. *Reel Spirituality: Theology and Film in Dialogue*. Grand Rapids: Baker Academic, 2000.

Kreitzer, Larry. *The New Testament in Fiction and Film: On Reversing the Hermeneutical Flow*. Biblical Seminar 84. Sheffield: Sheffield Academic, 1993.

———. *Pauline Images in Fiction and Film: On Reversing the Hermeneutical Flow*. Biblical Seminar 61. Sheffield: Sheffield Academic, 1999.

Lyden, John C. *Film as Religion: Myths, Morals and Rituals*. New York: New York University Press, 2003.

Marsh, Clive. *Cinema and Sentiment: Film's Challenge to Theology*. Studies in Religion and Culture. Carlisle, UK: Paternoster, 2004.

Niebuhr, H. Richard. *Christ and Culture*. New York: Harper, 1952.

Staley, Jeffrey L. "Meeting Patch Again for the First Time: Purity and Compassion in Marcus Borg, the Gospel of Mark, and *Patch Adams*." In *Screening Scripture: Intertextual Connections between Scripture and Film*, edited by George Aichele and Richard Walsh, 213–28. Harrisburg, PA: Trinity, 2002.

Vaux, Sara Anson. *The Ethical Vision of Clint Eastwood*. Grand Rapids: Eerdmans, 2012.

———. *Finding Meaning at the Movies*. Nashville: Abingdon, 1999.

———. "*Unforgiven*: The Sentence of Death and Radical Forgiveness." *Christianity and Literature* 47 (1998) 443–58.

Walsh, Richard. *Finding St. Paul in Film*. London: T. & T. Clark, 2005.

Wright, Melanie J. *Religion and Film: An Introduction*. London: Taurus, 2007.

Study Questions

1. To what extent can religion and film be deemed to comprise a relationship of equals, or should theology always have precedence over film?

2. To what extent does the cultural and religious vantage point of an author frame their interpretation of a text or film? Might an American audience, for example, understand a text in a different way from, say, their European counterparts?

3. Does a faith-based position facilitate or impede dialogue between religion and film?

13

Superhero Myth(s), Movies, and Scripture

Robert Jewett as Cultural Exegete

Robert K. Johnston

Abstract

IN HIS FIVE-DECADE ATTEMPT to have Paul become America's apostle, Robert Jewett has used biblical texts as his critical tool to engage and critique America's monomyth with its hyper-individualism and its rationalized violence. In this monomyth, a selfless superhero rejects relationships and responds to present evil with necessary violence, redeeming the community before disappearing. Missing in his analysis, however, has been the recognition of an emerging, more popular myth rooted in Marvel comics' superheroes—one more relational, more human, and less violent. This alternate myth could provide Jewett's proposed biblical "answer" the contextual grounding necessary to move beyond abstraction and find traction in the American experience.

Introduction

Robert Jewett is best known as a Pauline scholar. His lifetime of work on the book of *Romans* (2007) resulted in his major volume on the epistle to the Romans in the Hermeneia commentary series.[1] In that commentary, as in other of his writings, Jewett argues that Romans is a rhetorical letter that seeks to persuade those in Rome to support Paul's projected missionary campaign in Spain by challenging that church's false sense of superiority. Written in terms of the honor-shame culture of the first-century Roman Empire, the

1. Jewett, *Romans* (1986); Jewett, *Romans: A Commentary* (2007).

epistle reasons that there is no distinction between people either with regard to shame or with reference to honor, for all fall short of the glory of God, and all are made righteous by the gift of God in Christ Jesus.

There is a revolutionary impartiality in God's righteousness, which renders the honor-shame system (whether with regard to status, ethnicity, gender, or economics) null and void. As Jewett first argued over twenty-five years earlier:

> To bypass structural, rhetorical, and situational aspects of the letter will finally defeat theological understanding, since the seemingly contradictory details transcend modern theological systems and can be comprehended only by reconstructing the dialogical situation between Paul and his first century audience.[2]

In making his culturally rooted argument concerning Paul's epistle, Jewett's foil was a second contextualization, or "horizon," the dominant Eurocentric view of Paul argued by most modern interpreters. He believed that we, as Americans, should interpret Paul not with the Europeans, but in an American context.[3] In the introduction to his book, *Paul the Apostle to America* (1994), Jewett makes clear this second cultural agenda:

> Biblical scholarship today is an international enterprise . . . requiring colleagues in many countries, reflecting many different approaches and commitments. My effort to develop an American approach to Paul is not intended as a declaration of independence. It expresses instead the convictions that contextual interpretations are a necessity for every cultural setting for the gospel to be effective . . . My goal is to lend a tentative voice with an American timbre to the ecumenical chorus . . .[4]

With Paul, Jewett wanted to be a Greek to the Greeks and a Jew to the Jews (1 Cor 9:20–23).[5] He saw Paul as adaptable to cultural differences (Rom 1:14), and so, like Paul, desired to use Paul to throw light on attitudes and beliefs in the United States. If Paul could be an apostle to the Europeans, why not also to Americans?

---

2. Jewett, "Major Impulses in the Theological Interpretation of Romans," 31.

3. Note the titles of the first two chapters of his *Paul The Apostle to America: Cultural Trends in Pauline Scholarship* (1994): "Overcoming the Eurocentric View of Paul" and "Interpreting Paul in the American Context."

4. Jewett, *Paul the Apostle to America*, viii.

5. Cf. Jewett's prologue in *Saint Paul at the Movies*, 3.

Paul an Apostle in American Culture

In order to carry out this task, Jewett turns his exegetical skills not only to Romans, but also to analyzing American popular culture, particularly its dominant stories and myths as portrayed in movies, television, comics, and video games. In a number of books and articles spanning five decades, Jewett considered a wide range of popular stories in American culture, which together have produced a mythology that has helped shape our nation's subsequent behavior. In his words, his goal was to bring into dialogue "important trends in American culture, including popular entertainment and books" with "freshly discovered aspects of Pauline thought."[6]

Other chapters will comment on how original Jewett's understanding of "freshly discovered aspects of Pauline thought" really are. This essay will focus, instead, on his understanding of "important trends in American culture" and how Jewett used Paul's thought as his critical tool for unpacking these trends as observed in the stories of popular culture. Rather than using queer theory or feminist criticism, psychoanalytic thought or post-colonial insights as his critical tool, Jewett used Pauline theology.

Here, Jewett proved a trendsetter. Amos Wilder's *Theopoetic* (1976) and Bernard Brendon Scott's *Hollywood Dreams and Biblical Stories* (1994) were other early forays into the dialogue between Bible and story, along with Jewett's *The Captain America Complex: The Dilemma of Zealous Nationalism* (1973) and his *Saint Paul at the Movies: The Apostle's Dialogue with American Culture* (1993). Also to be mentioned is his book with John Shelton Lawrence, his colleague while at Morningside College, entitled *The American Monomyth* (1977).[7] In these and subsequent writings, both books and articles, Jewett did not claim to have the last word; instead, he was content to explore "a vast and significant terrain that Paul might well have traversed had the apostle to the Gentiles lived in our time."[8] As he somewhat colloquially put it in his introduction to *Saint Paul at the Movies*, "The apostle Paul would have wanted to extend his journey into the regions depicted by the movies had they been available in his time."[9]

At the 1994 Society of Biblical Literature (SBL) annual meeting, Jewett's book, *Saint Paul at the Movies*, was the subject of scholarly reflection. Ronald Roschke presented an insightful analysis of Jewett's understanding of Paul's

---

6. Jewett, *Paul the Apostle to America*, x–xi.

7. Wilder, *Theopoetic*; Scott, *Hollywood Dreams and Biblical Stories*; Jewett, *Captain America Complex*; Jewett, *Saint Paul at the Movies*; Jewett and Lawrence, *American Monomyth*.

8. Jewett, *Paul the Apostle to America*, xi.

9. Jewett, *Saint Paul at the Movies*, 3.

desire to relate the Christian kerygma to his multicultural world. This was understood as similar to Jewett's concurrent desire to relate Paul's epistles to modern twentieth-century readers. Roschke wrote in his handout to the participants in the "Bible in Ancient and Modern Media" section:

> There is an interesting and curious link here between *missionary* and *interpreter*, with each, in a different way, serving as a *guide*. The goal of interpretation, it would seem, is to allow Paul's texts now to reach across the centuries and engage contemporary Americans with the goals of the Pauline mission. Movies provide us with a distilled snapshot of our contemporary culture and help to define the context in which such a Pauline mission would take place within it. Movies show us what our culture considers to be "good, acceptable and perfect," but they also provide us with critical information for locating both the points of positive contact between the Christian kerygma and the culture as well as the places where the kerygma will want to challenge the culture.[10]

Such an intermedia approach is now firmly established in the SBL with multiple sections devoted yearly to the dialogue between Bible and both film and popular culture. A growing library of books and articles has also been written further developing these conversations.[11] But this was not the case in 1994. Here Jewett was a pioneer; he is to be applauded.

Exegeting Popular Culture

Jewett sought from the beginning to allow both Paul and the stories of popular culture to maintain their separate voices. At the same time, he believed that, as with Paul, the biblical critic could be a discerning judge of cultural "truth." His "dialogue in a prophetic mode" was thus largely unidirectional.[12] He was a biblical scholar and, thus, the biblical text was given precedence. Having considered some expression of American culture, Jewett then turned to Pauline text for confirmation or critique.

Jewett was, to be sure, too dependent on plot as the primary conveyor of the meaning of our culture's stories, not recognizing adequately

---

10. Roschke, "Review of Robert Jewett's *Saint Paul at the Movies*," 1.

11. Cf., the writings of Chris Deacy, John Lyden, Robert Johnston, Kutter Callaway, Elijah Davidson, Stefanie Knauss, Clive Marsh, Matt Rindge, Richard Walsh, Larry Kreitzer, Gerard Laughlin, Jolyon Mitchell, Adele Reinhartz, Garth Higgins, and an ever-expanding list of others.

12. Jewett, *Saint Paul at the Movies*, 8.

the importance of image or music, star power, or graphics as partners in conveying a story's meaning. He said, "I am not as much interested in evaluating films on the basis of aesthetic criteria as in discerning the message these interesting 'stories' disclose for our society." He said his task was not film criticism, but "culturally contextual interpretation."[13] Missing in this evaluation is the recognition that meaning is conveyed also through a movie's "aesthetics."

However, it is too easy simply to criticize. Jewett recognized correctly that Americans are shaped more often by popular culture than by Sunday school, by the movie theater more than the schoolroom. His turn as a major biblical scholar to popular culture for insight into how biblical texts might be being received was ahead of its time. Those of us following in his stead can only be appreciative of his leadership. Rather than critique Jewett for not being a better film critic, it is, I believe, more helpful to look at Jewett as the cultural critic he intended to be. Was Jewett's read of American culture adequately nuanced? Did he understand our myth of the American superhero well? It is here that perhaps our appreciative, yet critical, dialogue might best be centered.

As Jewett considered America's popular culture, whether movies, television, comics, or video games, he found a troubling foundational myth—a narrative the American public uncritically accepted, and which provided a model for interpreting current events. He called it the "Captain America" complex, or the "myth of the American superhero." America's national ideology was rooted in our fascination with Superman and John Wayne. This monomyth, argued Jewett, when operational, was antithetical to the American democratic ideal, creating "mythic dissonance." Its "elitism, irrationalism, zealous stereotyping, and appetite for total solutions instead of compromise" consistently undermined the American ethos at its best.[14]

The result, reasoned Jewett, was the cowboy politics all too evident particularly in the White House of both Bushes, first in the Gulf War and then in our response to 9/11 with our subsequent military action in Afghanistan. The events of September 11 did not create this myth; it only reawakened it. Although this myth arose in part from out of our nation's historical experience, its continuing expression through popular culture created, according to Jewett, "a reciprocal pressure on succeeding generations." That is, it provided

---

13. Jewett, *Saint Paul at the Movies*. For a helpful, brief review of Jewett's dialogue in a prophetic mode, see Nolan, "Books of the Films."

14. Lawrence and Jewett, *Myth of the American Superhero*, 338.

"a scenario or prescription for action, defining and limiting the possibilities for human response to the universe."[15]

Jewett, together with his sometimes co-author John Shelton Lawrence, noted that time after time in our American storytelling, there was an individual superhero who is contrasted with impotent people and corrupt public institutions. Lonely, selfless and sexless, the hero's sole interest is focused on his zeal for his mission. An outsider who is often aided by fate, this hero's redemptive mission sanctifies his use of reluctant violence and questionable ethics before victory is finally achieved, and the hero fades into the sunset. Think of John Wayne in *Shane*, though Jewett chooses to reference other of his movies. But the pattern is also true of Luke Skywalker (*Star Wars*), Captain Kirk (*Star Trek*), Chief Brody (*Jaws*), and Neo (*The Matrix*), as well as many of the movies of Mel Gibson (*Lethal Weapon, Braveheart*), Sylvester Stallone (all the *Rambo* movies), and Clint Eastwood (*Unforgiven*). It is even in the television hit *Touched by an Angel* and the children's classic from Disney, *The Lion King*. As the myth would have it, the public is so helpless that only outside, violent intervention can save it—someone (enter the US) with the wisdom, power, and resolve to solve the problems of democracy on their behalf.

This American monomyth, argued Jewett, had certain affinities with two Judeo-Christian dramas, combining elements of the selfless servant/savior who sacrifices his life for others with the zealous crusader who destroys evil. For Jewett, "The premise is that the vitality of democracy and a full understanding of contemporary religious consciousness depend on the intensive examination of these heroic redemptive images from popular culture."[16]

Perhaps the published picture of George Bush laughing at the cover of the German news magazine *Der Spiegel* says it all. In their political cartoon, we see the faces of members of George W. Bush's cabinet transposed onto the bodies of American superheroes. President Bush becomes Rambo, Colin Powell is Batman, Condoleezza Rice is Xena the warrior princess, Vice-President Chaney is the Terminator, and Secretary of Defense Donald Rumsfeld is Conan the Barbarian. Tellingly, when shown this cover by the US Ambassador to Germany, President Bush responded by ordering "thirty-three poster-size renditions of the cover to be conveyed back to the White House."[17] (Given the mythic structure of this cartoon, is it only accidental that thirty-three posters were ordered?)

15. Lawrence and Jewett, *Myth of the American Superhero*, 111, 233.
16. Jewett and Lawrence, "American Monomyth in a New Century," 11.
17. Jewett and Lawrence, *Captain America and the Crusade against Evil*, 43.

There are, however, less humorous examples. As Jewett pointed out, one can also find affinities between the monomyth and the lives of Timothy McVeigh, of the Unabomber, and of the real life "hero" of the movie *American Sniper*.[18] He compares Oliver North before the joint House-Senate hearing on the Iran-contra affair with Rambo, where North spoke with the language of a zealot, expressing no shame for going outside the law, for lying to government officials, for falsifying governmental records, and for displaying contempt for constitutional processes, given his desire to aid the Nicaraguan contras. Despite his bending of "ethical standards," many Americans found North to be, nonetheless, a real-life superhero. North had not just fought a play war with catsup blood. Devoted to an elevated cause— the American way—crimes committed as part of his redemptive crusade were judged by many to be incidental.

Jewett compared Ollie North's story to *Rambo: First Blood, Part II*. In that superhero movie, Rambo is sent to rescue POWs who have been left behind because of a corrupt democratic system. As Rambo prepares for his mission, he asks his officer, "Sir, do we get to win this time?" To which the officer replies, "This time it's up to you." Rambo is a fighting genius, now able to win a war others had earlier forced him to lose. But of course, Rambo is only a movie character! Nevertheless, writes Jewett, "It is as if the real Rambo had suddenly emerged on live television, conforming perfectly to the super-heroic ideal."[19]

While many Americans loved North for his super patriotism, Jewett did not. Having grounded America's response to Oliver North in the superhero tradition of Rambo, et. al., Jewett proceeds to criticize this zeal: "Patriotism of the type popularized by the fictional John Rambo and the real-life Ollie North is gravely threatening to a constitutional democracy."[20] To make his point, he puts "Ollie/ Rambo" into conversation with Paul in Romans. How might this real-life Rambo fit with Paul's self-critique of his former life as a Jewish zealot and with the life, death, and resurrection of Jesus who chose to reject such zeal, dying in place of the zealot Barabbas? North, like the unrepentant Paul, was someone for Jewett who had "zeal without understanding." (Rom 10:2) "Seeking to establish their own righteousness, they did not submit to the righteousness of God." (Rom 10:3; RSV)

Jewett's conclusion regarding his trialogue between Rambo, Oliver North, and Paul makes clear his priorities. It is ultimately Jewett the Pauline

---

18. Jewett and Lawrence, "Mythic Shape of *American Sniper*"; Jewett and Lawrence, *Myth of American Superhero*, 167, 176.

19. Jewett, "Zeal without Understanding," 755.

20. Jewett, "Zeal without Understanding," 754.

scholar, not Jewett the social scientist or film critic, who is paramount. "Those of us who understand what Paul was talking about," writes Jewett, "need to translate it into terms that our co-workers and family members can understand, helping them to enter this discussion with vigor and effectiveness. Christians need to become far more critical of the realm of popular entertainment, which has filled the minds of our children with the exploits of zealous superheroes who lack understanding."[21]

But my question is this. Is this unnuanced judgment fair to American popular culture? And particularly, to the superhero stories that populate it? More particularly, does Jewett's claim for the existence of an American monomyth, for one dominant mythic structure, which animates our popular culture, hold true today? Or might, in fact, a present, alternate mythic structure for our superheroes both undergird many of our tentpole movie's today and provide a better contextualized base on which to anchor his hope for a Pauline alternative?

In her review of Jewett and Lawrence's *Captain America and the Crusade against Evil* (2003), Claudia May perceptively asks, perhaps rhetorically:

> I am not an expert on the history and personality of superheroes, but it is my feeling that Captain America [and Rambo] fits nicely into the theoretical paradigm that Jewett and Lawrence put forward in their work. Would an examination into other American superheroes complicate, or at best add further dimensions, to Jewett and Lawrence's analysis . . . ?[22]

Paul Borgman is even more pointed in his appreciation, yet critique. Reviewing *The American Monomyth* (1977), he praises the authors for "their detailed, illuminating, and provocative analyses of television, film, comics, and *Playboy*." However, he also wonders, "Any single prism through which so much can be filtered is subject to the suspicion of having been artificially cut. Taking popular culture seriously is so important and so rare that this book needs to be read, though in the last analysis I would fault the authors for not taking it seriously enough."[23]

An Alternate Superhero Myth

Borgman and May are correct. On the one hand, the myth of the American superhero is certainly a central strand within popular culture's storytelling.

---

21. Jewett, "Zeal without Understanding," 756.
22. May, "Review of *Captain America*," 109.
23. Borgman, "Review of *The American Monomyth*," 60.

Jewett's judgment in 2002 concerning it has also proven tragically true: ". . . our mythic conformity in mounting military crusades (has been) ill-suited in response to terrorism" and has made our situation "ever more vulnerable."[24] Can anyone seriously question his conclusion after the last twenty years in Afghanistan? Nevertheless, central as well are other superhero stories, particularly those in the Marvel comics of Stan Lee, together with their film adaptations. DC Comics, with its Justice League of America triumvirate of Superman, Batman, and Wonder Woman, but also the early Captain America, dominated the Golden Age of comics beginning with the first Superman comic in 1938 and lasting into the early 1960s. Here is Jewett's focus. And though their monomyth has continued (one need only think of the extremely successful *Batman* movie in 1989, when attitudes of American superiority had resurfaced and Ollie North's ethic of cowboy justice again prevailed, or of the success of the film *Wonder Woman*), increasingly the alternate world of Marvel superheroes created by Stan Lee has tended to attract more fans. Consider the sizable franchises created by *Spider Man*, *X-Men and Wolverine*, *Daredevil*, *The Fantastic Four*, *Iron Man*, *Black Widow*, *The Hulk*, and *Thor*, not to mention *The Avengers* movies where multiple Marvel superheroes are present.[25] Moreover, if one went outside movie adaptations of the comic book world, not only would one find the movies of John Wayne and Sylvester Stallone, but other movies like *One Flew over the Cuckoo's Nest*. The film stars Jack Nicholson as Randall McMurphy, a flawed hero with mythic whales on his boxer shorts who is compared to the Lone Ranger and becomes a Christ figure.

As my doctoral student, Anthony Mills, has argued convincingly in his book, *American Theology, Superhero Comics, and Cinema: The Marvel of Stan Lee and the Revolution of a Genre* (2014), with Stan Lee, there developed significant differences between DC and Marvel comics as a revolution in the American understanding of a superhero happened. Mills perceptively shows how these changes were part of a larger shift in our understanding of being human, American theologians during this same period also moving from a more individualistic framework in their understanding of the human to a relational one.[26]

Jewett, however, seems to have been oblivious to this important, alternate "myth," perhaps because it did not on first blush fit well with his larger agenda to use Paul to criticize American culture, much as Paul had

---

24. Jewett and Lawrence, *Myth of the American Superhero*, 337.

25. It also should be noted that Marvel, not DC, has now been incorporated into the Disney brand.

26. In what follows, I am dependent on Mills for many of my insights.

implicitly criticized the arrogance of the Roman Empire in the epistle to the Romans. Jewett, thus, remained focused on the Golden Age of superheroes (on Superman and Batman), never noticing the powerful alternate myth of Marvel's universe (of Spiderman, Iron Man and Wolverine), a universe that might help us as Americans better understand aspects of a Pauline anthropology, one that we had neglected or mistakenly understood.[27]

With the comics of Lee's superhero stories and their film adaptations, we can observe the following themes:

1. Rather than a hyper-individualism that includes a refusal of intimacy, we are now given characters like Peter Parker/Spiderman, who loves his aunt May and uncle Ben who have raised him and is only truly himself when giving to others. Family is important in much of Lee's universe, even if it is artificially created. In the *X-Men* franchise, for example, the mutants at the school are more than a group; they are a community. It is in this context that we understand Logan reaching out to hug Rogue in order for her to experience his healing powers, even though this comes close to sapping all his life energy. In Lee's world, relationships are paramount.

2. Rather than there being a lack of romantic involvement among Lee's superheroes, in *Iron Man*, Pepper Potts becomes more than Tony Stark's assistant. Both can even express their vulnerability, saying to each other that they do not have anyone else. Moreover, by the release of *The Avengers*, they are a romantic couple. In Lee's comics, to cite another example, Bruce Banner/Hulk marries Betty Ross, after her redemptive love has saved him. And in *The Fantastic Four*, Mr. Fantastic marries Sue Storm/Invisible Girl.[28]

3. Rather than the monomythic hero being a superior male (Superman) and his female counterpart clearly subordinate (Lois Lane), Lee's superheroes are flawed men and women who struggle with their humanity and exhibit both strengths and weaknesses. Among other emphases, *X-Men* is built around this theme. In *X-Men* as well, the enhanced role of women is also noticeable. Though still a minority, and

---

27. In his two volumes, *Saint Paul at the Movies: The Apostle's Dialogue with American Culture* (1993) and *Saint Paul Returns to the Movies: Triumph over Shame* (1999), Jewett seems more open than with his Captain America writings to allow this conversation to go two ways, Hollywood's movie portrayal of honor and shame helping viewers also to unpack what Paul might have been saying to the Romans.

28. It is significant that, given the popularity of Lee's relationally-oriented superheroes, even DC's Superman eventually marries Lois Lane, and in the latest DC comics, the new Superman comes out both as gay and as concerned about the environment.

not without their flaws, like the male mutants, Jean Grey, Storm, and Rogue are all important members of the superhero team. Similarly, Sue Storm, the mother in *The Fantastic Four*, not only has superpowers of her own, but she is married to Reed Richards, with her vulnerability encouraging their loving relationship.

4. Rather than the monomythic villain being simply evil (consider the Joker in *Batman*), something deemed necessary to protect the purity of the superhero and the innocence of the community (consider the classic Superman movies), in Lee's stories, the villains are full human beings with backstories and contexts that add complexity and understanding to their roles. In *Spider Man*, for example, the man who kills Uncle Ben turns out to have attempted a robbery because he was desperate for his dying daughter, only for his gun to accidentally fire. This "villain" confesses that he lives daily with his guilt. Again, Magneto, the villain in the *X-Men* series, turns out to be a tragic figure, who lost his daughter in the holocaust and is a survivor himself. Lee was unwilling to dehumanize even his hero's nemeses.

5. Rather than a life void of the normal problems in life, with no real need of others to help out, Lee turned such superheroes on their heads, making these characters more realistic, truer to life. In Lee's words, he wanted "heroes plagued with the problems that torment us all."[29] Iron Man/Tony Stark, thus, has heart problems, and Daredevil/Matt Murdock is blind. Peter Parker/Spider Man grieves over the death of his Uncle Ben who has raised him. As Lee develops his stories, it is the "normal" person (e.g., Peter Parker and Tony Stark) who is his primary focus, and the "costumed" character (e.g., Spider Man and Iron Man) who is secondary.

6. Rather than the superhero having a total lack of doubt, always knowing the right course of action, Lee's superheroes are filled with self-doubt and angst, even as they recognize their duty to fight evil in the world. Think of the hero Logan in the film *Logan*, perhaps the last of the *X-Men* franchise, who is losing his superpowers but eventually acts to save his biological daughter, even at the cost of his life. Again, what of the guilt-ridden Peter Parker? Alternatively, consider Bruce Banner, whose fear, anxiety and paranoia transform him into a frightening Hulk before his massive strength is brought under control by the redemptive love of Betty.

---

29. Lee, *Son of Origins*, 9, quoted in Mills, *American Theology, Superhero Comics, and Cinema*, 107.

7. Rather than being somewhat shallowly drawn and timeless, like those in the monomyth, Lee's superheroes often developed over several issues, with their movies situated concretely in time and place. This allows Lee to tell the backstories of his characters and to situate them in real cities like New York (not Gotham City or Metropolis). There is character development in Lee's storytelling. Tony Stark, for example, provides weapons early in his story to kill the Vietnamese, but by 1968, he has serious reservations and eventually gets out of the business totally. Like many of his fans, Tony becomes less enamored with war.

As Lee described his superheroes, he tried to create "the kind of characters I could personally relate to; they'd be flesh and blood, they'd have their faults and foibles, they'd be fallible and feisty, and most important of all—inside their colorful, costumed booties they'd still have feet of clay."[30]

Conclusion: The Need for Stereoscopic Vision

These important differences between the superheroes of DC and Marvel comics, which carries over into their film adaptations (i.e., between the American monomyth that Jewett describes and the alternate mythic world of Stan Lee), qualify Jewett's claims with regard to the American *zeitgeist* in important ways. Jewett's monomyth is still present today, but it is not singular. In fact, Lee's mythic alternative is certainly the more influential in today's popular culture, particularly for those under forty. Less an abstraction, Marvel's characters seem more "human,"—more relational, more vulnerable, more fallible, more in touch with life as it presents itself today. The roots of this new mythology go back to the 1960s with the death of JFK and MLK, and the debacle of the Vietnam War. The innocence of America's "Camelot" became indelibly tarnished, and with it, America's self-definition as Eden-like. It is not surprising that it was during this same time that both Superman and the Western with its solitary hero began to lose their pride of place within American popular culture. Rather than continuing to be attracted to a myth that seemed both untrue to life and often destructive of it, moviegoers turned in increasing numbers to Lee's mythic archetype that offered, instead, a model of fragile hope found within life's messiness.

Asked decades later by the editors organizing a new book to reflect on the shadow that 9/11 cast on American cinema, Jewett, together with his writing partner Lawrence, finally noted the challenge to the American

---

30. Lee, *Origins of Marvel Comics*, 17, quoted in Mills, *American Theology, Superhero Comics, and Cinema*, 107.

monomyth that such blockbuster movies as *American Sniper* brought. Chris Kyle, the military sharpshooter in the story, was on one level an American hero, a real-life Clint Eastwood or John Wayne whom he watched at the movies. He shot those who would harm America or would undermine Iraq's new American-supported government. Kyle had fervent Christian beliefs about the rightness of his violent business; he could not kill enough Iraqis. Nevertheless, his four deployments also took their toll. When told by his commander not to shoot, he goes rogue, and his disobedience risks the lives of his companions. In the movie, as these soldiers scramble to escape, Bible, American flag, and guns are all symbolically left behind. The movie voices these questions to Chris: "When does glory fade away and become a wrongful crusade?" "When does it become an unqualified means by which one is completely consumed?"[31]

Jewett and Lawrence rightly recognize that, here, the monomyth is under attack. Turning to consider the Captain America comics themselves, they find a similar growing complexity as Captain America, himself, in the months following 9/11, now recognized the failure of institutions, including his own government, to act justly. Jewett expresses surprise. Overlooked, however, is the fact that the story in which Cap appears is now part of the alternate mythology of Stan Lee. Captain America is now appearing as part of a Spider Man comic. As you would expect of a Marvel superhero, Cap is now critical, raising self-doubts. Might America also be part of the evil that is threatening to bring the world to its knees?

In a second essay, also written forty years after *American Monomyth* first was published, Jewett and Lawrence were asked to reflect on the importance in our culture of hero and superhero stories more generally. As before, they are cautious, even if optimistic. In their chapter on "Heroes and Superheroes" for the *Routledge Companion to Religion and Film* (2009), they write:

> We hope to persuade our readers that heroic films can convey insights that form conduct. Yet we are cautious about the overall influence of film . . . Hollywood filmmakers often give pious garb to reigning versions of American civil religion . . . We nonetheless maintain that film's apparent power to touch human hearts ensures continuing optimism, even among the critically sophisticated . . .[32]

Jewett and Lawrence then proceed to illustrate their cautious optimism by turning first to ordinary "heroes" in the movies, to those like

31. Jewett and Lawrence, "The Mythic Shape of *American Sniper* (2015)," 35.
32. Jewett and Lawrence, "Heroes and Superheroes," 385.

Alvin Straight, who drives his lawnmower two hundred miles to reconcile with his estranged brother in *The Straight Story* (1999). They also describe Sister Helen Prejean in *Dead Man Walking* (1995), who accompanies those sentenced to death to their execution. These ordinary people, who might be any of their audience, become heroes by their willingness to care for others. But when Jewett and Lawrence reflect once again on superheroes, their focus returns to the monomyth with its larger-than-life heroes, to those like the Superman of *Superman IV* (1987), who takes it on himself to rid the world of all nuclear weapons. However, acting alone, he unintentionally creates a graver danger in the process. The writers caution, "Such fantasies lead audiences to follow leaders who act as vigilantes to rid the world of evil. The superhero of the American monomyth does not free us from violence but perpetuates it even as he claims to be a force for 'peace' in his own use of rationalized violence."[33]

Unfortunately, Jewett's description of the American superhero is too singular, failing to note that just as heroes on the screen include everyday men and women who rise to the occasion, so too is a growing list of our superheroes. While there are Marvel superheroes as well as DC superheroes; while there are Spider Man and the Black Widow, not just Superman; while the Lone Ranger has given way as the iconic cowboy figure to the multicultural *Magnificent Seven* (2016); and while James Bond would in 2021 die to save the life of his daughter, Jewett fails to note these more hopeful alternatives within the superhero genre. Rather, Jewett's single vision focuses only on the monomyth; he needs a more stereoscopic vision.

A Biblical Coda

What might all this have to do with Jewett, the biblical scholar? Those considering Jewett's handling of the biblical materials have noted Jewett's strong preference for the prophetic realism of the prophets and Jesus, rather than the zealous nationalism of the Bible's "apocalyptic" genre, a genre he believes carries over today in secularized form into the American monomyth. However, while many might be sympathetic with Jewett's sentiments as am I, his biblical "solution" lacks any compelling connection to the American context that he presents. Instead, it seems to float unanchored to reality. Within the American context, his positive conclusions seem more like wishful thinking and, thus, unconvincing.

However, the alternative, mythic, superhero tradition of Marvel comics and films, which Jewett surprisingly overlooked, provides a more

---

33. Jewett and Lawrence, "Heroes and Superheroes," 399–400.

grounded alternative—one, since the assassination of JFK, having greater connection with the American experience. If the stereoscopic vision that Jewett presented in his biblical discussion (both the apocalyptic and the prophetic) had been carried over to a stereoscopic vision of the two dominate mythic structures in American culture, Jewett would have been able to better anchor his positive conclusions, while maintaining his negative critiques. For Stan Lee's creations—while not eliminating for Americans all interest in the Rambos of the world with their righteous, violent certainty—challenge America's arrogant individuality and rationalized violence. In the process, they provide Americans a more fully human and biblical alternative, something Jewett would have applauded.

Bibliography

(* For Further Reading)

Borgman, Paul. "Review of *The American Monomyth.*" *Christian Scholars Review* 9/4 (1980) 60–61.

*Davidson, Elijah. *How to Talk to a Movie: Movie-Watching as a Spiritual Practice*. Reel Spirituality Monograph Series. Eugene, OR: Cascade Books, 2017.

*Forbes, Bruce David and Jeffrey M. Mahan, eds. *Religion and Popular Culture in America*. Berkeley: University of California Press, 2017.

Jewett, Robert. *The Captain America Complex: The Dilemma of Zealous Nationalism*. Philadelphia: Westminster John Knox, 1973.

———. "Major Impulses in the Theological Interpretation of Romans since Barth." *Interpretation* 34 (1980) 17–31.

———. *Paul the Apostle to America: Cultural Trends in Pauline Scholarship*. Louisville: Westminster John Knox, 1994.

———. *Romans: A Commentary*. Hermeneia. Minneapolis: Fortress, 2007.

———. *Romans*. Teacher Book and Student Book for the "Genesis to Revelation Adult Bible Series" 20. Nashville: The Graded Press of the United Methodist Publishing House, 1986.

*———. *Saint Paul at the Movies: The Apostle's Dialogue with American Culture*. Louisville: Westminster John Knox, 1993.

———. *Saint Paul Returns to the Movies: Triumph over Shame*. Grand Rapids: Eerdmans, 1999.

———. "Zeal without Understanding: Reflections on Rambo and Oliver North." *Christian Century* 104 (1987) 753–56.

Jewett, Robert, and John Shelton Lawrence. *The American Monomyth*. Garden City, NY: Doubleday, 1977.

———. *Captain America and the Crusade against Evil: The Dilemma of Zealous Nationalism*. Grand Rapids: Eerdmans, 2003.

*———. "Heroes and Superheroes." In *The Routledge Companion to Religion and Film*, edited by John Lyden, 384–402. Routledge Companions. New York: Routledge, 2009.

*Johnston, Robert K., Craig Detweiler, and Kutter Callaway. *Deep Focus: Film and Theology in Dialogue*. Grand Rapids: Baker Academic, 2019.

Lawrence, John Shelton, and Robert Jewett. "The American Monomyth in a New Century." *Perspectives* (August/September 2002) 8–13.

———. "The Mythic Shape of *American Sniper* (2015)." In *American Cinema in the Shadow of 9/11*, edited by Terence McSweeney, 23–44. Edinburgh: Edinburgh University Press, 2017.

———. *The Myth of the American Superhero*. Grand Rapids: Eerdmans, 2002.

Lee, Stan. *Origins of Marvel Comics*. New York: Simon & Schuster, 1974.

———. *Son of Origins of Marvel Comics*. New York: Simon & Schuster, 1975.

May, Claudia. Review of Robert Jewett and John Shelton Lawrence, *Captain America and the Crusade against Evil*. *Implicit Religion* 9/1 (2006) 105–122.

*Mills, Anthony. *American Theology, Superhero Comics, and Cinema: The Marvel of Stan Lee and the Revolution of a Genre*. Routledge Studies in Religion and Film 2. New York: Routledge, 2014.

Nolan, Steve. "The Books of the Films: Trends in Religious Film Analysis." *Literature and Theology* 12/1 (1998) 1–15.

*Rindge, Matthew S. *Bible and Film: The Basics*. The Basics. New York: Routledge, 2021.

Roschke, Ronald W. "Review of Robert Jewett's *Saint Paul at the Movies* and Bernard Brandon Scott's *Hollywood Dreams & Biblical Stories*." Paper presented at the Society of Biblical Literature, Bible in Ancient and Modern Media, Chicago, Illinois, November 21, 1994.

Scott, Bernard Brandon. *Hollywood Dreams and Biblical Stories*. Minneapolis: Fortress, 1994.

Wilder, Amos Niven. *Theopoetic: Theology and the Religious Imagination*. Minneapolis: Fortress, 1976. Reprint, Eugene, OR: Wipf & Stock, 2014.

Study Questions

1. Are you more attracted to the Batman movies or those of Spider Man, and why? How are they fundamentally different? Similar? Does one seem more connected to American life today? Why?

2. How might you compare a Superman movie with one of John Wayne's Westerns? Why do you think Westerns are not as popular a movie genre as they were in the 1950s and 1960s?

3. How might you put one of the Superhero movies of Marvel/Disney into dialogue with the Epistle to the Romans? How about the movie *Logan*?

Part III

Pauline Study and Contemporary Cultures

14

Hospitality as a Means to Further God's Reign

in the New Testament and Dominican Context

Aída Besançon Spencer

Abstract

A SPECIAL "KIND OF HOSPITALITY" was an important mark of the Jesus movement and subsequent Christianity, according to Robert Jewett. In this essay, several cultures are compared in regard to hospitality: New Testament teachings and practice, the Greco-Roman world, and the Dominican context. Private "hospitality" is the provision and reception of nourishment, protection, housing, and honor. Hospitality was an honorable trait among all ancients. Nevertheless, Christ's teachings caused tension with the Roman and Jewish manner of hospitality, because, in common practice, Roman hospitality was built on hierarchy, moral obligation, and seeking honor. Christian ethics supported welcoming all strangers in a manner of equality and generosity without obligation.

Introduction

Hospitality has many dimensions in the Bible and in the ancient Greco-Roman world. "Hospitality" is the provision and reception of nourishment (food and drink), protection, housing, and honor to strangers and believers alike.[1] It is modeled and taught by God and Jesus, God incarnate, as an exhortation to all. The act of hospitality may (and should) function in a

---

1. This essay focuses on "private hospitality," not public, temple, commercial, or theoxenic. Fitzgerald, "Hospitality," 522.

variety of ways beyond the basic act of physical wellbeing. Today, the New Testament and ancient Greco-Roman practices are still reflected in contemporary Dominican hospitality.

Hospitality in the New Testament with Reference to the Old Testament

The Greek New Testament uses numerous synonyms to discuss hospitality. Several composite words and cognate families are founded on the root "stranger" (*xenos*): "love of a stranger" (*philoxenia, philoxenos*),[2] which Robert Jewett aptly translates "stranger-love"[3] and "to welcome a stranger" (*xenodocheō*, 1 Tim 5:10). These composite words do not occur in the Septuagint, although their concepts certainly do. The simple verbs *menō* ("to remain, stay," "lodge")[4] and *epimenō*[5] may also refer to hospitality, as well as *xenizō*, formed from the root *xenos* ("stranger"), signifying "to show hospitality, receive as a guest, entertain,"[6] "to welcome" (*dechomai*,[7] *anadechomai* [Acts 28:7], *hypodechomai*),[8] *synagō* (to "gather, extend a welcome to, invite/receive as a guest"),[9] *kataluō* ("find lodging"),[10] and *epimeleomai* ("care for"; Luke 10:34–35).

Hospitality has a dual component: love extended out to the stranger and love received by the stranger. Both are essential components because love has to be both received as well as given; otherwise, there is no equality between the persons. For example, Jesus countermands the practice

---

2. Rom 12:13; 1 Tim 3:2; Titus 1:8; Heb 13:2; 1 Pet 4:9.

3. Jewett, *Letter to Pilgrims*, 229.

4. BDAG, 630–31; LSJ, 1103. *Menō* as hospitality occurs in Matt 10:11; Mark 6:10; Luke 1:56; 8:27; 9:4; 10:7; 19:5; 24:29; John 1:38–39; 4:40; 11:6, 54; Acts 9:43; 16:15; 18:3, 20; 21:7–8.

5. "To remain at or in the same place for a period of time, stay." BDAG, 375. *Epimenō* as hospitality may be found in Acts 10:48; 21:4, 10; 28:14; Gal 1:18.

6. BDAG, 683. *Xenizō* normally is more formal, elaborate, and preplanned than *menō*, e.g., Acts 28:7 vs. Luke 1:56. *Xenizō* as hospitality appears in Acts 10:6, 18, 23, 32; 21:16; 28:7; Heb 13:2. *Xenia* is "guestroom," Phlm 22.

7. *Dechomai*, signifying hospitality, appears in Matt 10:14; Mark 6:11; Luke 9:5; 10:8, 10; 16:4, 9; Heb 11:31.

8. *Hypodechomai* refers to hospitality in Luke 10:38; 19:6; Acts 17:7; Jas 2:25.

9. BDAG, 962–63. *Synagō* as hospitality may be found in Matt 25:35, 38, 43; Rev 19:17–18.

10. *Kataluō* signifies "rest, find lodging" or "to cease what one is doing, halt (lit. 'unharness the pack animals')" in Luke 9:12 and 19:7. *Katalyma* is the "lodging place" (Luke 2:7; 22:11; Mark 14:14). BDAG, 521–22.

of guests seeking the places of honor at wedding banquets: "Everyone exalting himself will be humbled, and the one humbling himself will be exalted" (Luke 14:7–11).[11] Moreover, the poor should be invited because they cannot repay (Luke 14:12–14). Jesus was renowned for being impartial (Matt 22:16; Mark 12:14; Luke 20:21).

The stranger is the outsider, visitor, and non-citizen. For example, those not Athenians were called "strangers" and their gods termed "strange" (Acts 17:18, 21). Gentiles were "strangers to the covenants of promise" (Eph 2:12, 19). Ruth, a Moabite, daughter-in-law of Naomi, an Israelite, calls herself a "stranger" who expects to be ostracized. Instead, when Boaz fulfills not only the legal requirements of nourishment to strangers (Deut 24:19–22) but goes beyond them to allow her to glean from the pre-gleaned barley, gives her drink, and protects her, she exclaims: "How is it that I have found grace in your eyes, that you should take notice of me, and I myself am a stranger?" (Ruth 2:9–17). David feels a "stranger" to his own people, belittled for his zeal for God's house (Ps 69:7–9, 12–21).[12] Travelers waited at the village square until provided shelter by someone (Judg 19:15–21), a courtesy Job always extended (Job 31:32).

The epitome of hospitality in model, practice, and teachings is God. God is the host for strangers and other potentially oppressed people (orphans and widows): "The Lord your God is the one who is God of the gods and Lord of the lords, the Mighty, the Great, the Strong, and the Wonderful, who is not partial and does not take bribes, executing justice for orphan and widow and loving every stranger, giving each one food and clothing" (Deut 10:17–18). God hosts all humans. Since God created the world, all the world belongs to God and all humans are thus strangers and guests in it. "The land is mine" God explains in Leviticus 25:23.[13] God's hospitality is shown by the provision of rain and sun and the resulting harvests and the promise of food and clothing.[14] Jesus, as God in the flesh, is both the host and the stranger. As the host, he feeds thousands of his listeners (e.g., Luke 9:10–17),[15] hosts the Last Supper (Luke 13:29; 22:7–38),[16] the Great Supper (Luke 22:30), the heavenly house (John 14:2–3), feeds his disciples after the resurrection

---

11. Unless otherwise indicated, all quotations from the biblical text are my own translation. See also Mark 12:39.

12. A "stranger" could be an enemy (Eccl 6:2; Lam 5:2).

13. See further, Spencer "God the Stranger," 97–100.

14. E.g., Matt 5:45; 6:11, 25–33; Acts 14:15–17.

15. Jesus, assisted by his disciples, feeds crowds of more than 5,000 and 4,000 (Mark 6:35–44; 8:1–9, 19–21). See also John 6:1–15, 23, 26.

16. See also Matt 26:17–35; Mark 14:12–26. Two disciples prepare the Passover meal, but Jesus arranges the guest room and blesses the meal.

(John 21:6–12) and is himself "bread from heaven" who grants eternal life (John 6:27–59). As the stranger, he accepts dinner invitations where he teaches.[17] When he is not welcomed by his own people (John 1:10–11), he becomes the estranged "stranger," the one who is not welcomed: "A stranger I was and you welcomed me" or "a stranger I was and you did not welcome (*synagō*) me" (Matt 25:35–43). The humble believer who is welcomed then becomes an image of welcoming Jesus himself (Matt 25:40, 45).[18] Moreover, believers, as well, are "strangers to this earth" because their citizenship is in heaven (Heb 11:13–16).

Jesus initiates the importance of hospitality to the Twelve and the Seventy-two as a crucial means in the process to further God's reign. The disciples are to find someone "worthy" and stay (*menō*) or remain in that one place and not move about from house to house for the "laborer deserves to be paid" (Matt 10:9–13; Mark 6:8–11; Luke 10:7–9). Good news is given as a gift, yet nourishment and housing or "wages" are received thankfully as gifts in return. Hospitality is thus given to the ministering Christians as thanks for receiving the good news. The hospitality is an occasion to heal the sick, raise the dead, cleanse the leper, and cast out demons (Matt 10:8).[19] When the Samaritan woman tells the village of Sychar about the Messiah's presence, the inhabitants urge him to stay (*menō*) and Jesus does stay there several days (John 4:5, 28–30, 39–42). Thereby, evangelism is combined with discipleship through receiving hospitality. John Koenig describes New Testament hospitality as "the establishment of committed relationships between guests and hosts in which unexpected levels of mutual welcoming occur . . . [It stimulates] a mutual giving and receiving that will bear fruit for all sides within the plan of God."[20]

The New Testament provides many examples where hospitality becomes an opportunity for ministry, while a host is providing provisions.[21] For instance, after the Emmaus travelers urge Jesus to "remain" (*menō*) with them, Jesus reveals his identity (Luke 24:13–32). Prisca and Aquila

---

17. E.g., Luke 7:36–50; 10:38–42; 11:37–53; 14:1–24; Rev 3:20; Mark 14:3–9.

18. See also Matt 10:14, 40–41; Luke 9:48.

19. See also Mark 6:10; Luke 9:4. Consequently, Donald Wayne Riddle concludes that Christian hospitality "was important as a factor in the gospel transmission . . . [It was] an ultimate medium of Christianity's growth." "Early Christian Hospitality," 153–54.

20. Koenig, *Hospitality*, 8–9.

21. Howard notes that, when the Ethiopian eunuch invites Philip to join him in the chariot (Acts 8:21), he brings the teacher Philip into the student's "space," thereby allowing the student's questions and concerns to guide the learning. See Howard, "Philip, the Ethiopian Eunuch," 13–14.

extended hospitality, work, ministry to Paul (Acts 18:2-3). Publius in Malta "received" (*anadechomai*) Paul, Luke, and Aristarchus for three days and entertained them (*xenizō*), which gave Paul opportunity to heal Publius's father (Acts 28:7-8). Sometimes travelers are invited, sometimes they seek invitations (e.g., Acts 21:4; 28:14, *epimenō*; Phlm 22, *xenia*), and frequently Christ's kingdom is advanced. While their ship is unloading in Tyre, Paul and his coworkers seek disciples, who in turn warn Paul of future troubles in Jerusalem and pray for them (Acts 21:4-6, *menō*). In Caesarea, while Paul visits the evangelist Philip and his prophet daughters (*menō*), Agabus warns Paul of future imprisonment in Jerusalem (Acts 21:8-14). Staying at Mnason's home in Jerusalem allows Paul to communicate with James and the elders and dispute over gentiles (Acts 21:16-25).

Hospitality functions as a practical opportunity for ministry or dispensing the good news. In addition, hospitality may in itself communicate a theological message. Robert Jewett notes that hospitality among Jewish and gentile Christians in Rome provided an opportunity for reconciliation between them. After the dispersion of the Jews by the Edict of Claudius (Acts 18:2), the gentile Christians came into control of the church(es) in Rome. While Jewish Christians expected the church to remain as it was before their departure, Jewett points out that Gaius welcoming all Christian travelers (Jewish and gentile) (Rom 16:23) adds "an ecumenical scope" to his hospitality that was "consonant with the theology and ethic of [Romans], so that his greeting provides an endorsement."[22]

The acceptance of gentiles by Jews as shown by joint meals also represents the traversing of the Jewish-gentile divide of ritual cleanliness and uncleanliness (Acts 10:9-14, 23; 11:1-3; Deut 14:3-21). When Peter receives as guests Cornelius's three gentile messengers, he begins his monumental change of attitude and action (vs. Gal 2:11-14) and ends by staying with Cornelius and his household (Acts 10:48, *epimenō*). Lydia appears to understand the significance of Paul's message of unity when she strongly encourages Paul, Silas, Luke, and Timothy: "After you come into my house, remain" and they, in turn, encourage Lydia, her household, and colleagues (Acts 16:15, 40).

Another example of hospitality communicating a theological principle comes when Jesus stays (*menō*, Luke 19:5) at the house of Zacchaeus, a "sinner," a tax collector, and a chief one at that. Zacchaeus "welcomed" him (*hypodechomai*, Luke 19:6). Jewish onlookers "grumble" when Jesus "finds lodging" (*kataluō*) at the home of a "sinner" because tax collectors were "unclean" in rabbinic thought, thereby causing Jesus to be unclean

---

22. Jewett, *Romans: A Commentary*, 765, 980-81.

ritually as well.[23] However, Jesus's main goal is transformation of the lost (Luke 19:9–10), not ritualistic cleanliness. Similarly, when Jesus accepts the dinner invitation of Levi, along with other tax collectors and sinners, the teachers are outraged, but Jesus responds that his goal is healing the sin-sick (Mark 2:15–17).[24]

What undergirds hospitality is that it expresses "the charismatic love ethic."[25] For instance, as an example of good neighborliness, the outsider Samaritan takes care of the half-dead traveler by first observing him, then filling with compassion, healing him, bringing him to an inn, and paying the innkeeper to take care of him (*epimeleomai*, Luke 10:29–37). In Romans 12, in the context of love, hospitality is enjoined for all (Rom 12:4–5, 9, 13–14). After listing the gifts that serve the body, Paul summarizes, "Let love be genuine, hating the evil, holding on to the good" (12:9). Two manifestations of genuine love are financially contributing to ease other believers' needs and loving strangers through hospitality. While others might persecute believers, love's response is to bless, so that hospitality provides a way to live peaceably with all people. As love repays persecutors with hospitality: feeding and giving drink, "you will heap burning coals upon their heads" and, in that way, "conquer evil with good" (Rom 12:14–21; Prov 25:21–22). The need for hospitality is the connecting idea between love of believers and love as a response to persecution by non-believers. Love contrasts with evil (12:9–21).

Hebrews follows the thoughts in Romans. The context is "brotherly love" (*philadelphia*): "Do not neglect the love of strangers (*philoxenia*), for on account of doing this some having entertained as guests *(xenizō)* angels" (13:1–2). The basis is love, and this love may benefit oneself. Paul's admonition is followed by an exhortation to "remember the ones in prison" (13:3). The context here is when some Christians are in prison, probably near the end of Nero's persecution when Timothy himself has been imprisoned and is now released (13:23). Also, in 1 Peter, hospitality occurs in the context of love, but Peter now adds "without grumbling" (4:8–9). Afterwards, he summarizes the two broad gifts of speaking and serving (4:10–11). He does not subsume hospitality under the gift of service.

While hospitality is enjoined in Romans under the larger context of admonitions to all the "brothers and sisters" ("all of you," "one body," 12:1–5), in the Pastoral Letters, Paul requires the practice especially of church

23. E.g., Mishnah Tohoroth 7:2, 5–6; John 18:28–29.

24. See also Jas 2:25; Heb 11:31, where Rahab "welcomed" the Jewish spies. See also Matt 11:19; Luke 15:22–24.

25. Jewett, *Romans: A Commentary*, 765. For the importance of the "relief of strangers" as an expression of love by the early church, see also Harnack, *Mission*, 1:177–98.

leaders, the overseer (*episkopos,* 1 Tim 3:2; *presbyteros* and *episkopos,* Titus 1:5–8).[26] Part of the goal is to be well regarded by outsiders (1 Tim 3:7). Hospitality shows in action what an overseer teaches (1 Tim 3:2). It models goodness, wisdom, righteousness, holiness, and self-control (Titus 1:8; 2:12). Though deacons, male or female, are *not* required to be hospitable (1 Tim 3:8–13), elder widows are included as leaders, bearing witness with good works demonstrated in actions, one of which is hospitality, while dedicating their last years to continual prayer, following the example of prophet Anna in the temple (1 Tim 5:5, 10; Luke 2:36–37).

Such emphasis on hospitality did open it to misuse. Some traveling ministers took advantage, spreading false doctrine (2 John 10; 3 John 6–8, 10). Eventually, the Didache (ca. end of first century–150) amassed elongated rules for hospitality toward itinerant apostles and prophets, including a three-day maximum stay (11:3–13:7).

Hospitality in the Greco-Roman World in Comparison with New Testament Teachings and Practice

Did a special "kind of hospitality" mark the "Jesus movement and subsequent Christianity"?[27]

On the one hand, hospitality was an honorable trait among all ancients. *Zeus Xenios* was considered the defender of strangers (2 Macc 6:2),[28] even as the God of Israel "loved every stranger" (Deut 10:18). Many ancient Greeks, Romans, and Jews were renowned for their hospitality. For example, Gallias of Agrigentum (fourth century BCE) posted slaves at the city gates to welcome strangers to his house.[29] Junia Theodora, a Roman living in Corinth in 43 CE, was honored for being "kind to all travelers, private individuals as well as ambassadors, sent by the nation or the various cities."[30] Plutarch considered Cimon's hospitality to surpass that of all other ancient Athenians, since he had a meal prepared at his home every day for visitors, including the poor.[31] Diodorus of Sicily noted that Spaniards entreated strangers to visit their homes, vying for the honor of hospitality and regarding "with approval" as "beloved of the gods" whomever travelers chose as host.[32]

26. The Shepherd of Hermas refers as well to the hospitality of overseers (*Sim.* 9.27).
27. Jewett, *Romans: A Commentary,* 765.
28. See also Dunn, *Romans,* 743.
29. Spicq, *TLNT,* 455.
30. Spicq, *TLNT,* 455–56.
31. Plutarch, *Cim.* 10; Spicq, *TLNT,* 456.
32. Diodorus Siculus, *Hist.* 5.34; Spicq, *TLNT,* 456.

Among the Jews, Abraham was a model of hospitality (Gen 18:1–8), as was Job, Rahab, Lot (Gen 19:1–3), Melchizedek (Gen 14:17–24), Rebekah (Gen 24:16–25), the Shunamite woman (2 Kings 4:8–17), Boaz, and Manoah (Judg 13).[33] Jose ben Johanan of Jerusalem is remembered for saying: "Let thy house be opened wide and let the needy be members of thy household" (Aboth 1:5). Even Herod's palace had bedchambers for one hundred guests.[34]

However, on several occasions, Christ's teachings caused tension with the Roman and Jewish manner of hospitality because, in common practice, Roman hospitality was built on hierarchy, moral obligation, and seeking honor. The Romans considered the city of Rome the social center of the Roman universe, and, thus, foreigners, beyond the frontiers, were objects of scorn. For example, Ammianus Marcellinus (fourth century CE) described members of the top Roman senatorial society as snobs who, "with empty bombast, treat anything born outside the city as simple dirt."[35] Ladislaus Bolchazy explains that, in order for a stranger to survive at Rome, he must demonstrate the "right of hospitality" (*ius hospitii*) as a *peregrinus* ("foreigner") having come from a community with which Rome had a treaty, thus, becoming a "guest-friend" (*hospes*), or place himself under the protection of a Roman citizen as a "client" (*cliens*), or go voluntarily into slavery.[36]

Roman historian J. P. V. D. Balsdon summarizes: "Roman society was built on the idea of deference (*obsequium*) in the family as in the State . . . In a class-ridden society all owed deference to those above them."[37] Jérôme Carcopino explains, when the Romans ate reclining, three couches would range around a square table, one side empty for the service. Each couch had space for two, often a man and woman side by side. The dining room might be planned for twenty-seven guests around three tables or thirty-six guests around four tables. On each of these couches, the most privileged position was that to the left, nearest the fulcrum or head of the couch. Seating had a hierarchical precedence. The couch of honor was opposite the empty side of the table (*lectus medius*), and on its right, the "consular" (*locus consularis*), the most honorable position. Next in honor came the couch to the left of the central one (*lectus summus*), and last was that on its right (*lectus imus*).[38]

---

33. Dunn, *Romans 9–16*, 744; Spicq, *TLNT*, 456; Elliott, *Home*, 184–87; 1 Clem. 10:7–11:1; 12:1–3.

34. Fitzgerald, "Hospitality," 524.

35. Balsdon, *Romans*, 25, 29.

36. Bolchazy, *Hospitality*, 22, 26, 34–35, 91.

37. Balsdon, *Romans*, 18.

38. Carcopino, *Daily Life*, 265–66.

Often the master of the house would treat his guests as inferiors to himself. Pliny the Younger describes a host who served himself and a few others very elegant dishes, while the rest had cheap and paltry food. The wines served were graduated according to the social status of the friends.[39] For example, one poor client had to settle with the coarsest wine, bits of hard moldy bread, toadstools of doubtful quality, a rotten apple, and other undesirable food. Carcopino adds, "Evidence from many sources places it beyond doubt that these practices were widespread."[40] John Dominic Crossan explains: "Distinctions and discriminations among foods or guests stand or fall with distinctions and discriminations among seats and salutations." Thus, three cultural levels are interlinked: food, table, and society. "To subvert either of the former is a calculated attack on the latter."[41]

Lynn Cohick elaborates:

> Though repeatedly couched in the language of friendship, the patron/client relationship was almost always asymmetrical. A patron might give a client money, food, an introduction to an important person, or advice. The client might reside in the patron's home. The patron might offer a low-interest loan to start a business or help the client find a spouse. The client was indebted to praise the patron publicly, for example, in the public greeting (*salutatio*) of the patron offered each morning at the patron's home. Often the client would praise the patron at the baths or as the patron traveled through the city. Patrons were expected to continue to support their clients, and clients were to remain loyal and provide whatever services the patron might require.[42]

She summarizes, "The institution of patronage structured society."[43] Crossan adds that the relationship between patron and client might be "horizontal or vertical depending on whether it is between social equals or unequals."[44] Such ethics of "friendship" (*amicitia*) entailed mutual indebtedness. Neither party could ever really be "paid up." The "bill" would be paid in installments, such as favors done for friends.[45] For instance, Marcus Cornelius Fronto tells Lucius Verus (166 CE): "All the favours I have had to ask from my Lord

---

39. *Pliny, Natural History* 14.91; Carcopino, *Daily Life,* 270; MacMullen, *Roman Social,* 111–12.
40. Carcopino, *Daily Life,* 270–71.
41. Crossan, *Historical Jesus,* 263.
42. Cohick, *Women in the World,* 289. See also Bolchazy, *Hospitality,* 40–46.
43. Cohick, *Women in the World,* 323.
44. Crossan, *Historical Jesus,* 60.
45. Crossan, *Historical Jesus,* 61.

your brother I have preferred to ask and obtain from you."[46] Patron-client networks in the Roman Empire permeated society from top to bottom with "accounts that could never be exactly balanced because they could never be precisely computed."[47] Bolchazy describes moral obligation as "contractual hospitality," which was binding not only for the duration of one's life but indefinitely, binding the children and their offspring as well.[48]

Consequently, hospitality as an ancient ideal was an excellent means for Christians to appeal to their pagan society, even in times of persecution. Bolchazy concludes that because of the right of hospitality, "Graeco-Roman society was capable of understanding, and predisposed to accepting, the social teachings of Christianity. The *ius hospitii* became a stem upon which Christianity could be grafted."[49]

However, Christian ethics supported welcoming all strangers and in a manner of equality and generosity without obligation. Food and seating were open to all. These factors created the special kind of hospitality that characterized Jesus and, subsequently, Christianity. The New Testament documents tensions created between Roman and Christian values. James criticizes the favorable seating of the wealthy and the dishonoring of the poor (2:1–9). Paul criticizes the honoring of rich Corinthians while neglecting poor believers. Gerd Theissen aptly explains how "the one eating and drinking without recognizing the body eats and drinks judgment to himself" (1 Cor 11:29) refers to the need to discern and include fairly all poor believers because the Lord's Supper is a symbol of unity rather than division (1 Cor 11:21–22, 33–34). When the wealthier ate by themselves, receiving larger portions and better quality of food, Theissen notes,

> the core of the problem was that the wealthier Christians made it plain to all just how much the rest were dependent on them ... Differences in menu are a relatively timeless symbol of status and wealth, and those not so well off came face to face with their own social inferiority at a most basic level.[50]

The wealthier humbled those who had nothing. What was appropriate in a socially stratified society was not appropriate among members of the body of Christ (cf. Acts 2:44–45).[51]

---

46. Crossan, *Historical Jesus*, 60.
47. Crossan, *Historical Jesus*, 65.
48. Bolchazy, *Hospitality*, 16–17, 38–40.
49. Bolchazy, *Hospitality*, 66.
50. Theissen, *Social Setting*, 151, 154–58, 160. See also Koenig, *Hospitality*, 66–70.
51. Theissen, *Social Setting*, 160.

Jesus exhorted his followers to be hospitable without obligating the person invited. Both the giving and responding to generosity are gifts. Instead of a hierarchy of wealth, power, nationality, purity, and righteousness, Paul follows Jesus's examples and teachings to regard and treat similarly the poor and wealthy, the powerless and powerful, the gentile and Jew, the ritually unclean and clean, the transformed and the self-righteous.

Hospitality in the Dominican Context in Comparison to Ancient Roman and New Testament Teachings

I chose to contrast ancient Roman and New Testament teachings on hospitality with those of the Dominican Republic for several reasons. I was born there and lived there throughout my elementary years. When my parents (from Puerto Rico and the Netherlands) retired there, I visited them several times a year and, after their deaths, my husband and I continue to visit there yearly. Dominicans are proud of their renown for hospitality. One promotional web site for the Dominican Republic begins: "Dominicans have a reputation for being among the friendliest people you'll meet . . . Courtesy and hospitality are core values, particularly in the countryside. Coming to the aid of visitors or a neighbor, and sharing a plate of food are considered normal." Thus, one of the ten reasons to travel to the Dominican Republic is "the warmth, hospitality, and vibrancy of the Dominican people."[52]

Thus, tourism is a natural national industry. The Dominican Republic is the most visited destination, with the largest tourist market, in the Caribbean. In 2019, the Dominican Republic had 6.5 million international arrivals and the highest number of hotel rooms (8,000) in the Caribbean.[53]

The Dominican Republic has three early cultural influences: the Taino natives, the Spaniard colonists, and the African slaves.[54] In 2017, the estimate was 72 percent of Dominicans have mixed African and Spanish descent, 11 percent are black, 16 percent are white, and 1 percent other.[55] Christopher Columbus arrived at the island of Haytí/Española in 1492[56] and found the Tainos to be very generous and hospitable. Columbus wrote: "They will give all that they do possess for anything that is given to them."[57] Predominantly Roman Catholic, the Dominican Republic is the

---

52. "Dominican Republic Has It All: Why Dominican Republic?"
53. Garcia, *Diario Libre*, 9.
54. Deive, "La Herencia Africana," 132, 138–39.
55. Wiarda, "Dominican Republic."
56. Dipp, *Raza*, 21.
57. Cintron, "The Taino Are Still Alive."

only country in the world with the Bible on its flag. Thus, Dominicans are consciously "Christian." Their appreciation of hospitality echoes both the Taino and Latin heritage from the Spaniards, but also yields some classism between the rich and middle class vs. the poorer laboring class.[58] Servants do not tend to eat with their landlords.

Like the ancient Romans, the Dominicans reflect the moral obligation from informal friendship and hospitality. My father worked for a Dutch company whose top leaders and administrators were from the Netherlands, but the other workers were from the Dominican Republic. He befriended one Dominican (Francisco) at work. As a result, Francisco graciously frequently did many favors for my parents. For example, he would pick me up at the airport whenever I arrived, sometimes with barely enough gas to travel back. When he died, his son, Juan, continued to help my parents in many ways; for instance, by taking care of their house when they moved to New Jersey. When he died and my father died, Juan's wife, Maria, was of great help when I tried to get errands done. She would frequently invite my husband and me to eat with her and her children at noon. The most efficient way for me to get errands done that required special help was to ask her to call her contacts after the meal while I waited next to her. For instance, the government required me to have a Dominican identification card for banking and business purposes, but I was not able to obtain one because they could not find my original birth records. My struggle went on for several years. I wanted to resolve this problem myself. However, finally, in exasperation (at a meal) I shared the bureaucratic impasse the government had placed me in. The government required me to have a Dominican identification card since I was born in the Dominican Republic, but they could not give me one! When Maria saw my distress, she gave me a reference to contact. As a result, I obtained an identification card in just days! Maria was most hospitable in providing food, lodging, and referrals.[59]

I have never found Dominicans, like Romans, offering inferior hospitality to some, but most do expect a moral obligation in extended relationships of "friendship." I think that devout Christian Dominicans, especially from the countryside, see their hospitality as gifts given without expectation of return. Yet guests gladly give favors in return.

Christians from all cultures can learn from the Dominicans to give and receive hospitality graciously. Nevertheless, we all can learn even more

---

58. Classism began in colonial society with the Spaniards who held to "purity of race" or "blood," traditionally discriminating against Moors, Jews, excommunicated persons, and converts. Dipp, *Raza*, 119–24, 235, 271, 300.

59. Nevertheless, friends are still advised to obtain their own lawyers in business relationships. See Collado, *Tíguere*, 13, 16–17, 26.

from Jesus to treat all people without favoritism and not expect a return for our own generosity, since "Love is not self-seeking . . . It always protects, always trusts, always hopes, always perseveres" (1 Cor 13:4; 7 NIV).

Methodology

Since "hospitality" is such a broad term, I chose to narrow the topic by beginning with the microcosm, word studies, while looking for Greek synonyms in each passage, then moved to the macrocosm, reading key New Testament books, especially narratives, for anything related to hospitality. In this manner, I extended the concepts studied by the specificity of words, but not limiting myself to these. Then I began the secondary study with Robert Jewett's own works and read his secondary references and other references in our school's library and elsewhere. My biblical study presupposes the Bible's claims for itself as to reliability and historical accuracy. I attempted to study words and passages in the historical and literary contexts of the New Testament letters. The electronic resources on the Dominican Republic were doublechecked for accuracy by consulting library and personal resources when I visited the Dominican Republic in April 2021.

Hospitality in the Gospels Related to Jesus[60]

Table 14.1: Jesus as Guest

Luke	Host	Theme	Mark	Matthew	John
4:38–39	Simon's mother	gratitude	1:31	8:14–15	
5:29–31	Levi	repentance	2:15–17	9:10–13	
7:36–50	Simon the Pharisee	forgiveness, love			
10:38–48	Martha	priorities			
11:37–53	Pharisee	cleanliness, justice, love			

60. The focus of the chart is the Gospel of Luke because it has more and many unique references to the theme of hospitality. Similar events are then listed parallel to Luke. The sequence of the Gospels listed are unrelated to source or chronology. The parallels were verified in *The NIV Harmony of the Gospels with Explanations and Essays*. Chart created by Aída Besançon Spencer, April 6, 2021.

Luke	Host	Theme	Mark	Matthew	John
14:1–24	Pharisee	Sabbath, healing, honor, no repayment, love			
19:1–10	Zacchaeus	saving the lost			
23:50–54	Joseph of Arimathea (plus Nicodemus)	offered tomb (plus spices)	15:42–46	27:57–60	19:38–42
24:29–35	Emmaus travelers	resurrected Jesus			
24:36–52	Disciples	prophecy fulfillment			
John 2:1–11	Wedding bridegroom	Jesus revealed glory (sign 1)			
4:7–28, 29, 39	Samaritan woman	cleanliness, living water, worship, Messiah, reveals inner nature			
4:40–43	Samaritans	savior of world			
12:1–11	Martha, Lazarus, Mary	Jesus's burial—to see resurrected Lazarus, love			
19:28–30	Soldier?	final act, duty	15:36	27:48	
Mark 14:3–9	Simon the leper	preparation for Jesus's burial, love		26:6–13	
15:23	Soldier?	crucifixion		27:34	

Table 14.2: Jesus as Host

Luke	Topic/theme	Mark	Matthew	John
9:12–17	5000-plus are fed with five loaves and two fish	6:35–44; 8:19	14:15–21; 16:9	6:1–15, 23, 26
13:29–30	Great Supper, global, honor		8:11–12	
22:8–38	Passover, new covenant for forgiveness of sins, love	14:12–26	26:17–30	13:1–17:26 meaning of love

	Topic/theme	Mark	Matthew	John
John 6:27–59	Jesus as bread from heaven, eternal life			
7:37–39	Spirit gives drink			
21:6–14	Jesus as provider			
Mark 8:1–9, 19–21	4000-plus are fed with seven loaves and a few fish		15:32–38; 16:10	

Table 14.3: Hospitality/Dinner(s) Used as Illustrations by Jesus

Luke	Topic/ theme	Mark	Matthew
6:1–5	eat grain, Jesus is Lord of Sabbath	2:23–28	12:1–8
7:34	Jesus's ministry, cleanliness		11:19
10:7–8	72/12, stay in house	6:10 (Twelve)	10:11 (Twelve)
10:27–37	good Samaritan, neighbor, love		
11:5–8	friend, provide for visitor, duty		
11:11–13	parent-child, good gifts, duty, love		7:10–11 generosity
12:37–38	master serves servant, duty		
15:22–24	father of prodigal son, forgiveness and restoration, love		
16:19–21	rich, lack of hospitality		
Matthew			
22:2–14	wedding feast, punishment, reception		
25:1–13	wedding banquet, be prepared		
25:34–46	king separates sheep from goats, whatever is done to the least of these is done for Son of Humanity		

Bibliography

(* For Further Reading)

Balsdon, J. P. V. D. *Romans and Aliens*. Chapel Hill: University of North Carolina Press, 1979.

Bauer, Walter, Frederick W. Danker, W. F. Arndt, and F. W. Gingrich. *A Greek-English Lexicon of the New Testament and other Early Christian Literature* [BDAG]. 3d ed. Chicago: University of Chicago Press, 2000.

*Bolchazy, Ladislaus J. *Hospitality in Antiquity: Livy's Concept of Its Humanizing Force*. Chicago: Ares, 1995.

*Carcopino, Jérôme. *Daily Life in Ancient Rome: The People and the City at the Height of the Empire*. Edited by Henry T. Rowell. Translated by E. O. Lorimer. New Haven: Yale University Press, 1940.

Cintron, David Ray. "The Taino Are Still Alive, Taino Cuan Yahabo: An Example of the Social Construction of Race and Ethnicity." *Electronic Theses and Dissertations, 2004–2019*, 22. http://purl.fcla.edu/fcla/etd/CFE0001325.

*Cohick, Lynn H. *Women in the World of the Earliest Christians: Illuminating Ancient Ways of Life*. Grand Rapids: Baker, 2009.

Collado, Lipe. *El tiguere dominicano: Hacia una aproximación de cómo son los dominicanos*. Santo Domingo: Collado, 2002.

Crossan, John Dominic. *The Historical Jesus: The Life of a Mediterranean Jewish Peasant*. New York: HarperSanFrancisco, 1991.

Danby, Herbert, trans. *The Mishnah*. Oxford: Oxford University Press, 1933.

Deive, Carlos Esteban. "La Herencia Africana en la Cultura Dominicana Actual." In *Ensayos sobre cultura Dominicana*, edited by Bernardo Vega et al., 107–41. 5th ed. Santo Domingo: Fundación Cultural Dominicana, 1997.

Diodorus of Sicily. 12 volumes. Translated by C. H. Oldfather. Loeb Classical Library [LCL]. Cambridge: Harvard University Press, 1939.

Dipp, Hugo Tolentino. *Raza e Historia en Santo Domingo: Los orígenes del prejuicio racial en América*. Santo Domingo: Editorial Búho, 2015.

"Dominican Republic Has It All: Our People." GoDomincanRepublic.com. https://www.godominicanrepublic.com/about-dr/our-people.

"Dominican Republic Has It All: Why Dominican Republic?" GoDomincanRepublic.com. https://www.godominicanrepublic.com/meetings-industry/why-dr.

Dunn, James D. G. *Romans 9–16*. Word Biblical Commentary 38. Dallas: Word, 1988.

Elliott, John H. *A Home for the Homeless: A Sociological Exegesis of 1 Peter, Its Situation and Strategy*. Philadelphia: Fortress, 1981. Reprint, Eugene, OR: Wipf & Stock, 2005.

Fitzgerald, J. T. "Hospitality." In *Dictionary of New Testament Background*, edited by Craig A. Evans and Stanley E. Porter, 522–25. Downers Grove, IL: InterVarsity, 2000.

García, Pablo. "Banco Central: la actividad turística volverá a la normalidad en el 2023." *Diario Libre* (March 31, 2021) 9.

Harnack, Adolf. *The Mission and Expansion of Christianity in the First Three Centuries*. 2 vols. Translated and edited by James Moffatt. Theological Translation Library 19. 2nd ed. London: Williams & Norgate, 1908. Reprint, Wipf & Stock, 1998.

Holmes, Michael W., ed., trans. *The Apostolic Fathers: Greek Texts and English Translations*. 3d ed. Grand Rapids: Baker, 2007.

Howard, Melanie A. "Philip, the Ethiopian Eunuch, and Student Hospitality." *Didaktikos* 4/3 (2021) 12–14.
Jewett, Robert. *Letter to Pilgrims: A Commentary on the Epistle to the Hebrews.* New York: Pilgrim, 1981.
———. *Romans: A Commentary.* Hermeneia. Minneapolis: Fortress, 2007.
*Koenig, John. *New Testament Hospitality: Partnership with Strangers as Promise and Mission.* Overtures to Biblical Theology. Philadelphia: Fortress, 1985. Reprint, Eugene, OR: Wipf and Stock, 2001.
Liddell, Henry George, Robert Scott, and Henry Stuart Jones. *A Greek-English Lexicon.* 9th ed. Oxford: Clarendon, 1968.
MacMullen, Ramsay. *Roman Social Relations: 50 B.C. to A.D. 284.* New Haven: Yale University Press, 1974.
The NIV Harmony of the Gospels with Explanations and Essays. Edited by Robert L. Thomas and Stanley N. Gundry. New York: HarperSanFrancisco, 1987.
Plutarch's Lives. Translated by Bernadotte Perrin. 10 vols. Loeb Classical Library. New York: Macmillan, 1914.
Pliny: Natural History. 10 vols. Translated by H. Rackham. Loeb Classical Library. Cambridge: Harvard University Press, 1968.
Riddle, Donald Wayne. "Early Christian Hospitality: A Factor in the Gospel Transmission." *Journal of Biblical Literature* 52 (1938) 141–54.
*Spencer, Aída Besançon. "God the Stranger: An Intercultural Hispanic American Perspective." In *The Global God: Multicultural Evangelical Views of God,* edited by Aída Besançon Spencer and William David Spencer, 89–103. Grand Rapids: Baker, 1998.
*Spicq, Ceslas. *Theological Lexicon of the New Testament.* 3 vols. Translated and edited by James D. Ernest. Peabody, MA: Hendrickson, 1994.
*Theissen, Gerd. *The Social Setting of Pauline Christianity: Essays on Corinth.* Edited and translated by John H. Schütz. Philadelphia: Fortress, 1982. Reprint, Eugene, OR: Wipf & Stock, 2004.
Wiarda, Howard J. "Dominican Republic." In Britannica.com. https://www.britannica.com/place/Dominican-Republic.

Study Questions

1. Compare Jesus's teachings and practice of hospitality with one culture with which you have acquaintance.
2. Observe one way in which your own reception and giving of hospitality might be improved.

15

Reimagining the Thessalonians at the End of the World with Ghost Dancers

T. Christopher Hoklotubbe

Abstract

ROBERT JEWETT STRESSED THE usefulness of a social-scientific approach for interpreting the Thessalonian correspondence, analyzing the situation at Thessalonica in light of sociological models derived from the cross-cultural, historical study of millenarian movements. In honor of Jewett's groundbreaking work, not only do I seek to reintroduce students of the Bible to this method but also, as a mixed Indigenous and settler biblical scholar myself, I consider how a closer focus on a nativist millenarian movement—namely the 1890s Ghost Dance movement—might help us further think about and (re)imagine the social dynamics at play within the Thessalonian situation.

Introduction

First Thessalonians seems like a straightforward letter as far as exegeting goes. Paul, Silvanus, and Timothy collectively write to the predominately gentile Christ-following assembly (*ekklēsia*) of Thessalonica (1 Thess 1:9) after Timothy catches up with Paul and Silvanus in Corinth (Acts 18: 18–25), having just returned from his visit with the Thessalonians (1 Tim 3:6). Paul and Silvanus are encouraged to hear from Timothy that the Thessalonians have remained resilient in their "faith and love" (3:6) in the face of the persecution they have faced from their neighbors and perhaps city officials (2:14; 3:3). The authors declare their solidarity in their mutual suffering (3:3–5), emphasize their mutual longing for one another and desire to be together (2:17–20; 3:6), reaffirm their values and moral principles for sharing life together in a manner pleasing to God as followers of Christ (4:1–12, 5:12–22), and clarify that those who are alive now will not precede those who have died when Christ returns to judge the world and to resurrect the dead, which will come suddenly "like a thief in the night" (4:13—5:11). First Thessalonians is an especially warm pastoral letter that attempts to make the authors' loving presence and consolation present among the fledgling Thessalonian assembly.

And yet, our curiosity to know more about the aims of the letter writers and what the situation on the ground looked like for the Thessalonians—especially regarding the nature of and reasons for the persecution they faced and their understanding and concerns around the return of Christ—has proven to be intractably ambiguous. Interpreters of 1 Thessalonians have wondered whether the Thessalonians' concern about the order in which followers of Christ will welcome their Lord's arrival belies their doubts in Paul's teachings on the resurrection itself—resulting from the failed expectation in Christ's imminent return. Others have wondered whether Paul, Silvanus, and Timothy offer a sly criticism of the Roman imperial order insofar as they describe Jesus's descent to Earth as a *parousia* ("coming")—a term used to describe a ruler's celebrated visit to a city— that will ironically undermine the confidence some Thessalonians placed in the "peace and security" (*pax et securitas*) established by Roman rule (1 Thess 5:3). Some have suggested that the authors' admonitions to "work with your hands . . . so that you may behave properly toward outsiders and be dependent on no one" (4:11; NRSV) indicate that some Thessalonians had stopped working in anticipation of the imminent return of Christ (see also 2 Thess 3:6–13). While scholars continue to debate how best to answer such questions, I want to draw attention to how such attempts to re-animate the people who wrote and received this letter inevitably mean importing a multitude of assumptions, biases, expectations, and cultural frameworks that inform how we re-imagine the characters, rhetorical aims, and social dynamics at play in Thessalonica.

Granted, it is impossible to have much certainty about the minds and motivations of people long gone from a culture foreign to our own and to deduce "what really happened." And yet, we do so anyways. We must imagine boldly because as preachers, as *story-tellers*, we inevitably re-imagine *something* to make the text come alive for ourselves and our audiences. It is essential then to consider the cultural assumptions and stories that inform how we connect the dots and fill in the gaps of the characters, theologies, and social situations of these silent texts and their worlds that are different and distant from our own. This is where the insights gleaned from the social-scientific criticism of biblical texts and the cultural anthropological study of millenarian movements can assist the exegete in thinking about 1 Thessalonians.

Reading 1 Thessalonians Alongside Millenarian Movements

A social-scientific approach seeks to make apparent and more intelligible the implicit cultural values, social codes and practices, and social-political hierarchies and organizations of the ancient Mediterranean society that shaped both the authors and audiences of 1 Thessalonians, which are often not intuitive to modern Western readers. This method utilizes insights and models developed by sociologists and cultural anthropologists who have analyzed cultures that bear compelling resemblances and resonances with the ancient Greek, Roman, and Hellenistic Judean cultures relevant to the study of 1 Thessalonians.[1] Social-scientific studies of the New Testament have drawn our attention to the presence and significance of social phenomena and cultural scripts in our biblical texts—such as honor and shame, patronage and clientage, ritual purity, kinship relations, social status, social and ethnic hierarchies, social capital, negotiation of colonial/imperial power, the "evil eye," and economic systems.

Models derived from cultural anthropologists' interpretations of nineteenth- and twentieth-century cultures can help readers reimagine the Thessalonian situation in helpful ways, but models also have their limitations and pitfalls. Bruce Malina has defined models as "abstract, simplified representations of more complex, real-world objects and interactions."[2] In the case of 1 Thessalonians, a cultural model serves as a heuristic or a lens to help us better understand how particular elements of the text—including inscribed persons and groups, behaviors and practices, technical terms, social hierarchies, social situations, and cultural stories and values—might relate together in typical or generally predictable ways that would be intuitive for ancient

---

1. Some classic studies include Malina, *New Testament World*; Meeks, *First Urban Christians*; Pilch and Malina, eds., *Handbook of Biblical Social Values*; Blasi, et al., eds. *Handbook of Early Christianity: Social Science Approaches*; see especially Horrell's "Social Sciences Studying Formative Christian Phenomena: A Creative Movement" (*Handbook of Early Christianity*, 3–28) for a fantastic overview of the history of scholarship, criticisms, and varieties of this approach. Space limits prohibit a comprehensive list here, but I strongly recommend Neufeld's annotated bibliography, "Social Sciences and the New Testament."

2. Malina, *New Testament World*, 18.

audiences of the text, but not for modern readers. Using models to reimagine the social situation of Thessalonica should not prescribe what *should* be there, but primes interpreters to look for particular social, political, and cultural dynamics in the text when they would not otherwise think to connect the dots in such a way. Of course, there is always the danger that interpreters might use models to explain, predict, and thus project *too much* into their interpretation of a text and, so to speak, overfill the gaps with social elements that are not present in or behind the text. Ideally, interpreters should ground and coordinate their modern cultural models with whatever analogous cultural data and models, however drafty, can be derived from studying the extant Greek, Roman, and Judean literary and material culture. But the reality is that interpreters always have *some* model in mind when they imaginatively reconstruct what is happening in and behind an ancient text. Usually, these models are simply based on our own life experiences, whether derived from something we directly experienced or the media we consume ranging from books, television, and news reports. Interpreters must be careful that their models do not overly predetermine and dictate what they "find" in texts like 1 Thessalonians, even though some form of this may always be operative in a conscious or unconscious way.

In *The Thessalonian Correspondence: Pauline Rhetoric and Millenarian Piety*, Robert Jewett has argued that cultural models derived from analyzing the beliefs and behaviors of millenarian movements, whose followers thought that they would soon experience the dawn of a new age, are helpful for reconstructing the concerns and practices of the Thessalonian assembly.[3] Jewett noted that past commentators seemed to have described the Thessalonian situation in terms of their own experiences in North American and European churches, as something akin to "modern Wesleyan or Baptist revivals,"[4] for example. According to Jewett, such models do not sufficiently account for the assembly's surprise and dismay over the death of recent members, their persecution, and their critique of Paul's leadership and challenge to his sexual ethics.[5] A millenarian model, however, informed by the research of sociologists Yonina Talmon and Stephen Sharot and the Jewish historian Sheldon R.

---

3. Jewett, *Thessalonian Correspondence*. See also Jewett, *Romans: A Commentary*, 1–4, to appreciate how he will eventually frame his methodology in terms of a "practical realism," which recognizes how interpreters inevitably interact with and shape their subjects of investigation and yet still offer interpretations that utilize critical analysis and theories (including one that looks for historical-religious parallels) that can qualify some readings as more persuasive and plausible than others.

4. Jewett, *Thessalonian Correspondence*, 136–42.

5. Jewett, *Thessalonian Correspondence*, 137.

Isenberg can better account for how a greater number of cultural elements relate to one another in these letters.[6]

Jewett argues that his application of a millenarian model to the Thessalonian correspondence helps him better understand how many of the behavioral expressions associated with some of the Thessalonians—including a renunciation of labor, theoretical embrace of sexual taboos, challenge to leadership, and experience of deprivation—relate to one another in a coherent and meaningful cultural matrix that is typical of millenarian movements. According to Jewett, some of the Thessalonians' presumed questioning of traditional sexual ethics (though not acted upon) can be regarded as akin to the ritual breaking of taboos and rejection of typical social norms often present among millenarian movements, including the Melanesian cargo cults.[7] That some Thessalonians abdicated from their social and occupational responsibilities, the so-called "idlers" (*ataktoi*; 1 Thess 5:14), parallels how many millenarian movements, like the Taborites in Hussite Bohemia and the Old Believers in Nizhny Novgorod, refuse to participate any longer in their respective social and economic orders.[8] Furthermore, given that millenarian movements are often led by charismatic individuals who are perceived to be endowed with supernatural powers and sometimes come into conflict with the leaders responsible for organizing the practical needs of the millenarian movement, it becomes more plausible to imagine some of the Thessalonians challenging the authority of those leaders whom Paul established for their perceived lack of charismatic or supernatural gifts.[9] Lastly, applying a millenarian model to the Thessalonian assembly leads interpreters to consider how the Thessalonians may have experienced various kinds of deprivation, that is, a feeling that their present experience of the world conflicts with their religious, socio-political, economic, and ethical expectations of how the world should be—a common social condition associated with the rise of millenarian movements.[10] According to Jewett, the economic struggles among lower-class Greeks to advance their social position, their experience of persecution, and, less persuasively, their

---

6. See Talmon, "Pursuit of the Millennium," "Millenarian Movements," and "Millenarianism"; Sharot, *Messianism, Mysticism, and Magic*; Isenberg, "Millenarism in Greco-Roman Palestine." Of course, numerous other sociological studies inform his complete analysis; see his bibliography on social-scientific studies, Jewett, *Thessalonian Correspondence*, 203–6.

7. Jewett, *Thessalonian Correspondence*, 172–73.
8. Jewett, *Thessalonian Correspondence*, 173–74.
9. Jewett, *Thessalonian Correspondence*, 175–76.
10. Jewett, *Thessalonian Correspondence*, 165–68.

frustrated expectations surrounding the cult of Cabirus,[11] the patron deity of Thessalonica, helps Jewett understand why some Thessalonians among the assembly became so attached to a "millenarian radicalism" that eschewed labor and resisted the established leaders of the assembly and traditional sexual morality.[12] In many ways, Jewett's millenarian model provides a useful and generally persuasive way to imagine the social dynamics at play among some of the Thessalonian assembly.

As a biblical scholar who descends from both Indigenous and settler heritages and a member of the Choctaw Nation of Oklahoma, I was particularly drawn to Jewett's reference to the Comanche tribe, whose confidence in White Eagle's millenarian visions and magic, which promised victory over the white men and protection from bullets, was quickly dashed with the deaths of fifteen of their warriors at the second battle of the Adobe Walls, Texas on June 27, 1874. For Jewett, the sudden disillusionment of the Comanche in White Eagle's message and power, whom they would re-name "Isa-tai" or "coyote's droppings," is analogous to some of the Thessalonians' becoming disillusioned with Paul's eschatological teachings after the death of members in their own community.[13] After reading this passing reference, I wondered what new questions might arise by reading and sitting with Indigenous millenarian movements in terms of how we imagine and think about the social dynamics at play within and around the Thessalonian assembly.[14]

As a mixed-Indigenous scholar, I am compelled by the opportunity to foreground the histories, stories, rituals, values, and experiences of Indigenous communities, past and present, in my biblical interpretation. It is an aim of Indigenous biblical interpretation to place Indigenous stories, values, and even models—our own "old testament"—in conversation with biblical texts to underline the inherent dignity of our traditions, the very retelling of which further spreads and preserves their legacies. Such juxtapositions of stories also become opportunities to (re)educate non-Indigenous communities about our collective histories and traditions.

---

11. Jewett's reconstruction of the Thessalonian situation is based on a historically problematic and speculative imagination of the cult of Cabirus in Thessalonica, about which not much is known, and what is known does not confirm Jewett's reconstruction. See Hendrix, Review of *The Thessalonian Correspondence*, 766.

12. Jewett, *Thessalonian Correspondence*, 176–79.

13. Jewett, *Thessalonian Correspondence*, 171.

14. For concise accounts of Indigenous millenarian movements, see Rosenfeld, "Nativist Millennialism," and Pesantubbee, "Native American Geopolitical, Georestorative Movements."

In what follows, I will briefly introduce another nativist millenarian movement that spread soon after White Eagle's movement and that also shares resonances with the Thessalonian situation, namely, the 1890s Ghost Dance movement. This movement was inspired by the visions of the Northern Paiute prophet, Wovoka, also known as Jack Wilson, and is perhaps most remembered for how it alarmed white settlers in South Dakota and through a series of events, culminated in the US army's massacre of between 150 and 300 Lakota men, women, and children at Wounded Knee. According to an account of Wovoka's message preserved in the so-called "Messiah Letter" obtained by James Mooney, an ethnographer commissioned by the government to investigate the widespread Ghost Dance movements, it may be the case that Wovoka himself was indirectly influenced by 1 Thessalonians! According to Mooney's free rendition of the letter, Wovoka taught:

> Do not tell the white people about this. Jesus is now upon the earth. He appears like a cloud. The dead are all alive again. I do not know when they will be here; maybe this fall or in the spring. When the time comes, there will be no more sickness and everyone will be young again.[15]

Admittedly, it is unclear whether Wovoka was directly referencing the description of Jesus coming in the clouds found in 1 Thessalonians 4:16–17, incorporating oral traditions influenced by 1 Thessalonians gleaned from his Presbyterian childhood friends or Mormon neighbors,[16] or simply describing Jesus in terms of clouds, which held great significance for someone acclaimed for his control of the weather clouds.[17] Whether or not Wovoka's prophetic instructions represent another chapter in the long reception history of 1 Thessalonians' apocalyptic visions,[18] analyzing the 1890s Ghost Dance movement as a comparable phenomenon can possibly help us look

---

15. Mooney, *Ghost Dance Religion*, 781–82. This "letter" ascribed to Wovoka may not actually come from Wovoka, who may or may not have identified the redeemer as Jesus. Rather, the "letter" may represent a development in the oral/literary tradition that is nonetheless credited to Wovoka. See Warren, *God's Red Son*, 174. The question of how much this letter reflects the historical Wovoka is ironic given similar questions surrounding the authenticity of 2 Thessalonians.

16. It is interesting to note that many members of The Church of Jesus Christ of Latter-day Saints expected that the world might end in 1890/91, according to Joseph Smith's prophecies, and so were enthralled with Wovoka's message; see Mooney, *Ghost Dance Religion*, 792–93; Hittman, *Wovoka*, 84–85.

17. On the centrality of cloud images and the cloud spirit for Wovoka, see Warren, *God's Red Son*, 109. On how Christianity may have influenced Wovoka and his exposure to the Bible, see Warren, *God's Red Son*, 99–100.

18. See Thiselton, *1 & 2 Thessalonians through the Centuries*, 115–60.

at well-trod paths with fresh eyes and reimagine the sociological dynamics at play within and behind 1 Thessalonians.[19]

The 1890s Ghost Dance Movement

The 1890s Ghost Dance movement was a continuation of established Indigenous millenarian/geo-restorative practices that was syncretized with Christian apocalypticism in response to widespread experiences of relative deprivation. The 1890s Ghost Dance movement was preceded both by the Prophet Dance revitalization movement of the Columbia Plateau, featuring dance in anticipation of a coming savior figure,[20] and the 1870s Ghost Dance movement, led by the Northern Paiute Wodziwob, a.k.a. "Fish Lake Joe." Wodziwob had received visions from the Great Spirit foretelling a coming earthquake that would swallow up the whites, leaving their buildings and goods to be claimed by the surviving natives and those returned to life, who were currently traveling by train from the East to be reunited with their native kin.[21] In anticipation of this climactic day, Indigenous peoples were to conduct an evening round dance, which spread across Oregon, Northern California, and Idaho. Wovoka was likely influenced by this movement, which spread among his fellow Paiutes along the Walker River Reservation in Nevada when he was a teenager. The relative deprivation experienced by the Paiutes of Nevada, which would be the seedbed for successive millenarian dance movements, consisted of, in part, a loss of lives from diseases and a loss of their traditional lifeways, ceremonies, land, and sources of food—including bison and pine nuts, since their ecosystems had been ravaged by the burgeoning mining and cattle industries of invasive white settlers.[22] Although Nevada had experienced an economic boom that benefited some Paiutes with new wage labor positions in the 1870s, by the 1880s,

---

19. My own interest in thinking about Christian apocalyptic traditions—like that found in 1 Thessalonians—alongside Indigenous traditions such as the Ghost Dance movement was precipitated by William E. Arnal's recognition of the potential for a careful study of the Ghost Dance movement to illuminate our understanding of ancient Christianity: "In terms of the actual situation of the proponents of this [Ghost Dance] movement; in terms of the use of tradition, syncretism, and innovation; in terms of ideology and structure; in terms of evangelization and the spread of the message; in terms of the variety of its various manifestations; and in terms of the reaction of the ruling military powers, I can think of no better analogue to ancient Christianities" (Arnal, "Doxa, Heresy, and Self-Construction," 85n.100). Alas, it would be a stretch to consider the present essay even a prologue to this desired work.

20. See Warren, *God's Red Son*, 97–98.

21. Mooney, *Ghost Dance Religion*, 702.

22. Warren, *God's Red Son*, 76–92.

with the decline in mining, many such dependent wage laborers would find themselves unemployed without any viable return to the way things had been before—at least not without divine intervention.[23]

In 1887 or 1889, Wovoka received his first vision and would proceed to receive many more foretelling an imminent renewal of the earth and revitalization of Paiute lifeways. His visions were accompanied by sacred teachings, which stated that his people:

> must not fight, there must be peace all over the world; the people must not steal from one another, but be good to each other, for they [are] all brothers . . . they must work all the time and not lie down in idleness.[24]

To bring about this geo-restorative climax of history, Wovoka instructed his audiences to participate in a five-night, pan-tribal round dance, wherein men and women would be interspersed and would interlock their fingers as they shuffled to songs sung without instruments, dancing their prayers for rain, health, and fecundity of game and seed. Sometimes participants experienced ecstatic trances and saw visions of their deceased kin who would soon return. The truth of Wovoka's prophetic status was confirmed through the divine/magical power or *booha* that the Creator had granted him, which made him invulnerable to guns and enabled him to predict and control the weather.[25] In resonance with Paul's admonition against "idlers" (1 Thess 5:14), Wovoka admonished his Indigenous audiences to work as wage laborers for the white people, which encouraged a strategic accommodation to the new economic realities while still holding out hope for a return to a traditional hunter-gathering lifeway.[26] According to Louis W. Warren, "the Ghost Dance

---

23. Warren, *God's Red Son*, 101–2. Cf. Hittman, *Wovoka*, 101–3, who argues that the kind of deprivation experienced by Paiutes in the 1890s Ghost Dance movement pales in comparison to what they had experienced in the 1870s. For Hittman, it is telling that Wovoka doesn't make temperance from alcohol a plank of his message (Hittman, *Wovoka*, 102). It is unclear whether Hittman considers the collapse of the mining industry; nonetheless his work urges caution in overreading the level of "deprivation" experienced among Paiutes.

24. Warren, *God's Red Son*, 104.

25. Warren, *God's Red Son*, 105–12. Hittman, *Wovoka*, 64–88.

26. Warren, *God's Red Son*, 121–22. Wovoka's emphasis on work sharply contrasted with the prohibition against work from a Wanapum prophet of revitalization, Smohalla. Across the Columbia River in Washington a half-century earlier, Smohalla similarly taught that if his people would return to their traditional ways and renew their dance, the Creator would eradicate the whites and return their Indigenous kin from the dead (122).

sanctified wage labor as a proper Indian way of living that Indians could take up without sacrificing their Indian identity."[27]

Representatives from over thirty tribes, ranging from Idaho (Shoshone, Bannock), Wyoming (Northern Arapaho), South Dakota (Lakota), and Oklahoma (Southern Cheyenne, Southern Arapaho, Kiowas), traveled to meet the Ghost Dance Prophet, each carrying back and (re)translating the tradition according to localized cultures and the needs of their respective tribes. Each of these tribes had known their share of deprivation—that was similar to, if not worse than, that of the Paiutes—with respect to military violence, relocation, illness, broken or unfair treaties, devastation to their lands, prohibitions against their ceremonies (e.g., Sun Dance), scarcity of work, and disruption to their traditional lifeways.[28] Indeed, many Great Plains Indians were primed for the Ghost Dance as other prophetic revitalization movements foretelling the return of the Bison and the removal of the white people had been promoted by successive Kiowa prophets in 1882 and 1887.[29] Some, like Porcupine (Cheyenne), regarded Wovoka as the return of Christ himself who sought to renew the world, resurrect the dead into their beautiful forty-year old bodies—the age where everyone would revert to—and bring together both whites and Indians as "one people."[30] Among the Sioux, Wovoka was also regarded as the messiah, but only to the Indians, not the whites, who had crucified him before and would be swallowed up by the land at its renewal.[31] The belief that the white people would be eradicated by divine intervention was also shared among the Cheyenne, Arapaho, Kiowa, Shoshoni, and others—but this belief went hand-in-hand with the admonishment to live at peace with the whites, that vengeance would be the Lord's.[32] And where Porcupine understood Wovoka to be the Christ, Lakota Sioux directly experienced Jesus themselves in the ecstatic trances brought about in the Ghost Dance.[33] Considering how quickly Wovoka's message was spread with localized variance, one can better appreciate and imagine how Paul's own millenarian message rapidly had a life of its own that reflected the localized concerns of its representatives.

27. Warren, *God's Red Son*, 122.
28. Warren, *God's Red Son*, 143–76.
29. Warren, *God's Red Son*, 166–68.
30. Mooney, *Ghost Dance Religion*, 793–96.
31. Mooney, *Ghost Dance Religion*, 796–98.
32. Mooney, *Ghost Dance Religion*, 786. See also Warren, *God's Red Son*, 185–91, on how the teachings and legacy of Short Bull, who introduced the Ghost Dance to the Lakota, has been misconstrued.
33. Warren, *God's Red Son*, 174.

Finally, it should be noted that US government agencies and forces responded differently to manifestations of the Ghost Dance movement among the Lakota of South Dakota and the Arapahos of Oklahoma, respectively. Whereas the Ghost Dance became a precursor of and justification for military mobilization and massacre of Lakota lives at Wounded Knee, government officials were relatively temperate of its practice in Oklahoma.

Reimagining Thessalonian Christ-Followers in Light of the Ghost Dance

So how might the 1890s Ghost Dance movement help us to think about 1 Thessalonians? Indeed, the messianic movement inscribed in 1 Thessalonians and the Ghost Dance movement share a number of commonalities, including an expectation of an imminent restoration of the world where the wicked would get their due, a prophetic/charismatic leader, numerous emissaries spreading and adapting the message to their localized communities, questions regarding the authenticity of the messages or competing interpretations of the meaning of a message, an emphasis on ethical behavior and continuing to work despite the imminent end, and experiences of deprivation and persecution. Of course, one of the many distinctive differences between 1 Thessalonians and the Ghost Dance movement is the latter's explicit concern about the return of Indigenous land from the hands of American settlers and a revitalization of their traditional lifeways. However, given the fascinating resonances, perhaps we have some warrant to ask questions, if not speculate, about the social-political dynamics that may be at play in 1 Thessalonians that are not as apparent in the epistle as they are within the Ghost Dance movement.

First, granting the inherent differences in the economic situation of first-century Thessalonian laborers and nineteenth-century Indigenous laborers, might we now have an intriguing cultural model that compels us to reconsider why some Thessalonians were being "idle," beyond simply attributing it to an excessive expectation for the nearness of the end? Could such "idleness" be attributed to difficulties that some Thessalonians faced in an evolving labor market analogous to what the Paiutes experienced? Might we also see the apostles' admonitions to "work with your own hands so that you may behave properly toward outsiders and be dependent on no one" (1 Thess 4:11–12; NRSV; see also 2 Thess 3:6–13) as sanctifying the "wage labor" as a dignified mode of Christian existence similar to how Wovoka's prophecy sought to dignify labor?[34]

34. On the stigmatization that was associated with various forms of labor in the

Second, given how swiftly the Ghost Dance movement spread across the Great Plains from South Dakota to Oklahoma and how the message and practice of the Ghost Dance experienced slight but significant reinterpretations as the message was orally transmitted among diverse communities, does our imagination change at all regarding how we envision the early Christ-following communities? If 2 Thessalonians is indeed by Paul, perhaps some of us should not be so surprised that Paul's millenarian message could be misconstrued so quickly and significantly, despite his previous confidence that the Thessalonians did not need to have anything written to them (1 Thess 5:1). Conversely, given questions over the authenticity of the "Messiah Letter,"[35] might we also hold with a loose hand our confidence over whether we can be sure about the (in)authenticity of 2 Thessalonians?

Third, if space allowed for a deeper study of the various fears and concerns that neighboring white settlers had toward the Ghost Dance movement, I suspect this would further enrich how we imagine the plurality of responses of distrust and suspicion that ancient Greeks and Romans had toward their millenarian Christ-following neighbors. Certainly many US officials and neighbors disregarded the apocalyptic beliefs as simply superstitious fervor and were quite charmed by Wovoka's charisma, morals, and work ethic[36]—as some Greeks and Romans may have been by Paul and his followers. And yet, some white settlers were so disturbed by what they interpreted as frantic and militaristic dances directed toward them that they pressured the authorities to intervene—sometimes with violent results.

Conclusion

In the end, I am left with more questions than answers regarding how I imagine the Thessalonian situation. But I also leave with more imaginative models and ways to think about the social dynamics present among the Thessalonian assembly. But perhaps most importantly for me, I come away with a greater understanding of native millenarianism, which is significant for me and other Indigenous peoples to remember. What I have grown to appreciate about biblical interpretations that foreground the interpreter's ethnic positionality, experiences, and traditions is that such readings become opportunities to learn about new stories from other cultures—however cursory—that open our minds and hopefully stimulate our appreciation and curiosity about the biblical world and our own.

Roman world, see Bond's *Trade and Taboo*.

35. See n. 15 above.
36. Hittman, *Wovoka*, 247.

For students of the Bible interested in replicating my sociologically informed (re)imagination of Scripture, I invite you to further familiarize yourself with the literature of this field.[37] Moreover, I invite students, especially those with traditional cultures, histories, and experiences that have been less privileged in Western society, to consider how stories and social dynamics from your heritage may share significant parallels with that of the biblical text. I encourage you to juxtapose your stories with those of the Bible and to consider how they might mutually invite new questions and new ways of seeing each "text." Of course, it is necessary to correlate your fresh insights of Scripture with what can be known from the literary and material culture of the ancient world, as limited as it may be, before making confident statements about how you imagine the world of the text. Nonetheless, it is important to recognize that our imaginations are only as informed and innovative as the stories and studies we learn. And we do at least a two-fold service to others by foregrounding our own stories: first, we emphasize the dignity and preserve the legacy of our ancestors' and those of our kin's experiences, as with the Ghost Dance movement; and second, we potentially discover new ways of seeing and appreciating the complex and often ambiguous social dynamics of our stories and Scripture.

Bibliography

(* For Further Reading)

Arnal, William E. "Doxa, Heresy, and Self-Construction: The Pauline *Ekklēsiai* and the Boundaries of Urban Identities." In *Heresy and Identity in Late Antiquity*, edited by Eduard Iricinschi and Holger M. Zellentin, 50–101. Texte und Studien zum antiken Judentum 119. Tübingen: Mohr Siebeck.

*Blasi, Anthony, Jan Duhaime, and Paul-André Turcotte, eds. *Handbook of Early Christianity: Social Science Approaches*. Walnut Creek, CA: Alta Mira, 2002.

Bond, Sarah E. *Trade and Taboo: Disreputable Professions in the Roman Mediterranean*. Ann Arbor: University of Michigan Press, 2016.

Hendrix, Holland. Review of *The Thessalonian Correspondence*, by Robert Jewett. *Journal of Biblical Literature* 107 (1998) 763–66.

Hittman, Michael. *Wovoka and the Ghost Dance*. Expanded, edited by Don Lynch. Lincoln: University of Nebraska Press, 1997.

Horrell, David. "Social Sciences Studying Formative Christian Phenomena: A Creative Movement." In *Handbook of Early Christianity: Social Science Approaches*, edited by Anthony J. Blasi, Jean Duhaime, Paul-André Turcotte, 3–28. Walnut Creek, CA: Alta Mira, 2002.

Isenberg, Sheldon R. "Millenarism in Greco-Roman Palestine." *Religion* 4 (1974) 26–46.

*Jewett, Robert. *Romans: A Commentary*. Hermeneia. Minneapolis: Fortress, 2007.

37. See note 1.

*———. *The Thessalonian Correspondence: Pauline Rhetoric and Millenarian Piety.* Foundations and Facets. Philadelphia: Fortress, 1986.
*Malina, Bruce J. *The New Testament World: Insights from Cultural Anthropology.* 3rd ed. Atlanta: Westminster John Knox, 2001.
Meeks, Wayne. *The First Urban Christians: The Social World of the Apostle Paul.* New Haven: Yale University Press, 1983.
Mooney, James. *The Ghost Dance Religion and The Sioux Outbreak of 1890.* Lincoln: University of Nebraska Press, 1991. A reproduction of the original report published in the *Fourteenth Annual Report of the Bureau of Ethnology.* Washington, DC: Government Printing Office, 1896.
*Neufeld, Dietmar. "Social Sciences and the New Testament." Oxford Bibliographies. https://www.oxfordbibliographies.com/view/document/obo-9780195393361/obo-9780195393361-0117.xml.
Pesantubbee, Michelene E. "Native American Geopolitical, Georestorative Movements." In *The Oxford Handbook of Millennialism*, edited by Catherine Wessinger, 457–73. Oxford Handbooks. Oxford: Oxford University Press, 2011.
Pilch, John J., and Bruce J. Malina, eds. *Handbook of Biblical Social Values.* 3rd ed. Matrix 10. Eugene, OR: Cascade Books, 2016.
Rosenfeld, Jean E. "Nativist Millennialism." In *The Oxford Handbook of Millennialism*, edited by Catherine Wessinger, 89–112. Oxford: Oxford University Press, 2011.
Sharot, Stephen. *Messianism, Mysticism, and Magic: A Sociological Analysis of Jewish Religious Movements.* Chapel Hill: University of North Carolina Press, 1982.
Talmon, Yonina. "Millenarianism." In *International Encyclopedia of the Social Sciences*, edited by D. L. Sills, 349–62. Volume 10. New York: Free, 1968.
———. "Millenarian Movements." *Archives européennes de sociologie* 7 (1966) 159–200.
———. "Pursuit of the Millennium: The Relation between Religious and Social Change." *Archives européennes de sociologie* 3 (1962) 125–48.
Thiselton, Anthony. *1 & 2 Thessalonians through the Centuries.* Blackwell Bible Commentaries. Malden, MA: Wiley-Blackwell, 2011.
*Warren, Louis W. *God's Red Son: The Ghost Dance and the Making of Modern America.* New York: Basic, 2017.

Study Questions

1. What do you think are the possibilities, pitfalls, and limitations of using models derived from sociology and cultural anthropology to interpret the social dynamics of ancient societies—in particular, those that contextualized Scripture?

2. What new questions and possible ways of (re)imagining the social situation 1 Thessalonians was addressing or about early Christianity in general were sparked for you after reading about the millenarian Ghost Dance Movement?

3. Have you ever felt that the history or experiences of your own ethnic heritage resonate with the social dynamics that animate the stories in the Bible? Perhaps it is worthwhile to inquire further whether juxtaposing stories from your own ancestors with those preserved in Scripture might help you to see either in a fresh light?

16

Reading Galatians with the Barbarians

West African and East European Perspectives

BRIGITTE KAHL AND ALIOU C. NIANG

Abstract

TRIUMPHANTLY REINED IN BY the *civilizing mission* of Roman colonialism, Paul's Galatians are the most notorious (ex-)barbarians of the ancient world. Reading the letter before the backdrop of nineteenth-/twentieth-century French and German imperialism and the Christian-occidental *mission civilisatrice* in "barbarian" territories like the tribal lands of the Senegalese Diola people, or "Slavic" Eastern Europe before and after WWII, offers striking cross-contextual insights into the elusive context and subversive texture of Paul's decolonizing project.

> To articulate the past historically does not mean to recognize it "the way it really was" (Ranke). It means to seize hold of a memory as it flashes up in a moment of danger . . . In every era the attempt must be made anew to wrest tradition away from the conformism that is about to overpower it.[1]

Stating the Problem

Traditionally, Paul's letter to the Galatians in Christian interpretation ranges among the least contextualized and most dogmatized documents in the New Testament. In fact, the lack of historical context and the overabundance of dogmatic assumptions drawn from it seem to complement each other.

1. Benjamin, "Theses on the Philosophy of History," thesis VI.

Though there were never-ending debates about North or South Galatia as the geographical location of the letter, they did not have much relevance for issues of interpretation. The question of circumcision as the focal controversy between Paul, the Galatians, and some anonymous-staying opponents, on the other hand, was treated in a rather decontextualized manner as a "purely theological" matter[2] and as Paul's conclusive farewell to Judaism. What Christian faith and Pauline faith-justification in this view originally stood up against was exclusively Jewish law and Jewish works-righteousness, while Roman law and Roman rule played a more or less benign fringe role. In this interpretational paradigm, Paul could all too easily morph into the canonical root source of Christian anti-Judaism and spokesperson for occidental imperialism and colonialism. And with astounding versatility, the Paul-derived Jewish Other as primal antagonist of Christianity was able to mutate into a plethora of other Others, including Muslims, pagans, Orientals, followers of indigenous religions, or secular humanists.

Robert Jewett belonged to a relatively small group of New Testament scholars who have challenged this one-sided contextualization of Paul in antithesis to Judaism, especially since the SBL "Paul and Politics" group started to stir up new debates in the 1980s. And he was the first one who systematically deconstructed the prevalent contextual myopia in a 1,000-page landmark commentary on Romans that appeared in the reputable Hermeneia series in 2007. Romans is widely recognized to be Paul's most foundational statement on the irresoluble antithesis between faith-righteousness and law/works-righteousness. Jewett's meticulous verse-by-verse exegesis, flawless in its historical-critical credentials, examined this antithesis not just before an isolated *Jewish* and *religious* background but consistently demonstrated how it was inseparable from its *Greco-Roman* and *political* context as well. This re-contextualization of Romans in its Roman context changes the interpretational codes dramatically. All of a sudden, "boasting," for example, is no longer the prerogative of the "works-righteous Jews" but of Rome as the true "boasting champion of the ancient world."[3] With this, the established understanding of faith, grace, law, and works, and the entire construct of the Other that Paul is wrestling with is in need of being redefined.

---

2. See, e.g., the 2016 study by Felix John who, after an extensive and insightful mapping of the first-century *"Lebenswelten"* of Asia Minor, arrives at the surprising conclusion that any "external evidence" from the real-life context of the Galatians is ultimately irrelevant to the subject matter of the letter in its purely theological nature: *"Ein innerer Bezug zwischen galatischer Krise und den lebensweltlichen Gegebenheiten der galatischen Gemeinden ist nicht zu finden . . ."* (John, *Lebenswelten*, 193).

3. Jewett, *Romans: A Commentary*, 295.

What we are presenting here is work in the wake of Robert Jewett and all those others who pioneered an alternative and more contextualized reading of the "apostle to the gentiles": Krister Stendahl, Dieter Georgi, Richard Horsley, Neil Elliott, Elsa Tamez, Jacob Taubes, and many more who have been aiming at understanding faith-justification within the framework of concrete social realities, and of justice-seeking.[4] With them, we are reading Galatians, the smaller twin-brother of Romans, not just in a Jewish but also in a Roman context. But we are adding a distinctly "indigenous" element: we are reading Galatians with the native "barbarians" as well.[5]

Method: A Contextual Hermeneutic of Dialogue

This approach is the result of several years of experimenting with a *contextual hermeneutic of dialogue between West Africa and Eastern Europe in the privileged "third space" of the US-American academy*. Initially, our encounter was a surprise: A postcolonial West African American and a post-communist East German American, both with strong democratic-socialist inclinations, found out that they had come up with, without knowing each other's work at first, strikingly similar questions about Paul and the Galatians.

We both had been puzzled by the pale blurriness and theological artificiality of the Galatians we encountered in standard commentaries: Those people, literally, had not a single other problem in their entire lives to handle than their foreskins! Nonetheless, we were equally skeptical about how Greco-Roman historiography, contrastingly, depicted these same Galatians in astonishingly vivid colors. According to Livy, Diodor, and others, the Galatians—or Gauls[6]—were the most notorious barbarians and enemies of civilization. They were irrational and lawless, belligerent, bibulous, blasphemous, and they sacrificed humans.[7] Their despicable bar-

---

4. For an introduction to this work, see the essays collected in Horsley, ed., *Paul and Empire*; also Stendahl, *Paul among Jews and Gentiles*; Tamez, *Amnesty of Grace*; Taubes, *Political Theology of Paul*.

5. Native contexts of Anatolia as background of Paul's Galatian controversy have been foregrounded in various ways by Elliott, *Cutting too Close*; Arnold, "I Am Astonished"; Niang, *Faith and Freedom*; Kahl, *Galatians Re-imagined*; Kamudzandu, *Abraham Our Father*. For an overall comprehensive introduction, see Mitchell, *Anatolia*; the Roman relevance of the circumcision debate within the framework of civic and emperor religion has been outlined by Winter, *Seek the Welfare*, 124–43; Hardin, *Galatians and the Imperial Cult*; Kahl, *Galatians Re-imagined*.

6. The terms "Galatians" and "Gauls" are largely synonymous in antiquity; cf. Kahl, *Galatians Re-imagined*, 48–51.

7. E.g., Diodorus 5.24–32; Livy, 38.17.

barianism justified, in both moral and military terms, centuries of warfare, territorial expansion, subjugation, and eventually the rightful position of Rome as world ruler at the apex of the civilized universe. We also found, independently, how deeply this pro-Roman reading of the ancient world in general and of the Galatians/Gauls in particular is still ingrained into New Testament scholarship, and how strong the admiration of "eternal Rome" runs in Western culture; it was consolidated through centuries of "classic" education, often crowned with a reading of Julius Caesar's "Gallic/Galatian War" in Latin that never doubted its factual truth.[8]

The foundation of the Roman province of Galatia in 25 BCE by emperor Augustus, only seven years after he had become single ruler in the Battle of Actium (31 BCE), was many things; but it was definitely *also* a grand-style declaration that the century-long "Gallic (or Galatian) War" was now over in the East as well. Situated on the territory of today's central Turkey, the province was vastly multi-ethnic in its composition and could have carried many names. Calling it precisely after the tribal minority of the Galatians/Gauls sent a message of Roman victory in the "Big Battle"—a battle that until today in the Western imagination has stayed the "mother of all battles," the archetypal war of occidental civilization against *Barbaria*.

Barbaria is a fictive entity that never existed on any political map, as far as we know. Nonetheless, throughout history, it has been continuously present as the ever-shifting country and culture of the ever-changing Others that the Western Self had to engage in combat. Edward Said in his landmark study on *Orientalism* described the antithesis between "our land" and the "land of the barbarians" as an example of "imaginative geography": while its demarcation lines are fictional and set up in our own minds, the "geographic boundaries" between "ours" and "theirs" in this arbitrary reality morph into firmly established "social, ethnic, and cultural ones."[9]

The clash between the civilized and the barbarians has been monumentalized with insuperable beauty and chilling realism at the Great Altar of Pergamon (ca. 170 BCE). Its world-famous Gigantomachy-Frieze depicts the victory of the Olympian gods and their local allies against the onslaught of primeval giants who represent chaos, lawlessness, godlessness, and rebellion. Yet behind the mythological veil, real-life combat is going on. The insurgent army of terrifying and subhuman monsters attacking Mount Olympus from below has a clear historical referent. It shows the historical Galatians/Gauls, the ancestors of Paul's Galatians, who entered Asia minor as migrant-mercenaries in 279 BCE and were seen as nothing

---

8. Cf. Wells, *Barbarians Speak*, 20–22.
9. Said, *Orientalism*, 54.

but robbers and raiders from the outset. Archetypal residents of *Barbaria* in the imaginary of the West, they are depicted in Pergamene iconography as not only trying to dethrone the gods but also to overthrow occidental civilization in its entirety.[10]

This takes us back to the question of method. It seems that both of us, though in very different ways, have some history as inhabitants of *Barbaria* that links us not only to these barbarian Galatians/Gauls, but also to Paul, who must have met the Galatians at some point of his journey in the middle of the first century CE. Though, as a Jew, he was distinct from the Galatians, in Roman eyes, he might have counted as resident of merely another province in the multi-faceted territory of ancient *Barbaria* marked by offensive Otherness.[11] It took us at least a decade to even start figuring out how our different native "moorings" might have shaped our approaches to Paul and the Galatians, and how ancient and present-day *Barbaria* could play into this.

One of us comes from French-colonized and Christian-missionized/ civilized Senegal, West Africa. Within a predominantly Muslim context, he grew up in a tribal Diola culture. Born to a Diola mother, Aliou Cissé Niang was raised by his Diola grandparents. He became a follower of Jesus and went on to study theology in the US, earning a PhD in New Testament at Brite Divinity School. Brigitte Kahl, on the other hand, was born and raised in post–World War II East Germany, a country simultaneously under Soviet supremacy and under siege by the West on the battlefield of the Cold War era. She studied theology and earned her PhD at Humboldt University in East Berlin and became ordained as a pastor of the Protestant Church of Berlin-Brandenburg. Within a programmatically atheist culture, she was shaped by both her minority Lutheran tradition and the debates about global decolonization, Christian-Marxist dialogue, liberation theology from a "second-world" perspective, and democratic socialism that were part of the failed twentieth-century socialist experiment in Eastern Europe.

Obviously, our contexts are different in a myriad of ways and located light years apart on the geopolitical map defined by the power-play between center and periphery. Still, there are astonishing similarities and

10. For the "invention" of the occidental construct of civilization in antithesis to barbarianism, see Hall, *Inventing the Barbarian*; for Galatian/Celtic "barbarity," cf. Strobel, *Die Galater*; Webster, "Ethnographic Barbarity"; Wells, *Barbarians Speak*; for a general overview and Pergamene backgrounds in particular: Kahl, *Galatians Reimagined*, 42–127.

11. Tacitus, *Histories* 5.4–5, for example, describes vividly how Jews lack everything that defines proper civic conduct: they pursue perverse religious practices, refuse worship to the images of the gods or of Caesar, separate themselves from their fellow-citizens, and are plagued by a general hatred of humanity.

congruencies in our readings of the "barbarians" we continue to discover. Our *contextual hermeneutic of dialogue* is just evolving. But there is another question we are trying to explore; namely, *How may the legibility of texts be facilitated or blocked by socio-contextual location?* or, more concretely, *How can analogous contexts open up texts in new ways?* Using elements of an *African tribal culture under French colonial domination* to read the *Galatian tribal context under Roman domination*, for example, may appear anachronistic measured by the standards of "objective" historiography as accurate fact-finding on a particular time and location. On the other hand, it may give us valuable socio-historical insight into the lost context of Galatia we otherwise have no way to reconstruct because the dominant historiography has erased any history "from below."

Cross-cultural reading of biblical texts is analogical. According to Daniel Smith-Christopher:

> [it] refers to biblical analysis that intentionally draws from the cultural background and experiences of the scholar him/herself in order to suggest analogies to historical phenomena in biblical history, propose alternative views on the context of a biblical passage, or otherwise nuance an interpretation of a text and/or artifact.[12]

To read biblical texts this way defies the myth of assured neutral objectivity that empiricist science proclaimed since the so-called Enlightenment. Smith-Christopher, like many liberationists reading from the Two-Thirds world, calls for an inculturation of biblical texts—an interaction between the historical and social milieu of texts and their recipients brought to bear on the context and lived experiences of the hermeneut.[13] In this *imaginaire*, the hermeneut engages in a cross-cultural analysis and translation of sacred texts in conversation with vernacular literature and orature in order to unmuzzle and liberate colonized "barbarians." Put differently, the interpreter navigates narrow and porous spaces of cultures, tribes, and ethnicities that empires constructed as inferior, superstitious, and barbarous in text and image in order to free and reclaim their humanity under the aegis of God. Similarly, Paul navigates Mediterranean seas,[14] cultures, tribes, and ethnicities to found

---

12. Smith-Christopher, "Cross-Cultural Exegesis," 138, 138–50; cf. also Wells, *Barbarians Speak*, 27.

13. Ukpong, "Reading the Bible in a Global Village," 17. See also Sugirtharajah, ed., *Vernacular Hermeneutics*.

14. Niang, "Contested Spaces," 102–105 and "Islandedness," 177–84. See also Aymer, "Islandedness," 25–36.

house-churches of liberated children of Abraham once characterized as fickle, superstitious, warmongering barbarians of Asia.

Mapping "Barbaria"

Space studies have shown that space is at least three-dimensional—space as experienced, perceived, and imagined.[15] Imperial cartography is never innocent but ideologically intentional. It maps spaces and human bodies. Already the Romans expressed and executed their mastery over foreign people and territories through sophisticated maps and territorial reorganization.[16] Similarly, the European powers (re-)drafted the colonial map of the African continent at the Berlin Conference in 1884–85. But even before that, French cartography in Senegal/West Africa had become one of the worst nightmares of the indigenous Diola people as it produced *maps of terror* that affected their sacred universe, namely culture.

The "*Quatres Communes*" in Senegal

The way humans experience and negotiate space is mapped out by occupying empires. In J. B. Harley's observation, imperial maps are powerful tools in the making of colonial geopolitics. He writes:

> As much as guns and warships, maps have been the weapons of imperialism. In so far as maps were used in colonial promotion, and lands claimed on paper before they were effectively occupied, maps anticipated empire. Surveyors marched alongside soldiers, initially mapping for reconnaissance, then for general information, and eventually as a tool of pacification, civilization, and exploitation in the defined colonies. But there is more to this than the drawing of boundaries for the practical political or military containment of subject populations. Maps were used to legitimize the reality of conquest and empire. They helped create myths which would assist in the maintenance of the territorial status quo. As communicators of an imperial message, they have been used as an aggressive complement to the rhetoric of speeches, newspapers, and written texts, or to the histories and popular songs extolling the virtues of empire.[17]

---

15. Sleeman, *Geography*, 43.

16. Cf. Nicolet, *Space, Geography, and Politics*.

17. Harley, "Maps, Knowledge, and Power," 57–58. Quoted in Niang, *A Poetics of Postcolonial Biblical Criticism*, 141.

Like their imperial predecessors in antiquity, French colonial officials who first set foot in Senegal mapped out the entire territory and then created cities—colonial centers we might call in modern parlance "Green Zones."[18] Although Catholic missionary presence in Senegal predates the French colonial efforts in the country, most of the missionaries during the colonial period believed in the colonial hegemony.[19] As argued in *A Poetics of Postcolonial Criticism*, prior to the Berlin Conference in 1884–85, which officially legitimated the colonial partition of Africa, French activity began with the creation of the so-called "*Quatres Communes*," the four "cities" of Saint-Louis and Gorée in 1872, Rufisque in 1880, and Dakar two years after the conference in 1887.[20]

Somewhat analogous to the Greek *gymnasia* in 1–4 Maccabees[21] that were meant to hellenize the Jews and assimilate them to the superior Greek civilization, the four cities in Senegal were established to provide the space where the French began the process of turning Senegalese people into French persons with black skin. They called this "*la mission civilisatrice*," the "civilizing mission" or *la paix Française*, "the peace of France." The assimilation process carried out in the cities from 1887–1960 resulted in a power differential, binary identity, and space construction that tore the communities apart. The *évolués*, meaning the "civilized or evolved," resided in the *Quatres Communes*, the Four Colonial Towns, while the rest of the uncivilized subjects and barbarians lived in the protectorate, called "*indigénat*." As such, the four cities constituted not only the center of political power but also the missionary headquarters. In contrast, the protectorate dwellers were subjects to be pacified, civilized through the colonial school curriculum, and converted to Christianity.

The Three Cities of the Galatians

Imperial cartography, ancient and modern, as a rule includes stratification of urban and even rural spaces. Colonial cities/towns comprise centers of education, politics, foreign architecture, and religion, all aimed at assimilating barbarians through the transfer of the colonists' cultural values. The four colonial towns of Senegal served that purpose. In the rural settings,

---

18. The term "Green Zones" here alludes to specific US-American spatial practices in Iraq, e.g., the creation of "American space" segregated from the rest of the city of Baghdad.

19. Foster, *Faith in Empire*, 94–98; Foster, "A Mission in Transition," 269.

20. Niang, *Poetics of Postcolonial Biblical Criticism*, 151–52; Foster, *Faith in Empire*, 23–29.

21. Cf. 1 Macc 1:14; 2 Macc 4:9, 12, and 4 Macc 4:20.

village chiefs were often enticed and turned into colonial collaborators. Missionaries assiduously transferred their Europeanized Christianity through literacy programs as they simultaneously chipped away at traditional religion by labeling it as satanic, pagan, evil, and idolatrous. This was the prevalent practice among most of the Catholic Order of the Holy Ghost Fathers toward the Diola people, rather than translating the gospel and cultivating an authentic inculturation process.

As the French had learned from the Greeks and Romans how to use urbanization for the higher ends of civilizing and colonizing the barbarians, the colonization of Senegal and of Galatia shows striking similarities. When the Roman province of Galatia was founded in 25 BCE, the tribal territories in the North were fundamentally remapped. The vast cultural and political transformations ahead were anchored in three main cities. Each was assigned to one of the three Galatian tribes that in turn got the honorary designation as *Sebasteni*, which meant "Augustan" in Greek and expressed their, and their territories,' symbolic appropriation by the emperor. The term "*Sebasteni*" also included strong religious overtones in terms of emperor religion that was promoted on a massive scale throughout Galatia.[22] With this, the *Sebasteni* Tectosagii, Trocmi, and Tolistobogii had their primary affiliation transferred from their tribe and local village to the divine emperor and to the imperial city. They were expected to leave their former barbarian identity behind and become civilized as worthy subjects of the *Pax Romana*, the Roman Peace. According to their formal titles as *Sebasteni Tectosagii Ancyrani, Sebasteni Trocmi Taviani*, or *Sebasteni Tolistobogii Pessinuntii*, they were not only adopted into Caesar's household and imperial order as "the Emperor's (*Sebasteni*) Tectosagii, Trocmi, and Tolistobogii" but also turned into urbanites identified through their respective cities of Ancyra, Tavium, and Pessinus, each of which were centers of the imperial cult.[23] These cities functioned as outposts of civilization in Galatian *Barbaria,* so to speak, the switch-points where not only the transmission of Greekness to the savages was organized but also the reverse transfer of taxes and tributes from their rural lands back to the imperial city of Rome.

We don't have any reports of how local communities in Galatia responded to this remapping of their land, culture, and economy, and to the vertical social stratification and separation that went along with it. Historiography from above has mostly erased such "useless" information from below. That's why an "analogous" approach might help us imagine possible Galatian responses. How did the Diola people in West Africa deal with a

22. Hardin, *Galatians and the Imperial Cult*.
23. Mitchell, *Anatolia*, 1:86–88.

similar imposition of colonial law and rezoning that declared them as inhabitants of *Barbaria* from the viewpoint of civilized urbanity and Christian-occidental superiority? But we have to take a brief look at the city of Berlin and its post-World-War-II partition first.

The Two-Partite City/Country of the Germans

Ironically, the city of Berlin, proud capital of the German Empire since 1871 and host of the infamous Berlin Conference of 1884–85 that partitioned the African continent, itself became divided into four parts after imperial Germany had unleashed and lost two horrifying world wars. After 1945, the then Allied Forces of Britain, France, the United States, and Soviet Union split Germany and Berlin into four occupational zones, one for each of them. Very soon, the four parts factually morphed into two. In 1949, the Federal Republic and, a bit later, the Democratic Republic of Germany were founded; in other words, West Germany (comprising the share of the three Western allies) and East Germany, the Soviet Zone.

This was a second profound irony. After losing all its colonies in Africa already as a result of World War I, Germany had increasingly looked toward Eastern Europe as the new space to colonize. The full arsenal of orientalizing ideology was employed to teach Germans that they were the superior Aryan race destined to rule over the inferior Slavic people in the East. After all, Germany needed "living space" (*Lebensraum*) and would gain it by defeating and exterminating Poles, Ukrainians, Russians, and other racially degraded Easterners. Hitler planned to detain Slavic people in huge labor camps for extracting and processing the rich natural resources of their lands.[24] Ideally, these labor camps were to be placed next to concentration camps, where workers after several months of grueling slave labor were to be eliminated, an approach pioneered by the *IG Farben* chemical and pharmaceutical company near Auschwitz between 1942–45.[25]

Instead, after 1945, Germany had not only lost the war but also large territories in the East, like East Prussia or Silesia. It also had to surrender one third of its "civilized" territory to the "barbarians," the Soviets.

One has to add that for centuries racism in Germany, though variegated, has had two main components, both of them not based primarily on skin color. The first type was anti-Semitism, the second anti-Slavism. Both went nicely together in Hitler's fascist ideology that defined Russian bolshevism as inherently "Jewish" and taught schoolchildren the physiological

24. Radkau, *Zweideutigkeit*, 533.
25. Roth, *Faschismus*, 51.

markers of Eastern inferiority in classes on the "biology of race," along with the dangers of Jewish alleged superiority claims. Like anti-Semitism, anti-Slavism goes back a long way in European and German history. Already the Middle Ages saw a flourishing business of catching people from beyond the Elbe river and further East (today's Poland, Lithuania, Sorbia, Bohemia) and selling them in large slave markets; for example, in Magdeburg/Germany.[26] In fact, there is debate whether the very word "slave" is etymologically derived from the ethnicon "Slavic."[27] At any rate, until today, Western European arrogance toward Poles, Bulgarians, Romanians, Russians, and other Easterners who often do menial jobs like house-cleaning or elder-care is a major part of European racism.

If in the German political imagination Eastern Europe was (and is) to a large degree *Barbaria*, this applied to East Germany as well, a liminal zone between "ours" and "theirs" on the one hand, yet firmly separated from the West by the "Iron Curtain" (Berlin Wall) after 1961. And soon another qualifier would be added to the standard repertoire of Orientalism. Blending in nicely with the alleged "despotism" of the Asians, the barbarians this time were "communist," representing a Russian-type socialism.[28] As Edward Said notes in passing:

> Anyone resident in the West since the 1950s, particularly in the United States, will have lived through an era of extraordinary turbulence in the relations between East and West. No one will have failed to note how the 'East' has always signified danger and threat during this period, even as it has meant the traditional Orient as well as Russia.[29]

As West Germany refused to pay war reparations to the Soviet Union in order not to strengthen a political antagonist, the East Germans alone had to shoulder all of Germany's debt to a country Hitler's army had invaded, leaving savage destruction and 21 million dead behind. The resulting (relative) poverty of the East became a Cold War trophy of the West that boasted of the overflowing abundance in luxury goods and commodities a free-market economy was able to produce. This economic miracle of capitalism was even more triumphantly celebrated after West Germany, rather than paying its war reparations, itself got the more than generous economic influx of the American Marshall Plan.

26. Lehr, *Zum europäischen Rassismus*.

27. Kluge, *Etymologisches Wörterbuch*, 566.

28. For despotism as one of the key features in the Western perception of the Oriental Other, see, e.g., Said, *Orientalism*, 4. 203.

29. Said, *Orientalism*, 26.

One has to weigh the words carefully here. I am not saying that East German socialism was good because the West called it "bad" and "barbarian," nor that the reparations to the Soviet Union were the only problem its economy was facing. Simple binaries rarely fit reality. East German state socialism had many and, as it turned out, ultimately irreparable flaws. It never could handle democracy well, nor ecology, for example. But what I am saying is that the East was not under siege because the West wanted a *better* socialism, but because it was not capitalism.

Yet many East Germans wanted precisely that when the Wall finally fell in 1989: a better socialism rather than capitalism. That is why the unification of Germany after forty years of split existence in a two-partite country was not a fundamentally democratic process either. For many East Germans, in hindsight, all things considered and after the initial enthusiasm had faded, it felt much more like a transition administered and imposed from outside and above. East Germany as a peculiar modern-day *Barbaria*, all of a sudden burdened with a hitherto unknown mass unemployment, de-industrialization, and wholesale de-valuation, was steered back into the orbit of Western capitalist civilization. Hopes for a "democratic socialism" or any kind of "third way" were categorically ruled out from the outset. The "barbarians" had no say in such matters. East Germans were invited to change into West Germans again and expected to be grateful—after all this most generous invitation was not extended to the rest of Eastern Europe. But the West itself refused to change.

At this point, we need to return to Galatia and the Galatians.

Cross-contextual Debates in Galatia: Paul, Aline Sitoé and Dietrich Bonhoeffer

Paul and the Galatians

We don't know what exactly happened to Paul and the Galatians when they met each other at some relatively remote outpost of Roman civilization and on a territory that Sir William Ramsay once described as a primary battleground in the fight between Orient and Occident. As British and Roman empires merge in his imaginary, Ramsay sees Paul as a combatant against ignorant and superstitious "native" Orientalism (including Judaism) on behalf of a superior occidental religion.[30] In Galatians 4:12–15, we get a glimpse of an encounter that Paul retrospectively describes as the pivotal

---

30. Ramsay, *Historical Commentary*, 195–96, 320–22; cf. Kahl, "Galatians and the 'Orientalism'" 209–13.

epiphany of Christ crucified in Galatia. Yet what apparently took place was not Paul's authoritative proclamation of a superior Christian-occidental gospel to dim-witted oriental idol-worshippers. Instead, the Galatians came across a most weak, vulnerable, and probably injured Jewish stranger whom they took in and nursed back to life as if he were one of their own. "You didn't do any injustice to me,"[31] Paul reminisces about his appearance at their doorstep in a most disheveled manner. He had given them all reason to despise him, to even spit at him, to turn their backs on him. They could have seen him as a piece of human trash, perhaps beaten up by the authorities and therefore better left alone, or a carrier of the evil eye magic that would do damage to their community. But no, Paul says, with amazement still ringing in his words: "You did not scorn or despise me, but welcomed me as an angel of God, as Christ Jesus" (Gal 4:14).

This whole event, according to Paul, was his initial gospel-proclamation to them: "You know that it was through weakness of the flesh that I first announced the good news to you." (Gal 4:13). It is not clear how missionary "words" and "works" of love toward a stranger were exactly related here. It could well be that the Galatians met the Messiah in the human wreckage of an alien before even hearing anything from Paul—it was primarily through an act of extraordinary hospitality that they encountered the weak and vulnerable Christ. Paul, it seems, at this point, did not have the physical capacity to deliver a grand-style missionary sermon anyway. It might well be that he only *post factum* calls a live-encounter with Christ-crucified what in reality was their acting as Good Samaritans towards the half-dead foreigner at a roadside of imperial Galatia (cf. Gal 3:1).

Let us assume for a moment that this indeed was the birth of messianic companionship between the Jew Paul and the non-Jewish Galatians—this exceptional act of ultimate hospitality that for Paul superseded all established boundaries keeping humans apart from one another. A "oneness in Christ" between a Jewish stranger and the Galatians was forged that no longer needed to be identified by foreskin or circumcision because it was verified by the crucified and resurrected Messiah (cf. Gal 3:28). This was the new "heterotopic" space beyond the borderlines segregating barbarian and civilized territories, "ours" and "theirs" on the imperial map, the space of Other-care where the mutilated body of Christ was healed and restored in an act of radical hospitality pertinent to all of humanity. For the Galatians, this perceived singularity of taking in the broken body of a nobody might have not looked as exceptional at first, because hospitality was "what they did" and was part of who they were. This takes us again to the Diola people

---

31. Gal 4:12, our translation.

in Senegal, West Africa, who comprised both what we call "religion" and "hospitality" under precisely this rubric of "what we do."[32]

Hospitality as "What We Do" in Aline Sitoé Diatta's Identity and Community Construction

The French newcomers in Senegal regarded Diola people—a name that means "visible human beings" or even "visible human beings among other human beings" in the native language—as anarchists and fickle barbarians who needed to be pacified and converted to a European-style Christianity. The encounter between colonialists, Catholic missionaries, and Diola people resulted in fierce conflicts. The textbook that the missionaries wrote to educate Diola people was the so-called *Diola syllabaire*.[33] It was the most effective tool in their literacy program that taught children how to write and read through sample sentences in which Diola religion was described as inferior or non-existent, while the missionary version of Christianity was presented as normative. Most of the missionaries who belonged to the Catholic Order of the Holy Ghost Fathers preached a God who sponsored colonization. Many tribal elders pushed back when they realized that their children were being taught to abandon Diola customs for French culture and Christian religion. At the same time, severe droughts were ravaging the country since the arrival of the French, causing famine and misery on a large scale. As Diola cosmology has it, such natural disasters and other social ills befalling the Diola community must have resulted from members failing to perform appropriate rituals, thus leaving the community vulnerable. All this increased social tensions inside the Diola communities and in their interactions with the colonial power.

While the elders were scrambling for answers amidst the pressures of French occupation, a woman prophet arose. Her name was Aline Sitoé Diatta (1920–1943 or 1944). She claimed that the supreme God "Emitai" had sent her to make rain, heal people, and liberate them from the French overlords. She had many Diola and non-Diola followers. Pilgrims came from neighboring Senegalese villages or cities, and from countries such as Mauritania, Mali, and Guinea to hear her.[34] Accused of political insurrec-

---

32. Since Diola people do not have a word for religion as Westerners do, they use the expression "What We Do" to capture their spirituality. So, what is Diola religion? It is "What We Do," lived experience.

33. Baum "Emergence of a Diola Christianity," 386.

34. Thomas, "Les 'rois' Diola," 164, 151–74. To our knowledge, her name is spelled as either Alinsitoue, Aline Sitoé or Alinsitüé.

tion and declared a threat to the civilizing reign of French colonial peace called *La Paix Française*, this prophetess nonetheless was able to create an alternative community that greatly baffled and angered the French.

Aline Sitoé, whose fame had spread after she performed successful rainmaking rituals, established a commonality that was both egalitarian and inclusive across gender, ethnic, and religious boundaries in striking ways. Men and women, old and young people, Christians, Muslims, and practitioners of traditional African religions from different regions and tribes came together to hear her proclaim Emitai's love for all people. God, the creator and first ancestor, does not condone oppression nor marginalization of any group of "visible human beings," she told them. Many stayed as long as they desired, while others made pilgrimages and disseminated her teachings as they returned to their respective home locations. Diatta's community, and by extension village, became a miniaturized *oikoumene*, a small-sized model of the "inhabited earth" functioning at different terms than the French colonial world mission. For the creator God, *Emitai* was not only the first ancestor but also the first to practice hospitality on a cosmic scale. Incipient forms of an economy of sharing were emerging.

According to Louis-Vincent Thomas, a French anthropologist who taught Senegalese people for many years, community members started to place themselves in God's hands and to "commune with all their meager possessions. This they practice not in despair but in joyful confidence... as a means and not an end."[35] The miracles Aline Sitoé performed authenticated her call and teachings that included the "universality of equality, fraternity, love and peace."[36]

> The cult gathers into a fellowship, almost a church, the totality of adherents to the truth of Alinsitüé, whatever their ethnic origins and their other religious practices, a kind of initiation on a human scale that takes on the appearance of a mystery open to all people of good will, regrouping them into a unitary movement focused on the Good. The latter responding to the economic aspirations of the era: meeting food needs through agriculture; the key to it remains the rain, dispensed by Alinsitüé on behalf of Ata Émit (God), to help suffering humanity. (Translation ours)[37]

The strangers or neighbors blown together by the wind/spirit in Diatta's goods-sharing community under the aegis of *Emitai* were offered hospitality, including the meals the prophetess herself helped cook. Meals for

---

35. Thomas, "Les 'rois' Diola," 164.
36. Thomas, "Les 'rois' Diola," 165.
37. Thomas, "Les 'rois' Diola," 164.

Diola people have ontological and epistemological dimensions. Sharing meals paves the way for building lasting relationships between families. As persons eat together, they learn to cultivate mutual relationships that shape their shared beliefs and practices and reflect on their differences. A song of Aline Sitoé that has been preserved from a long list of hymns she sang during these gatherings emphasizes this crucial importance of cooking and sharing food with strangers:

> Let us sing, to give us courage with joy
>
> For God invites all persons who live in this world
>
> To ask of him reasonable satisfaction for their needs,
>
> Even the most secret ones . . .
>
> The wind that blows carries our voices into the distance,
>
> And inspires the strangers to join us
>
> . . . take a cooking pot and prepare
>
> A meal for the strangers
>
> . . . cook the food for strangers.[38]

Diatta's practice of overflowing, boundless hospitality echoes the crucial theological themes of Galatians with surprising proximity. Like her community, the Galatians had extended ultimate hospitality to the stranger Paul who came from a different country, culture, and religion. Like the prophetess, Paul in turn insists that the radically inclusive table community between Jews and gentile strangers, circumcision and foreskin, at Syrian Antioch as well as in Galatia, was the core matter of proper faith (Gal 2:11–21). Within the body of the Messiah, all ethnic, religious, social, and gender distinctions were equalized into a new type of solidarity between Self and Other—the Self no longer needed to downgrade the Other as a barbarian to be assured of its own worth and "civilized" status (Gal 3:26–28).[39] Foreskin or circumcision didn't matter anymore. What mattered under the aegis of the crucified Messiah was the coalescing of people beyond the boundaries of religion, tribe, and nation toward global hospitality among diverse fellow-humans.

It is our assumption that this community across socially determinative borderlines and hierarchies became the reason that not only Aline Sitoé but also Paul were seen as a threat to the imperial construct of *Paix Française* or

---

38. Girard, *Genèse du pouvoir charismatique*, 348–49. This is Poem/Song 4 by Aline Sitoé Diatta recorded by Jean Girard, a colonial administrator. Niang, "Community and Identity Construction."

39. Niang, *Faith and Freedom*, 103–8.

Pax Romana respectively. His context opens up in new ways if it is overlaid with hers and contemplated through the lens of an analogous contextual historiography. Empire thrives on stoking local conflicts among the barbarians and among the conquered in general. For it rules by dividing. Pitting people(s) against one another, having them compete for superior status in the eyes of the conquerors as happened both in Senegal and Galatia, or dwelling on the superiority of one's own religion vis-a-vis the "uncircumcised"—all of this may produce compliance with imperial rule if the rulers play it well, as both the Romans and the French knew.[40] In his book on the geostrategic imperatives of American global primacy, Zbigniew Brzezinski summarized this imperial maxim of "Divide and rule" famously:

> To put it in a terminology that hearkens back to the more brutal age of ancient empires, the three grand imperatives of imperial geostrategy are to prevent collusion and maintain security dependence among the vassals, to keep tributaries pliant and protected, and to keep the barbarians from coming together.[41]

If those at the bottom become part of a commonality, it must be a unification based on the principles and belief systems of empire, not on political heresies like equality, hospitality, or justice for all "visible human beings." And definitely not under the aegis of somebody like Jesus from Nazareth, whom the empire had crucified as a political criminal with support from local collaborators. This is why Paul, in all likelihood, was executed under Nero in the early sixties of the first century CE in Rome. And this is why Aline Sitoé, betrayed by some of her own followers, was eventually caught by the French and deported to Timbuktu where she vanished. Until today, we don't know the end of her story.

Dietrich Bonhoeffer and a Church Becoming Hospitable to the Other in (East) Germany

After World War II, East German Protestantism faced tough choices it was barely prepared for. Used to its status as a powerful state church, and with roots reaching deep into the reactionary political establishment of Germany that had produced two World Wars and the Holocaust, it all of a sudden found itself in a position of utmost powerlessness. A worthy and

---

40. For an example of Galatian priests to god Augustus and goddess Roma trying to outperform each other, see the priest list at the imperial temple in Ancyra; cf. Mitchell, *Anatolia* 112; Kahl, *Galatians Re-imagined*, 191–204.

41. Brzezinski, *Grand Chessboard*, 40.

weighty representative of Christian Occidentalism at its heart, it abruptly was cast out into the "barbarian" world of an anti-Christian Orientalism that was also atheist and socialist. Turning the established order upside down, the new East German regime proclaimed the equality of men and women, the need to feed and house everyone, let no one go hungry or homeless or remain uneducated or without medical care, alongside the imperative to be in solidarity with anti-colonial movements in Africa and across the globe. None of this had been a theological priority for the majority of German Christianity so far, mildly stated, and it decided to focus on the atheist nature of the new social order and its undemocratic and repressive traits instead. Supported by its Western brothers and sisters, the East German church set out to become a bulwark and "mighty fortress" against Eastern communism and atheism.

But there were other voices that challenged this continued alliance with clerical conservatism and Occidentalism. Members of the Confessing Church that had resisted Hitler's fascist and racist agenda pledged for radical repentance and theological reconfiguration of German Protestantism in line with the "Barmen Declaration" of 1934 or the more radical "Darmstädter Bruderratswort" of 1947. Religious socialism that had some strong roots in Germany and in the resistance movement against Hitler established its presence in numerous ways.[42] But it was the voice of one theologian in particular who helped East Germans reconsider their position on the Cold War battlefield between West and East—Dietrich Bonhoeffer, whose *Prison Letters* appeared in East Germany in 1961, the very year the Berlin Wall went up.

Dietrich Bonhoeffer's metamorphosis from a conservative Lutheran to one of the most visionary German theologians of the twentieth century, forged by his time at Union Theological Seminary in New York, his work in the anti-Nazi resistance movement, his incarceration and subsequent brutal execution directly ordered by Hitler shortly before his own demise, had a momentous impact in East Germany. Interestingly, Bonhoeffer was read in East Germany with quite different eyes than in the West. Again, contrasting political contexts offered dissimilar reading lenses. Bonhoeffer's vision of a "Church for Others"[43] and his somewhat enigmatic notes on a "religionless Christianity,"[44] both concepts he developed in the prison letters, for many

---

42. Cf. Kahl, "Emil Fuchs."

43. "The church is the church only when it exists for others." Bonhoeffer, *Letters and Papers from Prison*, 382.

44. Bonhoeffer, *Letters and Papers from Prison*, 280–82.

East German Protestants changed the way they thought about what it meant to be church in an atheist and socialist context.

Bonhoeffer sparked a whole new way of rethinking Protestantism, as not just individual faith justification but also justice-seeking on a societal level. He taught East Germans that the traditional Lutheran separation between justification by faith "alone" and works of justice had made grace a cheap thing.[45] He enabled them to re-think the Protestant Self in its encounter with the non-Christian/atheist/Marxist Other and move towards an ethics of Other-care for the common good. Last but not least, Bonhoeffer helped East German Christians challenge their occidental bias and overcome a self-imposed parochialism by entering into a dialogue with the non-Christian Other for the sake of a better, more democratic, and humane socialism.

It is often overlooked how deeply Bonhoeffer was steeped in Pauline theology. For him, Paul's inclusive community of Jews and gentiles, circumcision and foreskin in Christ meant resistance against Hitler's "Aryan Law" that required the removal of Jews from public service and that a strong faction of German Protestantism (the "German Christians") also wanted to apply to the church. Splitting the church into two separate bodies of Christians, one of them with a Jewish and the other with an Aryan pedigree, was *anathema* to Bonhoeffer, as it was to Paul in an analogous configuration (cf. Gal 1:9). Bonhoeffer explicitly cites the break-up of the Antiochene table community in Galatians 2:11–14 to make his point that the whole existence of the church as the diverse and non-uniform body of Christ is at stake here.[46] For him, the Pauline question whether "circumcision" is a pre-requisite for gentile Christ-followers eventually morphed into the question whether "religion" as such was a precondition of being "in Christ." With this, he pointed a path toward collaboration and solidarity with the non-religious and atheist Other, as well as with the Other adhering to a different religion.[47]

Conclusion

Paul, Aline Sitoé, Dietrich Bonhoeffer—and their Galatian, Diola, East German, and present-day interlocutors—would have many things to discuss at a fictive table extending its hospitality across time and continents. There wouldn't be any disagreement among them that the law they resisted in the name of faith was not the law of any particular tribe, country, or religion,

---

45. Bonhoeffer, *Discipleship*, 459–61.

46. Bonhoeffer, *Aryan Paragraph in the Church*, 383; cf. also Kahl, "Justification, Ethics and the 'Other,'" 75–76.

47. Bonhoeffer, *Letters and Papers from Prison*, 281.

and certainly not Jewish law per se, but the law of empire as law of exclusion and competition—the time-tested law of victory, domination, and colonization. This, the law of power, was the law that in the end sentenced all three of them to death. Having them all seated at one imaginary fellowship table opens up new ways not only to understand Paul and the Galatians, but most of all our own world, our own state of emergency in light of global solidarity and hospitality—and in light of a *different world* all of them, as a matter of faith, experienced and envisioned as possible.

Bibliography

(* For Further Reading)

Arnold, Clinton A. "'I Am Astonished That You Are So Quickly Turning Away!' (Gal 1:6): Paul and the Anatolian Folk Belief." *New Testament Studies* 51 (2005) 429–49.

Aymer, Margaret. *Border Lines: The Partition of Judaeo-Christianity*. Philadelphia: University of Pennsylvania Press, 2004.

———. "Islandedness, Paul, and John of Patmos." In *Island, Islanders, and the Bible: RumInations,* edited by Jione Havea, Margaret Aymer, and Steed Vernyl Davidson, 25–36. Semeia Studies 77. Atlanta: Society of Biblical Literature, 2015.

Baum, Robert M. "The Emergence of a Diola Christianity." *Africa: Journal of the International African Institute* 60 (1990) 370–98.

Benjamin, Walter. "Theses on the Philosophy of History." In *Illuminations: Essays and Reflections*, edited by Hannah Arendt, translated by Harry Zohn, 253–64. New York: Schocken, 1969.

Bonhoeffer, Dietrich. *The Aryan Paragraph in the Church*. In *The Bonhoeffer Reader*, edited by Clifford J. Green and Michael P. DeJonge, 370–78. Minneapolis: Fortress, 2013.

———. *Discipleship*. In *The Bonhoeffer Reader*, edited by Clifford J. Green and Michael P. DeJonge, 455–513. Minneapolis: Fortress, 2013.

———. *Letters & Papers from Prison*. Edited by Eberhard Bethge. Translated by Reginald Fuller. New York: Mac-millan, 1972.

Brzezinski, Zbigniew. *The Grand Chessboard: American Primacy and Its Geostrategic Imperatives*. New York: Basic Books, 1997.

Diodorus. *Diodorus of Sicily*. Edited by T. E. Page. Translated by C. H. Oldfather. 12 vols. Loeb Classical Library. Cambridge: Harvard University Press, 1939.

Elliott, Susan M. *Cutting too Close for Comfort*. Journal for the Study of the New Testament Supplements 248. Sheffield: Sheffield University Press, 2004.

Foster, Elizabeth A. *Faith in Empire: Religion, Politics, and Colonial Rule in French Senegal 1880–1940*. Stanford: Stanford University Press, 2013.

———. "A Mission in Transition: Race, Politics, and the Decolonization of the Catholic Church in Senegal." In *God's Empire: French Missionaries and the Modern World*, edited by Owen White and J. P. Daughton, 257–77. New York: Oxford University Press, 2012.

Georgi, Dieter. "God Turned Upside Down." In *Paul and Empire: Religion and Power in Roman Imperial Society,* edited by R. A. Horsley, 148–57. Harrisburg, PA: Trinity, 1997.

Girard, Jean. *Genèse du pouvoir charismatique en basse Casamance (Sénégal).* Dakar SN: IFAN, 1969.

Hall, Edith. *Inventing the Barbarian: Greek Self-Definition through Tragedy.* Oxford: Oxford University Press, 1989.

Hardin, Justin K. *Galatians and the Imperial Cult: A Critical Analysis of the First-Century Social Context of Paul's Letter.* Wissenschaftliche Untersuchungen zum Neuen Testament 2/237. Tübingen: Mohr Siebeck, 2008.

Harley, John Brian. "Maps, Knowledge, and Power." In *The Iconography of Landscape: Essays on the Symbolic Representation, Design, and Use of Past Environments,* edited by D. Cosgrove and S. Daniels, 277–312. Cambridge Studies in Historical Geography 9. Cambridge: Cambridge University Press, 1988.

Horsley, Richard A., ed. *Paul and Empire: Religion and Power in Roman Imperial Society.* Harrisburg, PA: Trinity, 1997.

*Jewett, Robert. *Romans: A Commentary.* Hermeneia. Minneapolis: Fortress, 2007.

John, Felix. *Der Galaterbrief im Kontext historischer Lebenswelten im antiken Kleinasien.* Forschungen zur Religion und Literatur des Alten und Neuen Testaments 264. Göttingen: Vandenhoek & Ruprecht, 2016.

Kahl, Brigitte. "Emil Fuchs Römerbriefauslegung im Kontext gegenwärtiger Pauluskontroversen." In *Marxismus und Theologie: Materialien der Jahrestagung 2018 der Leibniz-Sozietät der Wissenschaften,* edited by Gerhard Banse, Brigitte Kahl, Jan Rehmann, 71–80. Abhandlungen der Leibniz-Sozietät der Wissenschaften 55. Berlin: Trafo Wissenschaftsverlag, 2019.

———. "Galatians and the 'Orientalism' of Justification by Faith: Paul among Jews and Muslims." In *The Colonized Apostle: Paul through Postcolonial Eyes,* edited by Christopher Stanley, 206–22. Paul in Critical Contexts. Minneapolis: Fortress, 2011.

*———. *Galatians Re-Imagined: Reading with the Eyes of the Vanquished.* Paul in Critical Contexts. Minneapolis: Fortress, 2010.

———. "Justification, Ethics and the 'Other'—Paul, Luther and Bonhoeffer in Trialogue." In *Luther, Bonhoeffer, and Public Ethics: Re-forming the Church of the Future,* edited by Michael P. DeJonge and Clifford J. Green, 63–82. Lanham, MD: Lexington/Fortress Academic, 2018.

Kamudzandu, Israel. *Abraham Our Father: Paul and the Ancestors in Postcolonial Africa.* Paul in Critical Contexts. Minneapolis: Fortress, 2013.

Kluge, Friedrich. *Etymologisches Wörterbuch der deutschen Sprache.* 11th ed. Berlin: de Gruyter, 1934.

Lehr, Fabian. *Zum europäischen Rassismus: Drei Thesen gegen den Import US-amerikanischer Rassismusdiskurse.* https://www.designing-history.world/en/theory/europaeischer-rassismus-amerikanische-rassismusdiskurse/.

Livy. *Histories of Rome.* Edited by T. E. Page. Translated by Evan T. Sage. 14 vols. Loeb Classical Library. Cambridge: Harvard University Press, 1955.

Mitchell, Stephen. *Anatolia: Land, Men, and Gods in Asia Minor.* Vol. 1. Oxford: Clarendon, 1993.

Nanos, Mark. *The Irony of Galatians: Paul's Letter in First-Century Context.* Minneapolis: Fortress, 2002.

Niang, Aliou Cissé. "Community and Identity Construction in the Life and Thought of Paul and Aline Sitoé Diatta: A Diola Christian Perspective." In *Reading the New Testament in the Manifold Contexts of a Globalized World Exegetical Perspectives*. Tübingen: Mohr Siebeck, forthcoming.

———. "Contested Spaces: Diola Christianity in Rural and Urban Sénégal." In *World Christianity, Urbanization, and Identity*, edited by Moses O. Biney, Kenneth N. Ngwa, and Raimundo C. Barreto, 3:101–22. World Christianity and Public Religion Series. Minneapolis: Fortress, 2021.

*———. *Faith and Freedom in Galatia and Senegal: The Apostle Paul, Colonists, and Sending Gods*. Biblical Interpretation Series 97. Leiden: Brill, 2009.

———. "Islandedness, Translation, and Creolization." In *Island, Islanders, and the Bible: RumInations*, edited by Jione Havea, Margaret Aymer, and Steed Vernyl Davidson, 177–84. Semeia Studies 77. Atlanta: Society of Biblical Literature, 2015.

———. *The Poetics of Postcolonial Biblical Criticism: God, Human-Nature Relationship, and Negritude*. Eugene, OR: Cascade Books, 2019.

Nicolet, Claude. *Space, Geography, and Politics in the Early Roman Empire*. Ann Arbor: University of Michigan Press, 1991.

Ramsay, William M. *A Historical Commentary on St. Paul's Epistle to the Galatians*. London: Hodder & Stoughton, 1899.

Radkau, Joachim "Die Zweideutigkeit des Kapitals gegenüber dem Faschismus. Einige Gedanken zum Verhältnis von Geschichtsforschung und Faschismustheorie und zum Vergleich zwischen Deutschland und Italien." *Das Argument* 146 (1984) 527–38.

Roth, Karl Heinz. "Faschismus oder Nationalsozialismus? Kontroversen im Spannungsfeld zwischen Geschichtspolitik, Gefühl und Wissenschaft." *Sozial Geschichte: Zeitschrift für historische Analyse des 20 und 21. Jahrhunderts* 19 (2014) 31–52.

Said, Edward. *Orientalism*. New York: Vintage, 1994.

Sleeman, Matthew. *Geography and the Ascension Narrative in Acts*. New York: Cambridge University Press, 2009.

Smith-Christopher, Daniel. "Cross-Cultural Exegesis." In *The Oxford Encyclopedia of Biblical Interpretation*, edited by Steven L. McKenzie, 138–50. New York: Oxford University Press, 2013.

Stanley, Christopher D., ed. *The Colonized Apostle: Paul through Postcolonial Eyes*. Paul in Critical Contexts. Minneapolis: Fortress, 2011.

Stendahl, Krister. *Paul among Jews and Gentiles: And Other Essays*. Minneapolis: Fortress, 1976.

Strobel, Karl. *Die Galater: Geschichte und Eigenart der keltischen Staatenbildung auf dem Boden des hellenistischen Kleinasien*. Berlin: Akademie Verlag, 1996.

Sugirtharajah, R. S., ed. *Vernacular Hermeneutics*. England, Sheffield Academic, 1999.

Tacitus. *The Histories and The Annals*. Translated by C. H. Moore and J. Jackson. 4 vols. Loeb Classical Library [LCL]. Cambridge: Harvard University Press, 1937.

Tamez, Elsa. *The Amnesty of Grace*. Nashville: Abingdon, 1993.

Taubes, Jacob. *The Political Theology of Paul*. Stanford, CA: Stanford University Press, 2004.

Thomas, Louis-Vincent. "Les 'rois' Diola, hier, aujourd'hui, demain." *Bulletin de l'Institut Fondamental d'Afrique noire* 34, no. 1 (1972) 151–74.

Ukpong, Justin S. "Reading the Bible in a Global Village: Issues and Challenges from African Readings." In *Reading The Bible in the Global Village: Cape Town*, edited by Justin S. Ukpong, Musa W. Dube, Gerald O. West, Alpheus Masoga, Norman K. Gottwald, Jeremy Punt, Tinyiko S. Maluleke, and Vincent L. Wimbush, 9–39. Atlanta: Society of Biblical Literature, 2002.

Webster, Jane. "Ethnographic Barbarity, Colonial Discourse and 'Celtic Warrior Societies.'" In *Roman Imperialism: Post-Colonial Perspectives*, edited by Jane Webster and Nicholas J. Cooper, 111–23. Leister: School of Archeological Studies, University of Leicester, 1996.

Wells, Peter S. *The Barbarians Speak: How the Conquered Peoples Shaped Roman Europe.* Princeton: Princeton University Press, 1999.

Winter, Bruce. *Seek the Welfare of the City: Christians as Benefactors and Citizens.* Grand Rapids: Eerdmans, 1994.

Study Questions

1. How might Aline Sitoé Diatta have received the Apostle Paul in her own colonial context, and what might they have talked about at the common table?

2. In what ways can Paul's Galatia, Aline Sitoé's Diola land, Eastern Europe, and post-World-War-II East Germany be perceived as neighboring provinces of a fictive *Barbaria* located on the imaginary map of the Christian Occident?

3. What is "cross-cultural" interpretation or "analogous historiography," and what can it do?

17

By Any Means Necessary, All Israel Will be Saved

Paul, Malcolm, and Community Identity in the Letter to the Romans

KEITH AUGUSTUS BURTON

Abstract

MANY OF THE RECIPIENTS of Paul's letter to the Romans were poor tenement dwellers in some of the most squalid areas of the capitol. Although multiethnic, they belonged to a fledgling Jewish-Messianic community that was on a quest for identity. Paul uses the LXX as an authoritative but malleable source to affirm their status as the renewed Israel of God. The Romans situation bears interesting parallels to the urban American context that gave rise to Malcolm X.

Introduction

Robert Jewett was intentional about forming relationships and building community. He was a beloved professor whom many students were privileged to call friend. Many ate at his table in his Evanston apartment, and his countless acts of kindness are recorded in the heavenly annals. I was the beneficiary of many expressions of tangible love when I served as his full-time research assistant for two productive years. "Bob" believed in community. Anyone familiar with Professor Jewett also knew a man who abhorred systems of cultural supremacy. Unwilling to confine himself to a theological Aeropagus distanced from the world in which real people lived, he donned the prophetic mantle as he chastised his native land for its excessive militarism and delusions of exceptionalism.¹ He was also known for critiquing culture by "bringing films and biblical texts into dialogue by means of an interpretive arch [that] . . . reaches between ancient and modern texts and stories."²

This study applies a similar cross-cultural hermeneutic in its reconstruction and analysis of the audience to whom Paul writes in Romans. The term "cross-cultural" is somewhat fluid and can have at least two suggested applications in biblical interpretation. First, it can refer to "the interpretive movement from ancient culture to contemporary cultures, beginning with the challenges of translation. It can also mean the way those from a culture not one's own interpret the Bible from their distinctive standpoint and experience."³ Both meanings apply to this study to a nuanced degree as readers are invited to look at the biblical culture through the lens of comparable events in contemporary culture. The task of pulling the cultures into conversation with each other encapsulates the conventional wisdom behind the imagery of "killing two birds with one stone." When appropriately applied, the student is provided with the experience of linking the familiar with the unfamiliar. Whether primarily acquainted with the biblical world or the parallel one, this approach provides a single lens to analyze both.

This essay explores Paul's efforts to build community among apparently disparate factions in Rome by alluding to the ministry of American civil rights leader, Malcolm X. Like the demographic to whom the Nation of Islam appealed, Paul's audience comprised urban dwellers who had chosen to identify with a controversial liberation movement.⁴ The urban aspect of their identity is discussed under the heading "Sociological Israel." The second section focuses on the rhetorical basis for establishing their identity as "Hermeneutical Israel." Here we highlight how Paul, like Malcolm, utilizes a rhetorical strategy of selectively appropriating the biblical text to achieve his aim of elevating community consciousness.

---

1. His critiques are found in Jewett and Lawrence, *Captain America*; Shelton and Jewett, *Myth of the American Superhero*.

2. Jewett, *Paul Returns to the Movies*, 4. See also Jewett, *Paul at the Movies*; and the influence it has had on some of my own work (Burton, "Regarding Henry.")

3. Cosgrove, Weiss, Yeo, *Cross-Cultural Paul*, 4.

4. See Hendricks, *The Politics of Jesus*, for an alternate view on the radical nature of early Christianity.

Sociological Israel: Believers in the Hood

In popular culture, the phrase "by any means necessary" is typically associated with assassinated civil rights leader, Malcolm X. This was a central theme in the speech he gave to launch his Organization of Afro-American Unity on June 28, 1964. Committed to the struggle for equal rights, he invited the masses to strive for freedom, justice, and equality "by any means necessary." The attempt to discern parallels between Malcolm X and the apostle Paul may at first seem hyperbolic, but while the details on their agendas may have differed, there was a common objective.

Malcolm's call for Afro-American unity was informed by Marcus Mosiah Garvey's vision for dispersed Africans to discover the power of the collective in their quest for racial equality.[5] For this to happen, Black people would have to move beyond obvious intersectional differences and find redemptive commonality in their shared experience of oppression. Similarly, Paul's quest was informed by the Messiah's vision of a countercultural society that faithfully reflected God's righteousness. This was only possible if those aligned with the new movement acknowledged their commonality, moved beyond ethnic and socio-economic barriers, and recognized their status as full citizens in God's realm.

The Projects

Like the audience to whom Malcolm X appealed, available evidence suggests that the Christian community to which Paul wrote was highly concentrated in the lower socio-economic neighborhoods in urban Rome. Building on Peter Lampe's research, Jewett believed that the churches were mainly located in Trastevere and Porta Capena, "swampy areas where the poorest population of Rome lived."[6] For the most part, these churches differed from the house church organizational structure that typified New Testament congregations. House churches were usually sponsored by a wealthy patron who provided the physical space for worship and fellowship and mirrored the hierarchical structure of Greco-Roman society.[7] Nonetheless, although there was wealth disparity between the patron and clients, the

---

5. For a discussion of the impact of Garveyite philosophy on the young Malcolm Little, see Decaro, *On the Side of My People*, 38–47.

6. Jewett, *Romans: A Commentary*, 62. See Lampe, *From Paul to Valentinus*.

7. See Meeks, *Urban Christians*, 76.

subordinating rules of society had no place among believers. Gerd Theissen calls this arrangement "love patriarchalism."[8]

The unique urban setting of some of the Roman churches did not easily allow for house-church arrangements since the area was dominated by multilevel tenement buildings. While the first floor may have served as a shop, the upper floors were packed to capacity with as many families as could be squeezed into the small rooms. Given habitual social dynamics, early believers in Christ would have migrated to each other and would eventually share living spaces. Of course, the social structure in these tenement churches would be much different from the ones in patriarchal "houses." These were poor people living independently with a common lack of financial resources and no access to a benevolent patron.[9] Theirs was a "one-dimensional" class structure, which Jewett terms "agapaic communalism."[10] Like the early Judean believers, they pooled their resources and regularly shared a common meal.[11]

The People

The lived and historical experiences of Malcolm's marginalized audience also mirrored that of many in the early Christian communities. In Malcolm's world, slavery had been abolished for less than a century, and Jim Crow laws deprived American Blacks of their citizenship. Similarly, in Rome, Jewett reminds us that, "Here, as elsewhere in the early church, the bulk of the members consisted of slaves and former slaves, with the rest coming largely from lower-class handworkers."[12] Many among these teeming masses were transplanted from different places in the empire, including a significant number of ancestral Jews whom Pompey had relocated to Jerusalem in 63 BCE.[13] By the time of Paul's letter, the Jewish community alone may have consisted of between 15,000 and 60,000 people.[14]

Although their rights were limited, Jews were legally permitted to practice their religion in the imperial capital. Consequently, there were many Jewish synagogues that were probably organized along the lines of the "storefront" churches that once frequented Black urban neighborhoods.

---

8. Theissen, *Social Setting*, 107.
9. Jewett, *Romans: A Commentary*, 65.
10. Jewett, *Romans: A Commentary*, 66.
11. Jewett, "Love Feast."
12. Jewett, *Romans: A Commentary*, 63.
13. Williams, "Shaping of the Identity," 34–35.
14. Lampe, *Paul to Valentius*, 84.

Whether through missionary activity or fascination, people from other ethnic groups joined the synagogues, resulting in a congregational admixture of ancestral Jews, "proselytes, God-fearers, and sympathizers."[15] Given the independent nature of the tenement synagogues, there would not have been much coordination among the individual leaders. The lack of a central organization made it easy for early Christian evangelists to penetrate individual units with their Messianic brand of Judaism. Eventually, their missionary success led to internal conflict that became so public that the authorities ordered some synagogues closed in 41 CE and eventually banned select Jewish leaders in 49 CE.[16]

The government restrictions resulted in an absence of generational Jewish leaders, providing opportunities for believers from other ethnic groups to occupy the vacant leadership positions.[17] It is generally believed that the change in leadership affected a demographic shift among the overall membership, a shift that was exacerbated by ethnic tensions in broader society.[18] Some who ascribe to this possibility deduce that when Paul writes his letter, "the Gentile majority was discriminating against the Jewish minority whom it was claiming to displace."[19]

The Problem

In a memorable speech, Malcolm categorized Blacks in America as either "house negroes" or "field negroes."[20] In spite of their common experience, the former had fully surrendered to their oppressed status, while the latter yearned for change. The believers in Rome were also ideologically divided. Scholars have tended to characterize the ideological division along ethnic lines, claiming that a conservative Jewish minority was at odds with a liberal

---

15. Jewett, *Romans: A Commentary*, 57–58. He also suggests that the synagogue of the Vernaclesians may even have been dominated by "native-born persons converted to Judaism."

16. See Schnabel, "Persecution of Christians," 530–31.

17. Jewett concludes, "it is appropriate to infer that the Christian groups originating inside the various Jewish synagogues in Rome had been deprived of their Jewish Christian leaders by Claudius's deportation order in 49 CE and that they continued as house congregations with Gentile leaders for the next five years" (*Romans: A Commentary*, 61).

18. Jewett comments, "The ethnic diversity of the Roman congregations enhanced a combative tendency that was present throughout the culture" (Jewett, *Romans: A Commentary*, 72).

19. Jewett, *Romans: A Commentary*, 70.

20. X, "The Race Problem."

gentile majority.[21] This tendency to align liberal and conservative along ethnic lines is based on anachronistic assumptions from later Christian generations when the parting of the ways between Judaism and Christianity was more pronounced.[22] The fact that the expulsion of Jewish leaders took place eight years after government closure of synagogues suggests that there was already a dynamic underground movement led by people who would have been familiar with the tenets of the Jewish faith.[23]

Even in the context of multicultural congregations, Jewish religious traditions would have directly influenced the liturgy and instruction.[24] The void created by the forced relocation of church leaders would have been filled by qualified leaders who themselves had been immersed in the tradition. In fact, in the final chapter of Romans, Paul takes it for granted that those to whom he wrote had been formally catechized (cf. Rom 16:17, 27). With this in mind, it should not automatically be concluded that inexperienced newbies manipulated their way into positions and completely abandoned their spiritual roots in just five years![25] As Mark Nanos has repeatedly demonstrated, even if theories about a gentile ethnic majority are correct, the church would have maintained its Jewish identity.[26]

While a rapid detachment from their core Jewish roots is unlikely, the impact of the loose organizational structure on individual congregational identities should be taken seriously. Ancestral Jews, descendants of proselytes, and the newly converted were bonding together into a new expression of Judaism that was subliminally revolutionary and a constant source of controversy. Like their siblings across the empire, and possibly beyond,[27]

21. Jewett writes, "It is likely that the majority of the strong were Gentile believers, with Jewish liberals such as Paul and his close allies included in this group. It is also likely that the weak included Jewish adherents to the law, but this group probably included some Gentiles who had been close to synagogues before becoming believers, or those drawn to the movement when it was still meeting in synagogues, that is, prior to 49 ce." (*Romans: A Commentary*, 56).

22. See Nanos, "Jewish Context"; Burton, *Laying Down the Law*, 125–28. For a discussion on the late first-century fissure between Christianity and Judaism, see Dunn, *Parting of the Ways*.

23. See Burton, *Rhetoric, Law, and the Mystery of Salvation*, 129–35.

24. See my discussion on the Jewish nature of the Roman church in Burton, "So That You May be with Another," 30–70.

25. In a simulation exercise, my doctoral colleague and Jewett's former student, Finger (*Roman House*, 144), indirectly implies that some liberal members may have even brought pork to a love feast.

26. For example, Nanos, *Reading Paul*; Nanos, "Jewish Context."

27. In part three of Burton, *The Blessing of Africa*, 111–44, I emphasize aspects of Christianity's concentric growth beyond the Roman Empire. The tendency is to view early Christianity strictly through the linear missions of Paul from the Levant to Europe.

they were still figuring out how they related to their parent religion. In penning his letter to the tenement churches, Paul coaches them along their journey as he uses their common document of faith to establish their status as a revamped Israel of God.

Hermeneutical Israel:[28] We Are Somebody

Malcolm X's success as the preeminent evangelist in the Nation of Islam was due in part to the organization's strategy of using Christian emblems to attract seekers to their faith. In addition to holding enthusiastic Sunday worship services, many of their teachings were derived from creative interpretations of the Bible.[29] When Paul writes to the tenement churches in urban Rome, he also utilizes sacred literature that he and the congregants deemed authoritative. Given the ease and frequency with which he quotes from the text, there was a basic expectation that the recipients would have been well familiar with the contents. Even if they were majority gentile, they would have maintained spiritual solidarity with their Jewish siblings even after the expulsion.[30]

A common language contributed to the attempt to build community among the believers. Although located in the capital of the Roman Empire, Greek was the lingua franca in these multiethnic urban areas.[31] Fortunately for Judaism, the Bible had been translated from Hebrew to the Greek "Septuagint" for more than a century so it was not difficult for the faith to be transmitted in a way the masses could understand.[32] They would have also understood the way in which Paul applied the Scriptures, which may raise the blood pressure of a modern seminary professor grading an exegetical paper, but was common in the rabbinic tradition in which the apostle was trained. His method is akin to proof texting, where certain "words" from Scripture can be connected to others like matching dominoes. The rules that govern this midrashic approach to hermeneutics are known as middot. In

---

28. Cosgrove, *Elusive Israel*, 26–45, uses the term "Hermeneutical Election" in his discussion of Romans 9–11.

29. Wilson speaks of the Nation of Islam using "biblical and Qur'anic exegesis" to support their doctrine of Black election ("Come Down of the Cross and Get under the Crescent," 498). See also Decaro, *Religious Life*, 48–58, on Malcolm's familiarity with the Christian Bible from childhood.

30. So Nanos, *Reading Paul*.

31. Jewett, *Romans: A Commentary*, 56.

32. Lanier and Ross assert that the term "Septuagint" is "used most ambiguously to refer to ancient Greek scriptures in general, with no specific text, boundaries, or historical phase in view" (*The Septuagint*, 35).

his description of Paul's approach, Richard Hays reminds us that the middot "do not tell the interpreter how to find out what a text means; instead, they suggest ways to make the text mean more than it says."[33]

The Faithful

Cain Hope Felder playfully critiques the license that many Black preachers take with the text.[34] This homiletical freedom that characterizes the dramatic storytelling in Black preaching has been embraced and expanded by ministers in the Nation of Islam. Like his disciple, Louis Farrakhan, Malcolm X would have embraced a biblical hermeneutic in which the application did not readily align with the scriptural context. Before we get too judgmental, Felder reminds us that "the earliest proponents of the Christian faith invariably appealed to arbitrary proof-texts to settle complex issues of community life."[35] Paul was no exception.[36] From the first citation from the LXX in his Romans letter, he alters the text of Habakkuk 2:4 in a small but significant way. Interestingly, the LXX translators had already altered the Hebrew text from "the righteous one shall live by *his* faith[fulness]," to "the righteous one shall live by *my* faith[fulness]." Paul goes a step further by dropping the personal pronoun altogether as he posits, "the righteous one shall live by faith[fulness]." (Rom 1:17b)

Paul's redaction has been interpreted as a radical replacement of *faithfulness* as a human activity, with *faith* as a fundamental of Christian belief. Along this line, Jewett writes, "the deletion . . . of the personal pronoun points indisputably in the direction of 'faith' as a theological formula for participation in the Christ movement."[37] Consequently, it is no longer the right *disposition* of the subject that indicates a righteous person, but the subject's right *belief*. This rationalization of "faith" is directly influenced by the rationalistic revolution in the Protestant Reformation, particularly Luther's faith-works dichotomy that has had a lasting influence on the negative concept of works-righteousness.

---

33. Hays, *Echoes of Scripture*, 12. Or as articulated by Neusner, "The painter cannot paint without the oils. But the colors do not make the painting. The painter does" (*Judaism and Scripture*, 123).

34. Felder, *Biblical Waters*, 79–80.

35. Felder, *Biblical Waters*, 80.

36. Campbell ("All God's Beloved," 69) explains, "Paul both interprets Scripture in relation to contemporary events of his own time, and in turn interprets these events in the light of Scripture."

37. Jewett, *Romans: A Commentary*, 145.

While this has become the dominant mode of understanding the text, we should not forget that the audience would have been familiar with the original citation and would not have understood his emendation through a future Protestant lens.[38] Instead, it appears that the decision to omit the personal pronoun is intended to connect the faithfulness of God with the faithfulness of the believer.[39] This establishes the inference in the previous clause that "God's righteousness is revealed in [the gospel] from [his own] faithfulness to the faithfulness [of the believer]" (1:17a). The recipients of the letter are not passive initiates into a new mystery cult but are active beneficiaries of God's faithfulness who in turn reflect that faithfulness in their daily lives and decisions. Like the people to whom Malcolm preached, their spiritual experience would not be confined to pews in stained glass cathedrals but would motivate them to actions of love within and without their fellowship.

The Flawed

In his memorable sermon, "The Ballot or the Bullet," Malcolm X provided a crash course in American history with the reminder, "We didn't land on Plymouth Rock, the rock was landed on us."[40] Whether they acknowledge it or not, every Black descendant in America has been hurt to some degree by the nation's racialized policies. Even while inspiring them to be faithful, Paul impresses upon the Roman congregations that all have been impacted by the sin virus, whether ancestral Jew or converted gentile. His argument is partly supported by a compilation of texts from the LXX that are widely believed to comprise a liturgical catena (Rom 3:10–18). Jewett believes the catena ". . . was probably created by Jewish sectarians, and was intended to buttress their claims against other groups whom they considered to be heretics."[41]

Paul's alteration of the catena totally transforms its role in promoting religious supremacy. It rejects the "us versus them" provincialism and embraces a soteriologically paradoxical inclusion. Before discussing the simple redaction that changed the meaning of the entire hymn, I cannot

---

38. In another place, Jewett cites Stegner who ". . . shows that in midrashic discourse, often supporting texts are cited only partially because the writer or speaker assumes that the audience knows the rest by heart and can identify the catchword connections by themselves" (*Romans: A Commentary*, 579). See also Stegner, "Romans 9:6–29," 40–41.

39. Also implied by Dunn, *Romans 1–8*, 45.

40. X, "Ballot or the Bullet."

41. Jewett, *Romans: A Commentary*, 264.

ignore that others have argued for further evidence of redaction. The original catena is generally seen as a collation of select proof texts from LXX Psalms 5, 9, 13, 35, and 139; and Isaiah 59.[42] Operating under this supposition, some have argued that when Paul writes, "a righteous human does not exist" in Romans 3:10, he is paraphrasing "a human doing good does not exist" from LXX Psalm 13:1c (which would have been preserved in the catena). They further suggest that Paul excises LXX Psalm 13:2 for theological and stylistic reasons, before harmonizing again in Romans 3:11 with the line from LXX Psalm 13:2b, "a human who understands does not exist." While this is tenable, it seems more reasonable that another verse informed the first line of the catena, namely Ecclesiastes 7:20a ("a righteous person (*anthrōpos*) does not exist").[43]

Whatever the case with the beginning of the catena, the final "significant alteration" is less ambiguous. This takes place in the last section where "a fear of God does not exist before his eyes" in LXX Psalm 35:2 becomes "a fear of God does not exist before their eyes" in Romans 3:18. In the context of the psalm, the "eyes" belong to the "lawless person" (*paranomos*) who obstinately opposes God. A strict reading of the text would contradict Paul's rhetorical intent, and so he changes the pronoun from the singular to the plural "to generalize and universalize responsibility for evil."[44] While the application may not have been exegetically correct, Paul was more concerned with establishing his assertion that nobody in the congregation has escaped the common experience.

The Favored

One of the names Wallace Fahd Muhammad gave to the religion he raised up was the Lost-Found Nation of Islam. The very name implied that a people whose humanity had been assaulted over centuries of racist oppression were now empowered to assert their true value. The final didactic section in Romans (9–11) is empowering news for both Jew and gentile. Paul repeats his affirmation of the central but paradoxical role of ancestral Jews in God's redemptive master plan. While acknowledging the trust placed in his forbears, he also aims to demonstrate that "... Israel's election as sons or children of God had always depended not on natural descent but on a selective

---

42. Jewett, *Romans: A Commentary*, 259.

43. As Dunn (*Romans 1–8*, 157) notices. All quotations from the biblical text are my own translation.

44. Jewett, *Romans: A Commentary*, 263.

divine promise."[45] In other words, God's purpose was never to establish for himself a nepotic nation, but to create a multiethnic community of people who are predestined for salvation.

Paul builds his basic case by establishing through the birth narratives of Isaac and Jacob that even some physical descendants of Abraham did not benefit from their genetic association (Rom 9:10–13). The inferences from these stories are self-explanatory. It is not until the perplexing reference to the hardening of Pharaoh's heart that the first significant redaction is observed. Here, Paul transforms "for this purpose <u>you have been preserved</u>" (Exod 9:16) to "for this purpose <u>I have raised you up</u>" (Rom 9:17). Here, as with the previous examples, the emphasis is not on the rejection of Pharaoh, Esau, and Ishmael, but on God's sovereign authority to elevate whomever he wants.

The divine authority is also the focus of the second significant redaction,[46] where Paul changes the words "I might demonstrate my <u>strength</u> (*ischys*) in you" (Exod 9:16) to "I might demonstrate my <u>power</u> (*dynamis*) in you" (Rom 9:17). This may seem like a simple synonymous substitution, but as Jewett perceives, *dynamis* is "a rhetorical echo of an absolutely crucial term."[47] When the congregants heard the term, their attentive minds would invoke the thesis where Paul declares that "the gospel is God's power (*dynamis*) to all who have faith, both to the Jew first and then to the Greek." (Rom 1:16)

The final redaction addressed in this essay involves a variant reading of LXX Hosea 2:25. It is widely agreed that in Romans 9:25b–c, Paul reverses the parallel stichoi from the original text so that he could replace the verb *erō* ("I will say") with *kalesō* ("I will call").[48] The deliberation behind the choice of "call" fits the theme of God's sovereign power to elect whomever he wills. Pressing home Paul's purpose of reconciling the competing factions in Rome, Jewett remarks, "Here an expression that Hosea had employed to refer explicitly to Israel is used to designate the new Christian community containing both Jews and Gentiles as God's people."[49]

---

45. Jewett, *Romans: A Commentary*, 577.

46. Jewett describes this as "the most significant of the alterations, from a rhetorical point of view" (*Romans: A Commentary*, 584).

47. Jewett, *Romans: A Commentary*, 584.

48. Jewett, *Romans: A Commentary*, 599–600.

49. Jewett, *Romans: A Commentary*, 600.

Conclusion

As we have seen in this essay, the apostle Paul was on a mission similar to brother Malcolm's. They may have had different audiences, but their aim was to affirm the sociologically dispossessed with a message of liberation. As a committed follower of Messiah and skilled rhetorician, Paul used the means available to him to empower the occupiers of the crowded tenements. Through his selective redaction of Septuagint texts, he assured them that their dismal surroundings echoing a common human depravity were no indicator of their spiritual reality. They comprised a faithful community that may be flawed but, through the power of divine favor, constitutes the redeemed Israel of God.

We will never know how successful Paul was in persuading his original audience to embrace his understanding of the Israel of God. If the tenement churches were fashioned after the segregated societies in which they were clustered, it would have taken a great deal of intentionality to create an authentic rainbow coalition. Nonetheless, even if the believers were not moved to action, they would have been buoyed with an affirmed identity. Whatever the ethnic balance between ancestral Jews and other expatriates, they would have seen how their elect status was rooted in the sacred text that informed their worldview. Despite their socioeconomic condition, they were the ones with whom God had sealed his covenant (Rom 11:26–27), and this served as a basis for unity—a unity that must be preserved "by any means necessary."

Bibliography

(* For Further Reading)

*Burton, Keith Augustus. *The Blessing of Africa: The Bible and African Christianity*. Downers Grove, IL: InterVarsity, 2007.
———. *Laying Down the Law*. Hagerstown, MD: Review & Herald, 2013.
———. "Regarding Henry and the Discovery of Grace." In *Celebrating Romans: Template for Pauline Theology*, edited by Sheila E. McGinn, 207–21. Grand Rapids: Eerdmans, 2005.
———. *Rhetoric, Law, and the Mystery of Salvation in Romans 7:1–6*. Studies in the Bible and Early Christianity 44. Lewiston, NY: Mellen, 2001.
———. "'So That You May Be with Another': The Status of *Nomos* in the Mystical Life of the Believer in the Rhetoric of Analogy in Romans 7:1–6." PhD diss., Northwestern University, 1994.
Campbell, William S. "All God's Beloved in Rome: Jewish Roots and Christian Identity." In *Celebrating Romans: Template for Pauline Theology*, edited by Sheila E. McGinn, 67–82. Grand Rapids: Eerdmans, 2005.

Cosgrove, Charles H. *Elusive Israel: The Puzzle of Election in Romans.* Louisville: Westminster John Knox, 1997.

Cosgrove, Charles H., Herold Weiss, and K. K. Yeo. *Cross Cultural Paul: Journeys to Others, Journeys to Ourselves.* Grand Rapids: Eerdmans, 2005.

Decaro, Louis A., Jr. *On the Side of My People: A Religious Life of Malcolm X.* New York: New York University Press, 1996.

Dunn, James D. G. *The Parting of the Ways between Christianity and Judaism and Their Significance in the Character of Christianity.* 2nd ed. London: SCM, 2006.

———. *Romans 1–8.* Word Biblical Commentary 38A. Dallas: Word, 1988.

———. *Romans 9–16.* Word Biblical Commentary 38B. Dallas: Word, 1988.

Felder, Cain Hope. *Troubling Biblical Waters: Race, Class, and Family.* Maryknoll, NY: Orbis, 1990.

Finger, Rita Halteman. *Roman House Churches for Today.* Grand Rapids: Eerdmans, 2007.

*Hays, Richard B. *Echoes of Scripture in the Letters of Paul.* New Haven: Yale University Press, 1989.

Jewett, Robert. "Are There Allusions to the Love Feast in Rom. 13:8–10?" In *Persuasive Artistry: Studies in New Testament Rhetoric in Honor of George A. Kennedy*, edited by Duane F. Watson, 265–78. Journal for the Study of the New Testament Supplements 50. Reprint, Valley Forge, PA: Trinity, 1998.

*———. *Romans: A Commentary.* Hermeneia. Minneapolis: Fortress, 2007.

———. *Saint Paul at the Movies: The Apostle's Dialogue with American Culture.* Louisville: Westminster John Knox, 1993.

———. *Saint Paul Returns to the Movies: Triumph over Shame.* Grand Rapids: Eerdmans, 1999.

Jewett, Robert, and John Shelton Lawrence. *Captain America and the Crusade against Evil: The Dilemma of Zealous Nationalism.* Grand Rapids: Eerdmans, 2002.

Lampe, Peter. *From Paul to Valentinus: Christians at Rome in the First Two Centuries.* Translated by Michael Steinhauser. Edited by Marshall D. Johnson. Minneapolis: Fortress, 2003.

———. "The Roman Christians of Romans 16." In *The Romans Debate*, edited by Karl P. Donfried, 216–30. Rev. ed. Peabody, MA: Hendrickson, 1991.

Lanier, Gregor R. and William A. Ross. *The Septuagint: What It Is and Why It Matters.* Wheaton, IL: Crossway, 2021.

Lawrence, John Shelton, and Robert Jewett. *The Myth of the American Superhero.* Grand Rapids: Eerdmans, 2002.

Meeks, Wayne A. *The First Urban Christians: The Social World of the Apostle Paul.* New Haven: Yale University Press, 1983.

Nanos, Mark D. "The Jewish Context of the Gentile Audience Addressed in Paul's Letter to the Romans." *Catholic Biblical Quarterly* 61 (1999) 283–304.

———. *Reading Paul within Judaism.* Vol 1. Eugene, OR: Cascade Books, 2017.

Neusner, Jacob. *Judaism and Scripture: The Evidence of Leviticus Rabbah.* Chicago Studies in the History of Judaism. Chicago: University of Chicago Press, 1986. Reprint, Eugene, OR: Wipf & Stock, 2003.

Schnabel, Eckard J. "The Persecution of Christians in the First Century." *Journal of the Evangelical Theological Society* 61 (2018) 525–47.

Stegner, William Richard. "Romans 9:6–29—A Midrash." *Journal for the Study of the New Testament* 22 (1984) 37–52.

Theissen, Gerd. *The Social Setting of Pauline Christianity: Essays on Corinth*. Translated by John Schütz. Philadelphia: Fortress, 1982. Reprint, Eugene, OR: Wipf & Stock, 2004.

Williams, Margaret H. "The Shaping of the Identity of the Jewish Community in Roman Antiquity." In *Christians as a Minority in a Multicultural City: Modes of Interaction and Identity Formation in Early Imperial Rome*, edited by Jürgen Zangenberg and Michael Labahn, 33–46. European Studies on Christian Origins. London: T. & T. Clark, 2004.

Wilson, Jamie J. "'Come Down of the Cross and Get under the Crescent': The Newspaper Columns of Elijah Muhammad and Malcolm X." *Biography* 36 (2013) 494–506.

X, Malcolm. "The Ballot or the Bullet." Audubon Ballroom. Washington Heights, New York, March 29, 1964. https://americanradioworks.publicradio.org/features/blackspeech/mx.html

*———. "The Race Problem." African Students Association and NAACP Campus Chapter. Michigan State University, East Lansing, Michigan, January 23, 1963.

Study Questions

1. What are the potential benefits and limitations of applying cross-cultural hermeneutics to biblical interpretation?

2. Nanos proposes that one does not have to be a "Jew" to be "Jewish." What do you believe he means by this and how helpful is this distinction in reconstructing the audience of Romans?

3. Paul's homiletical use of Scripture apparently involved redacting the words of the biblical text. Review select incidents where this occurred and evaluate whether the change in wording altered the intent of the original textual occurrence.

18

Christian Submission to Civil Authorities in the Ghanaian Context

Frederick Mawusi Amevenku

Abstract

Romans 13:1–7 teaches about church-state relations. What does it imply? This issue is debated among scholars. Using socio-rhetorical interpretation, this essay argues that Paul exhorts submission to the state to ensure peace and stability and to promote Christian evangelization. This does not imply absolute obedience to totalitarian regimes. When read in the Ghanaian context, the text does not preclude opposition to evil regimes.

Introduction

This essay uses socio-rhetorical interpretation (SRI) to read Romans 13:1–7 in the Ghanaian context. Vernon K. Robbins developed SRI, an approach that merges ideas from narrative criticism with insights from social-scientific criticism to explore the meaning of a text. Thus, SRI analyzes both text and context. In addition, the reader's context also is analyzed. As an interpretive analytic, SRI recognizes that a Bible text is like a tapestry with many threads. Different perspectives of the text are "textures." Five textures can be identified: the inner texture, the intertexture, the social and cultural texture, the ideological texture, and the sacred texture.

The inner texture explores linguistic patterns "like repetition, progression, opening, closure, analogies, giving reasons, disagreeing, contradicting, praising, blaming, accusing, commanding, and the like."[1] "This

---

1. Robbins, "Divine Dialogue and the Lord's Prayer," 131.

embodies linguistic patterns, voices, movements, argumentations, and structural elements of a text; the specific ways it persuades its audiences, and the ways its language evokes feelings, emotions, or senses that are in various parts of the body."[2] The inner texture includes repetitive, progressive, narrational, opening-middle-closing, argumentative, or sensory-aesthetic inner textures.

The intertexture demonstrates how a text characterizes, references, and applies "phenomena in the 'world' outside the text, including a text's citations, allusions and reconfigurations of specific texts, events, language, objects, institutions and other specific extra-textual contexts with which the text interacts."[3] The intertexture virtually rewrites other texts.[4] The oral-scribal, the cultural, the social, and the historical intertextures are identified.[5] The cultural intertexture represents other cultures. The social intertexture focuses on social intercourse, institutions, and roles. The historical intertexture cites historical events and locations. The phenomena of recitation, re-contextualization, and reconfiguration point to the oral scribal intertexture.[6]

The social and cultural intertexture "explores social responses to the world, social systems and institutions, and cultural alliances and conflicts."[7] Seven social responses to the world are recognized in SRI as conversionist, thaumaturgical, gnostic-manipulationist, utopian, revolutionist, introversionist, or reformist.[8]

"The sacred texture systematically probes the relationship between human beings and the divine."[9] It addresses issues of "redemption, commitment, worship, devotion, community, ethics, holy living, spirituality, and spiritual formation."[10]

The "ideological texture explores biases, opinions, preferences and stereotypes of specific authors and interpreters."[11] The way a text uses language tends to suggest and encourage certain alliances, conflicts, and points of view, which enables readers of the text to locate themselves in relation to

---

2. Robbins, "Glossary," xvii.
3. Gowler, "Textures of a Text and its Reception," 195.
4. Robbins, *Tapestry of Early Christianity*, 30.
5. Robbins, *Exploring the Textures of Texts*, 96.
6. Robbins, *Exploring the Textures of Texts* 102.
7. Robbins, "Divine Dialogue," 138.
8. Robbins, *Exploring the Textures of Texts*, 74–75.
9. Pillay, "Re-visioning Stigma," 65.
10. Robbins, "Glossary," xxiii.
11. Robbins, *Tapestry of Early Christianity*, 95.

individuals and groups within the text.[12] Interpreters identify with certain characters or points of views in the text. This happens anytime a Bible text is interpreted. Using SRI generates enormous data from a text that is difficult to thoroughly analyze. Therefore to delimit this study, we shall now focus on the ideological texture of Romans 13:1–7.

The Ideological Texture of Romans 13:1–7: The Problem

In Ghana, politicians often invoke Romans 13:1–7 to urge Christian submission to civil authorities. Does the text imply that Christians have no business opposing authoritarian, inept, and autocratic regimes? How do social location and presuppositions of the author and readers affect one's understanding of the text since meaning making is the product of the reader's interaction with the author's text? Therefore, to examine the ideological texture of this text from the Ghanaian perspective, my social location has to be mentioned first. The aim is to identify and point out how this text may or may not be used legitimately in Ghana.

My Social Location

As a Ghana-Eυe man living in a tiny West African country struggling to improve its economy, I have presuppositions that influence my view of things. My location as a scholar is a faculty member of a tiny, West African seminary with minimal research funding. My decision to study Romans 13:1–7 from an SRI perspective is ideological, if subtle, because alternatives exist. First, my choice of Romans is in honor of Prof. Robert Jewett. Second, my choice of SRI is due to Prof. Vernon K. Robbins's influence on me during my doctoral studies. Third, my experience of Ghanaian politics influenced my choice of Romans 13:1–7. My context makes it easy to identify with defiant rhetoric against evil rulers. Watching unjust civil authorities mismanage the affairs of my country, while appealing to Romans 13:1–7 to foster submission of citizens, is disgusting to me. The fact that my social location makes my interpretation identify with certain ideological points of view in the text is inevitable.

---

12. Gowler, "Textures of a Text and its Reception," 195.

My Relation to Other Groups

Eυe is a minority group with a complex political history in Ghana. Some Ghanaians regard Eυe people as foreigners in Ghana.[13] Some members of my seminary community despise me without saying it or acting it out explicitly. These experiences define my mode of discourse and shape my ideology of life as well. These realities shape my reading of Romans 13:1–7. Thus, this essay is not only to honor Robert Jewett, but also it is a conscious or unconscious effort to address my own social location and engage my ideology. Consequently, the ideological texture of Romans 13:1–7 involves an analysis of myself (as reader and writer), as well as the author and implied reader of the text. To be sure, there are ideological dimensions to every interpretation but in SRI, we are dealing specifically with the ideological texture.

Exegesis of the Text

The authorship of Romans is hardly in dispute. Most scholars agree that Paul is the author. However, when it comes to Romans 13:1–7, some claim it is an interpolation to Paul's logic. Nan goes as far as to say that Romans 13:1–7 is about Christian morality and does not deal with political theology.[14] The question of Christian morality is not in doubt because Paul's love ethic is about morality. But the love ethic has political implications. It requires the believer to relate to the authorities in a particular way. The date of Romans is also fairly determined. Most scholars accept a date of 57 or 58 CE. This places the writing during the early part of Nero's reign, about a decade after Claudius's edict in 49 CE to expel Jews from Rome (Acts 18:2).

The audience of Romans often is debated. Ademiluka cites Jewett as proposing a Jewish audience.[15] But Paul was an apostle to the gentiles, and there are references in the epistle to a gentile audience (cf. Rom 1:13; 15:14–19) as well. A mixed audience of Jews and gentiles is likely. Anum claims that Paul presents a church settling down to make peace in a world that is fully under God's control.[16] Anum, writing from a postcolonial perspective, further observes that intolerance of diversity and the labeling of opposition

---

13. K. T. Hammond, member of Parliament for Adansi Asokwa, made a public statement to the effect that the Eυe people are Togolese, not Ghanaians. He said this on June 28, 2020. See "K.T. Hammond's 'Ketu South Togolese' comment frightening, deeply disturbing."

14. Nan, "Submission to the Government," 118.

15. Jewett, *Romans: A Commentary*, 70.

16. Anum, "Post-Colonial Reading of Romans 13: 1–7," 68.

as "bad" are imperialist features in the text.[17] This suggests that the audience is "other" than the privileged rulers of Rome.

As Jewett notes, Paul's rhetoric in Romans 13:1–7 connects the purpose of his letter to court the help of the Christians in Rome for his intended mission to Spain. Thus, "Romans 13:1–7 was not intended to create the foundation of a political ethic for all times and places in succeeding generations . . ."[18] It must be read in its context. Romans is a "situational letter"[19] that is "highly abstract,"[20] and the "rhetorical approach allows the letter to speak for itself."[21] On the basis of these features, Jewett proposes a five-fold division[22] for the letter.

- Introduction (1:1–12)
- Narration (1:13–15)
- Thesis statement (1:16–17)
- Proof of case (1:18–15:13)
- Conclusion (15:14–16:27)

Romans 13:1–7 is part of the ethical implications of "living out the righteousness of God" based on the gospel, which does not depend on observance of law.[23] Paul had earlier called for transformed persons with renewed minds (Rom 12.1–2). Paul was still proving his thesis in 1:16–17 that the gospel is God's power to save whoever are believers, Jews or gentiles. For Paul, love is the central ethic that drives the conduct of the transformed person (Rom 12:9–10).

Romans 13:1–7

In Romans 13,[24] Paul states his imperative to the Roman Christians positively in verse 1:

---

17. Anum, "Post-Colonial Reading of Romans 13: 1–7," 68–69.
18. Jewett, *Romans: A Commentary*, 786.
19. Jewett, "Argument of Romans," 382.
20. Jewett, "Argument of Romans," 382.
21. Jewett, "Argument of Romans," 382.
22. Jewett, "Argument of Romans," 383.
23. Jewett, "Argument of Romans," 386.
24. Unless otherwise stated, all quotes of the Bible in English use the New Revised Standard Version (NRSV).

- Verse 1. Let everyone submit to the governing authorities because God instituted them.

Reasons

Paul articulates the reasons in verses 2–4:

- Verse 2. Whoever resists authority is resisting God and will be judged.
- Verse 3a. Rulers are not a threat to good conduct; they are a threat to bad conduct.
- Verse 3b. Whoever does what is good has no reason to fear the authorities.
- Verse 3c. The authorities commend those who do what is good.
- Verse 4b. The authorities are God's servants "for your good."
- Verse 4c. Whoever does what is wrong should be afraid because the authorities bear the sword of punishment and can execute wrath on the wrongdoer.

Rationale

Paul further develops his rationale in verse 5:

- Verse 5. Everyone must submit to the authorities not only because of fear but also because of conscience.

Implications

Paul describes the implications in verses 6 and 7:

- Verse 6a. It is because of this that everyone also pays taxes.
- Verse 6b. The authorities are God's servants busy with ruling.

Verse 7. Pay to all what is due them—taxes, revenue, respect and honor.

The Semitism *pasa psychē* (every soul) makes the imperative in verse 1 a sweeping one without exception. For Feinberg, Paul's command is absolute and unqualified. For Yeo, Paul points out that "for it is not an authority if (it is) not by God" (13:1b) implying God does not institute all authorities but only those rulers who serve God's purpose.[25] Indeed, there are rulers who are not of God and cannot make claims to obedience by

---

25. Yeo, "Paul's Way of *Renren*," 49.

their subjects. Paul calls for submission, not mere obedience.[26] Paul calls for submission and obedience to authorities (those instituted by God). Paul implies that God is the Lord of human affairs, and no one becomes a ruler without God's permission.[27]

Submission includes recognition and acceptance of the one wielding authority. This does not imply that Paul was making a universal, timeless command to apply to all Christ-followers in all ages in all places. If it were so, Paul's teaching would contradict the clear and categorical response of the Jerusalem apostles that they must obey God rather than human authorities (Acts 5:29). Norman L. Geisler cites seven instances[28] from the Scriptures where Christians must resist the civil authorities as follows:

1. When the government prohibits the worship of God (Exod 5:1)
2. When it requires taking of innocent life (Exod 1:15–21)
3. When it demands killing of God's servants (1 Kings 18:1–4)
4. When it requires the worship of idols (Dan 3:1–7)
5. When it commands prayer to a [hu]man (Dan 6:6–9)
6. When it prohibits the propagation of the gospel (Acts 4:17–20)
7. When it demands the worship of a [hu]man as God (Rev 13:4, 8).

In Romans 13:3, we learn that God established the authorities to do what is right. If they then do what is wrong, they undermine their own legitimacy and deserve to be resisted. God, from whom they derive their authority to govern, does not do what is wrong. Pilate told Jesus at the latter's trial that he had the power to release or execute him. Jesus responded, "You would have no power over me unless it had been given you from above" (John 19:11a). Paul could have taken from there the idea that there is no authority on earth that has not been established by God. If God is the source of authority, then all authorities exist to serve God's purposes on earth. The rulers hold delegated authority from God; they must exercise it in accordance with God's will.

Verse 3b suggests that the rulers praise those who do what is right, so how can they then turn around to do evil and not lose the moral authority to govern? In verse 4, the authorities are God's servants for "your good" (*soi eis to agathon*). As God's servants (*diakonoi*) who punish wrongdoing, the

---

26. Feinberg, "The Christian and Civil Authorities," 99.
27. Feinberg, "The Christian and Civil Authorities," 99.
28. Geisler, "Law and Government," 262. See also James, "Divine Justice and Civil Government," 199–210.

authorities are not permitted to do what is wrong (v. 4b). It is the duty of the civil authorities to reward good and punish evil. "When the state prohibits good and demands evil, it is no longer performing its God-ordained task."[29] Stanley Porter has argued that the instruction to submit does not cover unjust civil authorities because the word translated as "authorities" is preferably rendered "superior in quality."[30] However, his reasons are unconvincing. Submission requires recognition of someone's authority, but so does it recognize misuse of authority. The question is not about superiority in quality but responsible use of delegated authority.

Chapter 12:21 teaches Christ-followers to "overcome evil with good." This is the message preceding Romans 13:1–7. The message immediately following Romans 13:1–7 is for the Roman Christians to let love guide their choices to overcome evil with good. It is good to resist evil; therefore, to overcome despotic regimes by resisting them—through civil disobedience or public demonstrations for instance—undermines and breaks their will and resolve to do evil. To love also includes helping people to avoid being destroyed. Totalitarian regimes are ultimately accountable to God. God will punish their wrongdoing, immediately or eschatologically. If we love them, we will prevent them from perpetuating evil.

Governance that promotes suppression, domination, imperialism, hegemony, and other forms of human rights violation fly in the face of divine authority. To restore the intended divine order, the oppressive structures ought to be socially dismantled since they were socially constructed in the first place. The government of Paul's day was the superpower of the time.[31] If God established it, then it was not an autonomous superpower. Therefore, it could not do whatever it wished but rather the will of God.[32] There is a triangular relationship at play in this text: God the creator is the sovereign power, the people derive their sovereign will from God, and the authorities derive their authority from the God-given sovereign will of the people.[33]

As long as disobedience to the authorities will lead to obedience to God, it is a duty incumbent on such transformed and renewed Christians.[34] Romans 13:1–7 amounts to a call to freedom from the domination of overwhelming authorities,[35] but the apostle does not cover every

29. Feinberg, "The Christian and Civil Authorities," 99.
30. Porter, "Romans 13:1–7," 123.
31. Gusha, "Exegesis of Romans 13:1–7," 3.
32. Morris, *Romans*, 440.
33. Rediger, "Church and State: Romans 13:1–7," 17.
34. Jatau, "Submission to Governing Authority," 36.
35. Stubbs, "Romans 13 and the Market Economy," 240.

possible situation that may arise.[36] Paul no doubt knew it was the civil authorities who executed Jesus. He also knew what happened to John the Baptist and all the faithful believers who suffered persecution at the hands of the authorities. Rather than parrot the view of the civil authorities in Romans 13:1–7, Paul subverts it by presenting two different voices within the text: the official transcript and the hidden transcript. The hidden transcript is the hidden voice that insists that ultimately honor, respect, and authority belong to God alone.[37]

We find in verse 6 that "There are four obligations specified. They are presented in synonymous parallelism and 'rhyme.' Rulers are due 'taxes,' 'tribute,' 'respect,' and 'honor.'"[38] Why did Paul assume that the Roman Christians paid their taxes? Paul's exhortation in the preceding chapter (Rom 12:13–17) and Jesus's own practice in Matthew 17:24–27 (payment of the temple tax) may constitute a clue to Paul's assumption[39] that "it is for this reason that you also pay taxes" (v. 6 my translation). Coleman contends that Romans 13:1–7 reflects popular dissatisfaction with Nero's taxation,[40] noting that agitations were so severe that Nero considered abolishing indirect taxes altogether. This is not entirely supported by the history.

We find evidence in Acts through Jude of how NT Christians responded to the state.[41] Both submission and resistance are evident.[42] The NT does not present a single stance. In Acts, we learn that we must obey God rather than human authority (Acts 5:28–30). Romans 13:1–7 calls for submission perhaps in an antinomian context. Ephesians 6:5–8 teaches slaves to obey their earthly masters as they would obey God. Colossians 1:15–17 says that thrones, powers, rulers, and authorities are all under Christ. First Timothy 3:1–2 directs that prayers be offered for kings and all those in authority.

Furthermore, some scholars insist that we cannot read Romans 13 apart from Revelations 13.[43] The call to submission in Romans 13:1–7 is not the final word.[44] Acts 5:29 and other passages listed above "indicate quite plainly that Christians' first allegiance is to God, not the state, and that if

---

36. Morris, *Romans*, 441.
37. Lim, "A Double-voiced Reading of Romans 13:1–7," 7.
38. Feinberg, "The Christian and Civil Authorities," 97.
39. Feinberg, "The Christian and Civil Authorities," 96.
40. Coleman, "Binding Obligations in Romans 13:1–7," 326.
41. Nichols and McCarty, "When the State Is Evil," 596.
42. Nichols and McCarty, "When the State Is Evil," 600.
43. Nichols and McCarty, "When the State Is Evil," 613.
44. Nichols and McCarty, "When the State Is Evil," 622.

there is conflict between the two, then God must be obeyed."[45] Conflicts arise when human standards are set against God's standards to invalidate the worth of some human beings.

The Ghanaian Political Context as a Case Study

Ghana is in West Africa. West Africa is home to some of the world's poorest people. Continental Africa in general is frequently associated with poverty and deprivation. To be sure, many African countries, including Ghana, have been "independent" for many years but political and economic independence is far from the reality.

Recently, Ghanaian youth took to social media with the hashtag "fix the country," "fix mother Ghana," "fix the mess," etc. to voice their concerns about unemployment, corruption, and economic hardship. They accused the government of hiding behind COVID-19 protocols to deny citizens their right to peaceful assembly and protest. In response, government sympathizers hit back, saying to Ghanaians, "fix your attitude." This was followed by a heavy social-media backlash.

At his first term inauguration, the current president, in 2016, urged Ghanaians to be citizens, not spectators. Does this advice not mean that the president was encouraging citizens to exercise their right to free speech? Yet the same government has been accused of stifling free speech and closing down radio stations that criticize its policies. On January 16, 2019, investigative journalist Ahmed Hussein-Suale was murdered. He worked with the Tiger Eye media company. Since 2019, the government has not been able to find the perpetrators. Ghana held general elections in 2020 as well. Security forces shot and killed unarmed citizens during the process. No one has been punished so far. Abuse and arbitrary arrest of journalists by the police and other security institutions of the state is rampant. Instead of gathering intelligence to secure the country, "national security" is widely seen as an apparatus to terrorize and intimidate political opponents and vociferous journalists.

Worse still, since May 2021, a new trend in ritual killings has emerged. Thus, insecurity has been added to the precarious economic situation. The current president, while he was the opposition leader, once said at a local radio station, "*ye te sika so nso kom de yen*" ("we are sitting on gold and yet we are going hungry"). Opponents now remind the president of those comments as they draw attention to the challenges. Illegal mining is a major

---

45. Nichols and McCarty, "When the State Is Evil," 622.

problem too, and government officials are alleged to be involved. Youth unemployment is currently the biggest threat to security in Ghana.

Reading Romans 13:1–7 in the Ghanaian Context

In Romans 13:1–7, Paul urges the Roman Christians to submit to the authorities. As has been argued, Paul's instruction does not teach unconditional submission to any kind of civil authorities because he wrote in a historical context in which governance was benevolent. Paul was not naïve. He wrote during the early part of Nero's reign, which was benevolent. If Paul had written after 62 CE, he might have instructed his addressees differently because the conduct of the civil authorities had deteriorated badly by that time.[46]

Reading the text in the Ghanaian context requires that both Paul's social location and the social location of the interpreter be critically engaged. Lategan has noted that "problems associated with this passage have as much to do with the historical situation of Paul and his social location as with the experience of subsequent readers in their own dealings with governing authorities."[47] This coheres with the reading approach adopted for this study—ideological texture of SRI. Biblical texts are the products of a communication process that includes the voices of hearers or readers.[48] Governing authorities read the text affirmatively while those who are victims of abuse of authority read it with resistance.[49] Resistant reading shows in intertextual, evaluative, interpolative, relativized reading, or reading under different presuppositions.[50] Evaluative reading distinguishes between good and bad governments; relativized reading restricts the scope of the text to its historical context; different presuppositions enable readers to bring different questions to the text so as to come to different conclusions; if the text is evaluated from the perspective of twenty-first-century functional democracy, different questions will be raised and answered.

The ideological analysis is a relativized reading from the SRI perspective. The appropriation of Romans 13:1–7 depends on the context in which it is read.[51] In this case, one's social location and experience of civil authority tend to shape one's appropriation. Paul himself benefitted from

---

46. Ademiluka, "Romans 13:1–7," 6.
47. Lategan, "Romans 13:1–7," 259.
48. Lategan, "Romans 13:1–7," 260.
49. Lategan, "Romans 13:1–7," 264.
50. Lategan, "Romans 13:1–7," 264.
51. Gusha, "Exegesis of Romans 13:1–7," 9.

the development, laws, and policies of the regime.[52] Christians were in the minority in the historical context of the text, and their failure to submit and pay taxes to the government invited persecution.[53] Persecution endangered the spread of the gospel. Paul wanted the gospel to spread.

Reading this text in the context of the precarious economic, security, and political environment of Ghana requires that believers resist, speak against, and possibly subvert the authority that evidently undermines the will of God by failing to serve the interest of its citizens. If the government, which is expected to promote the good of the people, ends up making life hard and nearly impossible for the people, believers cannot be obligated to submit to it. On the contrary, believers are called to resist that inept and wicked regime. Thus, if the government is corrupt, evil, and self-serving, then it is illegitimate and must be resisted.

Because it presents many perspectives of a given text, SRI has the tendency to generate significant data that becomes burdensome to analyze. This is a limitation because the interpreter has to neglect some aspects of the text in favor of others. Helpfully however, SRI accommodates different methods of interpretation, both text-centered and context-centered. By analyzing one's social location as part of the interpretation process, one is able to arrive at a valid application of the text in context.

Conclusion

Romans 13:1–13 stimulates intense political discourse in Ghana. Politicians appeal to it to call for total submission by the citizenry, especially Christians. Christians, on the other hand, tend to read the text often with a caveat. When read in Ghana from the ideological texture perspective, the social location of Paul and his readers, as well as the social location of the Ghanaian reader, become crucial to its meaning. Paul wrote to a community of Christians in Rome in 57/58 CE for whom government functioned quite justly. Paul himself had benefited from the laws, policies, and infrastructural development of the regime. He desired to further take advantage of this to propagate the gospel and encourage other believers to do so. Paul's experience is contrary to the experience of the Ghanaian citizen, who lives in a precarious socio-economic and political context. To suggest to the Ghanaian that Paul gives a universal order of unconditional submission to any kind of government that rules them is to promote a gospel that perpetuates injustice. This is contrary to the spirit of the gospel of Jesus.

52. Gusha, "Exegesis of Romans 13:1–7," 4.
53. Gusha, "Exegesis of Romans 13:1–7," 7.

Bibliography

(* For Further Reading)

Ademiluka, S. O. "Romans 13:1–7 in Relation to Nigerian Christians' Attitudes Towards Social Activism." *In die Skriflig* 53/1 (2019) a2467. https://doi.org/10.4102/ids.v53i1.2467.

Anum, Eric Nii Bortey. "Post-Colonial Reading of Romans 13: 1–7 in the Context of Nation-Building." *British Journal of Humanities and Social Sciences* 11/2 (2014) 65–72.

Coleman, Thomas M. "Binding Obligations in Romans 13:1–7: A Semantic Field and Social Context." *Tyndale Bulletin* 48 (1997) 307–27.

Feinberg, Paul D. "The Christian and Civil Authorities." *The Master's Seminary Journal* 10 (1999) 87–99.

Geisler, Norman L. "A Premillennial View of Law and Government." *Bibliotheca Sacra* 142 (1985) 250–65.

Gowler, David. "Socio-rhetorical Interpretation: Textures of a Text and its Reception." *Journal for the Study of the New Testament* 33 (2010) 191–206.

Gusha, Ishanesu S. "Exegesis of Romans 13:1–7 and its Appropriation to the New Dispensation of the Second Republic of Zimbabwe." *HTS Teologiese Studies/ Theological Studies* 76/4 (2020) a6041. https://doi.org/10.4102/hts. v76i4.6041.

James, S. "Divine Justice and Civil Government." *Trinity Journal* 6 n.s. (1985) 199–210.

Jatau, Paul D. "Submission to Governing Authority in Romans 13:1–7: A Reflection in the Nigerian Context." *International Journal of Humanitatis Theoreticus* 2/2 (2019) 30–38.

Jewett, Robert. "Following the Argument of Romans." *Word and Word* 6 (1986) 382–89.

———. *Romans: A Commentary.* Hermeneia. Minneapolis: Fortress, 2007.

"K.T. Hammond's 'Ketu South Togolese' comment frightening, deeply disturbing." GhanaWeb, June 28, 2020. https://www.ghanaweb.com/GhanaHomePage/News Archive/K-T-Hammond-s-Ketu-South-Togolese-comment-frightening-deeply-disturbing-Azar-992488.

Lategan, Bernard. "Romans 13:1–7: A Review of Post-1989 Readings." *Scriptura* 110 (2012) 259–72.

Lim, Sung U. "A Double-voiced Reading of Romans 13:1–7 in Light of the Imperial Cult." *HTSTeologiese Studies/Theological Studies* 71/1 (2015) Art. #2475. http:// dx.doi.org/10.4102/ hts.v71i1.2475.

*Longenecker, Richard N. *The Epistle to the Romans: A Commentary on the Greek Text.* New International Greek Testament Commentary. Grand Rapids: Eerdmans, 2016.

Morris, Leon. *The Epistle to the Romans.* Pillar New Testament Commentary. Grand Rapids: Eerdmans, 1988.

Nan, Seng Tsin M. "Submission to the Government (Rom 13:1–7): Biblical Perspective with Christian Ethical Reflection for Present Day Myanmar." MTh Thesis, Norwegian School of Theology, 2011.

Nichols, Joel A. and James W. McCarty III, "When the State Is Evil: Biblical Civil (Dis) Obedience in South Africa." *St. John's Law Review* 85 (2011) 593–625.

Pillay, Mirinda N. "Re-visioning Stigma: A Socio-Rhetorical Reading of Luke 10:25–37 in the Context of HIV/AIDS in South Africa." DPhil [Theology] diss., University of Western Cape, South Africa, 2008.

Porter, Stanley E. "Romans 13:1–7 as Pauline Political Rhetoric." *Filologia Neotestamentaria* 3 (1990) 115–27.
Rediger, Milo A. "Church and State: Romans 13:1–7." Milo Rediger Writings and Addresses 17 (2020). https://pillars.taylor.edu/rediger-writings/17.
Robbins, Vernon K. "Divine Dialogue and the Lord's Prayer: Socio-Rhetorical Interpretation of Sacred Texts." *Dialogue* 28 (1995) 117–46.
———. *Exploring the Textures of Texts: A Guide to Socio-Rhetorical Interpretation.* Valley Forge, PA: Trinity, 1996.
———, "Glossary." In *Foundations for Sociorhetorical Exploration: A Rhetoric of Religious Antiquity Reader*, edited by Vernon K. Robbins, Robert H. von Thaden Jr., and Bart B. Bruehler. Rhetoric of Religious Antiquity Series 4. Atlanta: Society of Biblical Literature, 2016.
———. *The Tapestry of Early Christian Discourse: Rhetoric, Society, and Ideology.* New York: Routledge, 1996.
*Stein, Robert H. "The Argument of Romans 13:1–7." *Novum Testamentum* 31 (1989) 325–43. https://doi.org/10.2307/1560711.
Stubbs, Monya A. "Romans 13 and the Market Economy, Subjection, Reflection, Resistance: A Three-Dimensional Process of Empowerment." PhD diss., Vanderbilt University, 2005.
*VanDrunen, David. "Power to the People: Revisiting Civil Resistance in Romans 13:1–7 in Light of the Noahic Covenant." *Journal of Law and Religion* 31 (2016) 4–18. https://doi.org/10.1017/jlr.2015.41.
Yeo, K. K. "Paul's Way of *Renren* in Romans 13:1–10." In *From Rome to Beijing: Symposia on Robert Jewett's Commentary on Romans*, edited by K. K. Yeo, 48–53. Lincoln, NE: Kairos Studies, 2013.

Study Questions

1. How does your socio-political context affect your understanding of Romans 13:1–7?

2. How can a cultural reading of Romans 13:1–7 confront the problem of autocratic governments?

3. How does SRI of Romans 13:1–7 underscore the contextual nature of the task of biblical interpretation?

19

Reading Romans 13:1–7 as a Hidden Transcript in the Malaysian Context[1]

Kong Hock Hii and Kar Yong Lim

Abstract

Drawing insights from James Scott's notion of "hidden transcript" and Robert Jewett's commentary on Romans, this essay aims to offer a fresh reading of Paul's counter-imperial motifs in Romans 13 from the perspective of a Christian minority in the predominantly Islamic context of Malaysia. Special treatment also will be given to the implications of what it means to be responsible citizens in honoring the good and resisting evil when undergirded by the debt of love.

Introduction: History and Problems in the Interpretation of Romans 13:1–7

The opening verse of Romans 13:1–7 appears to suggest that Paul is advocating for an uncompromising endorsement of political authority and an

---

1. This essay is an exhaustive revision and major update building upon two previously published works: Hii, "Honoring the 'Good' and Resisting the 'Evil,'" 433–46 and Kok and Lim, "The Agape Meal," 447–54 (in Yeo, ed., *From Rome to Beijing*). At Garrett-Evangelical Theological Seminary (Evanston, Illinois, US), Robert Jewett mentored K. K. Yeo, who later mentored Kong Hock Hii. In 2008, three generations of Pauline scholars finally met at Sabah Theological Seminary (Malaysia), where Hii hosted a "Symposium on Romans" to celebrate and engage with Jewett's monumental commentary in the Hermeneia series. Kar Yong Lim first met Jewett as a PhD student when he was visiting Wales. One morning during breakfast, Jewett sat down with Lim and patiently listened to him struggling to articulate his research ideas. Jewett encouraged him and gave some suggestions for him to work on. Lim is very grateful to Jewett for his encouragement and support.

attempt to stifle any opposition to Rome's political systems of domination and oppression. Further justification for submission to governing authorities is often made by referring to later parallel texts found in 1 Peter 2:13–17; 1 Timothy 2:1–4 and Titus 4:1–3.

The difficulty in interpreting this passage is demonstrated by debates throughout the centuries.[2] Space does not permit us to review these various interpretations, which range from complete surrender to critical submission to the ruling authorities. Suffice to say that this passage has never failed to inspire the creativity of interpreters. Some of the more creative suggestions include: 1) Paul is warning Roman believers not to participate in Jewish Zealot activities;[3] 2) Paul is giving an exhortation not to create unrest that would adversely impact the Jewish population in Rome or his gentile mission;[4] 3) Paul is warning against Christian enthusiasm for opposing any ruling authority;[5] 4) Paul is addressing the Christian gentiles associating with the synagogues of Rome to be subordinate to the ruling authorities of the synagogues;[6] and the list continues.[7]

Whatever position one takes, the difficulties arising out of the various interpretations of Romans 13:1–7 have been noted. For example, J. C. O'Neill has claimed that this passage "caused more unhappiness and misery in the Christian East and West than any other seven verses in the New Testament by the license they have given to tyrants," as they "have been used to justify a host of horrendous abuses of individual human rights."[8] But perhaps what is equally shocking is that Paul could have spoken so positively of the Roman authorities and ascribed such an exalted status to Rome, as if he were oblivious to the brutality surrounding him. It is as if Paul is hypocritical and untrue to his entire theological position when he advocates submission and subordination to the ruling authorities. This led Jewett to caution that "Romans 13:1–7 was not intended to create the foundation of a political ethic for all times and places in succeeding generations—a task for which it has proven to be singularly ill-suited."[9]

---

2. See Reasoner, *Romans in Full Circle*, 129–42.

3. Bammel, "Romans 13," 365–83.

4. Elliott, *Liberating Paul*, 221–26; Wengst, *Pax Romana and the Peace of Jesus Christ*, 79–84; Das, *Solving the Romans Debate*, 147. See also Tobin, *Paul's Rhetoric in its Contexts*, 395–400.

5. Perriman, *The Future of the People of God*, 146–47.

6. Nanos, *The Mystery of Romans*, 289–336.

7. See Jewett, *Romans: A Commentary*, 785–87.

8. O'Neill, *Paul's Letter to the Romans*, 209.

9. Jewett, *Romans: A Commentary*, 786.

It is not until recent years that this passage has been viewed in light of the Roman imperial cult, which Jewett believes "could be a step toward taking fuller account of the political and cultural context of Paul's letter and its missional purpose."[10] Neil Elliott, who adopts this approach in reading Romans, argues that this epistle, especially Romans 1:18–32, constitutes Paul's critique of imperial injustice.[11] For Elliott, all the crime, outrageous and destructive sexual indulgence, and the ultimate depravity described in Romans 1:18–32 are evidence of God's punishment on the imperial rulers who continue to suppress the truth through their unrighteousness. If Elliott is correct, that Paul is pronouncing God's judgment on the imperial household, then this would make Paul's positive exhortation to be submissive to governing authorities in Romans 13:1–7 seem not only glaringly out of place but also contradictory. How then does one navigate through this difficult passage?

A Question of Method: "Hidden Transcript" in Resisting Dominant Discourse

In his commentary, Jewett adopts "all of the standard methods of historical-critical exegesis," and this includes "historical and cultural analysis of the honor shame, and imperial systems in the Greco-Roman world."[12] We are indebted to Jewett for his insightful commentary on Romans 13:1–7. Building on his work, we feel that more could be unearthed if we consider carefully the political and social reality of this passage.

One fruitful means of doing so is to employ the methodology developed by James C. Scott, a political scientist. According to Scott, in any discourse addressing the relationship between the ruling elites and those dominated, one should pay attention to both the public discourse and, in particular, the hidden transcripts put forward by both parties, as this can help us see how "competing ideologies" between the dominant group and the subordinated people interacted.[13] Scott developed his methodology based on fieldwork carried out to examine the relations between ruling elites and peasants in a rural setting in the northern state of Kedah in Malaysia. As citizens of Malaysia, we could readily identify with Scott's methodology, as we live

---

10. Jewett, *Romans: A Commentary*, 786.
11. Elliott, *The Arrogance of Nations*, 59–85.
12. Jewett, *Romans: A Commentary*, 1.
13. See Scott, *Weapons of the Weak* and *Domination and the Arts of Resistance*. Scott's methodology has been favorably applied to biblical studies. See Horsley, *Hidden Transcripts and the Arts of Resistance*.

as Christian minorities within a dominant and majority Islamic context. Scott's approach also helps us appreciate the relationship between the powers of the Roman imperial rulers and the weakness of the dominated Christ followers addressed in Paul's letter.

According to Scott, the public transcript is "a shorthand way of describing the open interaction between subordinates and those who dominate."[14] It employs mechanisms such as "public mastery and subordination (for example, rituals of hierarchy, deference, speech, punishment, and humiliation)" and "ideological justification for inequalities (for example, the public religious and political world view of the dominant elite)" to manage and secure "material appropriation (for example, of labor, grain, taxes)" for the purpose of domination.[15] In short, it is a discourse derived by the dominant elites to justify and propagate their own ideology in order for them to remain in power. Expressed in Scott's own words:

> The public transcript is . . . the *self*-portrait of dominant elites as they would have themselves seen. Given the usual power of dominant elites to compel performances from others, the discourse of the public transcript is a decidedly lopsided discussion. While it is unlikely to be merely a skein of lies and misrepresentations, it is, on the other hand, a highly partisan and partial narrative. It is designed to be impressive, to affirm and naturalize the power of the dominant elites, and to conceal or euphemize the dirty linen of their rule.[16]

Scott argues that the discourse in the public sphere can rarely be taken as a straightforward indication of what the subordinates truly believe. On the other hand, the public performance of the subordinates often shows the masks of obedience they wear to appeal to the expectations of the powerful, and this is done either out of prudence, fear, or the desire to curry favor. As such, Scott suggests that if we only pay attention to the formal relationship between the powerful and the weak, we only attend to the public transcript and thereby ignore the informal off-stage or hidden transcript of the subordinates, which is the true voice from the margins.

When they are beyond direct observation by powerholders, those who are dominated express themselves in a hidden transcript, which consists of "offstage speeches, gestures, and practices that confirm, contradict, or inflect what appears in the public transcript."[17] What they cultivate is a

---

14. Scott, *Domination and Resistance*, 2.
15. Scott, *Domination and Resistance*, 111.
16. Scott, *Domination and Resistance*, 18.
17. Scott, *Domination and Resistance*, 4–5.

shared "discourse of dignity, of negation, and of justice" that contains not only speech acts but a whole range of practices.[18] Some examples of hidden transcript can be found in the everyday conversations among locals during meal times in local eateries, expressions made through social media, art, poems, literature, and murals, and staged performances and stand-up comedy. Often veiled, subtle, and sarcastic, the message contained in the hidden transcript can only be appreciated by those who are contextually aware of the latest political developments in the local community.

Embedded within the hidden transcript is always a resistance by the subordinated group to confront ideologies that justify injustice and inequality.[19] Resistance entailed in the hidden transcript is always *social* and *active*. In the case of peasants highlighted by Scott, these practices of resistance may include "poaching, pilfering, clandestine tax evasion, and intentionally shabby work for landlords."[20]

Discovering the hidden transcript provides a window for us to see how Paul, through his letters written to the fledgling Christ assemblies, was resisting the dominant Roman imperial ideology. Using Scott's methodology, Richard Horsley illustrates well how a hidden transcript of resistance is evident in Paul:

1. Paul's "gospel" as a discourse itself "resonated deeply with the cultural meaning of many subjugated peoples' situation of humiliation."

2. Paul and his communities were under attack by the city authorities and/or other people, in particular cities; hence, "a key concern in some of Paul's letters is thus defense of the assembly-sites of the developing communities and their hidden transcript(s)."

3. Paul's letters show how a hidden transcript developed as a result of "power relations among subordinates themselves" and how Paul is "attempting to shape the developing hidden transcript of the respective assemblies."[21]

In short, Paul should not be seen as a passivist or political quietist but as an active human agent who creates and disseminates hidden transcripts in political resistance to the Roman imperial order through the rhetoric in his letters. Applied to Romans 13, we can see how Paul's *hidden* transcript is

---

18. Scott, *Domination and Resistance*, 114.
19. Scott, *Domination and Resistance*, 118.
20. Scott, *Domination and Resistance*, 14.
21. Horsley, "Jesus, Paul, and the 'Arts of Resistance,'" 19–20.

indeed subverting Rome's *public* transcript and envisioning a revolutionary transformation of the imperial order.

Hidden Transcript: Reconsidering the Two Imperatives in Romans 13

In order to discern the hidden transcript in Romans 13:1–7, we begin by considering the two imperatives that frame Paul's argument in the passage: *hypotassesthō* ("submit") in 13:1 and *apodote* ("pay or give") in 13:7. These two imperatives show us Paul's instructions for relating to the Roman authorities.[22] He begins the section with a general appeal to submit to authorities, supported by a series of statements as to why one should (or should not, if the authorities fail to do what is required of them) submit to the authorities. The section is then wrapped by another appeal to pay whatever one owes to the ruling authorities, whether taxes, respect, or honor. If read at face value, Paul seems to emphasize order, civil obedience, honor, and respect for civil authorities, suggesting that the Christ followers are instructed to be obedient citizens and subject to the ruling authorities. However, if we are to go deeper to discern the hidden transcript, we find that Paul may be saying otherwise.

The First Imperative: Submitting to All Authorities?

The basis for Paul's exhortation to submit (*hypotassesthō*) to the authorities is detailed in Romans 13:1b–3a. Paul's declaration that "there is no authority except from God, and those authorities that exist have been instituted by God" (Rom 13:1b; NRSV) clearly puts things in perspective for the Roman Christ followers. It is interesting to note that there is no recognition by Paul in this passage of what was commonly believed in his day—that the world is divided into rulers and ruled, masters and slaves. Paul simply attributes all authority to God. This God, according to Jewett, is "the God embedded in the crucified Christ . . . which turns this passage into a massive act of political cooptation."[23] To the Roman authorities, the god who granted power is not the God of Paul but Mars or Jupiter or one of the Greco-Roman deities. Seneca cites Nero as claiming that he had been chosen to serve on earth as vicar of the gods and also celebrated himself as a god.[24] However, Paul

---

22. For further discussion, see Pinter, "Josephus and Romans 13:1–14," 143–50.
23. Jewett, *Romans: A Commentary*, 790.
24. Seneca, *De Clementia* 1.2.

says otherwise by claiming that Nero was not God, and whatever power he had, it was given by the God and Father of Jesus Christ. Not only does Paul's statement turn its head against the imperial cult, but also it is counter-imperial. By stating that "there is no authority except from God," Paul hints of the possibility that there are governing authorities that are not from God. Therefore, what Paul is claiming is that if Rome's power were indeed from God, Rome should exercise its power honorably and rightly; otherwise, that authority was not deemed to be derived from God. This reading supports Jewett's understanding of the imperative *hypotassesthō*, which takes the middle voice of having the sense of "to submit voluntarily." This reading is in contrast to the idea of full obedience.[25]

Following this, Paul warns that the imperial sword was not idle—it would continue to threaten the most vulnerable population in Rome by provoking terror, fear, and the sword (Rom 13:3–4). This indicates that Rome would not hesitate to abuse its power.[26] Seneca recorded a speech by Nero that expressly echoed the same propaganda:

> I am the arbiter of life and death for the nations . . . all those many thousands of swords which my peace restrains will be drawn at my nod; what nations shall be utterly destroyed, which banished . . . this it is mine to decree. With all things thus at my disposal, I have been moved neither by anger nor youthful impulse to unjust punishment . . . With me the sword is hidden, nay, is sheathed; I am sparing to the utmost of even the meanest blood; no man fails to find favour at my hands though he lack all else but the name of man.[27]

What Paul does here is to expose the true colors of the imperial rulers as those who did not hesitate to carry out any act of terror in their favor. This serves as a warning for the Christ followers in Rome to always be prepared should they be persecuted for refusing to participate in the worship of the imperial cult. If the Roman authorities were responsible for the crucifixion of Christ, an event that could not have been forgotten by the Roman Christ followers, how much more the sword of Rome may be used against the followers of Christ one day. When he wrote that the imperial sword is "not in vain," little did Paul realize that destruction and bloodshed would be so imminent.

---

25. Jewett, *Romans: A Commentary*, 788. See also Keesmaat and Walsh, *Romans Disarmed*, 290–91. For a list of what *hypotassesthō* could and could not mean, see Harink, *Resurrecting Justice*, 179–84. Harink asserts that this word could not mean "obey" or "be loyal to" (181).

26. Grieb, *Story of Romans*, 124–25.

27. Seneca, *De Clementia* 1.2–4.

Nero would soon "nod his head" and draw his "hidden, unbloodied swords" unjustly against the Christ followers in Rome as history has shown.

The Final Imperative: Paying Taxes and Giving Honor?

How then would one understand Paul's other imperative, *apodote*, in paying what is due to the empire in the form of taxes, and particularly honor and respect (Rom 13:7)? Certainly, Paul would not have been too enthusiastic in his support of the empire. It is more likely that Paul would like to see the Christ followers display the public deference or respect that the oppressed show their masters. As Scott has said, the linguistic deference and gestures of subordination not only ensure survival but also act as a barrier and a veil that the dominant find difficult or impossible to penetrate.[28] In other words, Paul's words here are a response to a minority group who lived under the reality of Roman hegemony and power that seemed to be promoting injustice.[29] Paul is cautious, warning that his advice to practice the art of resistance must be carried out in ways that would not threaten the community. Paul may have sounded obedient, but he gives nothing to the empire except only what is due in Romans 13:7: "Pay to all what is due them—taxes (*phoros*) to whom taxes are due, revenue (*telos*) to whom revenue is due, respect to whom respect is due, honor to whom honor is due."

It is not too difficult to see why Paul would begin with the two forms of taxes that are to be paid to the authorities: the direct (*phoros*) and indirect (*telos*) taxes. What Paul is advocating here is in accordance with what has been historically documented in the middle of the first century by Roman writer Tacitus. Tacitus recorded that "direct taxes" (*tributum*; *phoros* in Rom 3:6–7a) were taxes levied on those living in provinces outside Rome, while "indirect taxes" (*portorium*; *telos* in Rom 13:7b) were levied on all Roman citizens.[30] He further notes:

> In the same year, as a consequence of repeated demands from the public, which complained of the exactions of the revenue-farmers, Nero hesitated whether he ought not to decree the abolition of all indirect taxation and present the reform as the noblest of gifts to the human race. His impulse, however, after much preliminary praise of his magnanimity, was checked by his older advisers, who pointed out that the dissolution of the empire was certain if the revenue on which the state subsisted

---

28. Scott, *Domination and the Arts of Resistance*, 32.
29. For further discussion on imperial injustice, see Elliott, *The Arrogance of Nations*.
30. Tellbe, *Paul Between Synagogue and State*, 179.

were to be curtailed: "For, the moment the duties on imports were removed, the logical sequel would be a demand for the abrogation of the direct taxes."[31]

Tacitus's account is important as it gives us a glimpse into the situation in Rome at the time Paul wrote Romans. There were complaints from the population about the taxes imposed on them by tax farmers. If Nero were to abolish this form of indirect taxes, demands might also be made to abolish direct taxes. This suggests that the population deemed both form of taxes as excessive.[32] It is therefore interesting that, in light of this historical insight, we see Paul exhorting the Roman Christians to exercise restraint by paying what is due to the authorities, be it direct (*phoros*) or indirect (*telos*) taxes, as reflected in the imperative *apodote*, which Jewett is right to suggest "implies a response to social obligations" in giving or paying back what is owed.[33]

When Paul exhorts Christians in Rome to pay *both* taxes (Rom 13:6–7), he possibly has in mind recent immigrants or those who had returned from other provinces after Claudius' expulsion and were still liable for the direct taxes.[34] That the authority "bears the sword" (Rom 13:4) most possibly reflected real situations, since Roman authorities did not hesitate to inflict severe punishment on those who violated their tax laws.[35] It is in view of their vulnerable status that Paul advises Christ followers in Rome to react appropriately toward the abusive taxation imposed by Imperial authorities.

However, what is often missed are the remaining two items Paul mentions that should be paid as well, *only* if they are due: respect and honor (Rom 13:7). In other words, if one lives under the injustice of Rome where respect and honor are *not* due, how should one respond to the authorities? Paul is less explicit, and this is where most interpreters have unfortunately missed the significance of Paul's hidden transcript. What Paul is advocating is a subversive call for Christ followers living under the Roman hegemony, power, and injustice to examine whether respect and honor should be reciprocated to those who failed to discharge their divinely appointed duties (Rom 13:1).

---

31. Tacitus, *Annals* 13.50.
32. Tobin, *Paul's Rhetoric in its Contexts*, 400.
33. Jewett, *Romans: A Commentary*, 801.
34. Coleman, "Binding Obligations in Romans 13:7," 312–13; McKnight, *Reading Romans Backwards*, 46, 48–49.
35. See Tellbe, *Paul Between Synagogue and State*, 180.

Love as the Only Debt: Honoring Good and Resisting Evil

We have seen the hidden transcript in Romans 13:1–7 reveal how subversive Paul can be. Both the imperatives, submitting to (*hypotassesthō*) and paying what is due (*apodote*) to the authorities, call the Roman Christ followers to evaluate carefully how they should live their lives as faithful witnesses for the gospel. In reading Romans 13:7, Jewett suggests that for the sake of proclaiming Christ, "Paul was willing to accept the system that demanded honor for the emperor and his officials whether they deserved it or not."[36] Does this mean Christians are to pledge unconditional allegiance to the imperial rule? Surely no, as we peer beneath the surface of Paul's rhetoric!

How then shall the Roman Christ followers live? It is unfortunate that in our modern English translations, Romans 13:1–7 is often treated as a passage or pericope by itself while Romans 13:8 is considered the beginning of a new paragraph or section.[37] While this is not inaccurate, it misses the force of Paul's argument and "cuts off the hands and feet of (Rom 13:1–7)."[38] The thematic link of Romans 13:7–8 could not be more pronounced. As Romans 13:7 ends by exhorting Roman Christ followers to pay what is owned (*opheilē*), Paul continues to challenge them in Romans 13:8–10 that they should not owe (*opheilō*) anything to anyone, except to love (*agapaō*) one another and to do no wrong to one's neighbor. Paul cites Leviticus 19:8, "Love your neighbor as yourself," in Romans 13:9, echoing the teaching of Jesus (see Mark 12:31) as one of the two greatest commandments, the other being the *Shema* (Deut 6:4). Furthermore, it is not a coincidence that Paul's wider exhortation is framed by the use of *agapaō/agape* in Romans 12:9 and 13:8–10 and climaxes in his notion of "owing no one anything except love," and that love fulfills the "law" (Rom 13:8). Therefore, the thematic link of *opheilē/opheilō* clearly implies the continuation of Paul's thought in Romans 13:7–8.[39] Paul reminds Christ followers that they are always debtors when it comes to loving one's neighbor. Yet on another level, the notion of *opheilē/opheilō* can be read as a hidden critique of Rome's taxation law, which yoked its subjects under the slavery of *debts*. Paul's command "to love" stands in clear opposition to Roman taxation, which was obviously deprived of love. What Paul envisions is a *free* and *loving* community when he appeals to Christ followers in Rome to not fall short of what they themselves can contribute to peace, to live on good terms with their neighbors,

---

36. Jewett, *Romans: A Commentary*, 803.

37. Jewett, *Romans: A Commentary*, 782. Jewett comments that "there is practically universal agreement among commentators" that the pericope "ends with v. 7."

38. McKnight, *Reading Romans Backwards*, 46.

39. So Tellbe, *Paul Between Synagogue and State*, 181–82.

relating with trust and respect on the basis of honesty and justice and, above all, with the overarching perspective of love.

Finally, Paul injects Romans 13:1–7 within the larger unit of Romans 12:9–13:14, the argument of which is knitted together by a coherent terminology. The three sections of Romans 12:9–21; 13:1–7; and 13:10–14 are linked by the contrast between "good" (*agathos*) and "evil" (*kakos*). This thematic contrast-pair of *agathos/kakos* runs throughout Romans 12:1–15:13, where *agathos* appears in Romans 12:2, 9, 21; 13:3, 4, 10; 14:16; and 15:2 while *kakos* in Romans 12:17, 21; 13:3, 4, 10; and 14:20.

These words should be read as a hidden transcript for obvious reasons. When Paul sandwiched Romans 13:1–7 between his discussion on "good" and "evil," the subjects he alluded to and whose deeds were reckoned as "evil" were clear to his audience. What is even more obvious is how Paul's exhortation runs counter to normal expectations in his call for the Christ followers in Rome to be patient in suffering (Rom 12:12), to bless those who persecute them (Rom 12:14), to do what is noble in the sight of all, not to repay evil for evil (Rom 12:17), but to overcome evil with good (Rom 12:21),[40] to treat their "enemies" by "heaping burning coals on their heads" (Rom 12:20).[41] Most notably, Paul wants them to "live peaceably with all" (Rom 12:18). In contrast to Romans 12:3–13, which depicts relations within Christian communities, all these are indications that Paul in Romans 12:14–21 is dealing with relations outside the Christ community, and he is calling for a positive response to hostility.

The basis for the Christ followers to honor good and resist evil can be found in the concluding verses of Romans 13:11–14. Paul boldly asserts that "salvation is nearer to us now than when we became believers," and "the night is far gone, the day is near." Because of this, there is an even greater urgency for the Christ followers in Rome to "lay aside the works of darkness and put on the armor of light" (Rom 13:11–12) and to "put on the Lord Jesus Christ" (Rom 13:14). Paul's use of the terminology of "salvation," "time," "hour," "near," etc. are indicators of the apocalyptic nature of this passage.[42] The *destiny of history*, says Paul, is not in the hands of the emperor, but ultimately in the hands of God and his crucified and resurrected Messiah, and embodied in the apocalyptic communities of God, which are more than

---

40. Jewett, *Romans: A Commentary*, 779, correctly points out that Paul's phrase is better rendered as "conquer evil with good," as it critiques Rome's idea of *Pax* and *Victoria*.

41. On possible interpretations of "heaping coals on enemies' heads," see Jewett, *Romans: A Commentary*, 777–78.

42. See also Keesmaat and Walsh, *Romans Disarmed*, 295–96.

conquerors under the lordship of Christ, with the empowerment of the Holy Spirit (cf. Rom 8:35–37). Finally, Porter's comment on this is worth noting:

> First, he (Paul) defines obedience in terms of willing submission, with the unstated though clearly understood assumption that this obedience is to be made to a just power and that submission is not to be made to an unjust power. Second, if all authority comes from a God who institutes justly, any authority which wishes to rule as God's instrument of justice must rule consistent with God's justice, otherwise that authority is rendered invalid . . . The important implication is that unjust authorities are not due the obedience of which Paul speaks, but rather are outside these boundaries of necessary obedience. Rather than being a text which calls for submissive obedience, Rom 13:1–7 is a text which only demands obedience to what is right, never to what is wrong.[43]

Reminding the emperor's subjects that the emperor is responsible to the true God is not a subjection to, but a diminution of, imperial arrogance. Written right under the Caesar's nose to Christians living in a hostile environment in the empire's center, this is indeed subversive.

Conclusion: Listening to the Text Again

Not everyone is convinced that the political reading of Paul is warranted. Some argue that the imperial cult was very much less important and significant in Paul's thought.[44] Some have also raised question of the methodology of hidden transcript we used in reading Paul.[45] We are deeply appreciative of Jewett and his excellent commentary on Romans that has shaped our further understanding of this epistle, especially his careful attention to the counter imperial rhetoric and the social historical background of Romans. We hope we have demonstrated that adopting a hidden transcript approach in reading Romans 13:1–7—reading from one's context and perspective but remaining faithful to the context out of which the Scripture was written—would yield a different understanding of this Pauline text that could speak

---

43. Porter, "Romans 13:1–7 as Pauline Political Rhetoric," 118.
44. See especially the works of Kim, *Christ and Caesar*.
45. For a critical review of using hidden transcript in reading Pauline texts, see Heilig, *Hidden Criticism?*, especially 50–67. Rather than abandoning the methodology, Heilig cautions that care must be exercised so that one does not read too much into the text.

powerfully to contemporary Christians living as a minority/dominated ones in a predominant Islamic context in Malaysia.

We are reminded that we are not to obey unconditionally *all* authorities, but to submit only to that which *first* submits to God's divine rule. Yet, Romans 13:1–7 is found within a block of materials in Romans 12–13 that calls believers to nonconformity to this present world. This call is not an advocate for the church to be completely withdrawn and detached from the world. In order for the church to be an authentic witness for the gospel, critical engagement with society is necessary. It is only then that the church can discern when and how to pay the dues of respect and honor. In addition, this passage also calls the church to speak prophetically to the state. The church is to take the courageous role in denouncing and calling for the elimination of specific abuses and practices that are contrary to the gospel—be it the increase in corruption and acts of injustice, the erosion of human rights, and the promotion of the supremacy of one particular ethnic group against others, etc.—and not to fear the power of the state, even if it means persecution for standing up for the truth (Rom 13:3–4). Above all else, in the existing situation, whereby our nation is still covered by clouds of political uncertainties, we need all the more to be guardians of God's *justice* (*dikaiosunē theou*), citizens who uphold the law of love, work for the common good of all, and be a voice for many other voiceless minority communities that consider this beloved nation a place to be called home.

The proclamation of the story of Jesus, the crucified and risen savior, has never been an easy task. As in Paul's day, the gospel of Jesus Christ remains a stumbling block and a scandal today. This serves as a reminder that the "sword" of the present-day empire can be wielded against the dominated ones. When one lives in this context, reading Paul's words prepares us to face any consequences that may include persecution and suffering as a minority Christian group. The Christian church in Malaysia is reminded that religious security and a quest for a safe haven of redemption without any risk are alien in Paul's gospel.[46]

Reading Romans 13:1–7 challenges us to evaluate whether our life and ministry conform to the prevailing social conventions and cultural expectations—or reflect a faithful and living exegesis of the gospel of Jesus Christ, especially what it means to be responsible citizens in honoring the good and resisting evil when undergirded by the debt of love.

---

46. For further treatment on the centrality of sufferings in Paul's thought, see Lim, *The Sufferings of Christ Are Abundant in Us*. See also Hii, "Contesting the Ideology of the Empire."

Bibliography

(* For Further Reading)

Bammel, Ernst. "Romans 13." In *Jesus and the Politics of His Day*, edited by Ernst Bammel and C. F. D. Moule, 365–83. Cambridge: Cambridge University Press, 1984.

*Blackwell, Ben C., John K. Goodrich, and Jason Maston, eds. *Reading Romans in Context: Paul and Second Temple Judaism*. Grand Rapids: Zondervan, 2015.

Coleman, Thomas M. "Binding Obligations in Romans 13:7: A Semantic Field and Social Context." *Tyndale Bulletin* 48 (1997) 307–27.

Das, A. Andrew. *Solving the Romans Debate*. Minneapolis: Fortress, 2007.

*Elliott, Neil. *The Arrogance of Nations: Reading Romans in the Shadow of the Empire*. Paul in Critical Contexts. Minneapolis: Fortress, 2008.

*———. *Liberating Paul: The Justice of God and the Politics of the Apostle*. Sheffield: Sheffield Academic, 1995. Reprint, Minneapolis: Fortress, 2005.

Grieb, A. Katherine. *The Story of Romans: A Narrative Defense of God's Righteousness*. Louisville: Westminster John Knox, 2002.

*Harink, Douglas. *Resurrecting Justice: Reading Romans for the Life of the World*. Downers Grove, IL: IVP Academic, 2020.

Heilig, Christoph. *Hidden Criticism? The Methodology and Plausibility of the Search for A Counter-Imperial Subtext in Paul*. Wissenschaftliche Untersuchungen zum Neuen Testament 2/392. Tübingen: Mohr Siebeck, 2015. Reprint, Minneapolis: Fortress, 2017.

Hii, Kong Hock. "Contesting the Ideology of the Empire: Paul's Theological Politics in Romans, with Preliminary Implications for Chinese Christian Communities in Malaysia." PhD diss., Garrett-Evangelical Theological Seminary, 2007. https://www.proquest.com/docview/304790743?parentSessionId=HHsId0UBqBfvKK4EKmB3lq07RfpDpb5loLUWaej0FEc%3D&pq-origsite=primo&accountid=12861.

———. "Honoring the 'Good' and Resisting the 'Evil': Reading Romans 13 as A *Hidden Transcript* in the Malaysian Context." In *From Rome to Beijing: Symposia on Robert Jewett's Commentary on Romans*, edited by K. K. Yeo, 433–46. Lincoln, NE: Kairos Studies, 2013.

*Horsley, Richard A., ed. *Hidden Transcripts and the Arts of Resistance: Applying the Work of James C. Scott to Jesus and Paul*. Semeia Studies 48. Atlanta: Society of Biblical Literature, 2004.

———. "Jesus, Paul, and the 'Arts of Resistance': Leaves from the Notebook of James C. Scott." In *Hidden Transcripts and the Arts of Resistance: Applying the Work of James C. Scott to Jesus and Paul*, Semeia Studies 48, edited by Richard A. Horsley, 1–26. Atlanta: Society of Biblical Literature, 2004.

*Jewett, Robert. *Romans: A Commentary*. Hermeneia. Minneapolis: Fortress, 2007.

*Keesmaat, Sylvia C. and Brian J. Walsh. *Romans Disarmed: Resisting Empire/Demanding Justice*. Grand Rapids: Brazos, 2019.

Kim, Seyoon. *Christ and Caesar: The Gospel and the Roman Empire in the Writings of Paul and Luke*. Grand Rapids: Eerdmans, 2008.

Kok, Ezra and Kar Yong Lim. "The Agape Meal: A Sacramental Model for Ministry Drawn from Romans 13:8." In *From Rome to Beijing: Symposia on Robert Jewett's Commentary on Romans*, edited by K. K. Yeo, 447–54. Lincoln, NE: Kairos Studies, 2013.

Lim, Kar Yong. *"The Sufferings of Christ Are Abundant in Us": A Narrative Dynamics Investigation of Paul's Sufferings in 2 Corinthians*. Library of New Testament Studies 399. London: T. & T. Clark, 2009.

McKnight, Scot. *Reading Romans Backwards: A Gospel in Search of Peace in the Midst of the Empire*. Waco, TX: Baylor University Press, 2019.

Nanos, Mark D. *The Mystery of Romans: The Jewish Context of Paul's Letter*. Minneapolis: Fortress, 1996.

O'Neill, J. C. *Paul's Letter to the Romans*. London: Penguin, 1975.

Perriman, Andrew. *The Future of the People of God: Reading Romans before and after Western Christendom*. Eugene, OR: Cascade Books, 2010.

Pinter, Dean. "Josephus and Romans 13:1-14" Providence and Imperial Power." In *Reading Romans in Context: Paul and Second Temple Judaism*, edited by Ben C. Blackwell, John K. Goodrich and Jason Maston, 143-50. Grand Rapids: Zondervan, 2015.

Porter, Stanley E. "Romans 13:1-7 as Pauline Political Rhetoric." *Filología Neotestamentaria* 3/2 (1990) 115-39.

Reasoner, Mark *Romans in Full Circle: A History of Interpretation*. Louisville: Westminster John Knox, 2005.

Scott, James C. *Domination and the Arts of Resistance: Hidden Transcripts*. New Haven, CT: Yale University Press, 1990.

———. *Weapons of the Weak: Everyday Forms of Peasant Resistance*. New Haven, CT: Yale University Press, 1985.

Seneca. *Moral Essays, Vol 1: De Providentia. De Constantia. De Ira. De Clementia*. Translated by John W. Basore. Loeb Classical Library 214. Cambridge: Harvard University Press, 1928.

Tacitus. *Annals: Book 13-16*. Translated by Clifford H. Moore and John Jackson. Loeb Classical Library 322. Cambridge: Harvard University Press, 1937.

Tellbe, Mikael. *Paul between Synagogue and State: Christians, Jews, and Civic Authorities in 1 Thessalonians, Romans, and Philippians*. Coniectanea Biblica: New Testament Series 34. Stockholm: Almqvist & Wiksell, 2001.

Tobin, Thomas H. *Paul's Rhetoric in its Contexts: The Argument of Romans*. Peabody, MA: Hendrickson, 2004.

Wengst, Klaus. *Pax Romana and the Peace of Jesus Christ*. London: SCM, 1987.

Yeo, K. K, ed. *From Rome to Beijing: Symposia on Robert Jewett's Commentary on Romans*. Lincoln, NE: Kairos Studies, 2013.

Study Questions

1. Reflect on Romans 13:1-7. How do you understand your relationship to your government or nation in terms of submitting to their authorities and paying taxes, respect, and honor?

2. How does Romans 13:1-7 challenge your convictions in the role you and your community of faith play in the political and public square?

Index of Authors

Aaron, David H., 75, 75n15, 76n18, 82
Adams, Edward, 78n31, 79n34, 82, 99
Ademiluka, S. O., 263, 270n46, 272
Agamben, Giorgio, 106n16, 111, 111n50, 112
Aichele, George, 170, 170n56, 171
Alexander, Philip S., 75n14, 76n17, 82
Anum, Eric Nii Bortey, 263, 263n16, 264n17, 272
Arnal, William E., 215, 215n19, 220
Arndt, W. F., xxviii, 157, 206
Arnold, Clinton A., 225n5, 242
Aymer, Margaret, 228n14, 242, 244

Bal, Mieke, 104n5, 112
Baldry, Harold C., 67n22, 69
Balentine, Samuel E., 142, 142n56, 143
Balsdon, J. P. V. D., 198, 198n35, 206
Bammel, Ernst, 275n3, 287
Barclay, John M. G., 89n13, 99, 132n8, 133n21, 143, 148n14
Barr, James, 47n6, 56
Barth, Karl, 109, 109n31, 112, 187
Barton, Carlin, 148n12, 157
Bauer, Walter, xxviii, 157, 206
Baum, Robert M., 236n33, 242
Belleville, Linda, 82
Benjamin, Walter, 143, 223n1, 242
Berg, Shane, 62n5, 69
Betz, Hans Dieter, 23, 23n17, 31, 54n46, 56
Beutler, Johannes, 32
Black, Max, 131, 143
Blackwell, Ben C., 287
Blasi, Anthony, 210n1, 220

Bolchazy, Ladislaus J., 198, 198n36, 199n42, 200, 200n48, 206
Bond, Sarah E., 219n34, 220
Bonhoeffer, Dietrich, 234, 239–40, 240n43, 241, 241n45, 242–43
Borgen, Peder, 76, 76n22, 82
Borgman, Paul, 180, 180n23, 187
Bornkamm, Günther, 22, 22n12, 31
Bourdieu, Pierre, 110n42, 113
Brewer, Raymond R., 51, 51n28, 57
Brooke, George J., 74n10, 77n24, 82
Brown, Schuyler, 46n2, 57
Brzezinski, Zbigniew, 239, 239n41, 242
Bultmann, Rudolf, 21, 104n3, 108, 109n30, 113
Burton, Keith Augustus, xxix, 246–59
Byrne, Brendan, 111n52, 113

Callaway, Kutter, 176n11, 188
Campbell, Douglas A., xxix, 3–18
Campbell, William S., xi, xxix, 39n11, 44, 85–101, 253n36, 257
Carcopino, Jérôme, 198, 198n38, 199, 199n39, 206
Carter, Warren, 149, 149n19, 157
Chia, Philip, xxi
Cintron, David Ray, 201n57, 206
Clark, W. Malcolm, 62n4, 69
Cohick, Lynn H., 199, 199n42, 206
Coleman, Thomas M., 268, 268n40, 272, 282n34
Collado, Lipe, 202n59, 206
Conzelmann, Hans, 23, 23n15, 31
Cosgrove, Charles H., 247n3, 252n28, 258
Cotter, Wendy, 55, 55n51, 56n51, 57

INDEX OF AUTHORS

Cranfield, C. E. B., 150n23, 157
Crook, Zeba, 148n12, 157
Crossan, John Dominic, 199, 199n41, 200n46, 206

Danby, Herbert, 206
Danker, Frederick W., xxviii, 157, 206
Das, A. Andrew, xxx, 72–83, 287
Daube, David, 77n27, 83
David, Noy, 37n8, 38n9, 40
Davidson, Elijah, 176n11, 187
de Ligt, L., 154n41, 157
de Mendoza, F. J. Ruiz, 131n6, 143
Deacy, Christopher, viii, xxx, 159–71, 176n11
Decaro, Louis A. Jr., 248n5, 252n29, 258
Deissmann, Adolf, 149, 149n17, 157
Deive, Carlos Esteban, 201n54, 206
Derrida, Jacques, 132n14, 133, 133n17, 140, 140n52, 143
deSilva, David A., 106n14, 113
Detweiler, Craig, 188
Dipp, Hugo Tolentino, 201n56, 206
Dodd, Brian, 111n49, 113
Donfried, Karl P., 3a, 86n1, 88n9, 90n17, 99, 258
Downing, F. Gerald, 106n14, 113
Du Bois, W. E. B., 110, 110n47, 113
Duhaime, Jan, 220
Dunn, James D. G., 109n34, 113, 150n23, 152n37, 154n44, 157, 197n28, 198n33, 206, 251n22, 254n39, 255n43, 258
Dyer, Bryan R., 32

Eberhardt, Christian A., 41n15, 44
Ehrensperger, Kathy, iii–iv, xiv, xxx, 34–44, 55, 55n48, 57, 91n21, 93, 93n23, 97n30, 99, 113
Elliott, John H., 148n14, 157, 198n33, 206–7
Elliott, Neil, 148n14, 157, 225, 275n4, 276, 281n29, 287
Elliott, Spencer, 148n14, 149, 152n33, 155n47, 157
Elliott, Susan M., 225n5, 242
Ellis, E. Earle, 77n23, 83

Eschner, Christine, 91n19, 100
Esler, Philip F., 88n9, 89n11, 100

Fanon, Frantz, 100, 100n48, 113
Fee, Gordon, 48n10, 51n27, 57
Feinberg, Paul D., 265, 266n26, 267n29, 268n38, 272
Felder, Cain Hope, 253, 253n34, 258
Finger, Rita Halteman, 251n25, 258
Fitzgerald, J. T., 191n1, 198, 206
Fitzmyer, Joseph A., 88n9, 100, 109n32, 113, 152n37, 157
Foerster, Werner, 150n27, 157
Foley, Eric, 157
Forbes, Bruce David, 187
Foster, Elizabeth A., 230n19, 242
Fowl, Stephen E., 50n25, 57, 144
Fredriksen, Paula, 36n4, 40n13, 44, 90n16, 100
Freud, Sigmund, 118n2, 125, 125n14, 126, 128
Frey, Jean-Baptiste, xxviii, 37n8, 38n9, 44
Fürer-Haimendorf, Christoph von, 147n5, 157

Gaca, Kathy, 113
Gadamer, Hans-Georg, 104n4, 113
Gamble, Harry Y., 29, 29n34, 32
García, Pablo, 143, 201n53, 206
Garnsey, Peter, 147n6, 148, 157
Gaventa, Beverly Roberts, 111n53, 113
Gehrie, Mark J., 119, 119n9, 126, 126n18, 128
Geisler, Norman L., 266, 266n28, 272
Geoffrion, Timothy C., 52, 52n35, 54n43, 57
Georgi, Dieter, 21, 21n6, 32, 225, 243
Gingrich, F. W., xxviii, 157, 206
Girard, Jean, 238n38, 243
Goh Meng Hun, xxx, 103–16
Goodrich, John K., 287–88
Gowler, David, 261n3, 262n12, 272
Grenholm, Cristina, 105, 105n9, 107, 107n22, 108n25, 113–14
Grieb, A. Katherine, 280n26, 287
Gundry, Robert H., 81n46, 83

INDEX OF AUTHORS 291

Gundry, Stanley N., 207
Gusha, Ishanesu S., 267n31, 270n51, 271n52, 272

Haddad, Najeeb T., xxx, 46–57
Hall, Edith, 227n10, 243
Hammond, K. T., 263n13, 272
Hardin, Justin K., 225n5, 231n22, 243
Harink, Douglas, 280n25, 287
Harley, John Brian, 229, 229n17, 243
Harnack, Adolf, 196n25, 206
Harrison, James R., 57, 67n23, 69, 89, 89n12, 100
Hawthorne, Gerald F., 49n13, 50n20, 51n30, 56, 56n53, 57
Hays, Richard B., 253, 253n33, 258
Heilig, Christoph, 285n45, 287
Hendrix, Holland, 213n11, 220
Hii, Kong Hock, xxx, 274–88
Hittman, Michael, 214n16, 216n23, 216n25, 219n36, 220
Hofius, Otfried, 78n31, 79n38, 83
Hoklotubbe, T. Christopher, xxxi, 208–22
Holder, R. Ward, 110, 113
Holloway, Paul, 50, 57
Holmes, Michael W., 206
Horbury, William, 37n8, 38n9, 44
Horgan, Maurya P., 77, 77n26, 83
Horner, Robyn, 132, 132n9, 143
Horrell, David, 37n7, 44, 201n1, 220
Horsley, Richard A., ii, 148n16, 157, 225, 225n4, 243, 276n13, 278, 278n21, 287
Howard, Melanie A., 194n21, 207
Hua Wei, xxi
Hughes, Frank W., xxvi, xxxi, 19–33

Instone-Brewer, David, 76, 76n19, 83
Irshai, Oded, 40n13, 44
Isenberg, Sheldon R., 212, 212n6, 220

James, S., 272
Jay, Jeff, 64, 64n14, 65, 65n15, 66, 66n20, 69
Jennings, Mark A., 50, 50n20, 51n27, 52, 52n36, 54n43, 56n52, 57
Jewett, Ellen, xvii–xx

Jewett, Robert, *passim*
John, Felix, 17, 224n2, 243
Johnson, Mark, 143
Johnston, Robert K., xxxi, 164, 171, 173–88
Jones, Henry Stuart, xxviii, 58, 144, 207

Kahl, Brigitte, xxiii, xxxi, 223–44
Kamudzandu, Israel, 225n5, 243
Käsemann, Ernst, 21, 78, 78n30, 83, 112n55, 114, 150n23, 158
Keck, Leander E., 80n43, 83
Keesmatt, Sylvia C., 287
Kennedy, George A., 24n20, 32, 258
Kern-Ulmer, Rivka, 76n17, 83
Kim, Seyoon, 284n44, 287
Kluge, Friedrich, 233n27, 243
Knox, John, 3, 17
Koenig, John, 194, 194n20, 220n50, 207
Kohut, Heinz, 118, 118n2, 119, 119n7, 120–23, 123n13, 125, 125n16, 126, 126n17, 128–29
Kok, Ezra, 274, 287
Kövecses, Zoltá, 179
Kreitzer, Larry, 163, 163n19, 170, 170n57, 171, 176n11

Lakoff, George, 132, 132n15, 143
Lampe, Peter, 248, 248n6, 249n14, 258
Lancaster, Sarah Heaner, 106n18, 114
Lanier, Gregor R., 252n32, 258
Lategan, Bernard, 270, 270n47, 272
Lawrence, John Shelton, xxv–xxvi, 159–71, 175, 177n14, 178–81, 184–88, 247n1, 258
Lawrence, Louise Joy, 106n14, 114
Lee, AHyun, 126n20, 128
Lee, Stan, 181, 184–88
Leenhardt, Franz J., 109n35, 114
Lehr, Fabian, 233n26, 243
Leitch, James W., 31
Levenson, Jon D., 139n47, 140n50, 143
Levinas, Emmanuel, 132, 132n11, 143
Lichtenberger, Hermann, 79n34, 83
Liddell, Henry George, xxviii, 58, 207
Lim, Kar Yong, xxxi, 274–88
Lim, Sung U., 268n37, 272
Lim, Timothy H., 78n29, 83

Lohmeyer, Ernst, 50, 50n21, 58
Longenecker, Richard N., 272
Lopez, D. C., 149n18, 158
Louw, Johannes P., 131n7, 141n55, 143
Luithui, Shimreichon, 146n4, 158
Lyden, John C., 164, 164n26, 171, 176n11, 187
Lyonnet, S., 78n30, 79n37, 83

MacMullen, Ramsay, 199n39, 207
MacMurray, Patrick, 94n26, 100
Mahan, Jeffrey M., 187
Malina, Bruce J., 106n14, 114–15, 210, 210n1, 221
Marion, Jean-Luc, 132, 132n14, 133, 133n17, 143
Marsh, Clive, 164, 164n25, 171, 176n11
Martin, Ralph P., 49n13, 50n20, 56–57
Martin, Troy W., xxiv, 32
Maston, Jason, 287–88
Mauss, Marcel, 132, 132n9, 133n22, 140n53, 141, 144
May, Claudia, 180, 180n22, 188
McCarty, James W. III, 268n41, 269n45, 272
McGinn, Sheila E., xxvii, xxxii, 59–71, 257
McKnight, Scot, 282n34, 288
Meeks, Elijah, 10n6, 17
Meeks, Wayne, 210n1, 221, 248n7, 258
Merleau-Ponty, Maurice, 104n2, 114
Mihoc, Vasile, 113, 115
Milbank, John, 138, 138n46, 144
Miller, Ernest C., 51, 51n29, 52, 58
Mills, Anthony, 181, 181n26, 183n29, 188
Milne, D. J. W., 81n44, 83
Mitchell, Jolyon, 176n11
Mitchell, Margaret M., 28, 32
Mitchell, Stephen, 225n5, 231n23, 239n40, 243
Moo, Douglas J., 79n36, 83, 109n32, 110n40, 111n51, 114
Mooney, James, 214, 214n15, 215n21, 217n30, 221
Moormann, Eric M., 64n13, 70
Morris, Leon, 267n32, 268n36, 272
Motyer, John A., 50, 50n21, 58

Moxnes, Halvor, 148n13, 151, 151n20, 152n34, 158
Murphy-O'Connor, Jerome, 6n4, 14n8, 17

Nan, Seng Tsin M., 263, 263n14, 272
Nanos, Mark D., 243, 251, 251n22, 252n30, 258–59, 275n6, 288
Neufeld, Dietmar, 210n1, 221
Neusner, Jacob, 75, 75n13, 82–84, 253n33, 258
Neyrey, Jerome H., 106n4, 114
Niang, Aliou Cissé, xxxii, 223–44
Nichols, Joel A., 268n41, 272
Nicolet, Claude, 229n16, 244
Nida, Eugene A., 131n7, 141n55, 143
Niebuhr, H. Richard, 160, 171
Nolan, Steve, 177n13, 188

O'Neill, J. C., 275, 275n8, 288
Oakes, Peter, 148n13, 152n33, 158
Odyuo, Iris, 148n13, 152n33, 158
Okorie, Ferdinand Ikenna, 153n21, 144
Olbricht, Thomas H., 32
Oliver, Kelly, 106n17, 114, 179, 187
Oropeza, B. J., 82–83

Page, T. E., 242–43
Patte, Daniel, xxii, 105, 105n9, 106n12, 107, 107n19, 108n25, 111, 111n54, 112, 112n56, 113–15
Peña, M. S., 131n6, 143
Perriman, Andrew, 275n5, 288
Perrin, Bernadotte, 207
Pesantubbee, Michelene E., 213n14, 221
Pilch, John, 115, 210n1, 221
Pillay, Mirinda N., 261n9, 272
Pinter, Dean, 279n22, 288
Pitt-Rivers, Julian, 106, 106n15, 115
Plevnik, Joseph, 106n13, 115
Pollock, Sheldon, 46–47, 47n3, 58
Porter, Stanley E., xxviii, 32, 116, 206, 267, 273, 285, 288
Porton, Gary G., 75n13, 76n16, 84

Rackham, H., 207
Radkau, Joachim, 232n24, 244

Ramsay, William M., 5, 207, 234, 234n30, 244
Reasoner, Mark, 89n15, 100, 275n2, 288
Rector, Lallene J., viii, xxii, xxxii, 117–29
Rediger, Milo A., 267n33, 273
Reed, Jefferey T., 49n13, 58
Rengstorf, Karl Heinrich, 134n27, 144
Reumann, John, 49n13, 58
Rhoads, David, xxii
Richards, I. A., 131, 131n3, 144
Ricoeur, Paul, 131, 131n5, 144
Ridderbos, Herman, 109n32, 115
Riddle, Donald Wayne, 194n9, 207
Rindge, Matthew S., 176n11, 188
Robbins, Vernon K., 260, 260n1, 262, 273
Robinson, James M., 22, 23n14, 32
Rodriguez, Rafael, 86, 87n4, 89n14, 100
Roetzel, Calvin J., 28, 28n32, 33
Roschke, Ronald W., 175–76, 176n10, 188
Rosenfeld, Jean E., 213n14, 221
Ross, William A., 252n32, 258
Rossing, Barbara, xxi
Roth, Karl Heinz, 232n25, 244

Sage, Evan T., 243
Said, Edward, 226, 226n9, 233, 233n28, 244
Saller, Richard, 147n6, 147n7, 148n11, 157
Scheid, John, 41n15, 45
Scheidel, Walter, 10n6, 17
Schenk, Wolfgang, 33
Schiffman, Lawrence H., 78n29, 84
Schmithals, Walter, 20, 20n3, 21, 32–33
Schnabel, Eckard J., 250, 258
Schneiders, Sandra M., 105, 105n11, 115
Schnelle, Udo, 108n29, 109n35, 115
Schrag, Calvin O., 139n48, 144
Scott, Bernard Brendon, 175, 188
Scott, James C., 274–78, 281, 287–88
Scott, Robert, xxviii, 58, 207
Segovia, Fernando F., 104n2, 115
Seifrid, Mark A., 109n37, 115
Sharot, Stephen, 211, 212n6, 221

Sheppard, Phillis Isabella, 120n10, 126, 126n20, 129
Shohe, Zakali, viii, xxxii, 145–58
Siegert, Folker, 76, 76n20, 76n21, 84
Silva, Moisé, 49, 49n13, 58
Sleeman, Matthew, 229n15, 244
Slingerland, Edward, 142n57, 144
Smith-Christopher, Daniel, 228, 244
Smith, Wilfred Cantwell, 106n12, 115
Soskice, Janet Martin, 130, 131n2, 144
Spencer, Aída Besançon, viii, xxxiii, 191–207
Spicq, Ceslas, xxviii, 197n29, 198n33, 207
Staley, Jeffrey L., 170, 170n55, 171
Stanley, Christopher D., 73n3, 84
Stegner, William Richard, 74, 74n8, 76, 76n22, 84, 254n38, 258
Stein, Robert H., 273
Stemberger, Günther, 40n14, 45
Stendahl, Krister, 225, 225n4, 244
Stern, Karen B., 64n13, 70
Stowers, Stanley K., 110, 110n44, 115
Strobel, Karl, 227n10, 244
Stuhlmacher, Peter, 79, 79n38, 84
Sugirtharajah, R. S., 228n3, 244

Talmon, Yonina, 211, 212n6, 221
Tamez, Elsa, 225, 225n4, 244
Tellbe, Mikael, 281n30, 282n35, 283n39, 288
TeSelle, Eugene, 110, 110n41, 113, 115
Teugels, Lieve, 75n14, 84
Theissen, Gerd, 78n30, 80, 80n39, 81n46, 84, 200, 200n50, 207, 249, 249n8, 259
Thielman, Frank, 109n36, 115
Thiselton, Anthony, 214n18, 221
Thomas, Louis-Vincent, 236n34, 237, 244
Thomas, Robert L., 207
Thurén, Lauri, 109n37, 116
Timmins, Will N., 109n37, 116
Tobin, Thomas H., 52, 52n37, 53, 53n39, 57–58, 275n4, 282n32, 288
Tolbert, Mary Ann, 104n2, 115
Tomson, Peter, 40n12, 45

Turcotte, Paul-André, 220
Turner, James, 47, 58

Ukpong, Justin S., 115, 228n13, 245
Ulmer, Rivka, 75n14, 76n17, 83–84

VanDrunen, David, 273
Varner, Eric R., 64n12, 70
Vaux, Sara Anson, 159–60, 167, 167n46, 168, 168n48, 169, 171
Vena, Osvaldo, xxii

Walsh, Brian J., 280n25, 284n42, 287
Walsh, Richard, 163, 171, 176
Wang Zi, xxii
Warren, Louis W., 214n15, 215n20, 216, 216n23, 217n27, 221
Webb, Stephen H., 137n43, 138n45, 140n51, 142n58, 144
Webster, Jane, 227n10, 245
Wedderburn, A. J. M., 79n37, 80n39, 84
Weiss, Herold, 247n3, 258
Welborn, L. L., 57, 113

Wells, Peter S., 226n8, 227n10, 228n12, 245
Wengst, Klaus, 275n4, 288
Wesley, John, 128n21, 129
Wiarda, Howard, 201n55, 207
Wilder, Amos Niven, 175, 175n7, 188
Williams, Margaret H., 249n13, 259
Wilson-Reitz, Megan, 70
Wilson, Jamie J., 252n29, 259
Winter, Bruce, 147n6, 148n11, 153, 153n39, 158, 225, 245
Wimberly, Anne Streaty, xxi
Wimberly, Edward Powell, xxi
Witherington, Ben III, 55n46, 58
Wright, Melanie J., 164, 164n29, 171

Yeo, K. K. (Khiok-Khng), iii, viii, xvii, xxi–xxv, xxxiii, 104n3, 113, 116, 130–44, 247n3, 258, 265, 265n25, 273, 274n1, 287–88

Ziesler, J. A., 80, 80n39, 84

Index of Subjects

Adam (and Eve), 72–84, 109, 109n38, 171. *See also* anthropology; human
aesthetic, beauty, 133, 142, 168, 177, 226, 261
    and glory of God, 43, 98, 137, 150, 166, 174, 185, 204
    and shame, xxi, 117–29, 146, 148n12, 157, 276. *See also* honor and shame
    and violence, 65, 70, 124, 142, 160, 166–69, 173, 178, 186–87, 217
Africa(n), xxix, xxxii, 105n6, 201, 201n54, 206, 228–32, 237, 240–45, 248, 257–59, 262, 269, 272, 287n27
    African American, 225, 248–54, 257, 259
    Ghana-Eve, Ghanaian context, xxix, 260–73
    Senegal, xxxii, 223, 227, 229–31, 236–37, 239, 242–44
    Timbuktu, 239
    West Africa(n), 223–45
America(n), 70, 83, 103–4, 110–14, 128, 151, 160–63, 165–67, 171–80, 184–87, 211, 221, 225, 230n18, 232–33, 239, 242, 246–47, 258
    Afro-American. *See* African
    Arab American, xxx
    apostle to America (United States), 31, 31n38, 32, 69, 103n1, 112n57, 173–75

    Captain America, 60, 69, 104, 113, 175–77, 180, 185–88, 247n1
    civil religion, xvii, 185
    civil rights, 247–48
    East German American, 225
    Hispanic/Latinx American, 207
    Japanese American, 119
    monomyth, 159, 159n1, 166, 171, 175, 178, 184
    movies. *See* film
    Native/Indigenous. *See* Native American
    society, xiii, 166
    superhero myth, 173–88
Ammianus Marcellinus, 198
Amyntas, King, 5
anakainōsei (renewing), 150–51
analogy, 61, 130–31, 134, 162, 257. *See also* rhetoric
anthropology, xii, xxv, 20–21, 31–32, 46–47, 57, 60, 69, 113–15, 118–19, 122, 127–29, 141, 165, 182, 210, 221. *See also* Paul
apocalyptic, 61n2, 113, 186–87, 214–15, 219. *See also* eschatology
Aristotle, 27, 130, 142
Aryan race, 232, 241–42
Augustine, 110, 115

barbarians, 105, 178, 223–45. *See also* Greco-Roman; Greek
Battle of Actium, 226
bears (*bastazeis*), 87, 96

INDEX OF SUBJECTS

Beijing, ii, xxi, xxiv, xxvi, xxxiii, 114–15, 144, 273–74, 287–88
belonging
    to a group, 48, 89, 93, 123, 127–28, 246. *See also* community
    to God/Christ, 96, 193, 268. *See also* God; Christ
    leaderless group, 126–27, 145. *See also* identity; church
beloved community, 60, 69, 74, 93, 153n36, 257
Bible, Scripture. *See also* IAD
    and culture. *See* culture
    and echoes, xxiv, 72–84, 256–58, 283
    biblical coda, 186–87
    biblical interpretation, xvii, xxii, xxiv, xxvii, 31, 46, 59, 70, 75, 82–84, 104–6, 108, 114–15, 130, 141, 144, 213, 219, 244, 247, 259, 273
    biblical metaverse, xvii
    biblical method/criticism. *See* criticism
    scroll and codex, 29–30, 19n14, 58, 74, 77–78, 82, 84
body of Christ. *See* church
Bolchazy, Ladislaus, 198, 206
Bonhoeffer, Dietrich, 234–36, 239–45
Bush, George W., 177–78

Cabirus, cult of, 213, 213n11
Caesarea Maritime, 8–12, 49, 195
Chicago, xix, 118n2, 119n9
China, xxi–xxii, xxxiii, 144. *See also* Hong Kong; Taiwan
Chinese, ii, xxiii, xxiv, xxvi
    church, Christian theology, 116, 144, 287
    cultures, traditions, xxiv, 130, 132
    ethics, religion, philosophy, 132, 141. *See also* Confucius
    Malaysian, 106–8, 274–88
Choctaw Nation of Oklahoma. *See* Native American
Christ. *See* Jesus Christ
Christian
    Christendom, 288

Christian-Marxist dialogue, 227
Christianity, 120, 135, 167, 191, 194n19, 197, 200, 210n1, 214n17, 215n19, 221, 224, 230–31, 236, 240, 247n4, 251n27. *See also* church
    Pre-Christian, 109–10
    tolerance, xi, xxv, 60, 69, 104, 114
chronology. *See* Paul
church, *ekklēsia*, xviii–xx, xxv, xxvii, xxx–xxxii, 4, 60, 69, 114, 211, 237, 242–43
    and colonialism, 173–74
    and state, 138–41, 156, 195–96, 227, 239–41, 260–73, 286
    as body of Christ, 134–37, 142, 200, 235, 241
    as people of God, 56, 99, 142, 154, 275n5, 288
    as new Israel, 52, 229, 251
    early church, 4, 7, 20–32, 44, 46, 56–57, 60, 120–22, 125, 133, 146, 158, 248–49
    Fathers, 107n21, 125, 206
    house church, 66, 117–29, 134
    tenement church, xiii, 117–29, 252, 257–58
    of God, 43, 134, 156
    global/universal church, xxxii, 115, 244–45
Cicero, 27
citizen (*politeuesthe*), 14, 46–58, 139, 147, 193–94, 198, 227n11, 245, 248–49, 262, 269, 271, 274, 276, 279, 281, 286. *See also* Greco Roman
circumcision, uncircumcision, 98, 120, 224–25, 235, 238–41
civil authorities, 260–73, 279–80
civilizing mission (*mission civilisatrice*), 223–34, 237–38
client and patron, 136, 148–49, 157, 198–200, 210, 248
colonial, post-colonial, xxxii, 175, 201, 202n58, 210, 223–32, 236–45, 263–64, 272. *See also* Roman Empire

community, xiv, xxxi, xxxiii, 6, 11, 29, 43, 48–55, 59, 90–97, 113, 125, 129, 133–58, 161, 165, 167, 173, 182, 198, 213, 218–19, 225, 241, 261, 263, 271, 278, 284–88. *See also* church
    and individualism, 80, 94, 103, 105–10, 112, 116, 119, 135, 137, 140, 146–51, 154, 167, 173, 178, 181–84. *See also* individual
    community-centered (relationality/ interpretation), 103–111, 116, 119, 281, 283
    communal (meal), communion, xxi, 34–35, 51, 56, 88n9, 147, 238. *See also* agape meal
    identity, 229–30, 236–37, 244–59
    other-centered (heteronomy), 103, 105–108, 111–12, 116
Confucius, Confucianism, 104n3, 116, 132, 141–44
    and *li* (propriety/gift), 132, 142
    and *ren*, and *ren ren*, 141
context, contextual
    contextual(ized) theology, ii, xii, 24–25, 33, 56, 59–60, 68–69, 71, 86, 103–7, 110, 112, 115, 133, 158, 174, 177, 180, 221–25, 234–41, 261, 273, 278
    hermeneutic of dialogue, xxii, xxvi, xxxi, 24–25, 31–32, 69, 100, 103–4, 110, 114, 133, 160–62, 164, 167, 169, 171–72, 175–77, 182, 187–88, 225–29
creation, xxii, xxix, xxx, 35, 42, 55n47, 57, 69, 81–82, 141, 144
criticism, critical method, xii–xiii, xxvii, xxxii, 5, 22, 46–47, 56, 58, 106n12, 108, 176, 224, 229n17, 230n20, 244. *See also* hermeneutics; interpretation
cultural interpretation. *See* culture
ethics in interpretation. *See* ethics
exegesis. *See* exegesis
feminist criticism. *See* female
form-critical study, 47
historical-critical. *See* historical and literary

indigenous interpretation. *See* indigenous
literary study. *See* literary method
metaphorical reading. *See* metaphor
movie criticism. *See* film
narrative criticism, 260. *See also* storytelling
philological criticism. *See* philology analysis
political reading, xxxii, 47, 149, 158, 273–88
postcolonial criticism, 230. *See also* colonial
psychological reading. *See* psychology
redaction criticism. *See* redaction
rhetorical criticism. *See* rhetoric
scriptural criticism, 103–116
social-scientific criticism, 210, 260. *See also* culture
cross, crucifixion. *See* Jesus Christ
culture, cultural
    and Christian faith, 127, 224, 253
    context, xxii, 43, 59, 62, 64, 118, 276
    cross-cultural, xx, 130, 141–42, 144, 208, 228, 244–45, 247
    cultural-critical reading, 130–44
    dynamics, 119–20, 211
    exegete, 173–88, 228n12, 244
    Greco-Roman culture. *See* Greco-Roman
    Jewish culture, 34–45, 51–52, 58–59, 61, 64–68, 70–84, 86–87, 89–93, 96, 98–99, 105, 111, 115, 117, 120, 122, 137, 142, 150, 191, 195, 198, 206, 211, 221, 224–25, 232–33, 235, 241–42, 249–52, 254, 257–59, 263, 275, 288
Cyprus, 4, 7, 11

Damascus, 4, 6, 10, 16–17, 31
democracy, 108, 134, 137, 177–79, 225, 227, 232, 234, 240–41, 270
Demosthenes, 27
dialogue in a prophetic mode, 162, 176–77
Dio Cassius, 7, 13–14, 17, 64, 70
Diola, xxxii, 227–45

Dominican context, 191–207. *See also* Roman Empire
Dominican Republic, xxxiii, 201–3, 206–7

economy, xii, 40, 68–71, 122, 155–57, 174, 210, 212, 216, 218, 231, 234, 237, 248, 257, 262, 269, 271, 273
   capitalism, 233–34
   divine economy. *See* God
   poor, 68, 140, 193, 197, 199–202, 246–49, 269
   wealth, 146–47, 153, 156, 200–1, 248
ego-ideals, 125. *See also* Freud
Emitai, creator God, 236–37
empathy, 118n2, 122–24, 127, 136. *See also* Kohut
end of the world, 208–222. *See also* eschatology
Ephesus, 8, 10, 12, 22, 49
eschatology, xxx, 52, 55n47, 77n24, 109, 141, 146, 213, 267. *See also* apocalyptic, millennial
ethics
   cultural ethics, 141, 144–45, 154, 167–68, 171, 178–81
   evil eye, 210, 235. *See also* hospitality
   gospel ethics, 43–44, 59, 149, 191, 199–200, 241, 243
   in biblical interpretation, 60, 103, 112, 114, 150
   Pauline ethics, 52, 58, 66, 68–71, 136, 149, 152–53, 195–96, 211–12, 218–19, 261, 263–64, 272, 275
   reciprocity ethic, 50, 132–33, 139, 147–48
European, xi, 103–104, 112, 172, 174, 211, 223–45
exegesis, xii, xiv, xvii, xxvii, xxix, 31, 47, 49, 54–56, 60, 75, 75n14, 76–78, 99, 104, 104n3, 105–7, 133, 138, 149, 173–88, 208, 210, 224, 252, 255, 263–69, 276, 286. *See also* criticism

female, woman, feminist criticism, xiii, 26, 129, 166, 168, 175, 181–82, 194, 197–98, 204, 236
film, movie criticism
   American Sniper, 179, 185, 188
   and religion, xvii, xxvi, xxx, xxxi, 60, 69, 104, 114, 159–88, 247, 258Avengers, 181–82
   Batman, 178, 181–83, 188
   Black Widow, 181, 186
   Captain America, xiii, xxv, xxvi, 60, 69, 104, 113, 175, 177–78, 180–82, 185, 187–88, 247, 258
   Clint Eastwood, 160, 164–68, 171, 178, 185
   Daredevil, 181, 183
   DC Comics, 181–82
   Fantastic Four, 181–83
   Hulk, 181–83
   Iron Man, 181–83
   James Bond, 186
   Justice League of America, 181
   Lion King, 178
   Matrix, 178
   movie's aesthetics, 177
   Rambo, 178–80, 187
   Shawshank Redemption, 164, 166–67
   Spider Man, 181–88
   superhero myth, xxvi, 173–88
   Superman, 177, 181–88
   Thor, 181
   Unforgiven, 167–69
   Wayne, John, 177–78, 181, 185, 188
   Wolverine, 181–82
   Wonder Woman, 181
   X-Men, 181–83
food, meal, xiii, xx, xxii, xxiv, 34–45, 88, 90–95, 118–21, 127, 135, 138, 140, 191, 193, 195, 197, 199–202, 215, 237–38, 249, 274n1, 278, 287. *See also* idol; love feast
foreigner (*peregrinus*), stranger (*xenos*), 55–56, 86, 147, 152–53, 156, 158, 191–98, 200, 207, 235–38, 263
forgiveness, 160, 164, 167–69, 171, 178, 203–5. *See also* Jesus Christ

freedom, xxxii, 21, 43, 47, 58, 87, 89,
    91–94, 96, 120–21, 135–36, 139,
    167, 225n5, 238n39, 244, 248,
    253, 267
French, 132, 223, 227–32, 236–39, 242
Freud, 118n2, 125–28
friendship (*amicitia*), v, xi, xv, xxi–xxii,
    199, 202

Galatians, Gauls or Celts, 5, 225–27
Gallias of Agrigentum, 197
Gallio, L. Annaeus, 6–7, 11–12, 15
gentiles, 34, 45, 51, 60, 65, 67, 86–93, 97,
    100, 110–11, 115, 117, 120–21,
    134–35, 137, 146, 154, 175,
    193, 195, 201, 208, 225, 238,
    241, 244, 250–52, 254–56, 258,
    263–64, 275. See also Jews
German(y)
    Berlin, xiv, xxxi, 227, 229–30,
        232–33, 240
    East Germany, xxxi, 225, 227, 232–
        34, 239–41, 245
    Heidelberg, xi, xx, xxv
    Tübingen, xi, xix, 20
    West Germany, 232–34
Ghana. See Africa
Ghost Dance. See Native American
gift, xvii, xxiii, xxiv, 130–44, 146. See
    also God; Jesus Christ
charis (grace/gift), 42, 63, 89n13, 99,
    132–34, 136–38, 174, 194
charisma (charismatic gift), 134–42,
    146–48, 151, 153, 157, 196,
    201–2, 205, 212, 218
dan, dô or *dâ, dōtinē, dosis, Gegebenheit,
    hostia, li*, 131–32
global(ization), 115, 204, 207, 227,
    228n13, 238–39, 242, 244–45
Gnostics, proto-Gnostics, 19–23, 29,
    32–33, 261. See also Schmithals
God, God's. See also Jesus Christ
    church. See church
    economy (*oikonomia*), xxix, 99, 132,
        136–40, 144
    grace, xxiv, 75, 86, 109, 121, 131,
        132n8, 133–42, 144, 157, 160,
        193, 224–25, 241, 244, 257. See
        also gift
image, xiii, 61, 67, 194, 227n11
impartiality, 60, 174, 193
love (*agapē*), xxiv, 94, 117–18, 138–
    39, 140n50, 141, 143, 166–67,
    249, 274, 283, 287
reign, 191–207
righteousness/justice (*dikaiosynē*),
    60–62, 65–71, 95, 109, 111n52,
    112, 115, 129, 135, 138–42,
    157–60, 165–68, 174, 179, 187,
    193, 197, 201, 203, 224–25, 235,
    239, 241, 248, 253–55, 264, 266,
    272, 276, 282–87
salvation, xxv, 21, 60–61, 67, 75,
    81n45, 111n52, 134–35, 165–67,
    246–59, 264, 284
suffering. See Jesus Christ
wisdom, 21–22, 29, 52, 62, 68
good (*kalon; agathos*) and evil (*kakos*),
    xvii, 42, 46–58, 62, 78, 93–98,
    103, 110–11, 133, 136, 141, 148,
    150, 153, 162, 165–66, 176, 194,
    196–97, 205, 216, 235, 237,
    241, 255, 265–67, 270–71, 274,
    283–88
gospel of Christ. See Jesus Christ
Great Altar of Pergamon, 226
Greco-Roman. See also Roman
    context, culture, world, 26, 44,
        46–47, 56–58, 67, 74, 105n7,
        130–33, 136–38, 144, 146–48,
        150, 169, 191, 197–201, 225,
        248, 276, 279
    economy. See economy
    Junia Theodora, 197
    rhetoric, 28, 32, 50–51
    politics, 224–25
    taxation. See taxes
Greek, Hellenistic. See also gentiles;
        Greco-Roman
    Achaia, 4, 6, 8, 11–12, 26
    and barbarians. See barbarians
    and Jews, 46–58, 76, 84, 166. See
        also Jews
    Athens, 8–9, 16

300   INDEX OF SUBJECTS

Greek (*continued*)
  Bible (LXX/Septuagint, GNT), 51, 51n26, 51n32, 73–74, 80, 150, 192–97, 210, 246, 252–58
  culture and people, 21, 41, 48–49, 69, 146, 148, 151, 158, 162–63, 197, 212, 219, 241, 252, 256
  Delphi, 6, 38
  Olympus, Mount, 226
  philosophy, 69–70, 115
  rhetoric, language, 5, 23, 46, 56, 58, 77, 83, 91, 107n21, 130–41, 143, 150, 211. *See also* metaphor
  religions, 43, 150n24, 151–55, 203, 206–7
guest-friend (*hospes*), 192–99, 202–204. *See also* foreigner; hospitality

hermeneutic, xvii, xxix, 31, 60, 76, 83, 99, 112–13, 161, 170–71, 244, 247. *See also* culture
  biblical, 103, 105, 107–10, 144–58. *See also* interpretation
  hermeneutical Israel. *See* Israel; Jews
  inter-disciplinary hermeneutic, 163
  of dialogue, 225–29
  of love, honor and hospitality, 145–58
hidden transcript, 268, 274–88
historical and literary, 48–50, 56, 60, 203. *See also* criticism
Hitler, 125, 232–33, 240–41
Hollywood, 9, 175, 182, 185, 188. *See also* film
Hong Kong, xxiii, xxvi
honor (*timē*) and shame, xi–xiii, xvii, xxi, xxvii, 34–37, 40, 43, 61–64, 89–90, 104–6, 111, 117–30, 137–39, 142, 145–58, 173–74, 182, 191, 193, 197–98, 200, 204, 208, 210, 231, 265, 268, 274, 276, 279–88
hope, v, xvii, xx, xxv, 73, 97, 111n52, 166–67, 180, 184–86, 203, 234. *See also* eschatology; salvation
hospitality, 132, 140, 145–58, 191–207, 235–42

acceptable (*euareston*), xx, xxxii, 42, 88, 94–99, 123–24, 127–28, 139, 149–51, 154n45, 158, 176, 195, 266
  welcome (*proslambanō* or *synagō*), xxiv, 25, 87–90, 95–98, 118, 149, 158, 191–97, 200, 209, 235
human, humanity, 42, 47n4, 58, 78, 80, 106, 134, 140–42, 181–82, 193, 205, 227n11, 228, 235, 237–38, 255, 272, 281. *See also* Adam; anthropology
agency, 278–79
Christ-like human being (fully human), xxiv, 41, 138, 141–42, 183–85, 193, 261
context/situation, 20, 122, 127–28, 131–32, 173, 178, 229, 266
nature, xxxii, 108, 110, 118, 123, 127, 129, 134, 165, 168, 187, 255. *See also* psychology
rights, 53, 229, 235–37, 267–68, 275, 286. *See also* barbarians
trafficking, 59–71

"I" of Romans (chapter 7), 78–81, 109–11
identity, xxix, xxxi–xxxii, 23, 34, 44, 51, 87n5, 90n16, 93, 96–100, 109, 116, 151, 156, 167, 194, 217, 220, 230–31, 236, 238, 244, 246–59. *See also* community
ideology, ideological analysis, xii–xiii, 60, 89–90, 105–108, 111–12, 145, 147, 149, 154–55, 177, 215n19, 229, 232, 250, 260–63, 270–73, 276–78, 286–87
idlers (*ataktoi*), 212, 216
idol(atry), 34–45, 61, 63, 67, 89–94, 231, 235, 266
image of God. *See* God
impiety (*asebeia*), 61, 68
incarnation. *See* Jesus Christ
indigenous interpretation, xxxi, 103–4, 158, 208–22, 224–25, 229. *See also* Native American; Diola

individual, 43, 80, 94, 98, 112, 119, 134, 137, 140, 146–51, 154, 167, 178, 181, 197, 212, 241, 250–51, 262, 275. *See also* community
individual-centered (autonomy), 103–10, 116
individualism, 135, 173, 182, 187
interanimation of thoughts, 130–31, 137–38. *See also* metaphor
  grounding, 103, 212, 220
  tenor, 124, 131, 133, 138
  vehicle, 131, 133, 138, 139
interpretation. *See also* criticism; hermeneutic
  biblical interpretation, xvii, 46, 59, 70, 75n14, 82–84, 104–106, 108, 114–15, 130, 141, 144, 213, 219, 244, 247, 259, 273
  critical engagement interpretation, xii, 286
  cross-cultural interpretation. *See* culture
  ideological interpretation. *See* ideology
Islam, 247, 252, 252n29, 253, 255, 274, 277, 286
Israel, xxx, 36, 39, 42–43, 51–53, 60, 63, 67–68, 73–75, 81n47, 82–83, 93–99, 113, 135, 140n50, 150n26, 193, 197, 243, 246–59. *See also* Jews
  hermeneutical Israel, 247, 252–57
  Jerusalem, xxxiii, 4–12, 15–17, 25, 90n16, 150n26, 154, 195, 198, 249, 266
  sociological Israel, 247–52

Jesus Christ
  cross of, 63, 112, 140, 167–68, 208, 252n29, 259
  death of (crucifixion), 16, 63, 66, 111–12, 142, 145–46, 179, 204, 217, 235, 238–39, 268, 279–80, 284, 286
  ethnē in Christ, 86–99, 137, 140
  faith(fulness) in/of, v, xvii, 53–54, 62, 89, 91, 95, 98, 106n12, 121, 127, 134–35, 164, 166, 169, 172, 208, 224, 238, 241–42, 256
  followers of (believers), xvii, 22, 25, 27, 29–30, 35–44, 49–50, 86–87, 94–95, 120–22, 136–37, 142, 145, 151–56, 161, 186, 197–201, 208–9, 218–19, 225, 227, 241, 248–49, 253–54, 256–57, 266–68, 277–88
  good news of, 69, 134, 145, 149, 160, 271. *See also* gospel
  hospitality. *See* hospitality
  imitate (put on) Christ, xxiv, 44, 54–55, 88, 96, 127, 133–34, 139–40, 142, 146, 151, 192–94, 203, 235
  incarnation of, 52, 127, 191, 193, 239
  kingdom of, 195. *See also* God
  lordship of, 86, 93, 97, 193, 266, 268
  love of, 196, 283–85
  movement (early church), xxxii, 7, 34–35, 127, 139, 191, 193n15, 253. *See also* church
  parousia (coming), xxi, xxv, 60, 92, 209, 214, 217. *See also* eschatology
  peace of. *See* peace
  resurrection of, 112, 127, 286
  salvation, xiii, xxv, 67, 174, 179
  suffering of, 167, 237, 286n46, 288
Jews, 7, 12–15, 35–43, 49, 51–52, 60, 64–66, 80–100, 105, 115, 120, 134, 146, 154, 163, 174, 195–98, 202, 224–25, 227, 230, 238, 241, 243–44, 249–51, 255–57, 263–64, 288. *See also* gentiles; Israel
justice
  injustice (*adikia*), 61, 65, 67, 135, 139, 235, 271, 276, 278, 281–82, 286
  of God. *See* God
  retributive justice, 165
  restorative order, 145, 215–16, 221
  social justice, 129

Kohut, 117-29. *See also* psychology
   basic needs of the self, 123
   empathy. *See* empathy
   idealization, xxxii, 123-27
   mirroring, 60, 117-18, 122-124, 248-49
   psychoanalytic. *See* psychology
   selfobject, xxxii, 117-29
   twinship, xvii, xxxii, 123, 126-27, 130, 138, 162, 225
Kyle, Chris, 185

law, the
   and love, 139, 152, 186, 286
   apart from the law, 78-81, 92-93
   divine/God's law, Jewish/Mosaic law (Torah), 51-53, 68, 78-81, 90, 105n6, 109, 109n35, 112, 224, 242
   fulfill the law, 53, 55, 94, 103, 109-10, 118, 138, 193, 283
   of empire, 242. *See also* Roman Empire
   of mind, 109
   of sin, 109, 112
   of life, 51
liberation theology, 26, 227-28, 247, 257
literary method, 20, 24, 26, 29-30, 33, 47, 48-50, 56, 60-61, 68, 74, 110n44, 133, 203, 211, 214n15. *See also* criticism
love. *See also* Jesus Christ; God
   and faith, hope, xvii, 94-95, 134, 169, 203, 208, 237
   beloved by God, 93, 140n50, 141, 166-67, 237. *See also* God
   brotherly love (*philadelphia*), 88, 138-40, 145-60, 168, 196, 204-5, 254, 264, 267, 283-86
   hesed (faithful love), 68, 139, 142
   love feast (agape meal), xiii, 34, 44, 117-22, 127-29, 138, 251n25, 274n1
   loving stranger and enemy, 118, 152-53, 156, 158, 165, 191-93, 196-97, 235, 284
   without pretense, xvii, 196
LXX. *See* Greek

Macedonia, 4, 8, 11-12
Malaysian context, 106, 108, 274-88
Malcolm X, 69, 246-59
Malta, 8, 12, 195
McVeigh, Timothy, 179
Messalina, Valeria, 63-64
metaphor, xxxi, 130-31. *See also* interpretation; hermeneutic
   figure of speech, trope, 26, 51, 67, 80, 130-31, 150-51, 160
   metaphoric imagination, 138-44
   metaphorical interpretation, 130-44
   of *charis* and *charisma*, 131-36
midrash, 72-78, 82, 84, 252, 254. *See also* Jews; interpretation; Qumran
millenarian, xvii, 208, 210-21. *See also* eschatology
Muhammad, Wallace Fahd, 255
music, and *yue*, xix, 41, 64-65, 67n22, 126, 142, 177
Muslim, 224, 227, 237. *See also* Islam

Nag Hammadi Library, 22-23, 32. *See also* Gnostics
Nagaland, Naga society, 146, 156
Narcissism. *See* psychology
nationalism, xiv, xxv-xxvi, 69, 113, 175, 186-87, 258
Native American, xxxi, 213n14, 221
   ceremonies, 132, 215, 217
   Choctaw Nation of Oklahoma, xxxi, 213
   eschatology, 213-20
   native "moorings," 227
   Ghost Dance, 208-222
   Sun Dance, 217
   tribes, 215-17
   White Eagle, 213-14
   Wodziwob, 215
   Wounded Knee, 214, 218
   Wovoka (aka Jack Wilson), 214-20
Nebraska, xviii, xix-xx
North, Oliver, 179, 187

Orient and Occident, 224, 226, 233-34, 240
Orosius, 7, 13-14, 17, 64, 70

INDEX OF SUBJECTS   303

Pamphylia, 4, 7, 11
parousia (coming). *See* eschatology;
    Jesus Christ
partition theory, 19–22, 27–31, 33
    frame letter, 22, 25, 29–30
    redaction, 21–23, 29–30
Paul the Apostle
    anthropology. *See* Adam;
        anthropology; human
    apocalyptic, 186–87, 214, 215n19,
        219, 284. *See also* eschatology
    biography, Acts-based approach,
        3–18
    chronology, xii, xxv, 3n1, 6n3,
        15–17, 31–32, 203n60
    eschatology. *See* eschatology
    missionary journey, 4–16
    Pauline scholarship, xii, xxvi, 28,
        103, 112, 169, 173
    Pauline theology and
        interdisciplinary study, 103–88,
        241
    primus inter pares ("first among
        equals"), 161
peace, 153, 155, 157, 230
    and joy, 94–95
    and justice, 166, 260
    and shalom (with all), 186, 196,
        216–17, 263, 275n4, 284, 288
    and security (*pax et securitas*),
        209, 231, 280. *See also* Roman
        Empire
    French colonial peace, 230, 237
    peace in Ghana, 269–71
perception/conscience (*syneidēsis*), 27,
    34–45, 87–93, 104, 106, 114,
    233n28, 265
philological analysis, 46–58. *See also*
    exegesis
political reading/dimension. *See*
    criticism
Prisc(ill)a and Aquila, 6–7, 12–15, 26,
    86, 194
psychology, xvii, xxii, xxxii, 81n46, 84,
    114, 117–29, 135, 175. *See also*
    Freud; Kohut
    narcissism, xxxii, 118, 118n2, 119,
        122–23, 127–28, 135

psychoanalytic, xxxii, 114, 117–19,
    125, 128, 175
self psychology, xxxii, 119, 122,
    128–29

Quatres Communes in Senegal, 229–30
Quintilian, 27
Qumran pesharim, 75, 77, 83

race, racial
    equality, 26, 138, 141, 191, 200,
        239–40, 248. *See also* justice
    multiracial, 108
    racism, superiority, 137, 192, 232–
        33, 254, 278
rationalized violence, 173, 186–87
resistance, resisting, 79, 85, 213, 240–41,
    265–78, 281, 283–88
rhetoric, rhetorical criticism, xii, xxvi,
    xxxi, 23–30, 32–33, 47, 57–58,
    71, 73–77, 83–86, 105, 110, 116,
    130, 140, 142, 144, 173–74, 180,
    209, 211, 221, 229, 247, 251,
    255–58, 262, 264, 272–73, 278,
    282–83, 288
    deliberative, 27, 50
    epideictic, 24, 27
    ethos, 34, 85, 89–90, 133, 167, 177
    handbooks, 27
    judicial, 10, 24, 27, 165
    narratio, 27, 79, 261, 264
    partitio, 19–21, 27
    peroratio, 25, 27
    probation, 25, 27, 54–55
    socio-rhetorical interpretation. *See*
        socio-rhetorical interpretation
    topos, 63–64, 67
Rice, Condoleezza, 178
rights, 13–15, 28, 33, 49, 53, 56, 65, 134,
    137–41, 153, 158, 163, 198, 200,
    226, 247–49, 266–69, 275, 286.
    See also human; justice
Roman Empire, xii, 4, 59, 62, 147–49,
    154, 157, 173, 182, 200, 234,
    244, 252, 287. *See also* Greco-
    Roman
    Augustus, 5, 62, 226, 231, 239n40

Roman Empire (*continued*)
  Claudius, 6–8, 12–15, 63, 70, 154, 195, 250n17, 263
  Gaius "Caligula," 14–15, 17, 63, 70
  imperial ideology, xxi, 9, 59, 62, 88–90, 104, 139, 145, 147, 149, 154, 209–10, 223–24, 229–30, 235, 238–39, 264, 267, 274–85
  Nero, 4, 8, 65n19, 67n22, 196, 239, 263, 268, 270, 279–82
  Tiberius, 14, 14n9, 63, 70
Russia, 232–33
  bolshevism, 232
  Soviet Union, 227, 232–34

salvation/redemption
  and Christ's work. *See* Jesus Christ
  national salvation, 269
Schmithals's Gnostic thesis, 20–22, 32–33. *See also* Gnostics
scriptural criticism. *See* Bible; criticism
Second Temple, 35, 72, 75–76, 78–80, 84, 91, 287–88
secular humanists, 224
Semitic, Semitism, 232–33, 265
Seneca, 7, 17, 89, 279–80, 288
Senegal. *See* Africa
Septuagint. *See* Greek
sexual
  ethics, 211–13. *See also* Paul
  immorality, 63–64, 66, 67n22, 68, 83, 276
  liberation, 26, 32
Silas and Timothy, 8n5, 9, 11, 52, 195–96, 208–9
sin
  against people, 39, 93, 139
  and idolatry, 92–93. *See also* idol
  and law (transgression), 78–81, 108
  as bondage. *See* slavery
  as faithlessness, 62, 68, 95
  as zealotism, totality, and coveting, 110–12, 195
  law of sin, 109, 112
  power of sin, 78–81, 109, 111, 166
  saving from sin and death, xxv, 111, 137, 196, 204, 254

  saving to life and wisdom, xiii, 62, 112, 127
Sitoé, Aline, 234–39, 241, 244–45
slavery, bondage, domination, xii, 33, 37–38, 48, 66, 109, 117, 142, 147, 149, 166, 187, 197–98, 201, 228, 232–33, 242, 249, 267–88, 279, 283
Slavs, Slavic, 132, 223, 232–33
Society of Biblical Literature (SBL), xv, xvii, 72–73, 75, 175–76, 224
socio-rhetorical interpretation (SRI), 58, 260–63, 270–73. *See also* rhetoric
  inner texture, 260–61
  intertexture, 72, 141, 170–71, 260–61, 270
  social and cultural texture, 99, 260–61
  ideological texture, 260–63, 270–71. *See also* ideology
  sacred texture, 60, 228, 257, 260–61
Spirit, the, 21, 53–54, 63, 94–95, 109, 127, 132, 134–37, 140–42, 144, 150, 205, 215, 237, 285
storytelling, xviii, 178, 180, 184, 253
submit (*hypotassesthō*), 154, 265, 267, 270–71, 279–80, 283, 286, 288. *See also* resistance
Suetonius, 7, 13–14, 17, 64, 70
super-mindedness, boasting, xii, 137, 179
Syria, 4–8, 11, 16, 64n13, 151, 238

table fellowship, 36–37. *See also* food
Taiwan, xxi, xxx, 108, 112
taxes, direct (*phoros; tributum*) and indirect (*telos*), 153–54, 231, 265, 268, 271, 279–82, 283, 288
temple meal, 37–40. *See also* food
third space, 225. *See also* cross-cultural
Torah, 13, 35, 51–53, 61, 63, 72, 76, 79, 93. *See also* Jews; law
Trinidad, xviii
Troas, xx
Turkey, xx, xxv, 5, 226
Two-Thirds world, 228

virtues and vice, 52–54, 67, 69, 114, 136, 142, 151, 162, 229. *See also* ethics
vocabulary, grammar, syntax, 46–47, 51, 59, 73, 90, 94. *See also* rhetoric

White Eagle. *See* Native American
Wodziwob. *See* Native American

World Wars I & II, 227, 232, 239
Wounded Knee. *See* Native American

Zealot, zealous, xxv–xxvi, 69, 105n6, 113, 122, 175–78, 180, 187, 258. *See also* film; nationalism; race/racism

Index of Ancient Documents

Hebrew Bible/Old Testament

Genesis

1–3	79
2–3	62, 69
2:15–17	81
2:15	79
2:17	78
3	61, 80
3:3	78
3:5–6	80
3:6	78
3:9	79
3:13	78
3:19	78
3:22	79
14:17–24	198
15:5	74
16:8	140n50
17:5	74
18:1–8	198
18:10, 14	74
18:27	140n50
19:1–3	198
21:12	74
24:16–25	198
25:23	74
32	79
37	79

Exodus

1:15–21	266
5:1	266
9:16	74, 256
9:26	74
33:19	74

Leviticus

19:8	283
19:18	139
25:23	193

Numbers

25	165

Deuteronomy

6:4	283
10:17–18	193
10:18	197
14:3–21	195
24:19–22	193
25:4	53
29:4	75

Judges

13	198
19:15–21	193

Ruth

2:9–17	193

1 Samuel

12:22	74

2 Samuel

18:5	74
21:7, 9	74

1 Kings

18:1–4	266
19:10	75
19:18	75

2 Kings

4:8–17	198

Ezra

3:7	79
7:11	79, 80

Job

31:32	193

Psalms

5	255
9	255
13	255
13:1, 2	255
13:2b	255
22:7	140n50
31:1	74
35	255
35:2	255
68:23	75
69:7–9, 12–21	193
75:5–6	73
89:21	73, 74
94:11	73
94:24	74
139	255

Proverbs

25:21–22	196

Isaiah

1–66	xxi
1:9	74
9:16–20	61
10:22–23	74
25:6	xxiv
29:16	74
59	255

Ecclesiastes

7:20a	255

Daniel

3:1–7	266
6:6–9	266

Hosea

2:1	74
2:25	74, 256

Micah

6:8	68

Habakkuk

2:4	253

Malachi

1:2–3	74

New Testament

Matthew

7:10–11	205
8:11–12	204
8:14–15	203
9:10–13	203
10:8	194
10:9–13	194
10:11	192n4, 205
11:19	196n24, 205
12:1–8	205
14:15–21	204
15:32–38	205
16:9	204
16:10	205
17:24–27	268
22:2–14	205
22:16	193
24:12	152
25:1–13	205
25:14	63
25:35–43	194

INDEX OF ANCIENT DOCUMENTS   309

25:35	192n9
25:38	192n9
25:40	194
25:43	192n9
25:45	194
26:6–13	204
26:17–30	204
27:9	154
27:26	63
27:34	204
27:48	204
27:57–60	204

Mark

1:31	203
2:15–17	196, 203
2:23–28	205
3:19	63
5:26	140
6:8–11	194
6:8	140
6:10	192n4, 194n19, 205
6:35–44	193n15, 204
8:1–9	193n15, 205
8:19–21	205
8:19	204
12:14	193
12:31	283
14:3–9	194n17, 204
14:12–26	193n16, 204
15:15	63
15:23	204
15:36	204
15:42–46	204

Luke

2:36–37	197
4:7–28	204
4:29	204
4:38–39	203
4:39	204
4:40-43	204
5:29–31	203
6:1–5	205
7:34	205
7:36–50	194n17, 203
9:10–17	193
9:12–17	204
10:7–9	194
10:7–8	205
10:29–37	196
10:34–35	192
10:38–48	203
10:40	73
11:5–8	205
11:11–13	205
11:37–53	194n17, 203
12:1–11	204
12:37–38	205
13:29–30	204
13:29	193
14:1–24	194n17, 204
14:7–11	193
14:12–14	193
15:22–24	196n24, 205
15:23	204
16:19–21	205
19:1–10	204
19:5	192n4. 195
19:6	192n8, 195
19:9–10	196
20:21	193
20:22	154
22:7–38	193
22:8–38	204
22:30	193
23	168
23:2	154
23:25	63
23:50–54	204
24:13–32	194
24:29–35	204
24:29	192n4
24:36–52	204

John

1:1–18	52
1:10–11	194
1:14	52
1:38–39	192n4
2:1–11	204
4:5	194

John (continued)

4:7–28	204
4:28–30	194
4:29	204
4:39–42	194
4:39	204
4:40–43	204
4:40	192n4
6:1–15	193n15, 204
6:23	193n15, 204
6:26	193n15, 204
6:27–59	194, 205
7:37–39	205
11:6	192n4
11:54	192n4
12:1–11	204
13:1—17:26	204
13:30	139
14:2–3	193
15:23	204
19:11a	266
19:16	63
19:30	63
19:38–30	204
21:6–14	205
21:6–12	194

Acts

1:1—8:40	10
2:38	131n7
2:44–45	200
3:21	150n26
4:17–20	266
4:34	154
5:28–30	268
5:29	266, 268
6:13	150n26
6:14	63
8:1	10
8:3	10
9:1–30	10
9:1–25	16
9:23	6, 16
9:26–30	16
9:31—11:18	10
10:9–14	195
10:23	195
10:48	192n5, 195
11:1–3	195
11:19–30	11, 16
11:19–26	15
11:27–30	6, 15
12:1–24	11
12:25—14:28	11, 15
13—14	7
15:1–35	11, 15
15:1–29	6
15:36—18:22	11
15:36—18:11	15
16:15	192n4, 195
16:40	195
17:13–15	9
17:18, 21	193
18:1b–18a	6
18:1	15
18:2–3	6, 195
18:2	13, 195, 263
18:3	192n4
18:5	9
18:11	6, 7
18:12–17	6, 15
18:18	25	208
18:23—21:17	12
18:20	192n4
19:19	154
21:4–6	195
21:4	192n5
21:7–8	192n4
21:8–14	195
21:10	192n5
21:16–25	195
21:17—26:32	12
21:28	150n26
27:1—28:31	12
28:14	192n5
28:7–8	195
28:7	192

Romans

1—16	xiii, 9, 12
1:1—15:6	98
1—4	134
1	65
1:1–12	264

INDEX OF ANCIENT DOCUMENTS 311

1:1–6	98	4:4	131n7
1:2	73	4:9	74
1:3	137	4:16	131n7
1:4b–6	86	5:1—8:39	60, 87n4
1:5–6	86	5:2	131n7, 134
1:5	131n7	5:12–19	78–79
1:7	60, 93, 131n7, 150n26	5:12	81
		5:13–14	80
1:13–15	86, 264	5:15	131n7, 134
1:13	86, 263	5:17	131n7, 134
1:14	174	5:20	80, 131n7
1:16–17	264	5:21	131n7
1:16	90, 256	6–8	134
1:17a	254	6:1	131n7
1:17b	253	6:2	109
1:18—15:13	264	6:14	109, 131n7, 134
1:18—4:25	60	6:15	131n7
1:18–32	59–69, 91, 276	6:17	131n7, 135, 251
1:19–20	61	6:22	109
1:21–23	61	7	86, 109n35, 110
1:21	73	7:1–6	81
1:24–28	68	7:7–25	53, 81, 81n46
1:24–27	66	7:7–13	72, 84, 109
1:24–25	61	7:7–12	72–84
1:25	61	7:7–11	79
1:26–32	62	7:7	79, 81, 111
1:26	62–63	7:8	80
1:28	62–63	7:9	78, 81
1:29–31	67–68	7:10	78
1:29	68	7:11	78
1:30	62	7:14–25	81, 103, 108–12
1:31	62, 68, 136	7:17	112
1:32	64, 94	7:20	112
2:12	92	7:22	112
2:21	165, 267, 284	7:25	112, 131n7
3:6–7a	281	8:24–25	166
3:10–18	254	8:26	73
3:10	118, 152, 255	8:29	93
3:11	255	8:32	63, 74, 142
3:18	255	8:35–37	285
3:21	112	9–11	60, 86, 99, 252n28, 255
3:23	127, 137, 166, 196		
3:24	127, 131n7, 134	9	93
4:1–25	74, 86	9:3	86
4:10	88	9:10–13	256
4:16	131n7	9:15	136
4:22	95	9:17	256
4:23–25	96	9:18	136

INDEX OF ANCIENT DOCUMENTS

Romans (*continued*)

9:23	136
9:25b–c	256
10:3	179
11:1–6	74
11:5	131n7
11:6	131n7
11:7–10	75
11:13	86
11:17–21	86
11:18	96
11:20	137
11:23	90
11:25–26	135
11:25	137
11:26–27	257
11:30–31	136
12–15	150
12:1—15:13	133, 284
12–13	133–34, 145–58, 286
12	43, 130–44, 150n24, 151–53, 196
12:1–5	196
12:1–2	134, 149–50, 264
12:1	136, 150
12:2	150, 165, 267, 284
12:3–13	133–34, 149, 151, 284
12:3	131n7, 134, 136, 137, 151
12:4–5	134, 137, 151, 196
12:5–6	134
12:5	137
12:6–8	134, 151
12:6	131n7, 134, 137
12:7	136
12:9—13:14	284
12:9–21	196, 284
12:9–13	151
12:9–10	xvii, 155, 264
12:9	152, 196, 283–84
12:10	151–52, 154
12:12	92, 284
12:13–17	268
12:13	152, 152n36, 153, 192n2
12:14–21	134, 149, 153, 196, 284
12:14	153
12:15–16	133
12:16	146
12:17–21	134, 149, 153
12:17	284
12:18–21	133
12:18	284
12:19	93, 165
12:20	284
12:21	267, 284
13	97, 268
13:1–13	271
13:1–10	149, 153
13:1–7	133, 134, 153, 260–71, 274–88
13:1–4	153
13:1–2	196
13:1	264–65, 279, 282
13:1b–3a	279
13:1b, 2–4	265
13:2	265
13:3–4	280, 286
13:3	266, 284
13:3a	265
13:3b	265–66
13:3c	265
13:4	266, 282, 284
13:4b	265, 267
13:4c	265
13:5–7	153
13:5	265
13:6–8	139
13:6–7	282
13:6	131n7, 268
13:6a	265
13:6b	265
13:7–8	283
13:7	153–54, 265, 279, 281–83, 283n37
13:7b	281
13:8–10	94, 134, 153, 283
13:8	138, 283
13:9–10	139, 155
13:9	79, 283

INDEX OF ANCIENT DOCUMENTS   313

Reference	Pages
13:10	118, 284
13:11–14	134, 284
13:11–12	284
13:14	127, 284
13:23	196
14:1—15:13	86, 97, 120
14:1—15:7	120
14:1—15:6	85–99
14	88, 90, 96–97
14:1	87–88, 96–98
14:2	92
14:4	90
14:5–12	90
14:5	97
14:5b	90
14:10b	88
14:13–23	91–94
14:14	91
14:15	91, 94–96
14:16	93, 284
14:17–23	94–95
14:17	95
14:18	95
14:19	94
14:20	92, 94, 96, 284
14:21–23	88
14:21	94
14:22	95
14:23	95
15	87, 96
15:1–6	96–97, 99
15:1	88, 90, 96–97, 99
15:2	96, 284
15:3–6	98
15:3	96
15:4–5	96
15:4	73
15:5	74
15:6	97–99
15:7–13	85, 97–90, 99
15:7–8	98
15:7	xxiv, 88, 97–98, 131n7
15:8–12	98
15:9–11	134
15:9	136
15:10	98
15:14—16:27	264
15:14–33	97–98
15:14–19	263
15:15	131n7
15:16–18	86
15:31	131n7
16	251
16:3–4	26
16:4	86
16:17	251
16:20	131n7
16:23	195

1 Corinthians

Reference	Pages
1–16	12, 19
1:1—6:11	20, 30
1–4	19
1:11–15	20
1:12	21, 28
4:17	135
6:12–20	26, 30
6:12	21
7:1—8:13	30
7:1	26
8	36–37, 39–40, 42
8:1	37
8:4–6	38
8:7	38–39
8:9	21
8:12	39
9:1–18	28, 30
9:1	21
9:19–23	30
9:20–23	174
9:22	162
9:24—10:22	30
9:4–6	21
9:8–12	53
10:14–22	35–36, 42
10:23–11:1	30, 36, 39–40
10:23–31	37
10:23	21
10:26—11:1	35–36
10:29	43
10:31	43
10:32–33	43
11:2–34	20, 27
11:2	30

1 Corinthians (continued)

11:3–16	30
11:7–9	79
11:17–34a	30
11:18	19
11:19	19
11:21–22	200
11:29	200
11:33–34	200
11:34b	30
12–14	134, 136
12:1–31a	30, 137
12:12–13	134
12:24	154
12:31b—13:13	30
13:1–13	25
13:4	203
13:7	203
14:1c–33a	30
14:29	135
14:33b–36	26
14:37–40	30
15:1–58	30
15:45	79
16:1–4	30
16:3	54, 131
16:13–24	30
16:19	26
16:5–12	30

2 Corinthians

1–13	12, 19
1:1—2:13	20, 25, 27, 30
1:8–9	10
1:9	10
2:4	19
2:6–11	25
2:14—6:13	25, 27, 30
6:6	152
6:14—7:1	25, 30
7:2–4	25, 27, 30
7:5—8:24	20, 27
7:5–16	25, 30
8:1–24	25, 27, 30
8:5	140
9:1–15	26, 30
10:1—13:13	19–20, 28

10:1—11:9	30
10:10	28
11:3	78–79, 135n33
11:10—13:10	30
11:9, 10, 11, 12	28
11:25	10
11:32–33	16
12:13, 14	28
13:11–13	30

Galatians

1–6	9, 11
1:9	241
1:12	135
1:18	192n5
2:1–10	6
2:11–21	238
2:11–15	86
2:11–14	36, 195, 241
3:1	235
3:17	80
3:26–28	238
3:28	235
4:12–15	234
4:12	235n31
4:13, 14	235
5:1—6:10	53
5:1	53–54
5:5–6	53

Ephesians

1–6	10, 12, 49
2:12	193
2:19	193
3:5	150n26
4:11–12	136
4:23	150
6:5–8	268

Philippians

1:7	49
1:13	49
1:14	49
1:17	55
1:27	53, 55
2:1—4:3	54

2:1	54
2:12	154
2:16	50
3:1-2	49
3:17—4:1	
3:17	55
3:19	56
3:20-21	55
3:20	46
3:21	55
3:6	109
4:1	54
4:15	131
4:17	131
4:22	9

Colossians

1-4	10, 12
1:15-17	268
1:28	135
2:6-7	135
2:7	135
3:1	135n33, 150
3:16	135

1 Thessalonians

1-5	9, 11, 209-10, 221
1:1	9
1:9	208
2:14	208
2:17-20	209
3:1, 2-6	9
3:3-5	209
3:3	208
3:6	209
3:8	54
4:1-12	209
4:11-12	218
4:11	209
4:13—5:11	209
4:16-17	214
5:1	219
5:3	209
5:8	xvii
5:12-22	209
5:14	212, 216
5:19-22	135

2 Thessalonians

1-3	9, 11, 214n15, 219
2:15	54, 135
3:6-13	209, 218
3:8	131n7

1 Timothy

2:1-4	275
2:14	78-79
3:1-2	268
3:2	152n36, 192n2, 197
3:6	208
3:7, 8-13	197
5:5	197
5:10	152, 192, 197
6:1	154

Titus

1:5-8	107
1:8	152n36, 192n2, 197
2:12	197
4:1-3	275

Philemon

1-25	10, 12
22	192n6, 195

Hebrews

1-13	196
11:13-16	194
11:31	192n7, 196n24
13:2	152n36, 192n2, 192n6

James

1:17	141
2:1-9	200
2:25	196n24

1 Peter

1:16	150n26
2:7	154
3:14	154
2:13–17	275
4:10–11	196
4:8–9	196
4:9	152n36, 192n2

2 Peter

3:2	150n26

2 John

10	197

3 John

6–8	197
10	197

Revelation

4:9	154
13	268
13:4	266
13:8	266

Other Ancient Texts

Apocrypha & Pseudepigrapha

Apocalypse of Abraham
23.1–14	80

Apocalypse of Moses
19.3	80

4 Ezra
3:7	79
7:11	79–80

Genesis Apocryphon	75–76
Jubilees	75–76
Letter of Aristaeus	53
1–4 Maccabees	51, 230

2 Maccabees
6:1	51
6:2	197

4 Maccabees	53

Sirach
1:9	62n5
11–30	62
17:7	81
17:11–12	81

Wisdom
3–14	61
4:10	150
9:10	150

Rabbinic Texts

m. Aboth
1:5	198

m. Avodah Zarah
3:4	41
4:2–3	40

b. Avodah Zarah
22b	80

b. Sabbath
145b–146a	80

b. Sanhedrin
56b	79

Targum Neofiti
1	79

m. Tohoroth
7:2, 5–6	196n23

b. Yebamoth
103b	80

Greek & Latin Writings

Aristotle, *Poetic*
1457b	130

Didache
11:3—13:7	197

Dio Cassius, *Roman History*
60.6.6	13, 14n10

INDEX OF ANCIENT DOCUMENTS   317

Diodorus Siculus, *History*
5.24–32   225n7
5.34   197n32
13.76.5   74

Dionysius Halicarnassus,
Roman Antiquities
5.10.7   74

Josephus
Antiquities of the Jews
1.41–47   79
12.141   154n40

Contra Apion
I.43   66n21

Historiae Adversus Paganos
7.6.15–16   13

Vita
1.12   51n34
16   65n19

Juvenal, *Satire*
VI:114–135   63

Livy
38.17   225n7

Philo
De Agricultura
113–21   65n15
35   64n14, 65n16

De Confusione Linguarum
78   51n33

De Mutatione Nominum
198   65n18

De Opificio Mundi
56   80

De Specialibus Legibus
4.78   53n41

In Flaccum
74–80   66n20

Legatione ad Gaium   14n9

Legum Allegoriae
1.90–97   79

Legum Allegoriae
2.18   80

Questiones et Solutiones in Genesiu
1.47–48   80

Pliny the Elder, *Natural History*
X   64n11

Plutarch, *Cimon*
10   197n31

Pseudo-Aristotle,
Rhetorica ad Alexandrum   27

Pseudo-Philo   75

Seneca
De Clementia
1.2–4   280n27
1.2   279n24

Letters from a Stoic
104.1   7

Shepherd of Hermas, *Similitudes*
9.27   197n26

Suetonius
Caligula 24   63n9

Claudius 25.4   13

Claudius 34   63n10

Tiberius 43–45   63n8

Tacitus
Annals 13.50   282n31
Histories 5.4–5   227n11

Chinese Classic

Analects
7:30   142
13:19   141
14:5   141
17:6   141

www.ingramcontent.com/pod-product-compliance
Lightning Source LLC
Chambersburg PA
CBHW061424300426
44114CB00014B/1538